THE NOBILITY UNDER AKBAR AND JAHĀNGĪR

The Nobility under Akbar and Jahāngīr

A STUDY OF FAMILY GROUPS

AFZAL HUSAIN
Reader in History, Aligarh Muslim University

CENTRE FOR ADVANCED STUDY IN HISTORY
Aligarh Muslim University

MANOHAR
1999

First published 1999

ISBN 81-7304-317-5

Published by
Ajay Kumar Jain for
Manohar Publishers & Distributors
2/6 Ansari Road, Daryaganj
New Delhi 110 002

Printed at
Rajkamal Electric Press
B 35/9 G T Karnal Road Indl Area
Delhi 110 033

TO
MY PARENTS

Contents

Preface

This book is a revised version of my Ph.D. thesis titled, *The Role of Family Groups of Nobles in Mughal Politics, 1556-1627* presented at Aligarh Muslim University in 1979. In the course of revision I have been able to collect some useful information relevant to my subject. This additional information has been incorporated in various chapters of this book. Chapters IV, V and VII in particular have been substantially revised in the light of the fresh data.

In the preparation and publication of the book I have received generous assistance from my teachers and colleagues for which I am deeply beholden to them. First of all, I am greatly indebted to my esteemed teacher, the late Professor M.A. Ansari, Professor Emeritus, Jamia Millia Islamia, New Delhi, from whom I received my first introduction to the subject and constant encouragement in my studies. I am equally indebted to the late Professor S. Nurul Hasan, former Head of the Department of History, on whose suggestion this work was undertaken and who had always been very kind and helpful to me. I am also grateful to the late Professor K.A. Nizami, who was generous to me both with his time and attention. My debt of gratitude to my supervisor the late Professor M. Athar Ali is not possible to express in words. Without his constant guidance and stimulating assistance the book could not have been prepared in the present form.

I express my profound and sincere thanks to Professor Irfan Habib who went through the complete typescript of the book and made valuable suggestions for improvement, including the change of the title to the one that this book now bears. Thanks are also due to Professor I.H. Siddiqui for his interest in the publication of this book. I am also thankful to Professor Shireen Moosvi during whose chairmanship the process of publication of the book started.

I am extremely grateful to Professor S.P. Gupta, Chairman and Coordinator, Centre of Advanced Study, Department of History, for his scholarly suggestions and keen personal interest in the publication of the book.

I take this opportunity to express my thanks to my colleagues and friends Dr S.M.R. Naqvi, Dr. I.A. Zilli, Dr. S.K. Abdul Latif, Professor Iqbal Husain, Professor S.P. Verma and Professor Asghar Abbas for their help of various nature in the preparation of the book. I should also acknowledge my gratitude to the staff of U.P. State Archives, Public Library and University Library, Allahabad; M.S. University Library, Baroda; Khuda Bakhsh Library, Patna; Maulana Azad Library, Aligarh and Research Library of my own department. All of them extended their sincere cooperation and allowed me to use their valuable collections. My thanks are also due to my young colleague Mr Reyaz Ahmad Khan for checking proofs, Mr Munir Uddin for processing the text and preparing Camera Ready Copy and Manohar Publishers and Distributors, for the cooperation extended by them in the publication of this book. However, for any errors or shortcomings, I alone am responsible.

Finally, I must acknowledge my deep gratitude to my wife Shama for her indulgence and patience during the writing of this book.

Aligarh, 1999 Afzal Husain

Abbreviations

'Arẓdāsht	*Maktūbat-i Khān-i Jahān Muzaffar Khān wa Gowāliar Nāma*
Bāyazid	*Taẓkira-i Humayun o Akbar*
De Laet	tr. J.S. Hoyland and annoted by S.N. Bannerjee: *The Empire of the Great Mogols*
Farishta	*Gulshan-i Ibrāhīmı* or *Tārīkh-i Farishta*
Iqbalnāma	*Iqbalnāma-i Jahāŋgīrī*
JRAS	*Journal of Royal Asiatic Society*
Maktūbat	*Maktūbat-i Allāmi*
Muntakhab	*Muntakhab-ut Tawarıkh*
Nafa'is	*Nafa'is ul Maasir*
Nevill	*District Gazetteer of United Provinces*
Tabaqāt	*Tabaqāt-i Akbarī*
Tuzuk	*Tuzuk-i Jahangīrī*
T.U.	*Haft Risāla-i Taqwīm al-Buldan* (*Taẓkirat-ul Umara*)
Von Nor	Fredrick Augutus, *The Emperor Akbar*
Z.K.	*Zakhirat-ul Khwānīn*

Introduction

The study of Mughal nobility has attracted a good deal of attention from scholars in recent years; three important works, M. Athar Ali's *The Apparatus of Empire* and *The Mughal Nobility under Aurangzeb*, and Satish Chandra's *Parties and Politics at the Mughal Court, 1707-1740*, have dealt with the nobility in the various phases of the empire. Important papers on various aspects of the working of the nobility have also appeared in learned journals. But barring these few articles or one or two monographs on the lives of important nobles and families of nobles, no comprehensive study of the structure of the nobility and the role of the nobles during the reigns of Akbar and Jahāngīr has been published so far.

The present study is an effort in this direction; its scope is limited to the study of certain important family groups as illustrative of the general norms and circumstances. Realizing that such a study might be one-sided, I have also tried to look at the nobility as a whole while assessing the role of individual family groups.

A study of this kind must necessarily begin with the nobility of Bābur and Humāyūn, on which also no detailed work had been done so far, since to understand the complex problem of the nobility under Akbar (particularly during his early years) a survey of the nobility during the previous two reigns is an essential pre-requisite.

Composition of Nobility under Bābur and Humāyūn

Bābur's nobles or *begs* were largely of Central Asian origin with the exception of a few Irānīs who might have joined his service in minor capacities after the fall of Timuride power in Hirat.[1] Even

[1] See Appendix A–I, List of Babur's nobles, *Bāburnāma*, tr. Beveridge II, 471-3; *Akbarnāma*, I, 96. Also see, *Life of Mun'im Khān*, ix.

before the conquest of Hindustan, he also came into contact with Indian nobles, since certain dissatisfied nobles of Sikandar Lodī actually invited him to invade India.[2] When he reached Dun (in *pargana* Jaswan), 'Imād Shīrāzī came from Araish Khān and Mullāh Muḥammad Mazhab with a letter, 'containing assurance of their attachment to my interest and urging me to continue resolutely the expedition I had commenced'. In reply Bābur assured them of 'protection and favours'.[3] About the same time 'Alam Khān, son of Bahlol Lodī, also came to him in a wretched condition. Bābur sent his nobles to welcome him; he was given horses as a mark of favour.[4] Such Afghān allies were, however, not taken into confidence and were kept away from the field at the battle of Panipat.

After the battle of Panipat, Bābur's attitude underwent a change, in that he realized the necessity of admitting Afghān and Indian nobles into his ruling class. Immediately after the battle, Malik Dād Karrāni, a prominent Afghān noble, was not only pardoned but also assigned several *parganas*.[5] Abū'l Faẓl adds that when Bābur established himself in Agra, 'with the strength of his liberality and justice composed the distractions of the country. Accordingly many of the officers of Hindustan and rulers of the country gradually entered his service.'[6] Among them was Shaikh Ghuran who brought with him as many as 'three thousand soldiers and quiver-weavers from Doab'.[7] Fīroz Khān, Maḥmūd Khān Nauhani, Qāzī Ziā and Shaikh Bāyazīd also joined his service after the battle of Panipat.[8] When Humāyūn was in Dalmau, Fatḥ Khān Sarwāni, son of 'Aẓam Humāyūn, a leading noble of the Lodīs, presented himself. Humāyūn sent him to the court, where Bābur received him favourably. He 'invited Fatḥ Khān Sarwāni to a wine party, gave him wine, bestowed on him a turban and robe of honour of my own wearing'.[9] He was given the title of *Khān-i Jahān* and

[2] *Bāburnāma*, tr. Beveridge II, 459-61.

[3] *Bāburnāma*, tr. Erskine, II, 175-6. Beveridge's translation is defective here. While Bābur was at Dun, Ismaīl Jilwani and Biban also wrote him letters. (*Bāburnāma*, tr. Beveridge, II, 463).

[4] *Bāburnāma*, tr. Beveridge, II, 464.

[5] Ibid., tr. Beveridge, II, 477.

[6] *Akbārnāma*, I, 101-2.

[7] Ibid. Abū'l Faẓl mentions that they were men of 'mark'. See also *Bāburnāma*, tr. Beveridge, II, 527.

[8] *Bāburnāma*, tr. Beveridge II, 527; *Akbarnāma*, 102.

[9] *Bāburnāma*, tr. Beveridge II, 537; *Akbarnāma*, I, 104.

'territory to the value of 1,60,00000 *tankās* over and above those assigned to his father'. He was permitted to go to his assigned territory but his son Maḥmūd Khān was asked to remain at the court.[10] Certain other officers of the Lodīs, like Niẓām Khān, Tatār Khān, and Muḥammad Zaitun also submitted and were admitted to service.[11]

From the *Bāburnāma* it becomes clear that Bābur not only admitted Indian nobles because of political compulsions, but also began to repose confidence in them. The Indian nobles who were admitted to service were given important assignments. For example, Fīroz Khān Sārang Khānī was given territory of the value in revenue of 1,46,05,000 *tankās* from Jaunpur, Maḥmūd Khān received territory worth 90,35,000 *tankās* from Ghazipur, and Qāzī Ẓiā, worth twenty lacs of *tankās*.[12] Similarly other nobles were also given large territories.[13] In all major engagements, following the battle of Panipat, Indian nobles fought in Bābur's army against Indian chiefs. The names of officers mentioned in the *Bāburnāma* at the time of the battles of Khanua, Chanderi and in the campaign in the eastern region bear testimony to this.[14] To establish personal affinities with them, Bābur invited Indian nobles along with Central Asian nobles to his assemblies.[15]

It also appears that Bābur made a beginning in establishing friendly relations with the local chiefs. The Raja of Kahlur, Sangur Khān Janjuha and Adham Khān Ghakkar accepted Bābur's suzerainty and the latter two served on his side in the battle of Khanua.[16]

[10] Ibid. The details of *jāgīr* assignment have been given by Abū'l Fazl only. Cf. *Akbarnāma*, I, 104.

[11] *Bāburnāma*, tr. Beveridge II, 539-40. [12] Ibid., tr. Beveridge II, 527.

[13] Ibid., 521, 527, 679. Cf. I.H. Khan, 'Bābur's Settlement of his conquests in Hindustan', *Indian History Congress*, 1967, 207-20.

[14] *Bāburnāma*, tr. Beveridge, II, 565-8; *Akbarnāma*, I, 107. In the battle of Khanua 'Araish Khān, Shaikh Ghuran, Jalāl Khān, Kamāl Khān (son of Sulṭān 'Alāuddin) Nizam Khān, Malik Dād Karrāni, Dilāwar Khān and Khān-i-Khānan were present. In the campaign against Biban and Bāyazid also Indian nobles like 'Alam Khān of Kalpi, Malik Dād Karrāni and Rao (Rawni) Sarwani took part (*Bāburnāma*, tr. Beveridge, II, 682).

[15] Ibid., tr. Beveridge, 627, 637.

[16] In 1529 the Raja of Kahlur waited on Bābur with a huge amount of *peshkash*. (*Tarikh-i Sher Shāhī*, 124.) Sangur Khān Janjuha, chief from Bhera, was killed in the battle of Khanua. Adam Ghakkar also fought against Rana Sanga. Cf. *Bāburnāma*,

In the light of this evidence, it may be inferred that the nobility of Bābur after the battle of Panipat no longer remained purely Tūrānī.[17] I have prepared a list of nobles of Bābur based on the *Bāburnāma* and other contemporary and near contemporary sources, which further corroborate this view. Out of a total of 116 nobles, 31 were Indians including Afghāns and Shaikhzadas.[18] Akbar's introduction of the Indian element in his nobility was not thus wholly an innovation.

During the early years of Humāyūn's reign, a number of Indian nobles remained in the service of the Mughals. The author of the *Qānūn-i Humāyūni*, while describing the festivities in the year 1534, gives a list of nobles who were given rewards. In that list the names of the following Indian nobles occur; Jalāl Khān (son of Sulṭān 'Alāuddin), Maḥmūd Khān Sarwāni, Jalāl Khān (son of Naṣir Khān), Jalāl Khān (son of Daryā Khān), Bāyazīd Khān and Gadāi Khān.[19] There are some other references to certain other nobles of Indian origin during the early years of his reign.[20] But as soon as the Afghān resistance grew stronger, the Afghān nobles started defecting. In addition, the infighting among the Mughal princes, sharp divisions in the Tūrānī nobility and Humāyūn's incapacity to deal with the situation firmly, also contributed to the thinning of the ranks of Indian nobles in Mughal service (it is well-known that many of the Afghān nobles went over to Gujarat).[21] Nevertheless, certain Afghāns and Shaikhzadas remained loyal to Humāyūn until his conquest of Bengal.

The Mughal nobility which had begun to resume a predominantly Tūrānī complexion after the accession of Humāyūn became

---

tr. Beveridge, I, 379, 383, II 547-8; *Akbarnāma*, I, 195-6. For more details about Bābur's relations with local chiefs, see A.R. Khan, 'Bābur's settlement of his conquests in Hindustan', *Indian History Congress*, 1967, 207-20.

[17] See *Life of Mun'im Khān*, IX-XII, Iqtidar Alam Khan believes that the Indian nobles joined Bābur for a very brief period only; he believes therefore that Bābur's nobility remained purely Tūrānī. But we find that a large number of the Indians remained with the Mughals even after Bābur's death and during the early years of Humāyūn. What can be nearer the truth will be that though a number of Indians remained within the nobility, the Chaghtāi tradition remained dominant, because the Indian nobles could not be fully assimilated.

[18] For the list of Bābur's nobles, see Appendix A–I.

[19] *Qānūn-i Humāyūnī*, 96-9.

[20] For instance, Araish Khān and Shaikh Jamāl.

[21] Cf. Iqtidar Husain Siddiqui, 'Political Role of the Refugees from Delhi under Sultan Bahadur Shah', *Indian History Congress*, 1972, 406.

purely Tūrānī shortly afterwards, with the exception, as before, of a few Irānīs.[22]

A great change in the composition of Mughal nobility occurred between 1540 and 1555 (after Humāyūn's defeat at the hands of Sher Shāh and the protracted civil war in Afghanistan). Most of Humāyūn's Tūrānī nobles left him and joined Mirzā Kamrān. A list of nobles, who accompanied Humāyūn to Iran, given by Abū'l Faẓl consists of only 26 persons in all. It is significant that out of these 7 were of Irānī origin.[23]

On the other hand during his stay in Iran, many people of Irānī origin joined Humāyūn's service. For instance, Walī Beg Zulqadar and his two sons, Ḥussain Qulī and Ismāīl Qulī; also Ḥaider Sulṭān Shaibāni and his two sons 'Alī Qulī and Bahādur Khān. Certain other relations and clansman of Bairam Khān also joined Humāyūn's service, though in minor capacities.[24]

When Humāyūn returned from Iran to take Qandhar and Kabul, a nucleus of Irānī nobles had thus already been formed. However, after the conquest of Qandhar, many of the old nobles of Humāyūn rejoined his service. A list of nobles provided by Bāyazid who accompanied Humāyūn in his march upon Kabul gives the names of several old nobles.[25] But the old nobles remained wavering in their loyalty; and, according to Abū'l Faẓl they indulged in intrigues 'with the evil idea that thereby their own greatness and affluence would be increased'.[26] In these circumstances, the old Tūrānī nobility tended to fade away from the political scene and the Irānī nobles improved their position. A number of people from Iran came to Kabul and entered Humāyūn's service.[27] Irānīs were also appointed to important central offices,

[22] Afzal Husain, 'Growth of Irani Elements in Akbar's Nobility', *Indian History Congress,* 1975, 166-79.

[23] *Akbarnāma*, I, 221-4. See Appendix A–II for the list of nobles. Bāyazīd Bayāt has also given a list, with 28 names in all. (*Taẓkira-i Humāyūn*, 4-7).

[24] These names may be found in the three lists provided by Bāyazid Bayāt. The first list includes nobles who accompanied Humāyūn on the conquest of Qandhar, the second of those with him when Humāyūn embarked on the conquest of Kabul, and the third, when Humāyūn invaded India (*Taẓkira-i Humāyūn*, pp. 4-7, 52-3, 177-87). See also Abū'l Faẓl's list, *Akbarnāma*, I, 342-3.

[25] *Taẓkira-i Humāyūn*, 52-5.

[26] *Akbarnāma*, I, 267. On the role of old nobles, see *Mirzā Kamrān*, 64 and *Life of Mun'im Khān*, 8-11.

[27] Bāyazīd refers to the arrival of Mir Sayyid 'Ali, Mulla 'Abdus Samad, Mullā Dost, Mulla Fakhr Mujjalid, Shaikh Qāṣim Astrābadi and his brothers, when

such as *Dīwān*, *Wazīr*, *Mīr Sāmān*, and *Musharif-i Dīwān*, in the period 1545-55 when Humāyūn was in Kabul.[28]

Along with the increased power of the Irānī nobility during this period, came the emergence of a new Tūrānī nobility which Humayun appears to have raised mainly to strengthen his position vis-a-vis the old nobility.[29] An analysis of the list of nobles given by Abū'l Fazl for those who accompanied Humāyūn to India shows that out of a total of 57 nobles, 27 were Tūrānīs and 21 Irānīs, while 9 of them cannot be identified. The Irānīs included Bairam Khān, Afẓal Khān *Mīr-Bakhshi*, Ashraf Khān *Mīr Munshī*, Khwājā 'Abdul Majīd *Dīwān*, Khwājā 'Atāullāh *Dīwān-i Bayūtāt*, Mīr Shahāb-uddīn *Mīr Sāmān*, Khwājā Abul Qāsim, Mirzā Nijāt and Mīr Ḥasan, who were all important nobles as is indicated by the offices they held.[30]

The list of nobles provided by Bāyazīd is more comprehensive. It includes even the menial servants and personal servants of the nobles. It gives names under three heads; nobles under Humāyūn, servants of Prince Akbar, and servants of Bairam Khān. A close scrutiny of the list also shows that important offices were filled by Irānī nobles.[31]

After the reconquest, Humāyūn, realizing the importance of including local elements in the ruling class, made a beginning by entering into a matrimonial alliance with Ḥasan Khān, the Mewati chief. But further efforts in this direction were cut short by his sudden death.

Royal Control over the Nobility

Before the conquest of India, Bābur was hardly in a position to organize a nobility fully disciplined and subservient to him.[32] The territory under his control was small and not very productive; in

Humāyūn reached Kabul after the conquest of Qandhar. Cf. *Taẓkira-i Humāyūn*, 65-7.

[28] Afzal Husain, op.cit.

[29] Cf. *Life of Mun'im Khān*, 8-11.

[30] *Akbarnāma* I, 342. For a different view on the same problem also see Iqtidar Alam Khan, 'The Nobility Under Akbar and the Development of his Religious Policy 1560-80', *Journal of the Royal Asiatic Society*, 1968, 30-5.

[31] *Taẓkira-i Humāyūn*, pp. 176-87. Also see Afzal Husain, op.cit.

[32] One of Bābur's begs is reported to have given himself royal airs, holding receptions and public tables, a court and workshop after the fashion of Sulṭāns. Another of his begs had a kettledrum beaten at his own gate, notwithstanding his

these circumstances it was not possible for him to attract and retain a stable nobility. The nobles who remained with him were treated more as associates. The situation became more complicated because of the presence of a large number of close relations and members of important Chaghatāī clans.[33] Certain customary rules, designated *Tūra-i Chengezī* were closely followed.[34] In these circumstances the position of the king remained very weak, and he could not control the ruling class very effectively. Although Babur accepted this position in Afghanistan, he was apparently averse to this kind of relationship between the ruler and his nobility. When he started on his expedition to northern India, he raised 'small men of little standing' to the status of begs, to keep them effectively under his control. But he was in for a close disappointment:

When I set out from Kabul this last time I had raised many of low rank to the dignity of beg, in the expectation, that if I had chosen to go through fire and water, they would have followed me back and forward without hesitation; and that they would have accompanied me cheerfully, march where I would. It never surely entered my imagination that they were to be the persons who were to arraign my measures, nor that, before raising from the council, they should show a determined opposition to every plan and opinion which I proposed and supported in the council and assembly.[35]

It also appears that admitting a large number of Indian nobles, and assigning them large areas, might have been done because of Babur's desire to strengthen his position vis a vis the older nobility.

acknowledging Bābur as *Pādshāh* (*Bāburnāma*, tr. Beveredge, I, 119, 249-50, 272). Cf. Iqtidar Alam Khan, 'The Turko Mongol Theory of Kingship', *Medieval India — A Miscellany*, II, 8-18.

[33] Cf. *Akbarnāma*, I, 65. 'If all the nobles serving under Babur who traced their ancestry to Bukhu Khataji, Bukhatu Salji and Boduauchar (figures whose birth was attributed to supernatural inspiration) are taken into account, it would appear that a vast majority of his nobles would be claiming a special status by virtue of their birth' (Iqtidar Alam Khan, 'The Turko-Mongol Theory of Kingship', *Medieval India — Miscellany*, II, 15-16).

[34] In his memories Bābur writes, 'My forefathers and family had always sacredly observed the rules of Changez. In their parties, their courts, their festivals and their entertainments, in their sitting down and rising up, they never acted contrary to the *Tūra-i Changez*. The *Tūra-i Changezī* certainly possessed no divine authority, so that any one should be obliged to conform to them; every one who has good rule of conduct ought to observe it. If the father has done what is wrong, the son ought to change it for what is right' (*Bāburnāma*, tr. Erskine, II, 7).

[35] *Bāburnāma*, tr. Erskine, II, 248. Beveridge's translation (524) is defective here.

But his attempts did not succeed because the Indian nobility which comprised largely of the former Afghān commanders, could not be completely relied upon. In these circumstances he had to fall back upon the Chaghtāī nobility.

After his death the problems of nobility assumed new dimensions. The nobles asserted their claim that 'the Empire belonged not to the ruler, but to the ruling family',[36] and allegedly conspired to enthrone Mahdī Khwājā setting aside the claims of Humāyūn.[37] Although the conspiracy did not succeed, Humāyūn had constantly to deal with the presumptions of his nobility. There were frequent rebellions of his nobles; Mirzā Kamrān's autonomous control over Afghanistan and the vacillating attitude of Askari and Hindal further contributed to the disruption of Humāyūn's control over his nobility.

After his defeat at Chausa and Kanauj, a large number of Humāyūn's nobles joined Mirzā Kamrān. During his march into Sindh and subsequent flight to Persia, the nobles remaining with him belonged with a few exceptions to the lower ranks only.[38] When he returned from Persia after the conquest of Qandhar as mentioned earlier a large number of his old Tūrānī nobles who had joined Mirzā Kamrān, came over to him.[39] These nobles entertained shifting loyalties.[40] But during his struggle with Mirzā Kamrān for control over Kabul between 1545 and 1555, Humāyūn was able to develop a nobility more closely loyal to himself. In doing so, as we have already explained, he promoted low ranking Tūrānī nobles and admitted a number of Persians and used them as bulwark against the old Tūrānī nobles.

The new nobility served him loyally throughout his contest with Mirzā Kamrān and followed him in the conquest of India. In recognition of their services important assignments were generally given to this section of the nobility.[41]

[36] Barthold, *Encyclopaedia of Islam*, 1st edn, Leyden, 1913, Vol.I, 861. See Iqtidar Alam Khan 'The Turko Mongol Theory of Kingship', 15-16.

[37] *Tabqāt-i Akbarī*, II, 28-9.

[38] See Appendix AII, list of nobles who accompanied Humāyūn to Persia.

[39] *Tazkira-i Humāyūn*, 60; *Akbarnāma*, I, 248. Also see *Life of Mun'im Khān*, 8, and *Mirzā Kamrān*, 31-3.

[40] For the incidents illustrating the old nobles' treasonable role, see Bāyazid, 84-6, 126-31; *Akbarnāma*, I, 245, 251, 254, 267, 272, 275, 293-7, 305-6. Cf. *Life of Mun'im Khān*, 9-10, and *Mirzā Kamrān*, 34-8.

[41] See Chapters I and III.

Although by raising Irānīs and low ranking Tūrānīs to higher ranks, Humāyūn was able to create a ruling class loyal to the king and was successful in reconquering Hindustan, the dominant sections in his nobility were still confined to a limited number of clan-and-family groups.[42] These clan groups were naturally averse to any centralization of authority. When Humāyūn died, he was still engaged in the process of reconquest. He therefore did not have yet to face the divisive pulls of factions among his creations, with their extensive clan loyalties.

The above discussion on the nobility of Bābur and Humāyūn shows that the Mughal ruling class was far from constituting a disciplined and effective organization to cope with the complex problems of a newly established empire in India. The attempts made by Bābur and Humāyūn to bring about some changes in its composition, to improve its working and making it loyal and subservient to the Crown were not fully successful. The most apparent reason seemed to be the presence of powerful clan and family groups of nobles with their roots in Central Asian traditions or claims of high descent. To break their power, some fundamental changes were required in the administrative structure, but this required time and security. Neither Bābur nor Humāyūn were able to enjoy these two advantages.

Akbar thus inherited a largely clan and family based nobility. During the early years of his reign, he was able to get first-hand knowledge of the working of the nobility, and came to the conclusion that for the establishment, consolidation and expansion of the empire, he must have a ruling class that should owe everything to the ruler; clan or family loyalties should not come in the way of their obedience to the sovereign. The future developments that took place under him and partly under Jahāngīr, were directed towards this objective.

Akbar enlarged his nobility by admitting local elements (mostly local chiefs) and foreign immigrants who belonged to prominent families in their own countries (Iran and Central Asia) and came here in search of employment. These newcomers and a number of his own personal servants who were already in service in minor capacities, were given the most important appointments. Besides, he also introduced important administrative reforms to curb the

[42] See Chapter III

growth of clannish tendencies in the nobility. However, as there was no scientific method of recruitment of the nobility, whole clans of local chiefs, the families of his personal servants and the families of foreign immigrants were admitted into service. But in due course of time the resultant clannish tendencies were controlled, if not fully curbed; newly risen clans and family groups too, by virtue of their devoted service to the emperor, came to enjoy a special status at the court.

The problem of a recalcitrant nobility was largely solved by Akbar after a considerable amount of effort, and an efficient and loyal bureaucracy was built up. But as Akbar failed to provide any solution to the problem of succession, the nobility tended to divide into factions supporting rival princes. This may be noticed in the reign of Akbar himself, and more clearly still during Jahāngīr's reign. The accession crisis at the time of Akbar's serious illness showed the anxiety among the nobles about the their future careers, forcing them to take important decision about imperial succession on their own. High Akbarshāhi nobles were apparently not sure whether they would be able to maintain their prominent position in the event of the succession of Salim (Jahāngīr); and so they decided to raise to the throne Khusrau, seemingly a prince of their own choice.

Although the conspiracy failed and Jahāngīr pardoned the erring Akbarshāhī nobles, he could not place absolute reliance upon them. Therefore, he too had to bring in new elements to counter the old nobility and give them extraordinary promotions. This naturally created rivalries and suspicions between Akbarshāhi and Jahāngīrī nobles. During Jahāngīr's later years, the reaction to the rise of the family of Nur Jahān, the rivalry among princes, and groups of nobles, all helped to shake the stability of the empire.

These are some important aspects of the nobility under Akbar and Jahāngīr that need to be studied in some depth. The present study aims at illustrating the contexts of these problems by detailed investigations of the fluctuating fortunes of nine leading families of nobles. To make the study more comprehensive, I have chosen at least one family from each of the important racial group that made up the nobility, viz., the Tūrānī, the Irānī, Rajputs, Indian Muslims and Afghāns. It is hoped that the descriptive accounts will do the work of jigsaws, by assembling which one can achieve an analytical view of the imperial apparatus as it actually functioned.

CHAPTER I

The Family of Bairam Khān, Khān Khānān

The name of Bairam Khān dominates the annals of the early years of Akbar's reign; and his son, 'Abdur Raḥīm Khān Khānān, renowned as a poet of Hindi, became a prominent grandee in Akbar's later years and in Jahāngīr's reign. Bairam Khān's ancestors had served the Timurid rulers; and his father, Saif 'Alī, was in the service of Bābur. After his father's death, Bairam Khān succeeded to his position, and from then onwards served three generations of Mughal emperors, Bābur, Humāyūn and Akbar till his dismissal in 1560. After Akbar's accession, Bairam Khān enjoyed for five years a unique position at the court as a regent. The family suffered an eclipse upon his dismissal; but his son, 'Abdur Raḥīm was able to revive its fortunes and obtained a high status under Akbar and Jahāngīr. In this chapter an attempt is made to trace the history of Bairam Khān's family, with particular reference to the position of its members (in terms of posts, *manṣabs*, etc.) during three distinct phases: when Bairam Khān was its head; the phase following his dismissal; and the period of ascendancy of 'Abdur Raḥīm Khān Khānān..

Bairam Khān belonged to the Baharlu clan of the Qaraqunlu Turks and was the fifth in descent from 'Alī Shukr Beg,[1] a prominent noble in the court of Mirzā Jahān Shāh (1437-67) the ruler of Azarbaijan, Faras, Kirman and the coast of Oman under the hegemony of the Qaraqunlu. 'Alī Shukr Beg ruled as a feudatory chief over the territories of Hamadan, Dinwar, Kurdistan

[1] *Muntakhab*, I, 190-1, Badāunī has given a brief biography of Bairam Khān. *Z.K.*, I, 11-19. A detailed biography of Bairam Khān is provided by Farīd Bhakkarī who, however, does not discuss his ancestry. *Mada'in-i Akhbār*, 171b-2ab, and *Ma'āsīr-i Rahīmī*, I, 57-9 give details of his ancestry and early life.

and its dependencies.[2] After his defeat and death at the hands of Uzun Ḥasan, the Aq-quyanlu chief, his son, Pīr 'Alī Beg joined the services of Sulṭān Abū S'āid of Herat, and after the death of the latter, entered the service of his son, Sulṭān Maḥmūd. Later on he joined Sulṭān Abū Bakr of Faras but being defeated by the Aq-quyanlu army at Garmsir, fled towards Khurasān where he was defeated and killed by Sulṭān Ḥusain Mirzā of Herat.[3] His eldest son, Yār 'Alī Beg, escaped to Sulṭān Maḥmūd in Badakhshan and, after his death, sought service with Khusrau Shāh, the Mongol chief of Qunduz. After Khusrau Shāh's downfall in 1504-5, Yār 'Alī Beg's son, Saif 'Alī, entered the service of Bābur.[4] The author of the *Mada'in-i Akhbār-i Ahmadi*, writes that after the conquest of Ghaznin, Bābur granted it to Saif 'Alī.[5] After his death his son Bairam Khān was confirmed to the governorship of Ghaznin.[6]

Bairam Khān was the son of Saif 'Alī. He was born in Bādakhshan. His father died when he was very young. He was brought up under the care of Pashā Begum, his grandfather's sister, and by Amīr Beg, his maternal uncle.[7] He joined Bābur's service at the age of 16 years.

The family ever since the time of 'Alī Shukr Beg had inter-married with the Timurids. Shukr Beg's son Pīr 'Alī Beg was married to the daughter of Mirzā Sikandar. The two sons of Mirzā Jahān Shāh were married to the two daughters of 'Ali Shukr Beg, while a third daughter married the son of the Timurid ruler Sulṭān Abu Sa'id. Later, Sulṭān Maḥmūd's daughter by Pashā Begum was married to Bābur.[8] On the basis of these marriages Bairam Khān could claim close relationship with the Timurids. A very significant marriage too was that of Saif

[2] *Haft Iqlīm*, III, Vol.I, 456, Amīn Aḥmad Rāzī states that till his ('Alī Shukr Beg's) time these territories were known as territories of 'Alī Shukr (*Qalamrawa-i 'Alī Shukr*). 'Alī Shukr Beg established himself as an independent ruler with Hamdan as his capital after the death of Mirzā Jahān Shāh at the hands of Aq-quyanlu chief Uzun Ḥasan in the battle of Azarbaijan in 1473.

[3] *Bāburnāma,* tr. Beveridge, I, 49, *Mad'ain-i Akhbār*, 171b, *Ma'āṣir-i Raḥīmī*, I, 65-6.

[4] *Mada'in-i Akhbār*, 171b, says that while Saif 'Alī Beg was serving Khusrau Shāh at Qandhar, Bābur visited the place, Saif 'Alī Beg along with his son Bairam Khān, joined his service. See also *Ma'āsīr-i Raḥīmī*, I, 64.

[5] Ibid., 172a, Ghaznin was conquered in 1504. [6] Ibid.

[7] *Mada'in-i Akhbār*, f.172b. Pashā Begum was married to Sulṭān Maḥmūd.

[8] *Bāburnāma,* tr. Beveridge, I, 48-9. Mirzā Iskandar was Qaraqunlu chief between 1429-37.

'Alī Beg who fetched a wife from 'the family of the Naqshbandi Khwājas'. The Naqshbandis were held in very high esteem by the Timurids and a number of marriages took place between the two houses in Central Asia and after that in Hindustan. Muḥammad Nūruddīn, son of Khwāja Ḥasan Naqshbandi, was married to Gulbarg Begum; and Salima Sulṭān Begum was their daughter.[9] These marriages took place in Central Asia.

It was in the context of these previous marriages that Humāyūn had apparently promised to marry Salima Sulṭān to Bairam Khān. This marriage was actually solemnized during Akbar's third regnal year. This marriage and that of Gulbarg Begum to Muḥammad Nūruddīn are both strongly criticized by Abū'l Faẓl as being unsuitable alliances.[10] But Bairam Khān's family had undoubtedly acquired high status: we may notice, for example, the marriage of 'Abdur Raḥīm Khān Khānān himself, to the sister of Mirzā 'Azīz Koka.[11] However, from the later years of Akbar's reign and during the reign of Jahāngīr, members of this family and the Tūrānīs began to move away from each other. Most of the marriages contracted by Bairam Khān's family members thereafter were with women of Irānī families. The family thus came to be allied with the families of the Safavid princes of Qandhar, of I'timad-ud daulah and the Injūs. 'Abdur Raḥīm Khān Khānān also took a wife from the Muslim Rajput tribes of the Sondhas of Amarkot. Later on, he married his son Mirzā Iraj to the daughter of Jānī Beg of Thatta (a Tarkhan, and so a Tūrānī) after the conquest of Sind. (This was the last known marriage alliance with the Tūrānīs). One of his other sons was married to the daughter of Niẓām Shāh. Besides these marriages, Bairam Khān had already married a daughter of Jamāl Khān Mewati, one of whose daughters had been married to Emperor Humāyūn. These marriages again indicate that the pattern followed by this family resembled the one followed by the royal family in Akbar's reign, and was later to be also adopted by a normal Irānī noble family.[12]

[9] *Akbarnāma*, II, 64-5; *Mada'in-i Akhbār*, 162b-6ab. The author of the latter work provides more details regarding marriages of Bairam Khān's family with that of the Mirzās.

[10] *Akbarnāma*, II, 64-5. [11] *Muntakhab*, II, 360-1, *Ma'āsīr-i Raḥīmī*, I, 51.

[12] For a detailed discussion on the pattern of marriages among Mughal nobles, see, Afzal Husain, 'Marriages among Mughal Nobles as an Index of Status and Aristocratic Integration', *Proceedings of Indian History Congress*, 1972, 304-12.

It seems necessary to identify the more important members of the family before going into other details. No attempt has been made so far to reconstruct a genealogical chart of Bairam Khān's family. Bāyazīd Bayāt while giving a list of nobles who accompanied Humāyūn from Iran has given the names of six persons related to Bairam Khān. Besides Walī Beg Zulqadar who was his brother-in-law and his two nephews, Ḥusain Qulī and Ismaīl Qulī, we are unable to determine the nature of his relationship with the other three of his kinsmen, Bazmi Khān, Muḥammad Beg and Shāh Bardi Beg.[13] In any case, after Akbar's accession, these persons are not noticed in our sources. Later on Bairam Khān's son, 'Abdur Raḥīm Khān Khānān, and his sons Shāhnawāz Khān, Darāb Khān, Mirzā Raḥmān Dāḍ and Mirzā Amrullah were granted *manṣabs*. The figures show that the numerical strength of the family was not very large. But the family had the support of other sections of the nobility. We will presently see that during Bairam Khān's regency, many of his personal servants were raised to high positions[14] and his friends, specially the Uzbek nobles, supported him to the last. Later on, 'Abdur Raḥīm Khān Khānān seems to have enjoyed the cooperation of Indian Muslims, particularly of the Barhā Sayyids and Lodī Afghāns.

Upon joining Bābur's service, Bairam Khān was attached to the retinue of Humāyūn. After Bābur's conquest of northern India, he accompanied Humāyūn to Kabul. The author of the *Ma'āṣir-i Raḥīmī* writes that Bābur had a very high opinion of him and placed him among his distinguished nobles. After Humāyūn's accession he was raised to the offices of *Muhardār* and *Wakīl*.[15] He is said to have played an important role not only in the campaign against the Afghāns, but also in the siege of Chittor, and the Gujarat and Bengal campaigns.[16] He was present in the ill-fated battle of Kannauj. After the defeat of the imperial armies he fled to Sambhal and became separated from Humāyūn for three years.[17]

[13] *Tazkira-i Humāyūn*, 185-7. Besides this, Bāyazīd provides a list of the servants of Bairam Khān who accompanied him to India with Humāyūn.

[14] *Z.K.*, I, 17, Farīd Bhakkarī writes that 25 persons of lower ranks were promoted to the *manṣab* of 5000 by Bairam Khān. Cf. *Akbarnāma*, II, 107. Menial servants of Bairam Khān were raised to the status of *Khāns* and *Sulṭāns*.

[15] *Ma'āṣir-i Rahīmī*, I, 64, *Z.K.*, I, 11, adds that he was granted *manṣab* of 5000.

[16] *Mada'in-i Akhbār*, 54b-5a, 172ab; *Akbarnāma*, I, 185; *Tarikh-i Gujarat*, 23.

[17] *Akbarnāma*, I, 185-6; *Ma'āṣir-i Raḥīmī*, II, 12-13.

In 1543, eluding Afghān surveillance, he joined Humāyūn at Jhun in Sindh.[18] At this time the Mughal emperor was in a wretched condition, and, having lost hopes of relief from every quarter, even contemplated retiring to Mecca. Bairam Khān patched up a treaty with the Arghuns and persuaded Humāyūn to proceed towards Qandhar. When Humāyūn met rebuff from Mirzā Askari at Mastang,[19] Bairam Khān induced Humāyūn to go to Iran and seek Persian help to recover his position. The author of the *Ma'āṣir-i Raḥīmī* naturally enough emphasizes Bairam Khān's role at this juncture, being concerned about exalting the antecedants of 'Abdur Raḥīm. Bairam Khān is said to have written letters to his kinsmen in Iran and to have sent a petition to the Persian emperor, for which he supposedly received a favourable response.[20] This is, however, not corroborated by any earlier source. It is true, though, that when he was sent as Humāyūn's ambassador to the Persian court, Bairam Khān was favourably received and was referred to as *Amīr-i Muẓẓam* in a Persian *farmān* and also accorded the title of *Khān*.[21]

In Humāyūn's recovery of Qandhar and Kabul, Bairam Khān played a very conspicuous role. After the conquest of Qandhar that fort was granted to him so as to placate the emperor of Persia.[22] It came to be reported to Humāyūn that he was contemplating rebellion and Humāyūn immediately rushed to Qandhar, only to find the suspicion to be false. Though Humāyūn yet wanted to transfer him and appoint Mun'im Khān in his place, the latter persuaded him to defer the move and requested that Bairam Khān be confirmed. Humāyūn finally agreed.[23]

When Humāyūn marched into Hindustan, Bairam Khān was summoned from Qandhar to accompany the emperor. In the battles of Sarhind and Machhiwara, Bairam Khān rendered conspicuous

[18] *Akbarnama*, I, 185-6 [19] *Tarikh-i Alfi*, 418; *Mada'in-i Akhbār*, 173a.

[20] *Mada'in-i Akhbār*, 66a; *Z.K.*, I, 11-12; *Ma'āṣir-i Rahīmī*, I, 575. Abū'l Bāqī Nihavandī further alleges that Bairam Khān was offered the government of Dayar Bakr in Azarbaijan which had belonged to his ancestors, Qarā Yūsuf and Mirzā Jahān Shāh. But he refused.

[21] *Taẓkira-i Humāyūn*, 32, 34; *Haft Iqlīm*, III, 154-7; *Z.K.*, I, 11-12.

[22] *Taẓkira-i Humāyūn*, 51. The nobles of Yādgār Nāsir Mirzā pleaded that Qandhar should be taken from Bairam Khān. Also see *Akbarnāma*, I, 241, *Ma'āṣir-i Raḥīmī*, I, 600.

[23] *Taẓkira-i Humāyūn*, 170-1. Bāyazīd adds that Mun'im Khān knew well that either the Safavids would conquer Qandhar or Humāyūn would transfer it to the Persian emperor as he had already promised it to him. He did not therefore want to have so transitory a charge.

service.[24] This Abū'l Faẓl himself acknowledges: 'The head of the faithful servants was Bairam Khān, who throughout waited on the stirrup of His Majesty as if he were his good fortune.'[25]

After the Mughal recovery of Indian possessions, Bairam Khān was appointed over Sarhind. There is no reference to any other administrative charge being assigned to any of his family members. Soon afterwards he was appointed *atālīq* (guardian) of Prince Akbar, in place of Mun'im Khān, and was deputed along with the prince to the Panjab to replace Shāh Abū'l Ma'ali, whose loyalty was suspect. While Bairam Khān and the prince were marching against Sikandar Afghān and had reached Kalanur, they received the news of Humāyūn's death. Bairam Khān summoned all the important nobles present in the camp and had Akbar crowned as emperor.[26]

At the time of his accession Akbar was only 14 years old. Being too young he was not in a position to take up in his own hands the reins of administration. In these circumstances, by virtue of being his *Atālīq*, Bairam Khān was appointed *Wakīl-us Salṭanat* (vicegerent). All the affairs of state and finances were made over to him. He used to sit in the *Diwān Khanā* twice a week and attended to all civil and military affairs. Whatever decisions were taken by him were reported to the emperor; and this was considered enough. Bairam Khān appointed and dismissed the highest officers of the state at his discretion. It was alleged that he even interfered in the personal matters of the emperor, and the emperor could incur personal expenditure only with his approval.[27]

The greatest problem before Bairam Khān was the threat from the Afghāns; in the east, Hemu, the commander-in-chief of 'Adil Shāh Sur, was threatening both Agra and Delhi and in the Panjab Sikandar could not be fully subdued. However, no serious challenge was posed from within to Bairam Khān's position as *Wakīl*. Only

[24] *Taẓkira-i Humāyūn*, 193-4; *Akbarnāma*, I, 343-7; *Tarikh-i Shāhi*, 336-7.

[25] *Akbarnāma*, I, 350.

[26] *Tārikh-i Akbarī*, 25; *Taẓkira-i Humāyūn*, 195; *Akbarnāma*, I, 351, 366-7.

[27] *Akbarnāma*, II, 5, 15, 57, 63-4, 70-1, Abū'l Faẓl tells us that Bairam Khān opposed Akbar's marriage to the daughter of 'Abdullah Khān Mughal. Badāunī at one place writes 'he (Akbar) had no voice in some of the transactions relating to the expenses of the Exchequer and because there was no privy purse at all, the servants of the emperor had poor fief'. *Muntakhab*, II, 8, 26-9, 36-9. *Z.K.*, I, 13. For detailed discussion on the powers of *Wakīl* specially during Bairam Khān's tenure of office, see Ibn Hasan, *The Central Structure of Mughal Empire*, 121-2.

Shāh Abū'l Ma'ali, a very senior Mughal noble, showed some sign of rebellion, when he refused to attend Akbar's coronation ceremony. He was imprisoned on the orders of Bairam Khān.[28]

In the meantime Tardī Beg Khān was defeated at Delhi and when the defeated commanders joined the imperial standard at Sarhind, he was charged with treason and, on the evidence of Khān Zamān and others, put to death. The execution was partly at least due to jealousy; Tardī Beg was considered by the regent to be a dangerous rival.[29]

After the victory over Hemu at Panipat, Bairam Khān rewarded and promoted chiefly his own servants and friends. This helped him to considerably enlarge his following. Areas in Doab were assigned to 'Alī Qulī Uzbek (*sarkār* of Sambhal and other *parganas* of Doab), 'Abdullah Khān Uzbek (*sarkār* of Kalpi), Sikandar Khān Uzbek (sent to Sialkot to assist Khizr Khwāja Khān in operations against Sikandar Sur) and Qayā Khān Gunj (Agra).[30] Sometime later 'Alī Qulī Khān's younger brother Bahādur Khān was appointed to Multan. By these appointments Bairam Khān was able to have complete control over the larger portion of the areas that had been brought under Mughal rule at the moment.

At the centre, Bairam Khān himself enjoyed the position of a *de facto* ruler. Pīr Moḥammad Khān Sarwāni, a personal servant of his, was attached to the person of the king in the capacity of the *Wakīl* of the regent and was a key figure in the administration.[31] Two old officers, Khwāja Sulṭān 'Alī and Mīr Asghar *Munshi*, were dismissed. Khwāja Amīnuddīn was appointed *Bakhshī* and Shaikh Gadāi Kamboh was appointed *Ṣadr*. Both these officers were proteges of Bairam Khān.[32]

[28] *Taẕkira-i Humāyūn*, 195; *Akbarnāma*, II, 15-16; *Muntakhab*, II 9-11; *Z.K.*, I, 77; *Ma'asir-i Rahimi*, I, 642. Cf. Iqtidar Alam Khan, 'The Mughal Court Politics During Bairam Khān's Regency' in *Medieval India — A Miscellany*, I, 23.

[29] *Tarikh-i Akbarī*, 50; *Akbarnāma*, II, 29-30. See 'The Mughal Court Politics during Bairam Khān's Regency', 26-7. Also see Chapter III.

[30] For instances of cooperation between Bairam Khān and the Uzbeks see, *Akbarnāma*, II, 45, 69, 82, 97, 105-6, 114; Badāunī, II, 14. See also for more details Chapter III.

[31] *Akbarnāma*, II, 45, 59; *Z.K.*, I, 101-3; *Ma'āsir-ul Umarā*, III, 182-6.

[32] *Muntakhab*, II, 14, Khwāja Sulṭān 'Alī and Mīr Asghar Munshi were arrested by Bairam Khān because they were considered supporters of Tardī Beg. For an account of Khwāja Aminuddīn and Shaikh Gadāi Kamboh, see *Ma'āṣir-ul Umarā*, I, 630, II, 29; also *Akbarnāma*, II, 96.

Thus we see that Bairam Khān and his group of nobles came to control the entire machinery of the state at the centre as well as in the provinces. His own relations received neither any office at the centre nor any appointment in the provinces, and no reason for this can be traced in our evidence. Nevertheless, it was alleged that they exercised considerable influence on the affairs of the state.[33] Walī Beg Zulqadar and his sons Ḥusain Qulī and Ismaīl Qulī, along with some other nobles, are specially mentioned. It was also alleged that these nobles were actually responsible for creating the crisis that arose later and brought about the downfall of Bairam Khān.[34]

The concentration of all authority in the hands of one group of nobles was naturally resented by other groups. Prominent among the opponents were Ādham Khān and his mother, Maham Anaga; Shahābuddīn Aḥmad Khān and other members of the Atka Khail. Not only were they resentful at being denied their due share in power, they had other complaints as well. They were assigned poor *jāgīrs*, often in distant and hostile regions. For example, Ādham Khān was assigned *a jāgīr* in Hathkanth near Agra which was inhabited by rebellious Rajputs, while Atka Khān was given the *jāgīr* of Bhera in the Panjab. Akbar accused Bairam Khān of disregarding claims of old and loyal nobles.[35] Certain incidents took place in which Bairam Khān suspected the hand of Atka Khān, Ādham Khān, Maham Anaga and others. One of these was an attempt on

[33] *Akbarnāma*, II, 93. 'Things became beyond bounds, on account of ill-fated maladaroit flatterers such as Walī Beg Zulqadar and Shaikh Gadāi Kamboh' (tr. 140-1). The *farmān* addressed to Bairam Khān, as given in *Akbarnāma*, II, 107: 'He himself knows what was the position and rank of Walī Beg among Qizilbashes, without considering his service, his lineage or his position, and mainly on account of relationship, viz., his being his (Bairam Khān's) brother-in-law, he brought him and put him over the great officers.... He gave Ḥusain Qulī who has not even fought with a chicken, equal position with Sikandar Khān, 'Abdullah Khān and Bahādur Khān and gave him cultivated fiefs, while he satisfied the great Khāns with waste land' (tr., II, 163).

[34] Ibid.

[35] Ibid., II, 106-7, *farmān* of Akbar.

To his own menial servants ... he gave the titles of *Sulṭān* and *Khān* and presented them with ... rich fiefs and productive territories, whilst he with total want of considerations made the Khāns, the Princes, the officers, and the trusted servants of H.M. Jannat Ashiyani whose rank, claims and qualifications are known to everyone to be in want of dry bread. Nay, he aimed at the life and honour of all of them and he took no thought for old servants and domestics ... and did not provide them with even the smallest offices which might have been a means of livelihood to them.

his life (July 1557). Bairam Khān was greatly enraged and Atka Khān along with his whole family had to take an oath that Atka Khān was not involved in the incident. Maham Anaga also sought to reassure him.[36] On account of continuous pressure from the nobility, Bairam Khān agreed to consult the prominent nobles of the court. It was agreed that he would meet the prominent nobles twice every week to discuss political and financial matters before submitting them to the king.[37]

A new source of weakness was the dissension among his own proteges. There arose a quarrel between Pīr Muḥammad Sarwāni and Shaikh Gadāi. Bairam Khān sided with the latter. Pīr Muḥammad Sarwāni felt greatly aggrieved and did not come to the court for several days.[38] On the other hand, 'Alī Qulī was involved in a scandal with a boy which was exploited by Bairam Khān's critics; Pīr Muḥammad took the initiative on their behalf. 'Alī Qulī was punished and Bairam Khān could not protect him.[39] In order to reassert his authority, Bairam Khān took action. In the second half of 1559 he dismissed Pīr Muḥammad and appointed Ḥajī Muḥammad Khān Sistānī as his personal *Wakīl*. Some low-ranking officers were raised to high positions. Shaikh Gadāi was given some more responsibility in political and financial affairs, in addition to his functions as *Ṣadr*.[40]

The assertion of power did no more than hide for a time the continuing erosion of Bairam Khān's authority. Ādham Khān, Shahābuddīn Āḥmad Khān, Mirzā Sharafuddīn Ḥusain, Atka Khān

---

See also *Akbarnāma*, II, 78: While granting the *jāgīr* of Hathkanth Bairam Khan thought that 'in this way he (Ādham Khān) might be removed from court, while at the same time rebels of that quarter would receive punishment and thus two good objects be carried out at once'. For Ādham Khān, see *Ma'āṣir-ul Umarā*, I, 67, See also Chapter II.

36 *Akbarnāma*, II, 60, 62. For details see Chapter II.

37 Ibid., II, 67. Also see, 'The Mughal court Politics during Bairam Khān's Regency', 32-3.

38 Ibid., II, 66.

39 Ibid., 82. 'Alī Qulī's *jāgīr* of Lucknow was confiscated and given to the Jalāirs. Later on, when he sent his agent Burj-i 'Alī to the court to attempt a reconciliation, on the orders of Pīr Ṃuhammad Khān, the agent was thrown from the palace top, and he succumbed to his injuries. For more details about 'Alī Qulī in this affair, see Chapter III.

40 Ibid., II, 86-7, *Z.K.*, I, 17, states that some 25 persons of lower ranks were promoted to the rank of 5000 under Bairam Khān. *Ma'āṣir-ul Umarā*, II, 540, Shaikh Gadāi used to put his seal on the back of court orders (Cf. *Akbarnāma*, II, 107).

and Maham Anaga, being close to the emperor gradually made him an accomplice in a conspiracy against the regent. Akbar himself was now tired of the bonds of tutelege, and the nobles convinced him that unless Bairam Khān was removed he would not be in a position to wield real power.[41]

A plan was worked out and in accordance with it Akbar together with Maham Anaga and Ādham Khān left Agra ostensibly on a hunting expedition; they then journeyed to Delhi where they were welcomed by Shahābuddīn Aḥmad Khān.[42] From Delhi, at the instigation of Maham Anaga and her colleagues, Akbar issued two *farmāns* to Bairam Khān dismissing him from office. He was ordered to proceed on a pilgrimage to Mecca.[43] Bairam Khān accepted the order and sent to the emperor his banner, kettledrums and all insignia of rank.[44] Although Bairam Khān surrendered his office, his own clansmen and allies, specially Walī Beg Zulqadar and Shaikh Gadāi Kamboh, wanted to resist by taking recourse to arms.[45] When Pīr Muḥammad Sarwāni with a body of troops was deputed against him, Bairam Khān's bitterest feelings were aroused.[46]

[41] *Muntakhab*, II, 35-7; Badāunī specifically mentions Ādham Khān, Maham Anaga and Ṣadiq Muḥammad Khān who often spoke to the emperor against Bairam Khān. Badāunī also at some other place mentions that Akbar was unhappy with the state of affairs (*Muntakhab*, II, 36). 'Arif Qandhari believes that Bairam Khān's main fault was giving undue favours to a section of the nobles at the cost of old nobles who were in the service of Mughals for a very long time. These nobles even during this period were on intimate terms with the emperor (*Tārikh-i Akbarī*, 57-8). *Akbarnāma*, II, 93-4. Abū'l Faẓl, however, writes that in the conspiracy against Bairam Khān, Akbar himself took the initiative and conveyed his intentions to Ādham Khān, Maham Anaga and Sharafuddīn Ḥusain. Shahābuddīn Aḥmad Khān was informed about the plot by Maham Anaga.

[42] *Akbarnāma*, II, 94-5, *Muntakhab*, II, 36-7, the *Tabaqāt*, II, 142-4, however suggests that though Ādham Khān, Maham Anaga and some other nobles were creating misunderstanding between Bairam Khān and Akbar, there was no premeditated plan. It was only by chance that when Akbar left Agra, Maham Anaga persuaded him to go to Delhi to see his mother Maryam Makani who was unwell. After reaching Delhi they persuaded him to dismiss Bairam Khān.

[43] *Akbarnāma*, II, 95-6; *Tārikh-i Alafī*, 600ab; *Muntakhab*, II, 35-9.

[44] *Akbarnāma*, II, 95-9.

[45] *Muntakhab*, II, 37-8. Badāunī writes that when Bairam Khān came to know of the states of affairs, he called a council of his nobles. The advice of Shaikh Gadāi with several others was this that 'before the balance of fortune should be turned against him, he should set out and get Emperor into his power'. Abū'l Faẓl also mentions that Shaikh Gadāi and Walī Beg Zulqadar wanted military action. Cf. *Akbarnāma*, II, 96-7; *Tārikh-i Alfī*, 600b-1a.

[46] *Tabaqāt*, II, 146; *Muntakhab*, II, 39-40.

Giving up the idea of pilgrimage he moved into the Punjab to punish those nobles who had brought about his downfall. But his desperate plan did not meet with success: he was defeated by Shamsuddīn Atka and had to take shelter in the Siwaliks.[47] He now sued for pardon which was granted. When he sought an assurance from Mun'im Khān for his safety, this too was conceded.[48] At his own wish he was permitted to proceed to Mecca.[49] He was, however, not destined to reach the holy city. He was murdered at Pattan in Gujarat by some Afghans.[50]

II

With the removal of Bairam Khān from the office of *Wakīl* and his subsequent murder, the prestige of his family declined rapidly. Some members of the family were arrested.[51] The nobles who had associated with the family in the lifetime of Bairam Khān now deserted it.[52] Even the Uzbek nobles, who had been greatly favoured by him, remained neutral during the entire crisis.[53]

Bairam Khān was accused of rebellion and the responsibility of inciting him was placed on Walī Beg Zulqadar, his sons and other relations. And yet, on the whole, members of Bairam Khān's family were not treated harshly after his downfall.[54] They were soon released and their offences were pardoned. They were also given fresh assignments. Thus, it can be inferred that Akbar was not personally hostile to the family. What he wanted was to get out of the tutelage of the regent.

[47] *Tārikh-i Alfī*, 601a-2ab; *Akbarnāma*, II, 103-6; *Tabaqāt*, II, 146-50; *Muntakhab*, II, 38-41. Also see Chapters II and III.

[48] *Akbarnāma*, II, 117-18, Bairam Khān was apprehensive of Chaghtāi grandees and other imperial servants.

[49] Ibid., *Tabaqāt*, II, 149-50.

[50] *Akbarnāma,* II, 117-18.

[51] *Akbarnāma*, II, 110-13, Ḥusain Qulī was arrested when he went to court along with the insignia of office of Bairam Khān. Sikandar Sulṭān, Ismaīl Qulī and Aḥmad Beg were arrested after the defeat of Bairam Khān.

[52] Qiyā Khān Ganj, Haji Muḥammad Khān Sistānī and Tarsūn Muḥammad Khān may be noted among many nobles who deserted Bairam Khān soon after the news of his downfall became known.

[53] For the role of Uzbek nobility, see Chapter III.

[54] *Tārikh-i Alfī*, 600b; *Akbarnāma*, II, 97-8. After being arrested when Ḥusain Qulī was given to the charge of Ādham Khān, Akbar was reported to have told Ādham Khān that 'he would be held responsible if any injury happened to Ḥusain Qulī'. Cf. *Akbarnāma*, II, 111.

The numerical strength of the group suffered a great setback during this period. Bairam Khān and Walī Beg Zulqadar were dead, and many other supporters of the family were also either killed in battle or joined the imperial forces. Ismaīl Qulī, Ḥusain Qulī, Aḥmad Beg and Ya'qūb Beg were the only noted members of the family left. Bairam Khān's son 'Abdur Raḥīm was very young. Ḥusain Qulī, who was later on given the title of Khān-i Jahān, was the seniormost member of the family.

The first appointment from amongst the family during this period was to a charge in the region of Ajmer and Nagor. Mirzā Sharafuddīn Ḥusain who held this area in *jāgir* had rebelled and fled from the court. The emperor assigned the area to Ḥusain Qulī and ordered him to chastise the rebel.[55] When Sharafuddīn Ḥusain came to know of Ḥusain Qulī's approach, he left Tarkhan Diwana to defend Ajmer and himself fled towards Nagor. The imperial forces captured Ajmer and proceeded towards Jalor pushing the Mirzā out of the imperial dominions.[56] At Sirohi he was joined by Shāh Abū'l Ma'ali who had recently returned from Mecca.[57] Both of them agreed to join forces.[58] Shāh Abū'l Ma'ali proceeded to Hajipur (near Alwar) to attack the family of Ḥusain Qulī which was lodged there, and thence to proceed to Kabul to incite Mirzā Hakim to invade Hindustan. A very grave situation was created by the rebels. Ḥusain Qulī faced the situation with great determination and despatched Aḥmad Beg and Sikandar Beg to defend the fort of Hajipur. Shāh Abū'l Ma'ali changed his route and proceeded to Narnol. He captured the fort, arrested its commandant and seized the treasure kept there. But soon afterwards, he was forced to flee towards the Panjab pursued by the imperial troops under Aḥmad Beg and Sikandar Beg. In one of the battles fought between Abū'l Ma'ali and the imperial armies, Aḥmad Beg and Sikandar Beg were killed, but Shāh Abū'l Ma'ali's troops also suffered heavy casualties, and he fled to Kabul.[59]

After making arrangements for the security of Ajmer, Ḥusain Qulī marched against Merta. The fort surrendered but it was again

[55] *Akbarnāma*, II, 195-6; *Mada'in-i Akhbar*, 216ab; *Muntakhab*, II, 59.
[56] *Akbarnāma,* II, 195-6.
[57] *Tazkira-i Humāyūn*, 277-8; *Akbarnāma*, II, 198; *Tabaqāt*, II, 164-5.
[58] *Akbarnāma*, II, 198-9. Cf. *Muntakhab*, II, 59-60.
[59] *Tārikh-i Alfī*, 610ab; *Tazkira-i Humāyūn*, 277-8; *Akbarnāma*, II, 198-9.

assigned to its previous possessor, Jaimal, upon orders of the emperor.[60] The other territories recovered by Ḥusain Qulī, which were previously held by Mirzā Sharfuddīn, were conferred upon him.[61]

While Ḥusain Qulī was in Ajmer, he was ordered to undertake an expedition against Jodhpur. After prolonged fighting the fort was captured. Ḥusain Qulī marched ahead and occupied Pali. Chandra Sen, the Rathor ruler, was forced to flee towards Bhadrajun, while the Sangra chief of Pali retired towards Mewar.[62]

In October 1567, Akbar marched against Chittor. Ḥusain Qulī who held the charge of Ajmer and Nagor was summoned to join the campaign. He invaded Udaipur and Kumbhalmir hoping to capture the Rana. Though the Rana escaped, Ḥusain Qulī ruthlessly devastated the country and much booty fell into his hands.[63]

In the year 1568, the Atka Khail was transferred from the Panjab and Ḥusain Qulī along with his brother Ismaīl Qulī was transferred from Ajmer and Nagor to the Panjab, with Ḥusain Qulī being made its governor.[64] In the meantime, he was also ordered to join in the expedition against Ranthambhor. At the request of Rai Surjan (who 'in order that his honour might be preserved begged that one of the intimate courtiers might come and introduce him to the court') the emperor sent Ḥusain Qulī into the fort to reassure him and bring him to the imperial presence to render homage.[65] Afterwards Ḥusain Qulī and Ismaīl Qulī were permitted to proceed to the Panjab.

The appointment of Ḥusain Qulī and his family in the Panjab and the transfer of Atka Khail was a significant event. Great prestige was enjoyed by the Atkas. But their concentration in one province, especially in the Panjab for a very long time, was seen as a source of danger.[66] On the other hand, Akbar apparently had great confidence in Ḥusain Qulī and his group, though they did not perhaps enjoy much support in the nobility.

[60] *Akbarnāma*, II, 196. [61] *Akbarnāma*, II, 196. *Mada'in-i Akhbār*, 216ab.

[62] *Akbarnāma*, II, 196. *Pargana ri Vigat*, I, 68; *Banki Das ri Wigat*, 202-4.

[63] *Akbarnāma*, II, 196. 313, II, 15, 58; *Tabaqāt*, II, 217-20; *Muntakhab*, II, 102-5; *Ma'āsir-ul Umarā*, II, 646-7. The fort of Chittor was captured in October 1567.

[64] *Akbarnāma*, II, 332-3; *Tabaqāt*, II, 223.

[65] *Akbarnāma*, II, 333, 336-8; *Tabaqāt*, II, 223; *Mada'in-i Akhbār*, 246a, 248b.

[66] For more details regarding the Atka Khail and the nature of their transfer, see Chapter II.

During Ḥusain Qulī's governorship of Panjab, two important problems were faced by him: the Nagarkot campaign and the rebellion of Ibrāhīm Ḥusain Mirzā.

Raja Jaichand of Nagarkot had incurred the displeasure of Akbar on some account. He was summoned to the court and was arrested. His territories were declared confiscated, and Ḥusain Qulī was ordered to capture and grant it to Raja Bir Bal. Raja Jaichand's son, Govind Das, received a false report that his father had been killed, and he accordingly rebelled.[67] Ḥusain Qulī invaded Nagarkot and laid siege to the fort. The siege lasted several months. While the siege operations were in progress and the surrender of the fort seemed imminent, it was reported from Lahore that Ibrāhīm Ḥusain Mirzā and other rebels had reached there from Gujarat and were creating trouble. The situation was naturally serious. Accordingly Ḥusain Qulī convened a meeting of the important nobles in the camp. There was a sharp division of opinion; the governor and his associates favoured decisive action against Nagarkot first and only after that against the rebel Mirzās. But the other group led by Moḥibb 'Alī Khān, Mirzā Yūsuf Khān and Khurram Khān proposed a settlement with the besieged and a withdrawal for immediate action against the rebels at Lahore. It appears that the opposite group was more numerous and Ḥusain Qulī had to accept their opinion, but on the condition that they would own responsibility for this decision in writing so as to absolve him of any risk of personal responsibility in case the emperor did not approve of the treaty. The officers agreed, and a treaty was made with the besieged.[68]

This episode brings into sharp focus the inherent weakness of Ḥusain Qulī's position. Though he held the charge of the *ṣūba* of Panjab, he could not take a decision without consulting other nobles who were appointed to help him, and his own opinion could be turned down by his colleagues.

Freed from the Nagarkot campaign, Ḥusain Qulī came back to Lahore to deal with the Mirzās. On the approach of the royal forces the rebel Mirzās fled towards Multan. Ḥusain Qulī pursued them

[67] *Akbarnāma*, II, 370; *Tabaqāt*, II, 256-57; *Muntakhab*, II, 161-2.

[68] *Akbarnāma*, III, 36-7. Badāunī gives a different version. He believes that the news of the arrival of Ibrāhīm Ḥusain Mirzā and the sufferings of the army of Ḥusain Qulī were responsible for the treaty. Cf. *Muntakhab*, II, 162-3; *Tabaqāt*, II, 256-9. For details of the terms of the treaty, see *Akbarnāma*, III, 36-7.

through the Panjab and overtook them at Tulamba. Ibrāhim Ḥusain Mirzā succeeded in escaping to Multan; but Masūd Mirzā was captured.[69]

In 1573, Ḥusain Qulī visited the court. He presented Masūd Mirzā before the emperor. In recognition of his service, Husain Qulī was granted the title of Khān-i Jahān. The government of Lahore and the whole of Panjab was re-entrusted to him. He was also favoured with additional *jāgīrs*;[70] Raja Todar Mal was deputed along with him to attend to the affairs of the *amirs* posted in the Panjab.[71]

During Ḥusain Qulī's tenure of office in the Panjab, Mirzā Sulaimān who was expelled from his native country took refuge at the court of Akbar. The emperor ordered Ḥusain Qulī to proceed to Badakshan and help Mirzā Sulaimān to get back his crown.[72] But in the meantime Mun'im Khān, governor of Bengal, died and Mirzā Sulaimān was offered governorship of Bengal.[73] Mirzā Sulaimān declined the offer as he was anxious to recover Badakshan. Therefore, Ḥusain Qulī was appointed governor of Bengal; his brother Ismaīl and Raja Todar Mal also accompanied him there.[74]

The charge of Bengal was yet another important assignment for the family. But Ḥusain Qulī was put in a very difficult situation because most of the officers already posted in Bengal were Mughals or Chaghtāis. The Chaghtāi officers apparently resented the appointment of a 'Qizlbash' as their commander.[75] His entire energy was spent in keeping the Chaghtāi officers in check and checkmate the Afghāns who were trying desperately to recover Bengal after Mun'im Khān's death.

After reaching Bengal Ḥusain Qulī along with Ismaīl Qulī and Raja Todar Mal persuaded the officers to join him in the campaign

[69] *Tārikh-i Akbarī*, 163; *Akbarnāma*, III, 37-8; *Muntakhab*, II, 163; *Tabaqāt*, II, 259.

[70] *Akbarnāma*, III, 39-40; *Tabaqāt*, II, 260.

[71] *Akbarnāma*, III, 39-40; *Tabaqāt*, II, 260.

[72] *Tārikh-i Akbarī*, 157; *Muntakhab*, II, 216.

[73] *Akbarī*, III, 161-2. Badāunī does not mention the offer of Bengal to Mirzā Sulaimān. On the contrary the author says, 'at his own request and for the peace of the kingdom', it was settled that Mirzā Sulaimān should go by sea on pilgrimage to Hijaz. Cf. *Muntakhab*, II, 216, 218.

[74] Ibid., III, 161-2.

[75] Ibid., III, 162, Abū'l Faẓl writes, 'some from evil disposition ... brought forward the affair of religion and began to chatter foolishly about headship of Ḥusain Qulī'. *Muntakhab*, II, 227, and *Tabaqāt*, II, 481, 83-4, do not mention differences between Chaghtāis and Khān-i Jahān over the latter's religious beliefs.

against the Afghāns. At Teliagarhi he defeated the Afghāns and captured the fort.[76] He then marched to Tanda to drive out Dāud Afghān who had shut himself up in the fort of Agmahal (the future Rajmahal). At this juncture the Chaghtāi officers refused to cooperate with him because they professed embarrassment at being headed by a Qizlbāsh.[77] When the emperor was informed about his weak position, he ordered Muẓaffar Khān, governor of Bihar, to proceed to help him. Although Muẓaffar Khān was a Persian and an old servant of Bairam Khān, he delayed carrying out this order. It was only after the assurance that the campaign was to begin immediately that he came.[78] The two commanders defeated the Afghāns at Agmahal. Many of the prominent Afghāns were killed and Dāud was captured. The remnants of the Afghāns were then defeated in Satgaon, and other places. Ḥusain Qulī also succeeded in reducing to submission Raja Mal Gosain, the *zamīndār* of Kuch Bihar.[79]

Ḥusain Qulī returned to Sihhatpur, a town which he had founded near Tanda. Here he took ill and died in December 1578.[80] While describing his death, Abū'l Faẓl says that emboldened by some of his great victories and the huge booty which he had collected in these campaigns, Ḥusain Qulī had contemplated rebellion.[81] These assertions are not corroborated by any evidence, and the suspicion might have been raised by Abū'l Faẓl himself since he shows himself to be a consistent critic of Walī Beg Zulqadar and his sons and relations, especially Ḥusain Qulī. What is obvious from Abū'l Faẓl's assertion is that the family of Bairam Khān was still under some cloud at the Mughal court.[82]

[76] *Akbarnāma*, III, 162-3; *Muntakhab*, II, 227.

[77] *Akbarnāma*, III, 178, 'The officers of the victorious army were for the most part Chaghtāis, and did not wish that so great an enterprise should be headed by Khān-i Jahān who was a Qizlbash.'

[78] Ibid., 179-80.

[79] For the details of Bengal campaign, see *Akbarnāma*, III, 179-83, 259-60, *Muntakhab*, II, 227-30, 237-8, *Riyaz-us Salatin*, 167, see also, Maulvi Muḥammad Akram, *Bengal aur Orissa men Raja Todar Mal ki Karguzari* (Urdu), 7-9.

[80] *Akbarnāma*, III, 263, *Muntakhab*, II, 267, *Ma'āṣir-ul Umarā*, I, 652-3.

[81] *Akbarnāma*, III, 263.

[82] Ibid., II, 132. When 'Abdur Raḥīm was brought to the court from Ahmadabad after the murder of Bairam Khān, Abū'l Faẓl states, 'His Majesty Shahinshāh in

III

We have seen that after the removal of Bairam Khān, the position of his family deteriorated considerably during the period of its leadership by Ḥusain Qulī. However, the emperor utilized the opportunity for retaining some of its members in high ranks and positions.

The eclipse of the family came to an end with the rise of 'Abdur Raḥīm Khān Khānān. It is a matter for consideration why so much favour was shown to the son of Bairam Khān and how a family numerically so weak became once again so important.

As we have seen, even Abū'l Fazl found very little that was blameworthy in Bairam Khān.[83] He puts all responsibility for Bairam Khān's rebellion on Walī Beg, his sons and other proteges.[84] When 'Abdur Raḥīm was brought to the court from Pattan, he was taken under the personal care of the emperor. Akbar appointed scholars and nobles like Maulana Amin Andjānī, Mīr Abū'l Fateḥ and Mān Singh as his tutors.[85] In a further act of recognition of his high rank, the emperor had him married to the sister of Mirzā 'Azīz Koka.[86]

The family remained numerically very weak in the 1580s and its representation in the nobility was very small. Ḥusain Qulī, Aḥmad Beg and Sikandar Sulṭān were already dead. Ismaīl Qulī held a *jāgīr* in Kalpi after being transferred from Bengal upon the death of Ḥusain Qulī. Thus now Ismaīl Qulī and 'Abdur Raḥīm were the only members of the family holding any position. Later on the family improved its position when 'Abdur Raḥīm's sons were granted *manṣabs* and a few other nobles became linked to the family through marriage.

'Abdur Raḥīm was brought up by Akbar and in his early years he accompanied the emperor in his campaigns.[87] In the first and second Gujarat campaign he accompanied the emperor and was assigned

---

spite of evil speakers and evil thinkers received that child of lustrous forehead in the lines of whose brows there were the notes of nobleness and truth with inborn kindness and reared him in the shadow of his own supervision' (tr. 203).

[83] See supra. [84] See supra.

[85] *Mada'in-i Akhbār*, 190b; *Akbarnāma*, II, 132-3; *Ma'āṣir-ul Umarā*, I, 693-4.

[86] *Z.K.*, I, 31.

[87] 'Abdur Raḥīm was taken with the emperor in the campaign against 'Alī Qulī Khān-i Zaman and other Uzbek nobles (*Ma'āṣir-ul Umarā*, I, 693-4).

Pattan under the tutelage of Sayyid Aḥmad Barhā.[88] During the second campaign in the battle of Sarnal he commanded the centre and distinguished himself.[89] After that he returned to the capital along with the emperor.

In 1576, Mirzā 'Azīz Koka who had disobeyed imperial orders in connection with the application of *Dāgh* regulations, was dismissed from the governorship of Gujarat. 'Abdur Raḥīm was raised to the *manṣab* of 4,000 and appointed governor of Gujarat in place of Mirzā 'Aziz Koka. As he had no experience, Wazīr Khān was appointed as his deputy. 'Abdur Raḥīm was ordered to give 'precedence in all affairs to Wazīr Khān's opinion and approval'.[90] Shortly afterwards Akbar visited Ajmer and summoned him to his presence and ordered him to join Bhagwan Dās and Mān Singh in the Mewar campaign.[91]

In 1581, he was appointed *Mīr-i 'Arz* [92] in charge of presenting petitions at the court. While still holding the office of *Mīr-i 'Arz*, 'Abdur Raḥīm was ordered to proceed to Ajmer, where a nephew of Rajā Bhārmal had killed Dastam Khān, an imperial official. He was granted the *jāgīr* of Ranthambhor and was asked to punish the miscreants and to establish peace in the area.[93] The details of the campaign are not available. However, he was called back to the court in 1582 to attend the annual darbar. All the important

[88] *Akbarnāma*, III, 6; *Muntakhab*, II, 139-40, does not, however, mention being assigned to 'Abdur Raḥīm. Cf. *Ma'āṣir-i Raḥīmī*, II, 210.

[89] For details of the Gujarat campaign, see *Akbarnāma*, III, 5-12; *Muntakhab*, II, 164-70; *Tabaqāt*, II, 237-45; *Ma'āṣir-i Raḥīmī*, II, 220-1.

[90] *Akbarnāma*, III, 165-6; *Mir'at-i Aḥmadī*, 113-14. But *Mir'at-i Sikandarī*, 457 does not designate him as governor. The *manṣab* has been mentioned in *Mira'at-i Aḥmadī*, only.

[91] For details of the campaign, see *Akbarnāma*, III, 198, 220-1; *Muntakhab*, II, 224.

[92] *Akbarnāma*, III, 297; *Ma'āṣir-ul Umarā*, I, 693-4 For a detailed discussion on the functions of *Mīr-i 'Arz*, see Ibn Hasan, *Central Structure of the Mughal Empire*.

[93] *Akbarnāma*, III, 326-7. G.N. Sharma, *Mewar and the Mughals*, 101, on the authority of some local source, gives some information about 'Abdur Raḥīm's activities in Ajmer. On 16 June 1580 he was appointed governor of Ajmer and commander in charge of the Mewar campaign. After leaving his family at Sherpur he led an expedition against the Rana. The Rana withdrew to his hill headquarters of Dohlana, pursued by 'Abdur Raḥīm, who finally captured the fort. In the meantime Amar Singh by his daring effort invaded Sherpur to divert the attention of the Mughals. He was also successful in capturing the Mirza's family. But at the instance of the Rana, he sent them back with honour.

nobles present at the court were asked to make one proposal each. 'Abdur Raḥīm pleaded for the preservation of small birds.[94] In the same year he was appointed the *atālīq* (guardian) of Prince Salīm. His predecessor in this office was Quṭbuddīn Khān Koka of the Atka Khail.[95] This appointment must have raised his status further in the Mughal hierarchy and brought him close to the prince.

During the period that he was in the capital performing the duties of *atālīq*, special officers were appointed for each market to look after its welfare. The administration of the horse market was given to 'Abdur Raḥīm, and Ismaīl Qulī was ordered to look after the offices of the grain market, along with Zain Khān Koka.[96] In 1583, princes of royal blood and leading nobles of the empire were given various departments to administer, and Sulṭān Salīm was ordered to look after the 'Divine task of severity and lexity and the superintendence of marriages and birthday feasts'; 'Abdur Raḥīm and Faizi were asked to assist Sulṭān Salīm in the task.[97] It is, however, difficult to explain the actual nature of these offices, and whether anything more than a nominal or ceremonial effort was involved.

After these assignments of relatively minor significance, 'Abdur Raḥīm was sent on a campaign to Gujarat against Muẓaffar Shāh.[98] But this appointment was disapproved by a section of the nobility at the court (left unnamed), who argued that when more experienced generals had failed, the appointment of a comparatively young and inexperienced commander was unwise.

Akbar was aware of the group rivalries within his nobility and, while deputing nobles with 'Abdur Raḥīm, he sent only those nobles who were closely allied with him or had no religious or racial affinities with the group hostile to him. Thus, the nobles posted with 'Abdur Rahīm included the Barhā Sayyids (Sayyid Hāshim, Sayyid Qāsim), Rajputs (Rai Durga, Rai Lonkaran, Medni Rai), and Indian Muslims (Shaikh Kabīr, Darvesh Khān, Rafi Sarmadi, Mian Bahādur and Nasib Khān). All of them were of Indian origin with

94 *Akbarnāma*, III, 380-1. 95 Ibid., 394. 96 Ibid., III, 396.

97 Ibid., 404-5.

98 *Akbarnāma*, III, 413-14; *Mir'at-i Aḥmadī*, 130; *Ma'āṣir-ul Umarā*, I, 11, 695. For the details of the event proceeding the appointment of 'Abdur Raḥīm, see Chapter II. *Tabaqāt*, II, 370-2, 373-4.

whom, as we have seen, 'Abdur Raḥīm's family had established good relations.[99] It is singular that no Irānī or Tūrānī official of any standing accompanied 'Abdur Raḥīm.

Another army under the command of Qulij Khān and Naurang Khān was also sent to Gujarat through Malwa to help 'Abdur Raḥīm. It is, however, significant that all the officers of this army came from the family of the Atkas and such nobles as were hostile to 'Abdur Raḥīm's family.[100]

After reaching the neighbourhood of Sarkhej on the Sabarmati, 'Abdur Raḥīm did not wait for the officers deputed from Malwa, but, at the suggestion of Daulat Khān Lodī and others, attacked the enemy and defeated Muẓaffar Shāh.[101] He gained another victory at Nandaud (Nandod). The emperor raised him to the *manṣab* of 5,000 and granted him the title of Khān Khānān, the title held by his father.[102]

Although 'Abdur Raḥīm defeated the rebels, he was not supported by all sections of the nobles present in the camp. His supporters insisted that the opponents be punished for not participating actively in the campaign. But before taking up any action, 'Abdur Rahim consulted Khwāja Niẓām Uddīn Bakhshi, a friend of the family, who advised him to observe restraint.[103] A very awkward situation was thus avoided. But his position in the camp remained weak; this is borne out by his correspondence with Hakīm Hummām and Abū'l Faẓl. He apparently wrote to Abū'l

[99] *Akbarnāma*, III, 413; *Tabaqāt*, II, 375.

[100] *Akbarnāma*, III, 414-15. Also see Chapter II.

[101] Details of the campaign may be checked in the following sources: *Akbarnāma*, III, 424-9, *Muntakhab*, II, 331-2, *Mirāt-i Ahmadi*, 130-4. Daulat Khān Lodī is reported to have said, 'At that time you will have partners in victory, if you want to be known as Khān Khānān you must win this victory alone.' Cf. *Z.K.* II, 70-1; also *Ma'āṣīr-ul Umarā*, I, 693-4.

[102] *Akbarnāma*, III, 428-30, *Tabaqāt*, II, 375-6, *Muntakhab*, II, 336, *Mir'āt-i Aḥmadī*, 130-4. For a detailed account of Daulat Khān Lodī, see Chapter VII.

[103] *Muntakhab*, II, 332-3. Niẓāmuddīn Aḥmad married Bairam Khān's foster-sister during his lifetime (Abū'l Faẓl, *Maktubāt-i Allami*, Delhi, 1846, II, 91-2). In a letter written to 'Abdur Raḥīm Khān Khānān in 1584-5, Abū'l Faẓl refers to the hostility of a section of the nobility towards him. Muḥammad Ḥusain Azad writes that 'Abdur Raḥim Khān Khānān wrote a letter to his son Mirzā Iraj who was at the court after his victory over Muẓaffar Shāh *(Darbār-i Akbarī*, 591). Without appending the copy of the letter, which he found in a large collection of letters, Azad says that in this letter, 'Abdur Raḥīm described his critical condition on account of the hostile attitude of the officers posted in Gujarat.

Faẓl as well as Hakīm Hummām asking them to intercede on his behalf with the emperor to recall him from Gujarat. The emperor, however, did not agree.[104]

'Abdur Raḥīm accordingly engaged himself in pursuing Muẓaffar Shāh and was successful in expelling him from the imperial territories.[105] At this time, it appears that Akbar was taking a keen interest in the Deccan affairs and that some correspondence between him and 'Abdur Raḥīm took place in this connection. In a *farmān* addressed to 'Abdur Raḥīm regarding the death of Rāja Bīr Bal, there is a long description of the Deccan problem. From references in the *farmān* it turns out that 'Abdur Raḥīm was then being consulted about the proposed campaign.[106] He even returned to the court, but the charge of the campaign was assigned to Mirzā 'Azīz Koka.[107] This appointment was resented by 'Abdur Raḥīm and his associates, and when Mirzā 'Azīz Koka, after his disastrous retreat in the Deccan, came to seek the help of 'Abdur Raḥīm, the latter refused him assistance.[108]

When the details of the campaign were reported to the emperor he took exception to 'Abdur Raḥīm's behaviour and immediately summoned him to court. For some time he remained at court, and later on was appointed *Wakīl*, a very high titular office. He was given the *jāgīr* of Jaunpur and ordered to take charge of the place.[109] Since he was posted at Jaunpur, he was more or less cut off from the court.

Akbar was now planning the conquest of Qandhar. 'Abdur Raḥīm seized the opportunity and with the help of Abū'l Faẓl was successful in getting charge of the campaign.[110] He took charge of the troops, but decided instead to attack Sind. Jāni Beg the ruler of Thatta was defeated and accompanied 'Abdur Raḥīm to the court. The defeated

[104] *Darbār-i Akbarī*, 591-2, Azad states that he saw the letters of 'Abdur Raḥīm written to Abū'l Faẓl and Hakim Ḥummām in this connection. But he had not reproduced them. However, the letters of Abū'l Faẓl to 'Abdur Raḥīm Khān Khānān corroborate Azad. Cf. *Maktubāt-i Allami*, II, 118-19.

[105] For the details of 'Abdur Raḥīm's activities in Gujarat, see *Akbarnāma*, III, 437-8, 452-3, 471-2; *Mir'āt-i Sikandarī*, 465, 466-7; *Mir'āt-i Aḥmadī* 132-4; *Z.K.*, I, 31-4.

[106] *Maktubat*, I, 43-5.

[107] *Akbarnāma*, III, 489-90.

[108] Ibid., III, 489-90; *Z.K.*, I, 33-4. For more details of the event, see Chapter II:

[109] *Akbarnāma*, III, 571-2.

[110] *Maktubat*, II, 118-19, 128-30. The reading of these letters suggests that some correspondence passed between Abū'l Faẓl and 'Abdur Raḥīm Khān Khānān, and that 'Abdur Raḥīm asked him to request the emperor to give him the charge of the

ruler also gave his daughter in marriage to Mirzā Iraj, 'Abdur Raḥīm's son.[111]

After returning from Thatta 'Abdur Raḥīm was deputed to serve under Prince Dāniyāl in the Panjab.[112] It was during this time that Sulṭān Dāniyāl was appointed together with 'Abdur Raḥīm, to lead the Mughal campaign in the Deccan. A council of nobles was convened to discuss the Deccan affairs. In the council 'Abdur Raḥīm represented that the charge of the campaign might be given to him, and Sulṭān Dāniyāl might be relieved of the burden. His representation was accepted and the command was given solely to him.[113]

The problem became complex, because Sulṭān Murād, then governor of Gujarat, had been ordered to join the campaign in the Deccan. He particularly resented the appointment of 'Abdur Raḥīm, since he was considered a close associate and ally of Sulṭān Salīm.[114] Ṣādiq Muḥammad Khān, the *Atālīq* of Sulṭān Murād, advised him to invade the Deccan before the arrival of 'Abdur Raḥīm, and the prince agreed.

'Abdur Raḥīm proceeded towards the Deccan along with the commanders from the clans of the Barhā Sayyids, the Lodī Afghāns and his Rajput allies.[115] After staying for a few days at his *jāgīr* of Bhilsa, he marched towards Khandesh. He took some time in deliberations with Rāja 'Alī Khān, the ruler of Khandesh. This was interpreted by Ṣādiq Muḥammad Khān and other nobles of Sulṭān Murād's camp as a deliberate attempt to spoil the campaign by slow movements. Sulṭān Murād accepted this interpretation and marched towards the Deccan without waiting for him to join.[116]

Qandhar campaign. But other historians do not refer to this projected Qandhar campaign. According to them 'Abdur Raḥīm was assigned the government of Multan and Bhakkar and ordered to conquer Sindh and Baluchistan. Cf. *Tarikh-i Ma'sumi*, 250; *Tabaqāt*, II, 375-6; *Ma'āsir-i Rahīmī*, II, 341-2; *Z.K.*, I, 34.

[111] For details of the campaign, see *Akbarnāma* III, 601-2, 606-9, 613-14, 633-5, 638; Ni'amatullah, *Tarīkh-i Khān Jahānī*, ed. Imam Alī Din, Dacca, 1960, I, 475-6, *Ma'āṣir-i Rahīmī*, II, 346-9.

[112] *Akbarnāma*, III, 645-6.

[113] Ibid., III, 646-8.

[114] Ibid., 648. Prince Murad also resented the appointment of Prince Dāniyāl. Saiyyed Alī Tabatabai, *Burhān-i Ma'āsir*, Jamia, Delhi, 1936, 616, specifically mentions that 'Abdur Raḥīm was considered a partisan of Sulṭān Salīm.

[115] For his relation with Rajputs, see *Z.K.*, I, 109.

[116] *Burhān-i Ma'āsir*, 616. The inordinate delay on the part of 'Abdur Raḥīm annoyed the prince to the extent that he wrote a letter to him to express his indignation. 'Abdur Raḥīm replied that since he was not quite sure of the friendly

When 'Abdur Raḥīm came and joined his camp at Jalna, the prince refused to meet him. 'Abdur Raḥīm thereupon left the camp, and only after much persuasion did he return.

In December 1595, the fort of Ahmadnagar was invested by the imperial army.[117] In the whole campaign the attitude of 'Abdur Raḥīm suggests that he was not keen on the seizure of Ahmadnagar. Rāja 'Alī Khān and Khwāja Muhammad Shirāzī, two known friends of 'Abdur Raḥīm, were suspected of secretly helping the garrison.[118] On one occasion when the garrison offered to surrender if 'Abdur Raḥīm came to the gates of the fort, he refused to do so.[119] Nevertheless, at the time of the negotiations for drafting the treaty, he was one of the plenipotentiaries of the prince.

The terms of the treaty were strongly disapproved by the emperor. Abū'l Faẓl alleges that the treaty was signed because 'a party of men owing to ignorance, and some, from interested motives, accepted these improper proposals'. He adds that 'owing to influence of bribes and listening to idle tales, the peace proposals were accepted'. Although he has not mentioned any names, it may be inferred that 'Abdur Raḥīm and his group of nobles were mainly responsible for the acceptance of the unfavourable terms.[120]

After the conclusion of the treaty, the Mughals raised the siege and retreated towards Berar, avoiding a contest with the joint forces of Bijapur and Golkunda. But soon afterwards the Mughal forces had to fight their opponents at Ashti[121], where in the beginning the

---

attitude of Rāja 'Alī Khān, he thought it prudent to wait for some time. Also see *Maktubat*, II, 182. Abu'l Fazl wrote letters to 'Abdur Raḥīm Khān Khānān, Ṣadiq Muḥammad Khān, Mirzā Shāh Rukh and Qāsim Khān Tabrīzī, the *Dīwān* of Murād, urging them to give up their differences.

[117] *Akbarnāma*, III, 698-9, Mu'tamid Khān, *Iqbālnāma-i Jahāngīrī*, Nawal Kishore, ed., 1870, 445-7.

[118] *Burhān-i Ma'āsir*, 618; *Iqbālnāma*, 447. Mu'tamid Khān writes that because of the negligence of 'Abdur Raḥīm from the eastern side of the fort which was under his charge, Abhanj Khān along with Mirān Shāh was able to enter the fort. Von Noer, *The Emperor Akbar*, Patna, Vol. I, 1973, II, 330-3. He has given a graphic description of the differences between 'Abdur Raḥīm Khān Khānān and Murād. For Rāja 'Alī Khān's role, see *Burhan-i Ma'asir*, 619, and for Khwāja Muḥammad Shīrāzī, see *Tarikh-i Farishta*, Nawal Kishore, ed., II, 160-2.

[119] *Z.K.*, I, 40.

[120] The treaty was signed on 23 February 1596, *Akbarnāma*, III, 700. Farishta, II, 161-2.

[121] *Iqbālnāma*, 450; *Ma'āṣir-i Rahīmī*, II, 468; *Akbarnāma*, III, 718-20. The battle was fought on 8 February 1597.

imperial army was defeated and Prince Murād had to be taken away from the battlefield. 'Abdur Raḥīm remained firm and drove away Suhail Khān, the commander of the Deccan forces.[122] The fortunes of the Mughals were thus retrieved. After this victory when Murād asked him to join in the conquest of Ahmadnagar, he declined stating that there were still many strong places to be taken in Berar and that it would be better to defer the assault on Ahmadnagar until the following years. As a result relations between Murād and 'Abdur Raḥīm again deteriorated. 'Abdur Raḥīm left the Mughal camp and went to his *jāgīr* at Jalna. When Akbar was informed of these developments, he summoned the prince for consultation and ordered 'Abdur Raḥīm to take charge of the Deccan during the prince's absence.[123] But Murād was prevailed upon not to go to the court; his courtiers argued that his absence from the Deccan might jeopardize his interests.[124] On the other hand, 'Abdur Raḥīm refused to join Murād's camp.[125] Abū'l Faẓl had therefore to be despatched to the Deccan to resolve the issue by bringing both the prince and 'Abdur Raḥīm to the court.[126] For some time 'Abdur Raḥīm remained out of favour. But after Murād's death, when Akbar decided to march to the Deccan personally, he was ordered to serve Prince Dāniyāl who had taken over as viceroy of the Deccan.[127]

The news of the approach of the imperial army caused great alarm among their opponents in the Deccan. As the Mughal forces advanced the territories of Burhanpur, Ahmadnagar and Berar were placed under a single charge of Prince Dāniyāl, although the actual management was placed in 'Abdur Raḥīm's hands.[128]

[122] *Iqbalnāma,* 450; *Z.K.*, I, 41-5. Farīd Bhakkarī gives more detailed account of the battle of Ashti. Sayyid Hāshim and Sayyid Qāsim Bārha, Daulat Khān Lodī and the Rajputs showed great valour in the battle.

[123] *Akbarnāma*, III, 739, Abū'l Faẓl says that Salbhan was sent from court for this task. He further adds that 'Abdur Raḥīm left the camp owing to 'the ill success of his evil wishes'.

[124] 'Murād declined to come to court when he was summoned but the leaders did not abandon their interested views and petitioned to the effect that the departure of the Prince would cause confusion' (Ibid., III, 744).

[125] Ibid., III, 744.

[126] Ibid., III, 744, 751. Von Noer, II, 348, believes that 'Abdur Raḥīm's recall from the Deccan was an injustice which Akbar compensated by favour at the time of his departure to the Deccan. Farishta, II, 163 writes that though the whole misunderstanding with Murad arose out of the prince's jealous disposition, the emperor's anger fell upon 'Abdur Raḥīm Khān Khānān.

[127] *Akbarnāma*, III, 756; Farishta, II, 164.

[128] *Akbarnāma*, 785.

However, the opposition in the Deccan soon regrouped itself, and during the last five years of Akbar's reign (1600-5) 'Abdur Raḥīm had to devote a major part of his attention to the struggle with Malik Ambar and Raju Deccani. Malik Ambar was largely successful in outwitting the Mughals as well as his Deccani rival Raju.[129]

After a repulse received from Shaikh 'Abdur Rahmān in Telengana, Malik Ambar sued for peace.[130] 'Abdur Raḥīm and others favoured an understanding with Malik Ambar in the teeth of Abū'l Faẓl's oppositions.[131] In thc same year Dāniyāl split the Mughal Deccan into two divisions, one under the command of Abū'l Faẓl and the other under 'Abdur Raḥīm.[132] 'Abdur Raḥīm took some initiative and his son Mirzā Iraj inflicted a heavy defeat on Malik Ambar.[133] After Dāniyāl's death in 1604 'Abdur Raḥīm took over as viceroy of Deccan. He now began to intervene in the struggle between Malik Ambar and Raju Daccani. Why he followed such a policy, which ultimately proved to be of no help to the Mughals, is difficult to explain. This was to lead in the end to Malik Ambar's triumph and in turn to the great dicomfiture of the Mughals. Perhaps, on this account, there grew some suspicion that 'Abdur Raḥīm was not loyal to Mughal interests.[134]

Sometimes in 1604 Akbar summoned 'Abdur Raḥīm to the capital with the intention of putting him in charge of a projected expedition to Central Asia. But 'Abdur Raḥīm excused himself urging that the affairs of the Deccan were more important.[135]

At the time of Akbar's death 'Abdur Raḥīm was serving in the Deccan along with his two sons, Mirzā Iraj and Darāb Khān, but the sons held only minor ranks. Among his other family members Ismaīl Qulī Khān had attained the rank of 4000,[136] and held such important

[129] See Radhey Shyam, *Life and Times of Malik Ambar*, Delhi, 1968.

[130] *Akbarnāma*, III, 789, 791; *Iqbālnāma*, 474, 476.

[131] The peace was made on 3 January 1602 (*Akbarnāma*, III, 794-5). Abū'l Faẓl disapproved of any understanding with Malik Ambar. Mu'tamid Khān is also in agreement with him. He says, 'His (Abū'l Faẓl's) dissatisfaction was justified as even in the fifteenth year of Jahāngīr reign, i.e. 18th year of the event, there is no peace between Malik Ambar and the Mughals' (*Iqbālnāma*, 479).

[132] Abū'l Faẓl's headquarters were at Ahmadnagar and 'Abdur Raḥīm was to be in charge of Berar, Telegana and to conduct campaign against Malik Ambar.

[133] *Takmila*, III, 807; *Iqbālnāma*, 484.

[134] *Z.K.*, I, 58, Farīd Bhakkari writes that 'Abdur Raḥīm had very friendly relations with the Deccani rulers, and Abū'l Faẓl declared him to be a rebel.

[135] *Takmila*, III, 834.

[136] *Akbarnāma*, III, 721. He was given promotion in 1598.

assignments as *Thānedārī* of Swat (1586),[137] co-governorships of Multan (1586) and Gujarat (1588), and *Wakīl* of Murād in Malwa and Gujarat (1591-3).[138] He also served under Dāniyāl in Allahabad (1598) and died sometimes in 1602.[139] But Ismaīl Qulī's career had not been a smooth one. He was repeatedly censured for disobedience and incompetence, so much so that orders for his exile had once been issued.[140] It appears that the main cause of his declining fortunes was the old family feuds with the 'Atka Khail', the family of Maham Anaga and Ṣadiq Muḥammad Khān.[141] In any case, although he was retained in service and no curtailment in his *manṣab* was made, his sons and the sons of his brother Ḥusain Qulī Khān-i Jahān were not given promotions.[142] Ultimately after Akbar's death, the only branch of Bairam Khān's family which retained any importance was that of 'Abdur Raḥīm Khān Khānān.

Towards the end of Akbar's reign, affairs in the Deccan had fallen into great confusion. The Deccanis threw off the Mughal yoke and the imperial armies under 'Abdur Raḥīm failed to protect the conquered territories.[143] Jahāngīr was preoccupied with more pressing problems, viz., the rebellion of Khusrau, and the Mewar and Qandhar campaigns, with the result that the imperial pressure on the Deccan slackened perceptibly. Although Jahāngīr confirmed 'Abdur Raḥīm to the viceroyalty of the Deccan, despatching dresses of honour to him and his sons, no substantial help was granted.[144] In 1608, 'Abdur Raḥīm visited the court and promised to complete the conquest of the Deccan provided he was assisted with re-inforcements numbering 12,000 cavalry and 100,000 rupees in

[137] Ibid., 492. *Ma'āṣir-ul Umarā*, I, 105-7.

[138] *Akbarnāma*, 511-12, 531, 598-600. In Multan he was co-governor with Ṣadiq Muḥammad Khān.

[139] *Akbarnāma*, 721; *Ma'āṣir-ul Umarā*, I, 105-7.

[140] *Ma'āṣir-ul Umarā*, I, 106-7. Shāhnawāz Khān writes that in the thirty-first regnal year of Akbar when Rāja Bhagwān Dās was recalled from the government of Zublistan (Afghanistan) owing to insanity, Ismaīl Qulī was appointed in his place, but he exhibited improper traits and fell out of favour. An order was given that he should be put into a boat and sent to Mecca (tr., I, 703).

[141] See supra.

[142] See Appendix A–III.

[143] *Tārīkh-i Khān-i Jahānī*, II, 504-5. Ni'amatullah writes that even those *mahāl* which were conquered by Prince Murād and Dāniyāl were reoccupied by Malik Ambar. Also see Chapter VII.

[144] *Tuzuk-i Jahāngīrī*, ed. Saiyid Aḥmad Khān, Ghazipur and Aligarh, 1863-4, 21, 46; *Ma'āṣir-i Rahīmī*, II, 513.

cash.[145] These demands being immediately complied with, he began his journey to the Deccan accompanied by Rajā Suraj Singh.[146] After reaching Burhanpur he did his best to improve the Mughal position; Shāhnawāz Khān and Darāb Khān achieved some initial success, but Malik Ambar captured Jinapur and forced 'Abdur Raḥīm to retire to Burhanpur.[147] Unable to cope with the forces at his command he requested the emperor for further reinforcements. Hence, Parvez was appointed to the supreme command and J'afar Beg Āṣaf Khān was deputed as his guardian.[148] But even after the prince's arrival, the Deccanis could not be expelled from the imperial territories. In these circumstances Āṣaf Khān suggested that the emperor should himself come to the Deccan. However, it was decided to send Khān-i Jahān Lodī, who pledged himself to conquer Deccan within two years.[149] But the Deccanis were successful again, and forced the Mughals to sign a dishonorable treaty.[150]

Regarding the attitude of 'Abdur Raḥīm in the Deccan at this stage there are two different versions. Jahāngīr followed by (Kāmgār Ḥusainī and Farīd Bhakkari) holds him responsible for the reverses, and says that Khān-i Jahān Lodī accused him of treachery and suggested his immediate recall.[151] As against this Khwāja Ni'amatullah

[145] *Tuzuk*, 70-1; Mu'tamid Khān *Iqbālnāma-i Jahāngīrī*, eds. Maulana Abd Al-Hai and Aḥmad Alī; Bibliotheca Indica, Calcutta, 1865, 34-5.

[146] *Ma'āṣir-i Rahīmī*, II, 513-16; cf. *Tārīkh-i Khān-i Jahānī*, II, 505.

[147] *Z.K.*, I, 45.

[148] *Tuzuk*, I, 74-5; *Iqbālnāma*, 36-7; Khāfī Khān, I, 260; *Z.K.*, I, 45-6; T. Roe, I, 90-1 writes, 'the prince hath the name and state but the Khān ('Abdur Raḥīm) governs all'.

[149] *Tuzuk*, I, 77-8; *Iqbālnāma*, 38-9; *Z.K.*, I, 46; *Tārīkh-i Khān-i Jahānī*, II, 509-10 adds that he was sent to the Deccan because of past experience of service in that region and intimate relations with 'Abdur Raḥīm. For more details see Chapter VII.

[150] *Tuzuk*, 68; *Iqbālnāma*, 38-9; *Tārīkh-i Khān Jahāni*, II, 510, clearly states that because of rainy season, shortage of food and fodder and the poor condition of the army, no advance could be made after reaching Deval-gam (in Balaghat). About the same time Malik Ambar proposed a truce. Although Prince Parvez and Khān-i Jahān Lodī were not happy with it, yet because of the prevailing conditions and hostile attitude of certain nobles, his terms were accepted. But *Basatin-us Salatin*, 268 and the *Aḥwāl-i Shāhzādgi* say that the prince called a council of war, in which 'Abdur Raḥīm suggested postponement of the campaign till after the rainy season. It was thereupon alleged that he was in league with the enemy, and his suggestion was rejected.

[151] *Tuzuk*, 68; *Iqbālnāma*, 38-9: Cf. *Z.K.*, I, 46, Farīd Bhakkari says that after the arrival of Khān-i Jahān Lodī, Mughal forces attacked the Deccanis from two sides. Malik Ambar could not withstand the assault and appealed to the Khān Khānān.

the biographer of Khān-i Jahān Lodī states that a section of the nobility hostile to 'Abdur Raḥīm convinced the emperor that he was in league with the Deccanis and had surrendered Jalna and other Lodī himself *parganās* to them. Ni'amatullah claims that it was Khān-i Jahān who personally interceded in 'Abdur Raḥims behalf by highlighting the great services rendered by him. Khān-i Jahān Lodi also stood surety for 'Abdur Raḥīm's good conduct.[152] But at the same time Ni'amatullah is also critical of 'Abdur Raḥīm's conduct of the campaign which led to the retreat of Mughal forces from Jalna.[153] Mahābat Khān was despatched to enquire into the circumstances of the defeat of the imperial army and to call 'Abdur Raḥīm to the court.[154]

After reaching the court he remained out of favour for some time. But in due course his son Darāb Khān was given a *manṣab* of 1000/ 500 and Mirzā Iraj received the title of Shāhnawāz Khān. Sometimes later Jahāngīr thought of appointing 'Abdur Raḥīm to the governorship of Kabul. But at the last moment Qulij Khān was appointed, and 'Abdur Raḥīm, along with his sons, was assigned *jāgīrs* in Kalpi.

The Deccan affairs showed no improvement even after the recall of 'Abdur Raḥīm.[155] Khwāja 'Abū'l Ḥasan and some other nobles, therefore, proposed that 'Abdur Raḥīm be sent once again to the Deccan, arguing that 'no one understood the business of that region as the Khān Khānān did'.[156] The emperor accepted the suggestion; he was promoted to the *manṣab* of 7,000 *ẕāt* and his sons, Shāhnawāz Khān and Darāb Khān, were also promoted to the *manṣabs* of 3,000 and 2,000/1,500 respectively. His younger son Raḥmāndād too was given a 'suitable' *manṣab*.[157] Some of his known opponents posted in the Deccan were either dead or were transferred by the time he reached

The latter treacherously stopped Khān-i Jahān for some time near Zafarnagar, Malik Ambar could fight with his full force with 'Abdullah Khān and force him to retire.

[152] *Tārīkh-i Khān-i Jahānī*, II, 494-5. It tells us that Khān-i Jahān went to the extent of saying that a person of the calibre of 'Abdur Raḥīm could not be found in the court of the Safavids, Uzbeks and other states. Cf. *Tuzuk*, 86: 'As many of those who were loyal had represented of the state of affairs whether true or false according to their ideas and I was displeased with him.'

[153] *Tārīkh-i Khān-i Jahānī*, II, 504-5. Also see Chapter VII.

[154] *Tuzuk*, 86; *Iqbālnāma*, 54-5; *Ma'āṣir-i Jahāngīrī*, 57a.

[155] See for details Chapter VII.

[156] *Tuzuk*, 108; *Tārīkh-i Khān-i Jahānī*, II, 494-5, says that on the recommendation of Khān-i Jahān Lodī he was sent again.

[157] *Tuzuk*, 108; *Iqbālnāma*, 67.

there.[158] Thus, he was better placed to pursue his own course of action. He opened an offensive against Malik Ambar with some vigour and created dissension in the Deccan army by offering bribes to defectors. A large number of Deccani nobles joined the Mughals.[159] Malik Ambar was severely defeated near Khirki (later Aurangabad) by the combined forces of Shāhnawāz Khān and Darāb Khān.[160] After the victory, Shāhnawāz Khān was promoted to the rank of 5,000.[161]

'Abdur Raḥīm continued to hold the supreme command in the Deccan till 1615. He was no doubt successful in retrieving the prestige of the Mughals, but no new territory was gained. He was still accused of accepting bribes from the Deccanis.[162] Hence, Jahāngīr transferred Parvez from the Deccan and appointed Khurram in his place. Orders for 'Abdur Raḥim's recall were also issued, but later events suggest that he remained in the Deccan and met the prince on the left bank of Narmada along with other nobles who were posted with him.[163] To seal his relations with 'Abdur Raḥim, Khurram married the daughter of Shāhnawāz Khān after reaching Burhanpur.[164]

After the submission of the Deccanis, Khurram appointed 'Abdur Raḥīm as his deputy to govern Berar, Khandesh and Ahmadnagar and deputed Shāhnawāz Khān with a cavalry of 12,000 to hold possession of the conquered territories. Darāb Khān accompanied him to the court.[165]

158 *Tuzuk.*, 108, 113-14, 130. Āsaf Khān J'afar Beg and Amīr-ul Umarā Sharīf were dead. Rajā Mān Singh died a year later and 'Azīz Koka was transferred to Mewar.

159 Ādam Khān, Ya'qut Khān, Jadao Ray and Babu Katiya came over to Shāhnawāz Khān and joined his service (*Tuzuk*, 152-3).

160 Ibid., 152-3; *Iqbālnāma*, 83-7.

161 *Tuzuk*, 153: the promotion in *manṣab* is not recorded. See *Ma'āṣir-ul Umarā*, II, 645-6.

162 *Iqbālnāma*, 479, T. Roe, II, 279-89, writes that Khān Khānān doubtless was acting in collusion with the Deccanis from whom he received pension.

163 *Tuzuk*, 159; T. Roe, II, 279-80. Roe tells us that 'The Emperor was well aware ... of the power of the Khān Khānān and was therefore desirous to accommodate all by accepting a peace and confirming the Khān Khānān in the government he held....' Farīd Bhakkari states that in the reign of Jahāngīr he was suspected of an alliance with Malik Ambar, hence he was dismissed. One of the confidential servants of Khurram, Muḥammad Ma'ṣūm came to the emperor and informed him that 'Abdur Raḥīm was in correspondence with Malik Ambar and the letters could be found with Shaikh 'Abdus Salam of Lucknow. When the Shaikh was asked about it, he refused to divulge anything and Mahābat Khān, tortured him to death (*Z.K.*, I, 56).

164 *Tuzuk*, 162; *Ma'āṣir-ul Umarā*, II, 645-6.

165 *Tuzuk*, 194; *Iqbālnāma*, 102-4; Khāfī Khān, I, 293-4.

In 1618 'Abdur Raḥīm's son Amrullah captured the diamond mines of Bairagarh from Panju, a *zamindār* of Khandesh.[166] The same year while the emperor was encamped at Ghati Ghanda (south-east Rajasthan) 'Abdur Rahim came to pay him homage. He was promoted to the rank of 7,000/7,000 and confirmed in his post.[167]

In 1619 Shāhnawāz Khān died. He then held the *manṣab* of 5,000. On the orders of the emperor his *manṣab* was distributed among his brothers and sons, thus maintaining the full strength of the family in the nobility. Darāb Khān was promoted to the rank of 5000/5000. He was despatched to the Deccan to take charge of the government of Berar and Ahmadnagar which had been held by Shāhnawāz Khān. Raḥmāndād was promoted to the rank of 2000/800. Manuchahar and Tughril, the sons of Shāhnawāz Khān, were raised to the *manṣabs* of 2000/1000 and 1000/500 respectively.[168]

As soon as Khurram left the Deccan, Malik Ambar formed a league with Bijapur and Golkunda, broke the treaty with the Mughals and launched an offensive. Although the Mughals were successful in direct engagements, they had to suffer heavy casualties in men and material. The Mughal forces retreated northwards and ultimately took refuge in Burhanpur.[169] 'Abdur Raḥīm repeatedly sent petitions for help and even threatened to immolate himself along with his family if quick help was not sent to him.[170] Hence, Jahāngīr immediately despatched Khurram who, after reaching there, successfully concluded peace with the Deccanis.

If we consider the two campaigns of Khurram in the Deccan, it would appear that 'he had only followed up the success of 'Abdur Raḥīm with a temporary truce'. Actually not an inch of territory was added beyond the limits of 1605.

The turning point in the career of the family group was the second visit of Khurram to the Deccan. In 1622 when Khurram began to contemplate rebellion he entered into an alliance with 'Abdur Raḥīm and other important nobles serving him in the Deccan.[171]

[166] *Tuzuk*, 236. [167] *Tuzuk*, 257; *Iqbālnāma*, 122.

[168] *Tuzuk*, 280; *Iqbālnāma*, 128; *Ma'āṣir-ul Umarā*, II, 14-5, 645-68, gives *manṣab* of Darāb Khān.

[169] *Tuzuk*, 305, 321-2; *Iqbālnāma*, 160-1.

[170] *Tuzuk*, 322; *Ma'āṣir-ul Umarā*, I, 700-1.

[171] *A Contemporary Dutch Chronicle*, trs. & eds. Brij Narain and S.R. Sharma, Calcutta, 1957, 55-7 states that after the invasion of Qandhar by the Persians, Khurram called the important commanders present in the Deccan and asked them to

The Persian attack on Qandhar in 1621 and the events which followed precipitated Khurram's revolt. He marched northwards from Mandu along with 'Abdur Raḥīm and his son Darāb Khān and some other commanders. Having failed to surprise Agra they proceeded towards Delhi but were defeated at Bilochpur. Many of Khurram's close associates, including Mirzā Manuchahar, son of Shāhnawāz Khān, now deserted him to join the royal army under Parvez and Mahābat Khān. 'Abdur Raḥīm too entered into correspondence with Mahābat Khān. One letter by him was intercepted, and Khurram had him detained along with his family.[172]

In the meantime 'Abdullah Khān acting as Khurram's deputy was defeated in Gujarat, and Khurram's negotiation with Ahmadnagar ended in a fiasco. At this time 'Abdur Raḥīm, who was still in correspondence with Mahābat Khān, offered to negotiate a settlement with the imperialists, leaving his sons and other family members with Khurram as hostages. He also suggested that if he failed in his mission, the prince should contact the Deccan rulers and invade the Mughal empire.[173] Seeing no other course open to him, Khurram made him swear on the Holy Quran and said, 'My times are hard, my position difficult, I make myself over to you and make you guardian of my honour. You must act so that I no longer go under contempt and confusion.'[174] When the news of the peace became known to Khurram's commander, Bairam Beg, who was defending the forts on the Narbada, he began to relax his vigilance. Taking advantage of it, the imperialists crossed over and fell upon the rebels. The time for negotiations was now past and 'Abdur Raḥīm joined Mahābat Khān.[175]

---

take an oath that they would be true to him. He adds, 'he wanted to rebel against his father and expected that they would gird him with the sword of his father'. De Laet writes that 'Abdur Raḥīm was a party to the murder of Sulṭān Khusrau. See *Z.K.*., I, 54, for 'Abdur Raḥīm's relation with Malik Ambar and Burhan-ul Mulk.

172 *Tuzuk*, 370-1; *Ma'āṣir-i Jahāngīrī*, 165b; *Z.K.*, I, 49. For more details see, Chapter VIII.

173 *Iqbālnāma*, 211; *Ma'āṣir-i Jahāngīrī*, 166b; *Z.K.*, I, 50. Jahāngīr in his memoirs writes that Khurram on his own first sent Sarbuland Rāy, son of Rāy Bhoj Hara, to negotiate with Mahābat Khān, but Mahābat Khān refused to discuss anything until 'Abdur Raḥīm came personally. Cf. *Tuzuk*, 378-9.

174 *Tuzuk*, 370-1; *Z.K.*, I, 50-1.

175 *Tuzuk*, 371-3; *Ma'āṣir-i Jahāngīrī*, 167a; *Z.K.*, I, 50-1 adds that Bairam Beg was in league with 'Abdur Raḥīm. *The Dutch Chronicle*, 66 says that 'Abdur Raḥīm wrote to Bairam Beg that he was successful in negotiating peace, his aim being to arrest the prince and despatch him to Mahābat Khān. See also De Laet, 212.

With the desertion of 'Abdur Raḥīm and the further advance of the imperial army, Khurram crossed the Tapti and proceeded towards Orissa and Bengal passing Golkunda territory. During the march Darāb Khān, and his sons and nephews remained under the custody of the prince as hostages. After the conquest of Bengal, Darāb Khān was released by Khurram, granted the rank of 6,000/5,000 and appointed governor of Bengal. His son Aram Bakhsh and Shakar Shikan, son of Shāhnawāz Khān, were given ranks of 1,000 and 1,000/1,000 respectively. A nephew and Mirzā Afrāsiyāb, son of Darāb Khān, were also promoted to the rank of 1,000 and left in Bengal to serve under him. However, Aram Bakhsh, the sons and daughters of Shāhnawāz Khān and Darāb Khān's wife, were kept under surveillance.[176]

When Khurram was defeated at Manikpur and Allahabad and retreated to Banaras, he summoned Darāb Khān with all the forces that he had at his command. Darāb Khān despatched a fleet of boats and one thousand of his troopers under his son Mirzā Afrāsiyāb to serve the prince, but excused himself.[177] The author of the *'Bahāristan-i Ghaibī* states that about this time three letters, two written by Darāb Khān to his son Aram Bakhsh and one by 'Abdur Raḥīm to Darāb Khān, were intercepted by the servants of the prince, their contents clearly indicating that Darāb Khān was planning to rejoin imperial service.[178]

Having again been defeated in a battle near river Tons, Khurram retreated to Rohtas and sent an account of his reverses to Darāb Khān asking him to hasten to Garhi. Darāb Khan expressed his inability to reach Garhi as he was surrounded by the local *zamindārs*.[179] Khurram treated this as an act of treachery and while returning towards the Deccan, handed over Darāb Khān's son and nephew to 'Abdullah Khān, who put them both to death.[180] After the conquest of Bengal by the imperial army, Mahābat Khān wrote

[176] Mirzā Nathan, *Bahāristān-i Ghaibī*, tr. M.I. Bohra, Gauhati, 1936, II, 690, 92, 94-5. *Iqbālnāma*, and *Z.K.*, I, 51-2 mention only Darāb Khān's appointment as governor of Bengal.

[177] *Bahāristān-i Ghaibī*, II, 709, 734, 749.

[178] Ibid., II, 737, 39.

[179] *Iqbālnāma*, 238; *Ma'āṣir-i Jahāngīrī*, 183a. De Laet, 220-1; *Bahāristān-i Ghaibi*, II, 766-7, 771-2.

[180] *Iqbālnāma*, 238; *Ma'āṣir-i Jahāngīrī*, 183ab. Mirzā Nathan says that 'Abdullah Khān on his own part put to death 1000 people who were suspected of treachery. Aram Bakhsh, son of Darāb Khān, was one of them. Cf. *Bahāristān-i Ghaibi*, II, 784-5.

to the *zamindārs* to capture Darāb Khān. Later on, upon receipt of Jahāngīr's orders he was executed.[181]

'Abdur Raḥīm himself was not treated well after joining the camp of Parvez and Mahābat Khān. Jahāngīr's statement that Mahābat Khān was interested only in detaching 'Abdur Raḥim from Khurram, seems to be correct. He was immediately arrested and put in prison close to the camp of Prince Parvez.[182] His daughter Janān Begum, who had been married to Prince Dāniyāl was asked to remain with him. When Parvez and Mahābat Khān marched towards Bengal and Bihar, they sent 'Abdur Raḥīm to the court whether he had been summoned. When he reached the court, the emperor treated him favourably, saying mildly, 'Whatever had happened was not to be ascribed to his own will but to the inscurtable decrees of Heaven.' He ordered the officers to admit him to his usual place among the nobles at the court. Soon after he was restored to the title of Khān Khānān, assigned Kanauj in *jāgīr* and granted rupees one lac in cash.[183]

This show of benevolence was probably due to the increasing estrangement between the court and Mahābat Khān.[184] When Mahābat Khān came to the court, and carried out his coup, he took care to apologize to 'Abdur Raḥīm for his past behaviour, but 'Abdur Raḥīm showed him little regard and proceeded towards his *jāgīr*.[185] In the meantime Mahābat Khān got the emperor to summon 'Abdur Raḥīm to Lahore. He also ordered Sayyid Bahwa the governor of Delhi to prevent him from proceeding further. 'Abdur Razzāq M'amurī and Balbhadr Kachhwaha Shekhawat with 400 horses were actually deputed to arrest him.[186] But before he could be arrested, Mahābat Khān had fallen from power.

'Abdur Raḥīm was now nominated to lead the campaign against him. The emperor transferred most of the *mahāls* from Mahābat Khān's *jāgīr* to 'Abdur Raḥīm and ordered him to march to Ajmer to intercept Mahābat Khān.[187]

181 *Ma'āṣir-ul Umarā*, II, 16-17.

182 *Tuzuk*, 378-9.

183 *Iqbālnāma*, 244-5, 47; *Z.K.*, I, 57-8.

184 *Iqbālnāma*, 245. Fidai Khān was despatched with the orders of the transfer of Mahābat Khān even before 'Abdur Raḥīm was summoned to the court. Also see Chapter VIII.

185 *Z.K.*, I, 58.

186 *Iqbālnāma*, 269; *Z.K.*, I, 59.

187 *Iqbālnāma*, 279-80; *Z.K.*, I, 59-60.

Before the campaign could really begin, 'Abdur Raḥīm died at the age of 72 early in 1627.[188] In spite of the formal restoration of his rank and the important charge given to him, towards the end of his career, his family hardly held any power in the empire at his death. It was a notable victim of Khurram's rebellion, many of its influential members lost their lives or ranks during the rebellion and the family did not regain its status or influence in the succeeding reign.[189]

[188] *Iqbālnāma*, 287.

[189] 'Abū'l Al-Hamīd Lāhaurī, *Bādshānāma*, eds. Maulvi Kabir Al-Din Aḥmad and Abdur Al-Rahim, Bibliotheca Indica, 1867, II, 121. Mirzā Manuchahar, son of Shāhnawāz Khān, who had joined Mahābat Khān and Parvez during the rebellion of Shāhjahān, was promoted to the rank of 3000/2000 after his accession. But nothing more is known about him or any other member of the family during the entire reign of Shāhjahān.

CHAPTER II

The Family of Shamsuddīn Atka

The family of Shamsuddīn—or the 'Atka Khail' as commonly designated in contemporary sources formed one of the largest family groups in the Mughal nobility during the reign of Akbar and the early years of Jahāngīr. The main reason for its sudden rise in the hierarchy under Akbar was the special relationship with the ruling family by virtue of two of its members being the Atka (husband of foster mother) and Koka (foster brother) of Akbar.[1] There were certain other families claiming a similar connection with Akbar, but none rose to as high a position as the family of Shamsuddīn Atka.[2]

Shamsuddīn Atka belonged to Ghaznin and was the son of Mīr Yār Muḥammad a 'spiritually minded householder'.[3] Shamsuddīn and his clansmen came to India with Mirzā Kamrān and were present in the fateful battle of Kanauj. He saved Humāyūn's life while the king was crossing the Ganges after the battle. Humāyūn took him into service after reaching Lahore and 'exalted him with princely favour'.[4] Sometime afterwards, he promised Shamsuddīn that his wife would have the privilege of nursing the child that Ḥamida Banu was expecting. Shamsuddīn's wife duly served Akbar after his birth, as wet nurse, and was styled Jiji Anga while Shamsuddīn was designated 'Atka'.[5]

[1] *Akbarnāma*, 1, 14, where characteristically a mystic anticipation of the coming good fortune of the family is recorded. See also ibid., 15.

[2] During the early years of Akbar's reign, families so connected with Akbar were those of Maham Anga and later on of Khwāja Maqṣūd Harvī. The latter had two sons Saif Khān Koka and Zain Khān Koka who became quite important. For Maham Anga, see also Chapter 1. For the biography of Saif Khān and Zain Khān see *Z.K.*, 1, 123.

[3] *Akbarnāma*, I, 14.

[4] Jauhar Aftabchi, *Tazkirat-ul Waqi'at*, B.M. Rieu, I, 14b, 27b-8ab; *Akbarnāma*, I, 166-8; *Muntakhab*, III, 308-9.

[5] *Akbarnāma*, I, 44.

When Humāyūn left for Iran from Mastang (December 1543) Shamsuddīn, his wife and certain other nobles were left behind to look after Akbar. Immediately afterwards, Mirzā Askari reached Mastang and took Akbar, Maham Anga, Shamsuddīn and the others to Qandhar.[6] After some time when in 1545 Humāyūn returned from Persia, and marched to Qandhar, Prince Akbar was brought to Kabul, where Shamsuddīn, who had accompanied him, was put into prison. During this period when Kabul changed hands between Mirzā Kamrān and Humāyūn, Shamsuddīn continued to watch over Akbar.[7] When after the final conquest of Kabul, Akbar was formally assigned Ghaznin under the tutelage of Khwāja Jalāluddīn Maḥmūd, Shamsuddīn was ordered to accompany him there.[8] It seems that during this period other members of Shamsuddīn's family also joined Humāyūn's service. The author of the *Ma'āṣir-ul Umarā*, in the biography of Mīr Muḥammad Khān-i Kalān states that he distinguished himself under Mirzā Kāmrān and in attendance on Humāyūn, but no exact date is given when he joined Humāyūn's service.[9] It is also not known when Quṭbuddīn Khān and Sharīf Khān joined Humāyūn.[10] However, when Humāyūn embarked on his expedition to India as many as 11 members of this family accompanied him according to the list of officers provided by Bāyazīd Bayāt. As against this, the list of high officers accompanying Humāyūn, provided by Abū'l Faẓl does not contain even a single member of the family. This is perhaps due to the fact that the Atkas as yet held minor positions among nobles and were more or less members of the personal staff of Prince Akbar, and so were not included in Abū'l Faẓl's list. Bāyazīd, on the other hand, includes even menial servants.[11]

[6] *Akbarnāma*, I, 186-94; *Muntakhab*, I, 443; *Ṭabaqāt*, II, 57-8.

[7] *Taẕkira-i Humāyūn*, 78; *Humāyūn-nāma*, 79; *Akbarnāma*, I, 258-9.

[8] *Akbarnāma*, I, 306, 315-16, 321-3.

[9] *Ma'āṣir-ul Umarā*, III, 211-16; *Z.K.*, I, 213, gives no information in this context.

[10] For Quṭbuddīn Khān and Sharīf Khān's biographies, see *Z.K.*, I, 213; *Ma'āṣir-ul Umarā*, III, 56-9, II, 601-3.

[11] *Taẕkira-i Humāyūn*, 176-87. These members of the family are named:

(1) Mīr Shamsuddīn Atka
(2) Yūsuf Muḥammad Khān s/o Shamsuddīn Atka
(3) Quṭbuddīn Muḥammad Khān brother of Shamsuddīn Atka
(4) Mīr Sharīf Ghaznavi brother of Shamsuddīn Atka
(5) Shāh Muḥammad Ghaznavi brother of Shamsuddīn Atka
(6) Mīr Muḥammad Ghaznavi brother of Shamsuddīn Atka

Shamsuddīn remained with Akbar during Humāyūn's campaign in India and was present at the battle of Sarhind.[12] When after reaching Delhi, Humāyūn distributed *jāgīrs* to his officers, the *sarkār* of Hissar Firoza and its neighbouring *parganas* were assigned to Akbar. Shamsuddīn was also assigned a *jāgīr* in that region.[13] He was with Akbar at the time of Humāyūn's death.[14]

After Akbar's accession, while Bairam Khān became the regent, considerable influence began to be exercised also by the nobles who had held the privilege of personal attendance on the emperor.[15] Apparently, in order to ward off rivalry from this quarter, Bairam Khān had Shamsuddīn and certain other nobles despatched to Kabul to bring the royal ladies to India.[16]

In 1557 Shamsuddīn and Mun'īm Khān along with the royal ladies started towards India. When they reached Jalalabad, they heard of Bairam Khān's ascendancy in the court and of Tardi Beg's execution. On this account Mun'īm Khān stayed back;[17] but Shamsuddīn and his kinsmen continued their journey, along with the imperial ladies, and presented themselves before Akbar at Mankot.[18] During the siege of that fortress, Akbar sent Shamsuddīn to negotiate with Sikandar, the Afghān pretender. At the same time Shamsuddīn and his relations seem to have been granted *jāgīrs* in the Panjab.[19]

Soon after the arrival of the royal ladies and Shamsuddīn from Kabul a struggle began at the court. Those nobles who had been the

---

(7) Faẓil Muḥammad s/o Shāh Muḥammad
(8) Nauranj Khān s/o Quṭbuddīn Khān
(9) Bāz Bahādur s/o Mīr Sharīf Ghaznavi
(10) Gujar Khān s/o Quṭbuddīn Khān
(11) Farrukh Khān s/o Shāh Muḥammad

For Abū'l Faẓl's list, see *Akbarnāma*, I, 342-3.

[12] *Akbarnāma*, I, 346-50; *Muntakhab*, I, 460-1.

[13] *Akbarnāma*, I, 351.

[14] Ibid., 352. The Atkas fought against Rustam Khān Lohani at Hissar. Shamsuddīn then went to join Akbar when Bairam Khān was made Akbar's guardian in place of Abū'l Ma'ali (*Akbarnāma*, I, 354-7; *Ṭabaqāt*, II, 37).

[15] See Chapter I.

[16] *Tazkira-i Humāyūn*, 208; *Akbarnāma*, I, 365-7, II, 17; *Muntakhab*, II, 12; *Ṭabaqāt*, II, 128.

[17] *Tazkira-i Humāyūn*, 213, 217-19, 221; *Akbarnāma*, II, 55.

[18] *Akbarnāma*, II, 58-9; *Ṭabaqāt*, II, 133-4.

[19] At the time of Bairam Khān's dismissal he is reported to have been stationed at Bhera. Cf. *Akbarnāma*, II, 95; *Ṭabaqāt*, II, 134-45.

personal servants of Akbar when a prince (particularly the families of Maham Anaga and Shamsuddīn) formed a group. They were unhappy with the immense power enjoyed by Bairam Khān and his associates, and tried to wean Akbar away from the tutelage of the regent.[20] While at Mankot, Bairam Khān's camp was attacked by a royal elephant. Suspecting foul play, Bairam Khān protested to Maham Anga, who persuaded him to drop the matter.[21] But Bairam Khān was not fully satisfied; and when he reached Lahore, he reopened the issue and held Shamsuddīn responsible for the disfavour shown to him by the emperor.[22] Thereupon Shamsuddīn collected all his relations, went to Bairam Khān to render him the necessary assurances.[23]

After this incident we have no information about the Atkas for the next three years. Apparently they served in the Panjab; and Shamsuddīn seems to have held Bhera in *jāgīr*. But the subsequent events suggested that the Atkas and the group of Maham Anga continued to work in close cooperation until Akbar dismissed Bairam Khān from the office of *Wakīl*.[24] Shamsuddīn was now summoned to court, ordered to proceed immediately to Lahore, assume charge of that city, and then leaving his elder brother Mīr Muḥammad there, come to Delhi.[25] At his arrival Shamsuddīn was warmly received and awarded the standard and *tuman togh* previously held by Bairam Khān. He was also entrusted with the government of the Panjab. The office of *Wakīl* was not given to him; it seems to have been held jointly by Shahābuddīn Aḥmad Khān and Maham Anga.[26] This division of power was, however, not easy for either party, and Shamsuddīn and Maham Anga soon fell out. Despite the opposition of Maham Anga and her associates, who urged the emperor to lead the campaign personally, the command of the expedition against Bairam Khān was given to Shamsuddīn.[27] He was thereupon accused of deliberately moving

[20] *Akbarnāma*, II, 59-60, 62, 95, *Ṭabaqāt*, II, 142. Nizāmuddīn writes: 'At every opportunity they said to His Majesty words which might produce disfavour in his mind' (towards Bairam Khān).

[21] *Akbarnāma*, II, 60; *Ṭabaqāt*, II, 134-5.

[22] Ibid., II, 62.

[23] Ibid.

[24] Ibid., II, 93-4.

[25] Ibid., II, 95.

[26] Ibid., 95-6.

[27] Ibid., II, 110, 119; Abū'l Qāsim Namakin, *Munshāt-i Namakīn*, MS: Maulana Azad Library, Aligarh, 20a-2b. A royal letter dated July 1560, addressed to certain nobles in the Panjab. This indicates that Shamsuddīn Atka was a joint commander against Bairam Khān. Muḥammad Qāsim and Mahdī Qāsim also held important positions in the expeditionary force (*Ṭabaqāt*, II, 145-7, Nizāmuddīn makes no reference to this controversy).

slowly and providing Bairam Khān with an opportunity to flee.[28] However, Bairam Khān was defeated and his relations were either killed or taken prisoner.[29] After the victory, Shamsuddīn was 'exalted with royal favour and the choicest parts of the Panjab were assigned to him and his kinsmen'.[30] About the same time Mun'īm Khān came from Kabul and was appointed *Wakīl*.[31]

These favours did not satisfy the ambitions of Shamsuddīn because he coveted the office of *Wakīl* for himself. Sometimes after the appointment of Mun'īm Khān, Shamsuddīn wrote a letter to Akbar. He accused Maham Anga and her associates of hampering him during the campaign against Bairam Khān. Many persons who participated in the campaign against Bairam Khān were given presents and pensions 'tenfold more than their service', yet Yūsuf Muḥammad's award of one crore *dams* remained only on paper because no *jāgīr* was assigned to him. Similarly he (Shamsuddīn) was also assigned one crore *dams*, but a *jāgīr* carrying only 40 lakhs *dams* per year was assigned to him. In the end he requested that as Bairam Khān's rank and other titles had already been awarded to him, the office of *Wakīl* should also be conferred on him.[32]

Shamsuddīn came from the Panjab to Agra in November 1561.[33] He was given the title of A'ẓam Khān and entrusted with the task of reorganizing the army and the finances of the empire.[34] Probably by this step Akbar wanted to vest the highest authority in the hands of Shamsuddīn, without formally dismissing the *Wakīl*. But the step evoked the jealousy of Maham Anga who considered herself as the *de-facto* regent of the empire; Mun'īm Khān too, was dissatisfied. The arrangement could not work satisfactorily under these circumstances and soon afterwards Shamsuddīn was formally appointed *Wakīl*.[35]

[28] *Akbarnāma*, II, 119-20; Letter of Atka Khān to Akbar.

[29] Ibid., 112, Bairam Khān was defeated near Sultanpur on 23 August 1560; *Tazkira-i Humāyūn*, 226; *Ṭabaqāt*, II, 147-8.

[30] *Akbarnāma*, II, 115-16; *Ṭabaqāt*, II, 148.

[31] *Akbarnāma*, II, 114; *Tabaqāt*, II, 148.

[32] The letter was written presumably in May 1560, *Akbarnāma*, II, 119-20. *Ma'āṣir-i Raḥīmī*, I, 667-8. Akbar had earlier promised the *tuman togh* to Mun'īm Khān, but it seems that after having decided to appoint him *Wakīl*, the king considered it prudent to satisfy the vanity of Shamsuddīn by conferring upon him the prestigious standards till then enjoyed by Bairam Khān. See also *Ma'āṣir-ul Umarā*, II, 531-5.

[33] *Akbarnāma*, II, 149; *Ṭabaqāt*, II, 155.

[34] *Akbarnāma*, II, 174; *Ma'āṣir-ul Umarā*, II, 531-5.

[35] Shamsuddīn is described as *Wakīl* in the sources but it is difficult to find out

This further exacerbated the relations between Shamsuddīn and his rivals. Matters came to a head when certain administrative measures, notably scrutiny of *jāgīrs*, were taken up by Shamsuddīn.[36] As the factional struggle at the court intensified, Ādham Khān's rashness added fuel to the fire.[37] Finally, while he was transacting state business in his office Shamsuddīn was attacked and murdered by Ādham Khān; he was believed to have done so at the instigation of Mun'īm Khān, Shahābuddīn Aḥmad Khān and certain other nobles.[38]

When the murder became known to the Atka Khail, Yūsuf Muḥammad, Shamsuddīn's eldest son, immediately armed himself and collected his clansmen. They did not believe that Ādham Khān had been killed by Akbar until they were shown his corpse. Akbar personally consoled members of the Atka family and 'promoted them to higher ranks'.[39] The ill-feeling of the Atka Khail against Shahābuddīn Aḥmad Khān, Mun'īm Khān and other suspected conspirators would have led to bloodshed if the Atkas not been removed from the court. Accordingly, Mīr Muḥammad, Quṭbuddīn Khān and Sharīf Khān, the brothers of Shamsuddīn, along with the other *jāgīrdārs* of the Panjab, were immediately employed in the campaign against Sulṭān Ādam Gakhar in the Salt Range. After the successful completion of that campaign, they returned to their *jāgīrs*.[40]

During this period the whole of the Atka clan held all their *jāgīrs* in the Panjab; and Shamsuddīn's brother, Mīr Muḥammad, was the governor of that province. Yūsuf Muḥammad and Mirzā 'Azīz Koka

the date of his appointment. *Ā'īn*, I, 595; *Akbarnāma*, II, 151, 180; *Mun'īm Khān*, 64n. 3.

[36] *Akbarnāma*, II, 179; *Iqbālnāma*, 171. For a detailed discussion of these reforms, see *Mun'īm Khan*, 66 n. 1.

[37] Haji Arif Qandhari, *Tārīkh-i Akbarī*, Rampur 1962, 70. *Tārīkh-i Alfi*, 70 and Farishta, I, 252 support 'Ārif Qandhārī's statement that there was a long drawn struggle which finally resulted in the murder of Shamsuddīn.

[38] *Akbarnāma*, II, 179-80; tr. 278. Abū'l Faẓl while discussing the flight of Mun'īm Khān clearly states that 'his motives in instigating Ādham Khān was that after this affair, the binding and loosening of the transaction of the sublime family and the control of all matters political and financial would be in his hands'. The *Ṭabaqāt*, II, 158; and *Muntakhab*, II, 52 also maintain that Shamsuddīn's murder was the result of a conspiracy of Mun'īm Khān. Iqtidar Alam Khān, however, argues against the existence of a wider conspiracy. Cf. *Mun'īm Khān*, 66-7.

[39] *Akbarnāma*, II, 191-2.

[40] Ibid., II, 191-4; *Ṭabaqāt*, 159-62; *Muntakhab*, II, 54-5.

remained at the court under the personal care of the emperor and accompanied Akbar in his campaign against 'Abdullah Khān Uzbek in Malwa and 'Alī Qulī in the east.[41]

While the Atkas were posted in the Panjab, Mirzā Sulaimān invaded Kabul (1564). Mirzā Hakīm thereupon fled from his capital, crossed the Indus and appealed to Akbar for help. He also despatched Khwāja Beg Muḥammad *Dīwan* and Maqsūd Khān Jauhari to Mīr Muḥammad. The latter sent Qāzī 'Imād to Mirzā Hakīm 'with presents and encouraging messages'.[42] Akbar appointed Quṭbuddīn Khān as the 'guardian' (*atālīq*) of Mirzā Hakīm and ordered Mīr Muḥammad and other officers of the Panjab and Multan to join the prince on the banks of the Indus. After establishing Mirzā Hakīm at Kabul, Quṭbuddīn (Mīr Muḥammad's younger brother) was to remain as his guardian. When the imperial officers along with Mirzā Hakīm reached Jalalabad, Mirzā Sulaimān gave up the siege of Kabul and retired to Badakhshan. Mirzā Hakīm occupied Kabul without any resistance.[43]

After arranging affairs at Kabul, Mīr Muḥammad sent back the officers under Quṭbuddīn to India and himself assumed the office of the Mirza's *Wakīl*. This was in violation of imperial orders. However, soon afterwards, differences arose between Mīr Muḥammad and Mirzā Hakīm, and their relations finally broke down when Mirzā Hakīm got his sister married to Khwāja Ḥasan Naqshbandi against the wishes of Mīr Muḥammad. Ultimately, Mīr Muḥammad left Kabul without intimating anybody, and after reaching Hindustan sent a detailed report to the court. Abū'l Fazḷ, while summarizing these events, considers his action uncalled for, and holds him responsible for the confusion at Kabul.[44] About the same time Yūsuf Muḥammad, the eldest son of Shamsuddīn, died.[45]

In 1566 Mirzā Hakīm having been expelled by Mirzā Sulaimān, again fled from Kabul and sought imperial help. The emperor immediately ordered the Panjab officers to proceed to his assistance.

[41] *Akbarnāma*, II, 223-9, 252-3, 291; *Muntakhab*, II, 96.

[42] *Tārīkh-i Alfi*, 616b-17b; *Akbarnāma*, II, 71-2.

[43] *Tārīkh-i Alfi*, 617; *Akbarnāma*, II, 239-42; *Ṭabaqāt*, II, 178; *Muntakhab*, II, 72-3.

[44] *Tārīkh-i Alfi*, 617b; *Akbarnāma*, II, 242-3. *Muntakhab*, II, 88, states that after taking possession of Kabul, Mirzā Ḥakīm dismissed the nobles who were sent to help him from India; and Mīr Muḥammad, becoming unhappy at Khwāja Ḥasan Naqshbandi's supremacy, also came back to the Panjab.

[45] *Akbarnāma*, II, 272; *Ṭabaqāt*, II, 195-6. Yūsuf Muḥammad died at Delhi on 24 May 1566.

But in the meantime Farīdūn, a maternal uncle of Mirzā Hakīm who had been at the court for some time and was on the way to Kabul, met him and persuaded him to invade Lahore.[46] Sulṭān 'Alī and Ḥasan Khān, two other rebels from the court, also joined Farīdūn.[47] According to Abū'l Faẓl, Mirzā Hakīm himself thought that perhaps he might bring over the Panjab officers to his side.[48] Apparently he was relying upon the impact of the Uzbek rebellion in the east and the resentment of the old Tūrānī nobles. However, the Panjab officers, Mīr Muḥammad, Quṭbuddīn Khān and Sharīf Khān, prepared themselves to defend Lahore, and Akbar himself started for Lahore on 17 November 1566. When he reached the banks of the Sutlej, Mirzā Hakīm took to flight. Quṭbuddīn Khān and other officers were deputed to the borders in pursuit.[49]

While Akbar was at Lahore, the Uzbeks again rebelled and proclaimed their allegiance to Mirzā Hakīm. The emperor hurriedly confirmed arrangements for the government of the Panjab and marched back to Agra. As before, the charge of the province was assigned to Mīr Muḥammad, Quṭbuddīn and their sons and brothers under the supreme command of Mīr Muḥammad himself.[50]

Mindful of the Atka family's acquisition of power in the Panjab Akbar transferred the Atka Khail from the province in 1568, as soon, apparently, as his mind was free of anxieties regarding the Uzbek rebels. While discussing this measure, Abū'l Faẓl remarks that 'whenever a large body is gathered together of one mind and one speech, and show much push and energy, it is proper to disperse them firstly for their own good, and secondly, for the welfare of the community'.[51] Akbar himself is reported to have said later that they had grown quite powerful, and he considered their transfer from the Panjab as one of his greatest achievements.[52] Moreover, during Mīr Muḥammad's stay in Kabul and at the time of Mirzā Hakīm's invasion of the Panjab, according to Abū'l Faẓl, 'wonderful stories

[46] *Akbarnāma*, II, 275-6; *Muntakhab*, II, 89-90.

[47] *Muntakhab*, II, 90. Ḥasan Khān was brother of Shahāb Khān.

[48] *Akbarnāma*, II, 276. Nizāmuddīn and Badāunī's accounts suggest the same opinion. See *Ṭabaqāt*, II, 201; *Muntakhab*, II, 90.

[49] *Tārīkh-i Akbarī*, 142-3; *Akbarnāma*, II, 274-7; *Ṭabaqāt*, II, 198-203; *Muntakhab*, II, 90-1.

[50] *Akbarnāma*, II, 285-6; *Ṭabaqāt*, II, 208; *Muntakhab*, II, 92-3.

[51] *Akbarnāma*, II, 332-3. *Ṭabaqāt*, II, 223 and *Muntakhab*, II, 106 briefly mention the transfer without comments.

[52] *Tazkirah-i Humayun*, 253.

had been told about these loyal men'.[53] But there is no actual indication of any disloyal action on their part.

The Atkas were summoned to the court and fresh assignments were given to them. Mīr Muḥammad, Quṭbuddīn Khān and Sharīf Khān were assigned Sambhal, Malwa and Kanauj respectively.[54] Mirzā 'Azīz Koka's *jāgīr* of Dipalpur was, however, not transferred. Mīr Muḥammad was transferred to Nagaur in 1570. This shows that when fresh appointments were given, the Atkas were deliberately so posted as to be placed at a distance from each other. Akbar himself says that they were spread all over the empire 'like the constellation of the Bear in the sky'.[55]

This dispersal of the Atkas from the Panjab naturally affected the power and prestige of the family. But Mirzā 'Azīz Koka, the playmate of Akbar, apparently continued to be in favour; we have seen that his *jāgīr* was not transferred. This fact seems to have been well known even outside the country. A little before the conquest of Gujarat (1572), 'Abdullah Khān Uzbek wrote a letter to Akbar, in which he particularly mentioned Mun'īm Khān and Mirzā 'Azīz Koka apparently as the two most influential nobles and also sent presents to them.[56]

Akbar thus tried to break the power of this family even as he raised at the same time as its most prominent member, Mirzā 'Azīz Koka, to a very high status. The case of the Atka Khail and 'Azīz Koka is actually illustrative of Akbar's policy towards his nobility. Without destroying any important family, or even greatly deflating its status, he managed to establish his own authority.[57]

In 1572 when Akbar embarked on the expedition to Gujarat, Mīr Muḥammad Khān was sent as head of the advance guard. Almost the whcle of the Atka Khail also accompanied the emperor. After the conquest of Gujarat,[58] the government was entrusted to Mirzā

[53] *Akbarnāma*, II, 332.

[54] Ibid., III, 332-3; *Muntakhab*, II, 106. Mir Muhammad Khan-i Kalan was given charge of Sambhal and Bareli.

[55] *Tarikh-i Humayūn*, 253.

[56] *Akbarnāma*, II, 368; *Muntakhab*, II, 198-9. It is significant that in about 1569-70 'Aziz Koka had enough influence to intercede successfully with the emperor on behalf of Shaikh Mubarak and his sons Faizi and Abu'l Faẓl securing them from persecution and getting them permission to return to Agra (*Muntakhab*, II, 198-9).

[57] *Akbarnāma*, III, 33. This subject is further discussed in our Conclusion.

[58] For the details of conquest of Gujarat see *Akbarnāma*, II, 372, III, 8-9, 17-18, 24-7; *Mir'āt-i Aḥmadī*, 102-3.

'Azīz Koka, and the city of Ahmadabad and the *parganas* of Petlad and Haveli along with several other *parganas* were assigned to him in *jāgīr*. The other members of the family were also assigned *jāgīrs* in the province. Pattan was assigned to Mīr Muḥammad and his sons, Fāẓil Khān and Farrukh Khān. The *sarkār* of Baroch and its neighbouring regions were given to Quṭbuddīn Khān; Naurang Khān was given Baroda. Sharīf Khān and his sons, 'Ārif and Zāhid, were also assigned *jāgīrs* in Gujarat.[59]

From these appointments one may infer that Akbar reversed his earlier policy of not posting officers of one family in the same province. But a close study of these appointments indicate that Akbar desired close cooperation among his commanders in a recently conquered land, and, at the same time, took care to choose a member of the family closest to him personally as its head. In the presence of senior members of the family (Mīr Muḥammad and Quṭbuddīn Khān) Mirzā 'Azīz Koka was appointed governor of Gujarat and his uncles were posted to serve under him. Abū'l Faẓl reacts to the obvious supersession of seniority here by arguing that 'the foundation of appointment is talent and virtue and the quality of ancestors is not required'.[60]

In September 1575 Akbar sent Muḥammad Rafi Qurchi with a *farmān* to Mirzā 'Azīz Koka summoning him to the court. Simultaneously a secret letter was sent to Mīr Abū Turāb Walī. In this letter Akbar instructed Abū Turāb that contrary to his previous practice, he should regularly send confidential detailed reports on the situation in Gujarat particularly about the behaviour of Mirzā 'Azīz Koka, Mīr Muḥammad and Quṭbuddīn.[61]

Mīr Abū Turāb was embarrassed by this order. He did not want to complain against the Mirzā and at the same time had no desire to annoy the emperor. He, therefore, replied that since he wanted to come and pay his respect at the court, he would personally make a report on the situation in Gujarat.[62] Mirzā 'Azīz, though in the dark about Akbar's secret instructions, still took from Abū Turāb the assurance that the latter would not make any complaint against him.[63]

[59] *Akbarnāma*, III, 33; *Mir'āt-i Aḥmadī*, 102-3, provide the details of appointment. See also *Muntakhab*, II, 142, and *Ṭabaqāt*, II, 253.

[60] *Akbarnāma*, III, 33. Surprisingly enough, there is no element of criticism in the narration of these events in either Nizāmuddīn Aḥmad Bakhshī or Badāunī.

[61] Abū Turāb Walī, *Tārīkh-i Gujarat*, Asiatic Society of Bengal, 1909, 91-2.

[62] *Tārīkh-i Gujarat*, 92.

[63] Ibid., 93.

Mirzā 'Azīz started for the court with Mīr Abū Turāb and after stopping for a while at Pattan, bid farewell to Mīr Muḥammad. This was the Mirzā's last meeting with Mīr Muḥammad as the latter died in Pattan in December 1575.[64] He reached Fatehpur on 10 October 1575. There Mīr Abū Turāb gave a full report to the emperor in a way that Akbar's suspicions regarding the administration of Gujarat were largely allayed.[65]

While Abū Turāb's account suggests that Akbar's dissatisfaction with the way 'Azīz Koka had governed Gujarat was responsible for his recall, Abū'l Faẓl gives two different reasons: firstly, since Mirzā Sulaimān was expected at the court, Akbar wanted the Mirzā to be present at the entertainments in his honour. Secondly, towards the end of 1574-5 Akbar had introduced the most far-reaching reforms of his reign, viz., the branding regulations (*dāgh*), the conversion of assignments (*jāgīrs*) into directly managed territory (*khalisa*) and fixing the grades of officers of state. Many of the nobles were opposed to these regulations.[66] Akbar now wanted to discuss the question of these reforms with the Mirzā and seek his cooperation.[67]

It is probable, that while recalling the Mirzā for consultation, Akbar did not intend to remove him from the governorship of Gujarat. It was only when the Mirzā fell from favour and showed no repentance, that he decided fully six months after his recall to make other arrangements. 'Azīz Koka expressed very strong disapproval of the new regulations for the branding of horses and the *'Karorī* experiment; and made references to the distressed conditions of the peasantry. He used such harsh language that Akbar, notwithstanding his affection, was annoyed. He, therefore, decided that the Mirzā should not be permitted to 'lead the nobles astray'. Consequently, the Mirzā was removed from service and put in virtual confinement in his garden at Agra.[68] Quṭbuddīn Khān and Naurang Khān were also apparently summoned to the court, for both of them joined the emperor in the campaign against the Rana of Mewar in the same year. Quṭbuddīn Khān was also promoted to the rank of 5,000.[69]

[64] Ibid., 92-3; *Akbarnāma*, III, 163. [65] *Tārīkh-i Gujarat*, 93.

[66] *Akbarnāma*, III, 69; *Iqbālnāma*, II, 298; *Mir'āt-i Aḥmadī*, 113.

[67] *Akbarnāma*, III, 69-70; *Ṭabaqāt*, II, 315; *Muntakhab*, II, 214-15; *Ma'āṣir-i Raḥīmī*, I, 837.

[68] *Akbarnāma*, III, 147; *Muntakhab*, II, 214-15; *Mir'āt-i Aḥmadī*, 113.

[69] *Akbarnāma*, III, 184, 191, 195. During the Mewar campaign both Quṭbuddīn and Rāja Bhagwan Das were censured as they failed to capture Rana Pratap.

After returning from Mewar, Qutbuddīn Khān and Naurang Khān were despatched against Rāja 'Alī Khān of Khandesh under the command of Shahābuddīn Aḥmad Khān. When Rāja 'Alī Khān came to know of the advance of the army, he offered to surrender. But in the meantime Quṭbuddīn was informed of the rebellion of Muẓaffar Ḥusain Mirzā at Baroch, Baroda and other places of his *jāgīr*. He thereupon proceeded towards Gujarat. On account of his departure, the settlement with Khandesh could not be made properly.[70]

Sharīf Khān, another uncle of Mirzā 'Azīz Koka, seems to have remained at the court; he served in the Mewar campaign between 1576 and 1578.[71]

Mirzā 'Azīz Koka remained in confinement for about five years. A passage in the *Akbarnāma* suggests that attempts were made to persuade him to accept Akbar's new measures. He was also promised great favours, but he declined to be swayed.[72] In 1578 Akbar sent Mīr Fatḥullah Shīrāzī to bring Quṭbuddīn to the court and seek his help in persuading Mirzā 'Azīz Koka.[73] In any case, Mirzā 'Azīz Kokā at last started visiting the court, and was apparently treated with favour. But in the same year an earlier incident involving Mirzā 'Azīz Koka came to be reported to Akbar. Mirzā 'Azīz Koka, it was said, had handed over Mīr 'Alauddīn to one of his servants upon some suspicion about his honesty; the servant, tortured the man to death. When Mirzā 'Azīz came to know of this, he had the servant executed. At this time, Mīr 'Alauddīn's father came from Persia and demanded justice. Akbar ordered an enquiry into the matter, firmly insisting that there should be no 'glossing over' of the truth.[74] 'Azīz Koka naturally 'suspected that he had lost favour and went into retirement'; he, however, took care to win over 'Alauddīn's father with large sums of money.[75]

'Azīz Koka's suspicions about Akbar's motives were probably ill-founded. Moreover, Quṭbuddīn in the same year was appointed guardian (*atāliq*) of Prince Salim.[76] Although the office was of little administrative significance, it was indicative still of high court status. He was also given command of the forces appointed to attack the Portuguese ports of Gujarat.[77]

[70] *Akbarnāma*, III, 199; *Ṭabaqāt*, II, 338.
[71] *Akbarnāma*, III, 194; *Muntakhab*, II, 242; *Ṭabaqāt*, II, 340-1.
[72] *Akbarnāma*, III, 250. [73] Ibid., 250, 261. [74] *Akbarnāma*, 111, 266.
[75] Ibid., 326. [76] Ibid., 274.
[77] Ibid., 280-1; Cf. V.A. Smith, *Akbar the Great Mughal*, 145-6, for his expedition to Daman.

In 1580 Mirzā 'Azīz was at last pardoned; he was given the rank of 5,000 which he had previously held and was appointed governor of Bengal in succession to Muẓaffar Khān.[78] Abu'l Faẓl states that he was pardoned at the request of the ladies of the ḥarem, but apparently, the serious revolt of nobles in Bengal also called for the service of a commander of some status.[79] He was, however, to be in company of the Indian noble, Shahbāz Khān Kambū.[80] The two could hardly have been expected to get on very well together. Mirzā 'Azīz Koka's hostility to the *dāgh* system was well known, and this system was alleged to have been introduced at Shahbāz Khān's suggestion. Besides, Mirzā 'Azīz was very hostile to the Shaikhzādas.[81] From the outset, therefore, the two commanders took their own separate ways, and a joint campaign could not be launched against the rebels.[82] As if to match their opponents, the rebels also became victims of disagreement. Mirzā 'Azīz thereupon opened negotiation with the Qāqshāl nobles and won them over. The rebel noble Ma'ṣūm Khān thereupon became alarmed and fled.[83] But before the rebels could be fully brought to heel, Mirzā 'Azīz, who was unhappy with his position, requested the emperor to send him to some other territory on the plea that the climate of Bengal did not suit him. Akbar accordingly appointed Shahbāz Khān as governor of Bengal; and 'Azīz Koka was ordered to go to his *jāgīr* in Bihar.[84]

During this time, Akbar promulgated certain administrative reforms. As part of this, the department of dyes was given to Naurang Khān a member of the Atka family.[85] Further reforms in the administration were introduced in 1583. Princes of royal blood and leading nobles of the empire were given various departments to

[78] *Akbarnāma*, III, 326. [79] Ibid. [80] Ibid., 314; *Muntakhab*, II, 285.

[81] For the introduction of *Dagh-o Mahall*, see *Muntakhab*, II, 173, 190-1; for 'Mirzā 'Azīz Koka's hostility to Shaikhzadas, see his *Arzdāsht* to Jahāngīr, in Appendix C-II.

[82] On account of the independence displayed by Shahbāz Khān, Mirzā 'Azīz Koka and Todar Mal, who was also sent to assist him, left every thing to Shahbāz Khān and subsequently went to Tirhut on the pretext of subduing Bahādur; 'in reality they sought to get away from Shahbāz Khān'. But Shahbāz Khān himself left his charge by going off to Jaunpur on the pretext of checking Ma'ṣūm Farankhudī who had also revolted. For more details see *Akbarnāma*, III, 323-5, 329-31; *Muntakhab-ut Tawārīkh*, II, 287. Also see A.J. Qaisar, 'Shahbāz Khān Kamboh', *Medieval India — A Miscellany*, I, 60-2.

[83] *Akbarnāma*, III, 400-1. [84] Ibid., 405-7; A.J. Qaisar, op.cit.

[85] *Akbarnāma*, 396; Naurang Khān was son of Quṭbuddīn Khān. See Appendix B–II. For these administrative reforms, also see Chapter I.

administer. Sharīf Khān Atka, along with Rāja Askaran, was now ordered to look after the property of deceased persons and hand it over to the heirs. Naurang Khān was appointed to the department of buildings.[86]

In 1583 Gujarat once again became the centre of sedition. The trouble started with the appointment of I'timād Khān as governor in place of Shahābuddīn Aḥmad Khān. Muẓaffar Shāh revolted, with the help of the retainers of Shahābuddīn Aḥmad Khān, who had been replaced by I'timād Khān. Muẓaffar Shāh captured Ahmadabad and marched on to Baroda and Baroch, which were under the command of Quṭbuddīn Khān. Under the pressure of the rebels Quṭbuddīn Khān agreed to surrender the fort on the condition of safe passage. But the rebels treacherously arrested and killed him near the town of Sarnal on 2 November 1583.[87]

When Akbar was informed about the rebellion, 'Abdur Raḥīm son of Bairam Khān, was appointed to quell it. Sharīf Khān, Naurang Khān and Zāhid, son of Sharīf Khān, who were posted in Malwa under Qulīj Khān, were ordered to join 'Abdur Raḥīm. About the same time, Mirzā 'Azīz Koka came to the court from Hajipur, Bihar (March 1584); Akbar decided to post him near the province of Gujarat, and with this in view Garha and Raisen in Malwa were given to him in *jāgīr*.[88] He was ordered to go to Hajipur to collect his troops and then come to the court.[89]

After returning to the court, Mirzā Azīz Koka was appointed to command a campaign against the Deccan states (in 1586). Shahābuddīn Aḥmad Khān and Sharīf Khān from Malwa were also ordered to join him in the campaign. Mirzā 'Azīz Koka proceeded to Handia and took the fort of Sanoli from Nahar Rao. Thereafter, Akbar appointed him governor of Malwa.[90] But after these initial successes the campaign completely failed owing to the differences that arose between Shahābuddīn Aḥmad Khān and Mirzā Azīz Koka and then between Mirzā 'Azīz Koka and 'Abdur Raḥim Khān Khānān. These differences were largely on grounds of past family feuds.[91]

[86] *Akbarnāma*, III, 404-5.

[87] *Akbarnāma*, 405-7, 421-4; *Ṭabaqāt*, II, 373-4; *Mir'āt-i Aḥmadī*, 122-4, 127-9. See also Chapter I.

[88] *Akbarnāma*, III, 423-4. [89] Ibid., 422-3, 436. [90] Ibid., 489; *Z.K.*, I, 95.

[91] *Muntakhab*, II, 343, 347, 361-2. *Akbarnāma*, III, 489-91. See also *Ṭabaqāt*, II, 383-5; *Z.K.*, I, 95-6.

During the same year when two co-governors were appointed over each *ṣūba*, the Atkas were assigned only one *ṣūba*, Nauranj Khān was placed as the additional governor over Malwa, with 'Azīz Koka as the 'first' governor. Some other minor administrative charges were also given to them during this period; their *manṣabs* were not reduced, and apparently the family remained an important group at the court. As an additional sign of favour, in May 1587 Mirzā 'Azīz Koka's daughter was married to Prince Murād.[92]

Mirzā 'Azīz Koka remained in Malwa till 1589 when he was transferred to Gujarat. He was not willing to go to Gujarat and represented against his posting. But his request was turned down and he was asked to leave for Gujarat immediately. Mirzā 'Azīz is said to have considered this transfer to be equivalent to exile. During his governorship of Gujarat almost all of his sons and relations came to be posted in the *ṣūba*. In his campaign against Muẓaffar Shāh, 'Azīz Koka was accompanied by his kinsmen, Sharīf Khān, Naurang Khān, Gujar Khān, Fidāi Khān, Mirzā Anwar, Mirzā 'Abdullah and Mirzā Khurram.[93]

After his victory over Muẓaffar Shāh in 1593, the Mirzā was called to the court which he had not visited for the previous two years. But he believed that Akbar was unhappy with him and wanted to punish him. Hence he made a pretended march towards Diu held by the Portuguese, while dismissing Naurang Khān and Gujar Khān to their *jāgīrs*. Then he took a ship to Mecca along with his six sons and six daughters.[94]

There is no conclusive evidence in the chronicles regarding the circumstances that compelled Mirzā 'Azīz Koka to leave India. But

[92] *Akbarnāma*, III, 511-12.

[93] For details of Mirzā 'Azīz Koka's activities in Gujarat, see *Akbarnāma*, III, 578, 620, 628-31; *Mir'āt-i Aḥmadī*, 151-6.

[94] *Akbarnāma*, III, 638. In *Ṭabaqāt*, II, 422 Nizāmuddīn writes, 'At this time some malicious persons had communicated to him some unkind words which they had said had been spoken in respect of him by Akbar'. *Muntakhab*, II, 386-7 gives details of the causes of disagreement between Akbar and Mirzā 'Azīz Koka. According to him religion was the main point of difference. He also states that Mirzā 'Azīz had not visited the court for the previous six years. *Z.K.*, I, 96, writes that Mirzā 'Azīz had not visited the court for the previous ten years.

[95] In all there are four letters written to Mirzā 'Azīz Koka after his departure to Mecca in the *Maktubāt-i Allāmi*. Of these one was written by Abū'l Faẓl on behalf of Akbar and the other are by Abū'l Faẓl himself. Cf. *Maktubāt*, I, 56-7, II, 91-2, 155-6, 157-8. See also Athar Abbas Rizvī, *Religious and Intellectual History of Muslims in Akbar's Reign*, Delhi, 1975, 319-20.

the letters contained in Abū'l Faẓl's *Maktubāt*,[95] suggest that an estrangement between Mirzā 'Azīz and Akbar had been growing since the introduction of the *dāgh* regulations. It also appears that there had been an exchange of letters between the Mirzā and Abū'l Faẓl in this connection. Clearly too there was considerable resentment in the nobility on account of the rise of new entrants in it. In one of the letters 'Azīz Koka complained that his enemies had influenced the emperor's mind against him and sought his ruin. Mirzā 'Azīz Koka further protested against Akbar's attempt to throw into shade the old nobility and give more importance to those who followed his policies. In a letter written to Akbar, Mirzā 'Azīz Koka took exception to the prominence accorded to Abū'l Faẓl, Faizi, Ṣādiq Khān and Qilich Khān. He went to the extent of saying that Akbar had raised Abū'l Faẓl and Faizi to the position of Caliphs 'Uṣman and 'Alī. He also denounced Akbar's religious beliefs and added that those who had alienated Akbar from Islam were not his friends, but flatterers and time-servers. He claimed that the Sulṭān of Turkey would give him the title of Azām Khān if he asked for it.[96] Abū'l Faẓl in reply sought to clarify the true significance of the four degrees of devotion which was expected of the royal servants under the new spiritual doctrines espoused by the emperor.[97] He advised 'Azīz Koka to take up the charge of Gujarat immediately and send some one on whom he had confidence to the court, so that Abū'l Faẓl might privately convey to him the actual state of affairs and give him his faithful opinion.[98]

These charges of 'Azīz Koka especially his complaint regarding the dominance of a new nobility at the court may be examined in the light of the position of the Atka Khail itself.

As already discussed the family enjoyed a very high position from the very beginning of Akbar's reign. But after the transfer of the

[96] For the letter of Mirzā 'Azīz Koka to Akbar, see Cambridge University Library, King's College Collection (fols. 5b-8b). An English translation of the letter has been published by me in the *Proceedings of the Indian History Congress*, 1978, 353-9, see also Appendix C–II.

[97] *Maktubāt*, II, 156-7.

[98] Ibid., II, 155-6. One of the reasons for 'Azīz Koka's annoyance was the taking away from him of the charge of affixing the imperial seal on *farmāns*. In one of his letters Abū'l Faẓl writes that his complaint about some one also being put in charge of affixing the imperial seal on *farmāns* was frivolous. This duty was assigned to some other person only on account of the Mirzā's absence. For details, see *Maktubāt*, II, 158.

Atkas from the Panjab and certain other measures taken to break their family ties, the position of the family declined. We see that since their transfer from the Panjab, no member of this family except for Mirzā 'Azīz Koka and Sharīf Khān was given charge of a *ṣūba*[99] or an important post at the centre. The strength of the family in terms of *manṣabs* also continued to decline, because after the death of senior members of the family, their sons and relations were either not given *manṣabs* or the *manṣabs* given were too small to be recorded in the contemporary works.[100]

Thus it may be suggested that Akbar did not have full confidence in the Atkas. Presumably on that account other senior members of the family were not appointed to high posts, although their *manṣabs* were not curtailed. But Mirzā 'Azīz Koka had a distinct position; Akbar himself says 'a stream of milk connected him and 'Azīz'.[101] Apparently on that account and as a result of the great influence enjoyed by him in the imperial ḥarem, he was able to maintain his position in spite of his conduct causing annoyance to Akbar.[102]

When Akbar came to know of the flight of Mirzā 'Azīz Koka to Mecca, he professed great regret at his doing so without seeking permission of the emperor or the approval of his mother. Akbar reassured him of imperial favours and advised him to return immediately at least for the sake of his mother. The letter concludes by saying that Akbar had long been planning to send an ambassador to the Sulṭān of Turkey in order to strengthen the bonds of friendship between them. It was, therefore, desired that the Mirzā should return to the court before the ambassador reached Turkey.[103] As a matter of fact no ambassador was sent to Turkey and this remark appears to be a threat that if he did not leave Mecca immediately, Akbar would have to ask the Sulṭān through an embassy to expel or punish him.

After the Mirzā's departure, Akbar took care of his sons who remained in India. Mirzā Shamsī, his eldest son, was promoted to the rank of 1,000 and Shādmān was given the *manṣab* of 500. A fertile *jāgīr* was also assigned to them.[104] However, when Naurang

[99] Afzal Husain, 'Provincial Governors Under Akbar', *Proceedings of Indian History Congress*, Jabalpur, 1970, 269-77.

[100] See infra. Also see, the two lists of nobles of Atka Khails at the end of this chapter.

[101] *Ṭabaqāt*, III, 231.

[102] See supra.

[103] *Maktubāt*, I, 56-7.

[104] *Akbarnāma*, III, 638

Khān died in 1594 the ranks given to his sons, if any, were so low that Abū'l Faẓl omitted any mention of them.[105]

In 1594 Mirzā 'Azīz returned from Mecca to Gujarat and sought permission to present himself at the court.[106] According to Badāunī, having 'suffered much harm at the hands of the Sharīf, and throwing away the blessing which he had derived from the pilgrimage, he joined immediately on his return, the divine faith.[107] Abū'l Faẓl covers the entire episode, as usual, with lofty philosophizing:

> In a short space of time his heart emerged from darkness, but he remained in the state of bewilderment. He had not the effrontery to return and he could not think of staying. Suddenly he became aware again of His Majesty's graciousness, and giving up all other ideas he set out on the ocean. In twenty-four days he came back from the port of Balawal and gathered eternal bliss by paying his devotions to Akbar. A new aspect was given to submission.[108]

From now on Mirzā 'Azīz accepted Akbar's new policy. His change of heart was accepted and he was given his previous rank of 5,000 and offered a choice between the Panjab, Gujarat and Bihar for his *jāgīr*. He selected Bihar.[109] About the same time (1594) the only other surviving senior Atka noble Sharīf Khān, who had held his *jāgīr* in Malwa since 1580, was transferred to Ghaznin at his own request. He remained in command of Ghaznin, his ancestral home, till 1602 when Shāh Beg Khān was appointed in his place. Nothing further is known about him.[110]

In 1595 Mirzā 'Azīz Koka was appointed to the office of *Wakīl*. The seal was given to him and his *jāgīr* was transferred from Bihar to Multan.[111] Thereafter we have no information about him until 1600. Apparently all these years he remained at the court.[112]

In 1600 upon the death of Prince Murād, 'Azīz Koka was appointed governor of Gujarat. He was promoted to the rank of 7,000/6,000 and his sons 'Abdullah and Anwār were each raised to

[105] Ibid., 651. [106] Ibid. [107] *Muntakhab*, II, 398.

[108] *Akbarnāma*, III, 655-6.

[109] Ibid., 655. *Muntakhab*, II, 398, writes that he was given Ghazipur and Hajipur in *Jāgīr*.

[110] *Akbarnāma*, III, 654, 659.

[111] Ibid., 672, 717, while referring to his transfer, Abū'l Faẓl writes, 'As he wanted to make amends for his former misconduct (in going to Mecca) he asked to have his *jāgīr* near the court. His request was granted.'

[112] Ibid., 749-50, 769-70, 779.

the rank of 1,000 and Shamsuddīn to 2,000. Mirzā 'Azīz, however, was not permitted to go to Gujarat. His son Shamsuddīn was appointed *Nāi'b* of the *ṣūba* and his second son Khurram *faujdār* of Junagarh.[113] In 1602 the *ṣūba* of Gujarat was granted in *jāgīr* to Mirzā 'Azīz and his sons. At the same time, Shamsuddīn was recalled and Shādmān was appointed deputy governor of the *ṣūba*, and 'Abdullah, another son of Mirzā 'Azīz, was appointed to Junagarh in place of Khurram. They were promoted to the rank of 1,700/500 and 1,500/700 respectively. Mirzā 'Azīz continued to hold charge of Gujarat till 1605 but as an absentee governor. He was then transferred to Bihar.[114]

Thus towards the end of Akbar's reign the total *manṣabs* known to be held in the family of Mirzā 'Azīz Koka (as shown in Table 2.2) amounted to 14,200/7,200. If we compare this total with the total *manṣabs* held by the family in 1583 (Table 2.1) it would be obvious that the Atka Khail suffered a great setback in *manṣabs* as well as in their numerical strength.

Table 2.1

Total *manṣabs* held by the family in 1583

1. Mirzā 'Azīz Koka	5,000
2. Quṭbuddīn Khān	5,000
3. Sharīf Khān	3,000
4. Naurang Khān	3,000
5. Mirzā 'Abdullah	1,000
6. Mirzā Shamsuddīn	900
7. Mirzā Khurram	800
8. Bāz Bahādur	700
9. Gujar Khān	700
10. Mirzā Anwār	600
11. Mirzā Shādmān	500
12. Farrukh Khān	500
13. Fidāi Khān	500
Total *mansabs*	22,200

[113] *Takmila*, III, 806; *Mir'āt-i Aḥmadī*, 159.
[114] *Takmila*, III, 825; *Mir'āt-i Aḥmadī*, 159.

The decline in the number of *manṣabs* held by the Atka family was accompanied by an almost complete eclipse and elimination of the family (i.e. sons of Shamsuddīn Atka's brothers). The total number of nobles of the Atka Khail in Mughal service fell from thirteen in 1583 to five in 1605. As a matter of fact, the Atka Khail was practically reduced to the family of Mirzā 'Azīz Koka.

Although, during the last years of Akbar's reign the numerical strength of the family was thoroughly reduced, Mirzā 'Azīz Koka himself was at the height of his influence at the time of Akbar's death.[115] But the support which he gave to Khusrau's candidature undermined his position completely during the reign of Jahāngīr. He and his sons were retained in service, but it was obvious that he exercised no influence over the emperor.

Jahāngīr, after ascending the throne, pardoned all those nobles who were involved in the effort to supersede him by Khusrau.[116] But the Mirzā's relations with the emperor and the favourites of the new emperor remained full of mutual suspicions. The rebellion of Khusrau soon after the accession further undermined his position. He was suspected as being one of the chief instigators and when Jahāngīr started in pursuit of Khusrau he thought it necessary to take the Mirzā with him.[117] Farīd Bhakkarī states that Mirzā 'Azīz feared that he might be killed any moment; and he even used to come to the court along with a coffin.[118]

Certain other events connected with the early years of Jahāngīr's reign indicate his hostile attitude towards Mirzā 'Azīz Koka. The

Table 2.2

Total *manṣabs* held by the family in 1605

1. Mirzā 'Azīz Koka	7,000/6,000
2. Shamsuddīn	2,000
3. Shādmān	1,700/500
4. Khurram	2,000
5. 'Abdullah	1,500/700
Total *manṣabs*	14,200/7,200

The Tables are based on Appendix A–III.

[115] For details of Mirzā 'Azīz Koka's role in the accession crisis at the time of Akbar's death, see Conclusion.

[116] *Tuzuk*, 4-5. [117] Ibid., 25; *Z.K.* I, 97; De Laet 179. [118] *Z.K.*, I, 85.

author of the *Zakhīrat-ul Khawānīn* writes that once in full darbar hot words passed between Sharīf Khān Amīr-ul Umarā, and Mirzā 'Azīz Koka and the matter was referred to Jahāngīr in private chamber. The emperor immediately summoned Sharīf Khān, Mahābat Khān, Muqarrab Khān and Khān-i Jahān Lodī. Sharīf Khān urged that Mirzā 'Azīz should at once be executed. Mahābat Khān too spoke in a belligerent vein. Muqarrab Khān advised the emperor to follow the path of moderation. Khān-i Jahān too opposed the suggestion of execution on the ground that wherever His Majesty's fame had gone, 'Azīz Koka's name had also gone by virtue of being the Atka of the late emperor. If he was killed, the whole world would regard him as a victim. While this meeting was in progress Salima Sulṭana Begum called from behind the *purdah*, saying that all the Begums were assembled in the ḥarem for the purpose of interceding on behalf of Mirzā Koka. She requested the emperor to come in to hear them, otherwise the ladies would come out. The expostulation of the ladies forced him to overlook the remarks of Mirzā 'Azīz and to forgive him and even to give him opium from his own special pellets.[119]

In the first year (1606) of Jahāngīr's reign a letter alleged to have been written by Mirzā 'Azīz Koka to Rāja 'Alī Khān of Khandesh was produced in the court. In the letter Mirzā 'Azīz Koka had violently denounced Akbar. Jahāngīr writes that when he was asked to read the letter he 'with shamelessness and impudence (he) read it as though he had not written it and was reading it by order'. Jahāngīr thereupon ordered him to be deprived of his *jāgīr* and *manṣab*. But soon after he was again pardoned. Jahāngīr simply writes: 'For certain consideration I passed it over.'[120] The imperial *Dīwan* was ordered to give him a *jāgīr* according to his rank of 7,000.[121]

While Khān-i Jahān Lodī's defence of 'Azīz Koka is in line with his defence of the Rajputs about the same time (reported by another source),[122] the demand for his execution voiced by Sharīf Khān and Mahābat Khān shows the depth of feeling that divided the new from the older Akbarshāhī nobility. Significantly, none of the four nobles

119 *Z.K.*, I, 85-6. For Amīr-ul Umarā Sharīf Khān's hostility towards Mirzā 'Azīz Koka, see *Z.K.*, II,186-7.

120 *Tuzuk*, 38; *Iqbalnāma*, 20-1; *Z.K.*, I, 98.

121 Ibid., 70; *Ma'āṣir-i Jahāngīrī*, 48b.

122 For details see Chapters IV and VII.

summoned by the emperor, was from the Akbarshāhī nobility. At the same time it also becomes quite clear that 'Azīz Koka too had his own supporters, in the nobility and the imperial ḥarem, which explains how he could recover his *manṣab* without reduction, and his sons could be given promotions.[123]

Though not affected financially (and in formal status) Mirzā 'Azīz Koka and his sons lost in terms of real power. They were not given any assignment for the first two years of Jahāngīr's reign. But in 1608 'Azīz Koka was appointed governor of Gujarat, though asked to remain at the court; he sent his eldest son Shamsuddīn (later given the title Jahāngīr Qulī Khān) as his deputy. Jahāngīr Qulī was promoted to the rank of 3,000/2,500 and one of Azīz Koka's other sons Khurram was given title of Kāmil Khān and assigned Junagarh.[124] 'Azīz Koka remained the absentee governor of Gujarat till 1611.

In 1611 Mirzā 'Azīz Koka was transferred to Malwa and given the command of operations in the Deccan in order to cooperate in the 'grand offensive' against Ahmadnagar.[125] He reached Burhanpur and joined Prince Parvez in May 1612. In September he proceeded towards Daulatabad to attack Malik Ambar. Khān-i Jahān Lodī, Sharīf Khān, 'Abdullah Khān and Man Singh were supposed to serve under him. But differences arose from the very beginning between him and Khān-i Jahān Lodī. Man Singh and Khwāja Abū'l Ḥasan also fell out with the latter. As a result of these differences the campaign proved a disastrous failure.[126]

Jahāngīr now entrusted the supreme command of the Deccan once again to 'Abdur Raḥīm Khān Khānān (1612). Mirzā 'Azīz Koka thereupon sent a request to the court that he might be given permission to render service against the Rana of Mewar. Jahāngīr granted the request and ordered the Mirzā to proceed to his *jāgīr* in Malwa and prepare for the expedition against the Rana.[127]

[123] For details of *manṣab* promotion see list of nobles promoted during the first six years of Jahāngīr's reign (Appendix A-VI).

[124] *Tuzuk*, 73; *Ma'āṣir-i Jahāngīrī*, 50a.

[125] Ibid., 93.

[126] *Tuzuk.*, 107-8; *Ma'āṣir-i Jahāngīrī*, 57a; *Tārīkh-i Khān-i Jahānī*, II, 512-20. See Chapters VII and VIII.

[127] *Tuzuk*, 110. But the '*Arzdāsht* (petition) of Mirzā 'Azīz Koka to Jahāngīr indicates that he was reluctant to take up the command and actually suggested that other noble be assigned that service. *Gawaliarnāma,* fols., 17a-18a. See also Appendix C–II.

Towards the end of 1613 Mirzā 'Azīz took over the command of the Mewar expedition. At his request Khurram was also sent to join him at the head of 12,000 troops. Jahāngīr himself went to Ajmer to be near the scene of action.[128] Differences arose between Mirzā 'Azīz and Khurram as to who was to be the effective commander.

When this was reported to Jahāngīr, he sent Ibrāhīm Ḥussain to Mirzā 'Azīz Koka to tell him that since every wish of his was granted he should cooperate with the prince. These instructions proved to be of no avail. Khurram complained to Jahāngīr that on account of being Khusrau's father-in-law, the Mirzā was not acting properly and spoiling the situation. The prince even took 'Azīz Koka into custody.[129]

Jahāngīr accepted Khurram's version and despatched Mahābat Khān to bring Mirzā 'Azīz from Udaipur. On 5 April 1614 Mirzā Azīz was presented at the court and Jahāngīr ordered that he should be imprisoned in the fort of Gwalior.[130]

Mirzā 'Azīz was released from Gwalior in 1615 after about one year. Jahāngīr has given a very interesting account of the circumstances which led him to release Mirzā 'Azīz. One day Akbar appeared to Jahāngīr in a dream and said, 'Baba forgive for my sake the faults of Mirzā 'Azīz Koka, who is Khān-i 'Aẓam.'[131] When he was produced at the court, 'I perceived', adds Jahāngīr, 'more shame in myself than in him. Having pardoned all his offences gave him the *shawl* I had round my waist.' The Mirzā was given Rs.10,00,000 in cash, and it was ordered that the *pargana* of Dasna and Kasna stated to be equivalent to 5,000 *ẓāt* be made over to him in *jāgīr*.[132] He was not restored to his previous rank of 7,000 immediately. But in the following year (1616) he was promoted to 7,000 *ẓāt* and an order was issued that a *jāgīr* be assigned to him.[133]

During these years (1616-22), when Mirzā 'Azīz Koka apparently remained at the court, his sons were assigned important administrative charges. In 1615 after the release of his father, Jahāngīr Qulī Khān was promoted to the rank of 3,000/2,500.[134] In the same year, he was appointed governor of Allahabad. His other brothers were also deputed with him and were given *jāgīrs* in the *ṣūba*. Two years

[128] *Tuzuk*, 126; *Iqbalnāma*, 72; *Ma'āṣir-i Jahāngīrī*, 88a-9a.

[129] *Tuzuk*, 126: *Iqbalnāma*, 73; *Z.K.* I, 88-9.

[130] *Tuzuk*, 127-8; *Iqbalnāma*, 74; *Z.K.*, 89-90.

[131] *Tuzuk*, 131-2.

[132] Ibid., 142.

[133] Ibid., 163; *Z.K.*, I, 90-1.

later (1617) he was transferred to Bihar.[135] But within a year, he was removed on the charge of oppressive administration. When he returned to the court in 1619, he was posted to Jaunpur. When Khurram's army marched to Jaunpur after the capture of Patna, Jahāngīr Qulī Khān fled to Allahabad and joined Mirzā Rustam in the defence of the fort.[136] After the departure of the rebels, Jahāngīr Qulī was made governor of Allahabad.[137] 'Azīz Koka's other sons were also given *manṣabs* but they were never given any important administrative assignment.

In 1622, when Khurram rebelled and marched northwards, Jahāngīr again thought of calling up Mirzā 'Azīz for active service. 'Azīz Koka's son-in-law Khusrau had been murdered by Shāhjahān, and it could be assumed that 'Azīz Koka would be most hostile to Khurram, who had already been once responsible for his imprisonment. He was promoted to the rank of 7,000/5,000 and appointed *atāliq* of Dāwar Bakhsh, son of Khusrau, who had been appointed governor of Gujarat.[138] On 3 July 1623 Dāwar Bakhsh and Mirzā 'Azīz entered Ahmadabad, which the local officers had successfully defended against Khurram's troops. In November 1623 Mirzā 'Azīz received orders from the court recalling him to Ajmer and asking that Dāwar Bakhsh should be kept at Ahmadabad in the charge of Ṣafī Khān. Mirzā 'Azīz, however, remained in Gujarat till the middle of 1624, when he died there.[139] Presumably he resented the imperial order and did not proceed to court in the interest of his grandson, Dāwar Bakhsh.

After the accession of Shāhjahān, the family went into oblivion. Jahāngīr Qulī was confirmed in his previous rank of 3,000/3,000, but was removed from the governorship of Allahabad.[140] He was sent to take charge of Sorath and Junagarh, where he died in the fifth regnal year.[141] According to Lahori, Shāhjahān raised Jahāngīr Qulī's eldest son to the rank of 2,000/2,000 and confirmed him in the charge held by his father.[142]

[134] Ibid., 128-9. [135] Ibid., 142.

[136] *Iqbalnāma*, 221-4, *Bahāristān-i Ghaibi*, II, 718.

[137] *Ma'āṣir-ul Umarā*, I, 524-5.

[138] *Tuzuk*, 361-2; *Ma'āṣir-i Jahāngīrī*, 162b; *Z.K.* I, 91-2.139 *Iqbalnāma*, 229-30; *Ma'āṣir-i Jahāngīrī*, 184b-5a; *Z.K.*, I, 92.

[139] *Iqbalnāma*, 229-0; *Ma'āṣir-i Jahāngīrī*, 184b-5a; *Z.K.* I, 92.

[140] *Ma'āṣir-ul Umarā*, I, 519-20. [141] *Z.K.*, II, 325.

[142] *Bādshāhnāma*, II, 737; *Ma'āṣir-ul Umarā*, I, 524-5.

Mirzā Khurram (Kamīl Khān) another son of Mirzā `Azīz was at Burhanpur when Jahāngīr died. He died at an advanced age during the reign of Shāhjahān and held the rank of 1,000/400.[143] It is, however, significant that of his property rupees five lakhs worth was confiscated and only twenty thousand rupees in cash were allowed to his sons. Of his many sons, Mirzā 'Abū'l Khair was in the imperial service under Shāhjahān and held the charge of the fort of Jola or Choka. His rank, however, is not known to us.[144]

[143] *Bādshāhnāma*, I, 185.

[144] *Z.K.*, II, 327-8.

CHAPTER III

The Family of 'Ali Quli Khān-i Zamān

The prominent members of 'Alī Qulī's family during the reign of Akbar included besides himself, Bahādur Khān, 'Abdullah Khān Uzbek, Ibrāhīm Khān and Sikandar Khān. A chart of the family is provided in the Appendix. The total *manṣabs* held by members of the family as recorded in the *'A'in* was 22,500 which apparently was higher than the total *manṣabs* held by any other important family group during the period.[1] Although the *manṣab* system was not introduced by that time, and the *manṣabs* assigned to them by Abū'l Faẓl are post-facto or fictitious, they are yet indicative of the high position which the Uzbeks then commanded. As 'Ārif Qandhārī puts it,

> The members of this clan had been given high promotions. They received much high honours and titles as Khān, Khān-i Zamān, etc. and were given the contiguous *wilāyats* and *parganas* such as the *sarkār* of Jaunpur, Awadh, Saruar (Gorakhpur) and the whole of the east, of which every *wilāyat* had been (at one or the other time) the seat of the Sultans of India.[2]

'Alī Qulī and Bahādur Khān were the sons of Ḥaidar Sulṭān who was a step-brother of Qasīm Ḥusain Shaibānī and 'Abdullah Khān Uzbek.[3] Sikandar Khān and Ibrāhīm Khān are mentioned by Bāyazīd

[1] *Ā'īn*, ed. Blochmann. These Uzbek nobles related to 'Alī Qulī have been listed by Abū'l Faẓl.

(i)	'Alī Qulī Khān-i Zamān	5,000
(ii)	'Abdullah Khān Uzbek	5,000
(iii)	Bahādur Khān	5,000
(iv)	Sikandar Khān	3,000
(v)	Ibrāhīm Khān	2,500
(vi)	Darwesh Muḥammad Uzbek	2,000

See also Appendix B–III.

[2] *Tārikh-i Akbarī*, 95.

[3] Bāyazīd, 36, 86-7; *Tārikh-i Alfi*, 620; *Akbarnāma*, I, 142, states that 'Abdullah Khān was a relation of Qasīm Ḥusain Khān. Gulbadan Begum, *Humāyūn-nāma*, 17, writes that Sulṭān Ḥusain Mirzā was the maternal grandfather of Qasīm Ḥusain Khān. Of 'Abdullah Khān it is

as close relations of 'Alī Qulī. Sikandar Khān claimed descent from Uzbek princes.[4] However, their exact relationship to each other is not clear in our sources. Some of them were Shias; others Sunnis. Some of them like 'Alī Qulī and Bahādur Khān were for all practical purposes Khurāsanīs as they were born and brought up in Persia.[5] But 'Abdullah Khān, Sikandar Khān and Ibrāhīm Khān had spent their entire career in the service of the Timurids and had no links with Iran.

The Uzbeks' conduct at the Mughal court indicates that they were a well knit family group and always acted in close cooperation among themselves. Their own ethnic affinities transcended political, or religious differences. For this very reason, perhaps, they failed to evoke even a little support from the other Irānīs or Tūrānīs, though some individual nobles from other sections sided them at some point or the other.[6]

Ḥaidar Sulṭān Shaibānī, father of 'Alī Qulī and Bahādur Khān, belonged to Sistan and was connected with the family of Shaibānī Khān.[7] In the battle of Jam fought between the Uzbeks and the Safavids, Ḥaidar Sulṭān joined the Persians and attained the rank of an *amir*. He settled in Isfahan and married into a Persian family.[8] When Humāyūn was returning from Persia, Ḥaidar Sulṭān joined him, along with his two sons, 'Alī Qulī and Muḥammad Sa'id Bahādur Khān and other clansmen.[9] Ḥaīdar Sulṭan's entry into Humāyūn's service might well have been the result of an earlier association of the family with Bābur. Qasīm Ḥusain Khān Uzbek, a brother of Ḥaider Sulṭān, had been in the service of Bābur and had held the *jāgīr* of Awadh.[10] Along

stated that he was married to the daughter of Qasīm Barlas, a well known Chaghtāī noble of Bābur. Also see, *Life of Mu'nim Khān*, 22-3, 30-1 for the biographies of 'Alī Qulī, Bahādur Khān and Qasīm Ḥusain Khān Shaībānī. *Z.K.*., I, 26, Farid Bhakkari simply says that they belonged to the family of Shaībānī Khān.

[4] *Tārikh-i Rashidi*, tr. D. Ross, 1895, 474. Sikandar Khān was a former servant of Mirzā Kāmrān and remained in Mughal service from the early years of Humāyūn's reign. *Tārikh-i Alfī*, 620a. Ibrāhīm Khān was the seniormost among the Uzbek officers under Akbar. 'Alī Qulī treated him like an uncle. Cf. *Ma'āṣir-ul Umarā*, I, 84-7.

[5] *Tārikh-i Farishtā*, II, 214.

[6] *Tazkira-i Humāyūn*, 74.

[7] *Tarikh-i Farishta*, II, 217. 'Alī Qulī and Bahādur Khān both were born in Persia.

[8] *Z.K.*, I, Kewal Ram, *Taẓkirat-ul Umarā*, 51a-2ab; *Ma'āṣir-ul Umarā*, I, 622. See also *Life of Mun'īm Khān*, 22-3.

[9] *Akbarnāma*, I, 218-19, 229-30, adds that he was an intimate of Mirzā Kāmrān and was with him at Tus. Bāyazīd, 35-6, states that he was a commander in the Persian army which had accompanied Humāyūn on his return from Iran under the command of Prince Murād.

[10] Ibid., I, 148.

with 'Abdullah Khān Uzbek, he had served Humāyūn in the Gujarat and Bengal campaigns.[11] When Humāyūn fled towards Lahore after his defeat at the hands of Sher Shāh, Qasīm Ḥusain joined him in Delhi and accompanied him in his further marches.[12] However, in 1542 he deserted Humāyūn and joined Yādgār Naṣir Mirzā at Rohri.[13]

Ḥaidar Sulṭān and his sons rendered valuable service in the conquest of Qandhar; and the territory of Shal (Quetta) was assigned to him.[14] About the same time Qalat and its neighbouring areas were assigned to Qasīm Ḥusain Shaibānī who had apparently rejoined Humāyūn at the time of the conquest of Qandhar.[15] During the march from Qandhar to Kabul, plague broke out and Ḥaider Sulṭān along with many others died on the way.

At this time 'Alī Qulī and Bahādur Khān were serving in the capacity of *safarchi* and *parwanchi*.[16] They were among the six Uzbek nobles who were now in Humāyūn's train.[17] 'Alī Qulī and other Uzbeks remained loyal to Humāyūn during this most critical period when he was making frenzied efforts to deal with Mirzā Kāmrān, Mirzā Sulaimān and other opponents.[18]

Humāyūn started on his expedition to India in November 1554. 'Alī Qulī, Bahādur Khān, Sikandar Khān and 'Abdullah Khān accompanied him along with other officers. During this time 'Alī Qulī and Bahādur Khān held the posts of *safarchi* and *muhardar* respectively, and Sikandar Khān was appointed to the advance guard of the army.[19] The Uzbeks played a distinguished role in the campaign

[11] Ibid., 129, 133-4, 140-1, 148. After the conquest of Gujarat, Qasīm Ḥusain had been given charge of Baroch (*Humāyūn Nāma*, 39, 41).

[12] Ibid., I, 167, 171. [13] Ibid., 178.

[14] *Tazkira-i Humāyūn*, 41-3; *Akbarnāma*, I, 229-30, 235.

[15] *Tazkira-i Humāyūn*, 51.

[16] *Akbarnāma*, I, 244; *Tazkira-i Humāyūn*, 52, 57.

[17] On the occasion of Kamran's surrender at Taliqan, 'Alī Qulī and Bahādur Khān were among the six leading Uzbek nobles who were sent in the second batch of officers to welcome the Mirzā (*Akbarnāma*), I, 281; *Tazkira-i Humāyūn*, 97.

[18] *Akbarnāma*, I, 252, 259. Bahādur Khān served Humāyūn in Badakhshan against Mirzā Sulaimān. Later on he was imprisoned by Mirzā Kāmrān at Kabul where he had been sent by Humāyūn after the battle of Tirgiran (*Tazkira-i Humāyūn*, 92). In 1548 at the time of the rebellion of Qarcha Khān, 'Alī Qulī and Bahādur Khān stood firmly with Humāyūn. They accompanied Humāyūn once again to Badakhshan to quell a rebellion. Bahādur Khān, Sikandar Khān and 'Abdullah Khān accompanied Humāyūn in the Balkh expedition (*Tazkira-i Humāyūn*, 123-4; *Akbarnāma*, I, 290). 'Alī Qulī and Bahādur Khān also served in operations against the Afghān tribes (*Tazkira-i Humāyūn*, 150).

[19] *Tazkira-i Humāyūn*, 177; *Akbarnāma*, I, 342.

that followed.[20] In reward for their services Humāyūn assigned Agra, Sambhal and Kalpi respectively to Sikandar Khān, 'Alī Qulī and 'Abdullah Khān.[21] Bahādur Khān was apparently despatched to take charge of Zamindawar. These assignments they continued to hold under Humāyūn, and after Akbar's accession they were confirmed in their charges.[22] Their position was now so high that, if Bāyazīd Bayāt is to be believed, they were actually considered next only to the Mirzās in the hierarchy.[23]

At the time of Humāyūn's death, 'Alī Qulī was engaged in a battle with Shā'dī Khān Afghān, one of the chief officers of Mubāriz Khān who held Sambhal and its neighbourhood. An army despatched by 'Alī Qulī was defeated; hence he decided to march in person against the rebels.[24] But, in the meantime, Tardī Beg and other officers posted at Agra and Etawa informed him that Hemu was marching on Delhi at the head of a huge army. Thereupon 'Alī Qulī suspended his campaign and marched towards Delhi. Before his arrival Hemu had defeated Tardī Beg near Tughlaqabad on 7 October 1556. The defeated Mughal officers, Tardī Beg, Sikandar Khān and 'Abdullah Khān together with 'Alī Qulī, who had arrived Delhi a day after the battle, withdrew to join the imperial camp at Sarhind. Despite the rather undistinguished conduct by the Uzbek nobles themselves, 'Alī Qulī threw the whole blame of the Mughal reverses upon Tardī Beg, possibly with encouragement from Bairam Khān, and Tardī Beg was executed on a charge of treachery.[25]

At the battle of Panipat the command of the van was given to 'Alī Qulī and other Uzbek officers. After the victory, in which he undoubtedly had a role, 'Alī Qulī was confirmed in his *jāgīr* of *sarkār* Sambhal and other *parganas* in the Doab. 'Abdullah Khān was assigned the *sarkār* of Kalpi; Sikandar Khān was assigned Sialkot and ordered to reinforce Khizr Khwāja Khān.[26] In the meantime Bahādur Khān came from Zamindawar, and at the request of Bairam Khān, was

[20] *Tazkira-i Humāyūn.*, 190; *Akbarnāma*, I, 335.

[21] *Tazkira-i Humāyūn*, 194; Ibid., 351-2. [22] *Akbarnāma*, II, 14, 27-8.

[23] *Tazkira-i Humāyūn*, 99. Abū'l Fazl's list of nobles who accompanied Humāyūn to India, includes all the Uzbek nobles mentioned. This list includes only important officers. There is no reference to any of the Atka nobles. *Akbarnāma*, I, 278-9.

[24] *Akbarnāma*, II, 27-9; *Ṭabaqāt*, II, 213; *Muntakhab*, II, 13 *Tārikh-i Farishtā*, II, 184-5, writes that 'Alī Qulī himself was badly defeated by Shadi Khān and only two hundred of his men escaped.

[25] *Muntakhab*, II, 14. [26] *Akbarnāma*, II, 33, 45-7.

appointed to Multan. This was in spite of the fact that Bahādur Khān was responsible for the surrender of Qandhar to the Persians and might have been thought deserving of some punishment.[27]

During his tenure of office at Sambhal which was a stronghold of the Afghāns, 'Alī Qulī defeated Rukn Khān Lohānī and the combined forces of two other Afghān chiefs Jalal Khān Sur and Ḥasan Khān Bachgoti near Lucknow.[28] The territories from Sambhal to Lucknow came under the possession of the Mughals and were assigned to 'Alī Qulī and his clansmen.

The appointment of Uzbek nobles to the charge of the empire's eastern region as well as the Panjab and Multan, gave them a distinct position in the nobility. Being so favoured by Bairam Khān, the Uzbeks became his close allies. But the regent also gained many enemies, and both Bairam Khān and his allies had to face hostile measures brought about by their opponents.[29]

At the pretext of a scandal involving 'Alī Qulī and Shaham Beg a royal bodyguard, Pīr Muḥammad Sherwānī, in open disregard of the wishes of Bairam Khān, confiscated 'Alī Qulī's *jāgīr* of Sandila and assigned it to Sulṭān Ḥusain Jalair. Sandila had already been granted by 'Alī Qulī to Ismail Khān, son of Ibrāhīm Khān Uzbek. This led to an armed conflict between Ismail Khān and the imperial forces under the Jalairs. Ismail Khān was expelled from Sandila by force. In the engagement, Shāh Budagh Bulaqi, a relation of 'Alī Qulī, was killed. 'Alī Qulī was enraged and decided to take military action against Sulṭān Ḥusain Jalair. Bairam Khān, whose own power had declined at the court and was unable to protect the interests of his ally, tried to obtain a reconciliation. On the one hand, he stopped Pīr Muḥammad Khān from despatching an army against 'Alī Qulī, and, on the other, he advised 'Alī Qulī to send one of his faithful servants to the court to clear up the misunderstanding. However, when Burj-i 'Alī, a servant of 'Alī Qulī, came to the court, he was not permitted to meet the emperor on the orders of Pīr Muḥammad Sherwānī. While these drastic

[27] Ibid., 52. Bahādur Khān who had been assigned Zamindawar, conspired to seize Qandhar. At the last moment Shāh Muḥammad Qandhārī who held Qandhar for Bairam Khān, came to know of it, applied for help to the Persians, no aid from India being possible. The Persians sent him help on the condition that he would surrender Qandhar (*Akbarnāma*, II, 29-30; *Ṭabaqāt*, II, 129-30; *Tārikh-i Farishta*, II, 184-5).

[28] *Akbarnāma*, II, 56; (with critical observations) *Muntakhab*, II, 25; De Laet, 142.

[29] See Chapter I. Cf. Iqtidar Alam Khan, 'The Mughal Court Politics during the Regency of Bairam Khan', 8-11.

steps were taken against his closest supporters, Bairam Khān was apparently in no position to act against his enemies. 'He (Bairam Khān) cherished revenge for it in his heart, and put off the punishment to another time.'[30]

In 1559, 'Alī Qulī was once again ordered to expel Shaham Beg from his *jāgīr*, proceed to Jaunpur and capture it from Ibrāhīm Sur. His *jāgīr* in the Doab was confiscated and Qayā Khān Ganj, Sulṭān Ḥusain Jalair, Muḥammad Khān Jalair and Hājī Muḥammad Khān Sistānī were despatched to take charge of Lucknow, which had been under the charge of the Uzbeks. Dire consequences were threatened if he refused to comply with imperial orders.[31] 'Alī Qulī obeyed the imperial orders and marched to Jaunpur as he had presumably realized the weak position of Bairam Khān at the court.

Unable to withstand 'Alī Qulī, Ibrāhīm Khān Sur vacated Jaunpur and fled to Orissa (1559).[32] In the same year Bahādur Khān of Bengal attacked Jaunpur, but 'Alī Qulī was successful in driving him away.[33] Thereafter 'Ali Quli remained in Jaunpur, until his rebellion. All of his clansmen and relations were granted *jagirs* in that region, with the exception of 'Abdullah Khān. 'Alī Qulī entered into some sort of understanding with the Karrānī Afghāns, possibly to protect his own position which had been weakened at the court.

In 1559, Bahādur Khān was ordered to conquer Malwa; but the campaign was suspended because of Bairam Khan's rebellion and he was recalled.[34] In the meantime court politics took a new turn; the groups of Maham Anaga, the Atkas and others combined together to bring about Bairam Khan's dismissal. It is significant that none of the Uzbek nobles joined Bairam Khān at any stage of his rebellion. Among the contemporary sources only Abū'l Faẓl suggests that Bairam Khān was planning to go to Bahādur Khān and with his help, conquer Malwa. He adds that Bairam Khān also thought of joining 'Alī Qulī and enlisting the help of the Afghāns of the eastern region.[35]

30 *Akbarnāma*, II, 67-9; *Tārikh-i Farishtā*, II, 192.

31 *Akbarnāma*, II, 82.

32 Ibid., Farishta, II, 194-5, believes that Khān-i Zamān in order to protect himself and effect a reconciliation, with the king invaded Jaunpur and Banaras.

33 *Akbarnāma*, II, 138-9; *Muntakhab*, II, 48; De Laet, 142.

34 *Akbarnāma*, II, 89-90; *Muntakhab*, II, 35; *Ṭabaqāt*, II, 235; Farishta, II, 195. Bada'uni writes that Bahādur Khān returned and joined Akbar on the advice of Bairam Khān.

35 *Akbarnāma*, II, 96-7; *Tārikh-i Alfī*, 601a. Iqtidar Alam Khan also accepts the opinion of Abū'l Faẓl (*Life of Mun'īm Khān*, 75). Also see 'The Mughal Court Politics during Bairam Khan's Regency', 36, n. 61.

Later events, however, do not support either of these suspicions.[36] The Uzbeks, during Bairam Khan's revolt, remained aloof and did not join either side. After the final defeat of Bairam Khān, it became clear that the groups which emerged as the most powerful at the court were hostile to the Uzbeks. The Uzbeks countered this by trying to win over a section of the Tūrānī nobility which included such nobles as Qayā Khān Gang, Sulṭān Ḥusain Jalair and Muḥammad Amīn Diwanā. With their support and with the support of such other nobles as were unhappy with Maham Anaga and the Atkas, the Uzbeks were able to retain or strengthen their position for the time being.

Since the circumstances were favourable to them, Bahādur Khān now laid claim to the office of *Wakīl*. The court party had no alternative but to concede him the office in order to keep him away from supporting Bairam Khān.[37]

Bahādur Khān remained *Wakīl* for a very short period. No contemporary work, except the *Akbarnāma*, notices his appointment. During the period when Bahādur Khān was *Wakīl*, real power at the court lay in the hands of Maham Anaga and her supporters and every attempt was made to undercut Bahādur Khan's position. As soon as Bairam Khān was defeated Sulṭān Ḥusain Jalair and a number of other nobles were imprisoned. Qayā Khān Gang was transferred to Bahraich, and Muḥammad Amīn Diwanā fled from the court. Ultimately Bahādur Khān was dismissed from office and granted a *jāgīr* in Etawah.[38]

The removal of Bahādur Khān from the office of *Wakīl* and the harassment of his supporters created bad blood between the court party and the Uzbek clan. Mun'īm Khān, the new *Wakīl*, therefore, made an attempt to placate the Uzbeks. At his suggestion a *farmān* was issued confirming 'Alī Qulī in his *jāgīr* of *sarkār* Jaunpur, Ghazipur and some *parganas* in the *sarkār* of Awadh. The area up to river Son and *sarkār* Manikpur were also granted to him. He was further assured that if he conquered Bengal from the Afghāns, that province too would be assigned to him.[39] Despite this overture certain elements in the nobility, notably the influential group of Maham Anaga, remained hostile to the Uzbek cause. Bahādur Khān brought matters to a head by killing the *Tawāchī* who had brought the head of Wali Beg Zulqadar.

[36] *Muntakhab*, II, 35-6. Cf. *Akbarnāma*, II, 96-7; *Tārikh-i Alfi*, 601a.

[37] *Akbarnāma*, II, 99-100.

[38] Ibid., 100.

[39] *Tazkira-i Humāyūn*, 239. It appears that along with the territories of Bahādur Khān those of 'Alī Qulī had also been confiscated, earlier.

This was regarded as an act of rebellion, and his *jāgīr* was confiscated.[40] He fled to Jaunpur and took refuge with 'Alī Qulī. When Mun'īm Khān informed the emperor of this, it was decided to despatch Bāyazīd Bayāt to reassure Bahādur Khān and persuade him to return to the court. But Bahādur Khān refused; and 'Alī Qulī assigned him Banaras, which was part of his own *jāgīr*. Although Bahādur Khān and 'Alī Qulī thus disobeyed imperial orders, they were not punished, and Bahādur Khān was apparently even confirmed in his charge of Banaras.[41]

In the meantime the Afghāns of the eastern region took the opportunity to recover their lost position. Ādil's partisans placed his son Sher Khān (Sher Shāh II) on the throne at Chunar and in 1561 marched upon Jaunpur. 'Alī Qulī collected his clansmen, and in a battle fought outside the fort of Jaunpur defeated the Afghāns.[42]

While 'Alī Qulī was engaged in war with Sher Shāh II, Fatḥ Khān with his brother Ḥasan Khān, seized Bihar and some other territories belonging to his *jāgīr*. They enthroned 'Awaz Khān, son of Islām Shāh, at Rohtas. After the defeat of Sher Shāh II they advanced towards Jaunpur, only to be repulsed at Andhiari.[43]

After this failure, Fatḥ Khān entered into friendly relations with 'Alī Qulī and subsequently helped the latter during his rebellion. The Afghāns of Bengal after their defeat in 1558 also maintained friendly relations with 'Alī Qulī. They remained passive spectators during Sher Shāh II's incursion towards Jaunpur. Tāj Khān Karrānī of Bihar, who later became ruler of Bengal and Bihar, continued to have friendly relations with him and used to send him presents.[44]

'Alī Qulī's successes against the Afghāns of the eastern region and the friendly relations which he developed with them subsequently, were viewed with great alarm at the court. Nizāmuddīn indeed states that after 'Alī Qulī's victory over the partisans of Sher Khān II, people began to harbour suspicions about his intentions.[45]

40 *Akbarnāma*, II, 115. 41 *Tazkira-i Humāyūn*, 244.

42 *Tazkira-i Humāyūn*, 138-9; *Tārikh-i Alfī*, 604a, 604b; *Akbarnāma*, II, 138-9; *Muntakhab*, II, 48; see also Abdur Rahim, *The History of the Afghāns in India*, 136-7.

43 *Akbarnāma*, II, 219-20; *Muntakhab*, II, 48-9; *Ṭabaqāt*, II, 255-6.

44 Bahadur Shah ruler of Bengal was defeated by Ali Quli near Jaunpur in 1558 (*Muntakhab*, II, 25). In 1559 Tāj Khān sent 'Alī Qulī the present of a few elephants and pieces of muslin. Bāyazīd also believes that 'Alī Qulī after conquering Bengal handed it over to Tāj Khān (*Tazkira-i Humāyūn*, 239).

45 *Ṭabaqāt*, II, 255-6.

While 'Alī Qulī's campaign against the Afghāns was in progress, the emperor had already despatched Shahābuddīn Aḥmad Khān, Wazīr Khān and Maulana 'Alauddin Lāri 'to establish him ('Alī Qulī) on the path of fidelity by good counsels and by royal favours'. An attempt was also made to befriend Sulaimān Karrānī, who had so far maintained an understanding with 'Alī Qulī; Sulaimān Karrānī now read the *khutba* in the name of Akbar.[46]

After these steps, Akbar decided to make a gesture himself. He marched eastward and reached Kara; 'Alī Qulī and Bahādur Khān came immediately to offer homage. The emperor accepted their submission, confirmed them in their assignments and returned to Agra.

Uzbek power within the Mughal empire reached its apex at this time: Uzbek nobles were in control of Malwa and the large eastern region. But this very fact caused them to be suspected and led to allegations about their lack of fidelity to the imperial cause right from 1556.[47]

Akbar's own reserve was partly rooted in personal dislike of the Uzbek nobles since he believed that his father's troubles were due to their intrigues and conspiracies during his exile. 'Ārif Qandhārī suggests that 'Alī Qulī had designs to capture Akbar and seize the country.[48] The relations the Uzbek nobles maintained with Changez Khān of Gujarat and the Afghān rulers of Rohtas, Bihar and Bengal only further inflamed suspicion.[49] Each of thesefactors must have its part; but a close study of the political conditions of the empire after the dismissal of Bairam Khān reveals that the basic cause of the Uzbek rebellion lay rather in Akbar's attempt to bring all sections of the Mughal nobility under centralized control.

As soon as Akbar took the reins of government in his hands in 1560, the administration of finances attracted his attention. The reorganization of revenue administration created general discontent in the nobility, especially among those nobles who held charge of distant regions. The officers posted in outlying provinces were practically autonomous in collecting revenue and taxes. But as a result of these reforms they were required to submit complete accounts of their revenues.[50]

[46] *Akbarnāma*, II, 219-20. [47] Ibid., II, 97-9. [48] *Tārikh-i Akbarī*, 81-2.

[49] *Tārikh-i Akbarī*, 129; cf. A.L. Srivastava, *Akbar the Great*, I, 99-100. Also see *Life of Mun'im Khān*, 75-6.

[50] For a discussion on the early reforms see, Iqtidar Alam Khan, *Life of Mun'im Khān*, 76-7, and Chapter II of this book.

During the same period, Akbar initiated some changes in the composition of the nobility, bringing in Rajputs and Shaikhzadās. He was also anxious to eliminate the dominance of clan groups inside the nobility, which could remotely parallel his own authority. One device employed to check clan power was to scatter *jāgīr* assignments. Pīr Muḥammad Khān Sherwānī, presumably acting in Akbar's interest, had even during the period of regency, twice resumed *jāgīrs* of 'Alī Qulī and other Uzbeks which were concentrated in one region.[51]

Akbar's centralizing measures were bound to cause resentment particularly among the old nobility which was largely of Tūrānī origin; and of these, the Uzbeks were liable to be affected more than any one else. They were by far the largest clan group and had large holdings of contiguous *jāgīrs* in the eastern region, where, except for 'Abdullah Khān, all the other Uzbeks were posted.[52]

A confrontation then was inevitable, since the Uzbeks, given their power, could not conceivably see it constricted and destroyed piecemeal. Moreover, they possibly felt that senior Tūrānī nobles like Mun'īm Khān were sympathetic towards them.[53]

First of all, professing a suspicion that 'Abdullah Khān was meditating rebellion,[54] Akbar proceeded towards Malwa on the pretext of a hunting expedition in July 1564, and despatched Ashraf Khān and I'timād Khān to force 'Abdullah Khān to submit.[55] 'Abdullah Khān became apprehensive and fled, but the two officers met him at Liwani. 'Abdullah Khān sought to be excused from personal presence and to be continued as governor of Malwa. These terms were accepted at the intercession of Mun'īm Khān.[56] But in the meantime a woman complained to Akbar of the atrocities committed by a Qurbegi of 'Abdullah Khān, and Akbar personally assured her of justice.[57] 'Abdullah Khān lost his nerve, and fled to Gujarat to take shelter with Changez Khān.[58]

51 *Akbarnāma*, II, 67-78, 82. See *Life of Mun'īm Khān*, 76; Iqtidar Alam Khan, 'The Nobility under Akbar and Development of his Religious Policy 1560-80' *JRAS,* 1968, 29-30. Cf. Chapters IV and V of this book.

52 See supra.

53 *Life of Mun'īm Khān*, 75-7.

54 *Akbarnāma*, II, 221; *Ṭabaqāt*, II, 172; *Muntakhab*, II, 67.

55 *Akbarnāma*, II, 221; *Tārikh-i Alfī*, 613b.

56 *Akbarnāma*, 223-5; *Ṭabaqāt*, II, 172; *Muntakhab*, II, 68.

57 *Akbarnāma*, II, 225.

58 Ibid., 226-30; *Ṭabaqāt*, II, 173; *Tārikh-i Alfī*, 613b; *Muntakhab*, II, 68, Nizāmuddīn writes that Changez Khān requested Akbar to forgive the offences of 'Abdullah Khān, in response to Akbar's order to expel 'Abdullah Khān from Gujarat.

'Abdullah Khan's flight signalled the beginning of the revolt of the Uzbek clan which continued for three years (July 1564 to June 1567). First of all, Akbar decided upon a plan to march to the eastern region to keep vigil on 'Alī Qulī and his clansmen. The Uzbeks, on their part, 'made this incident a pretext for staging their revolt'.[59] Akbar despatched Qulij Khān to Rohtas to get the support of Fatḥ Khān, who promised to assist the royal forces if Akbar came to Jaunpur; and he despatched his brother Ḥasan Khān to the court.[60] Ashraf Khān was now sent to summon Sikandar Khān, *jāgīrdār* of Awadh, to clear past misunderstandings. A robe of honour and an inlaid sword were sent to him. Akbar obviously wanted to isolate 'Alī Qulī from his relatives; but Sikandar Khān detained Ashraf Khān and proceeded to consult with 'Alī Qulī, Ibrāhīm Khān and other Uzbek nobles.

The Uzbek officers decided upon defiance, and expelled the other imperial officers posted in the region, while Akbar was still at Narwar in central India. They planned to make two inroads into the Doab: one from the side of Manikpur under 'Alī Qulī and Bahādur Khān, and the other towards Qannauj under Sikandar Khān and Ibrāhīm Khān.[61] Muḥammad Amīn Diwanā was defeated by Ibrāhīm Khān and Sikandar Khān near Nimkhar and Majnūn Khān Qaqshal was forced to take shelter in the fort of Manikpur.[62] When these developments were reported to Akbar, he despatched Mun'īm Khān to lead the van, and followed him himself. At the approach of imperial army the rebels fled and fortified themselves at Kundanah somewhere near Hajipur[63] and approached both Sulaimān Karrānī and Fatḥ Khān Batani for succour. Akbar, on his part, sent Hājī Muḥammad Khān Sistānī to Sulaimān Karrānī to make him turn from such a course. When the latter envoy reached Rohtas on his way, he was handed over by the Afghāns to 'Alī Qulī.[64] Hājī Muḥammad had very old relations with 'Alī Qulī; because of that Abū'l Fazl believes, he was ultimately successful in persuading 'Ali Quli to submit. The emperor despatched

[59] *Tārikh-i Akbarī*, 81; *Tārikh-i Alfī*, 617b; *Ṭabaqāt*, II, 174; *Muntakhab*, II, 74.

[60] *Akbarnāma*, II, 243; *Ṭabaqāt*, II, 185. At this time Fatḥ Khān was besieged by Sulaimān Karrānī, the ruler of Bengal.

[61] *Tārikh-i Akbarī*, 81-4; *Akbarnāma*, II, 249; *Ṭabaqāt*, II, 180-1; *Muntakhab*, II, 74-5; *Tārikh-i Alfī*, 618a.

[62] *Akbarnāma*, II, 250; *Tārikh-i Alfī*, 618a; *Muntakhab*, II, 75; *Ṭabaqāt*, II, 181.

[63] *Nafā'is*, 49a; *Tārikh-i Akbarī*, 85-6; *Tazkira-i Humāyūn*, 286; *Akbarnāma*, II, 251-3; *Ṭabaqāt*, II, 182. Kundanah belonged to the Afghān kingdom of Bengal.

[64] *Akbarnāma*, II, 254-5; *Muntakhab*, II, 76.

Ḥasan Khān Khazānchi and Mahapatra to Raja Madhukar Dev of Orissa with the same purpose.[65] Another mission was sent to Fatḥ Khān of Rohtas.[66] These diplomatic maneuvres were not successful, and to assist the Uzbeks Sulaimān Karrānī despatched an army under Sulaimān Mangali and Kala Pahar, who were joined by Fatḥ Khān along with his brother Ḥasan Khān.[67]

In the meantime Āṣaf Khān fled from the imperial camp[68] which further weakened the position of the royal army. But 'Alī Qulī soon realized that the Uzbeks could not improve their position as long as the emperor was in the east, and he opened negotiation with Mun'īm Khān.[69]

After prolonged negotiations a meeting between 'Alī Qulī and Mun'īm Khān was held in which 'Alī Qulī, Mian Kalāpahār, Sulaimān Mangali, Ḥasan Khān Batani and Sulaimān Uzbek participated. It was decided that the emperor should send Khwāja Jahān with orders of pardon for the rebels. 'Alī Qulī was also to be excused from personal presence. Ibrāhīm Khān was to escort 'Alī Qulī's mother to the court to offer submission on behalf of her sons. Regarding their *jāgīrs*, it was agreed that so long as the imperial camp was in the neighbourhood, they could not cross the river to reoccupy them. After the return of the camp to Agra a *farmān* would be issued for the confirmation of their *jāgīrs*.[70]

While these peace negotiations were in progress, Muiz-ul Mulk the imperial commander was defeated in the area of Saruar (Gorakhpur) by Bahādur Khān. Although on the orders of 'Alī Qulī and Mun'īm Khān, Bahādur Khān gave up the elephants and other valuables,[71] the success nevertheless emboldened the rebels. Hence, in contravention of his promise 'Alī Qulī crossed the Ganges and sent his men to occupy

[65] *Akbarnāma*, *Muntakhab*, II, 76-7; *Ṭabaqāt*, II, 183-4.

[66] *Akbarnāma*, II, 257-8; *Muntakhab*, II, 78-9.

[67] *Tazkira-i Humāyūn*, 291; *Akbarnāma*, II, 255, 257-8; *Ṭabaqāt*, II, 183-4; *Muntakhab*, II, 78-9.

[68] *Tazkira-i Humāyūn*, 293. *Akbarnāma*, II, 255-6, 261-2; *Muntakhab*, II, 77, 80-1; *Ṭabaqāt*, 183.

[69] *Tazkira-i Humāyūn*, 290. 'Alī Qulī sent Agha Sarv-qad an ex-maid of Bābur's ḥarem to hold secret discussion with Mun'īm Khān regarding the possibility of peaceful end of the conflict. *Muntakhab*, II, 79, says that 'Khān Khanan ... in his old way of intimacy kept sending soldiers with messages of peace'. Cf. *Akbarnāma*, II, 257-8. See *Life of Mun'īm Khān*, 82-3.

[70] *Nafā'is*, 48b; *Tārikh-i Akbarī*, 87; *Tazkira-i Humāyūn*, 290-1; *Akbarnāma*, II, 259-60; *Muntakhab*, II, 82. It appears that the emperor was apprehensive about the attitude of Mun'īm Khān; hence Khwāja Ghayās-u'ddīn was sent from Jaunpur to watch over the proceedings.

Jaunpur and Ghazipur. When the emperor came to know of this, he left the camp at Banaras and rapidly marched towards the rebels.[72] Bāyazīd here gives a different version of the course of events from that of the *Akbarnāma*. He writes that while Akbar was at Banaras certain nobles, who were not happy with the terms of the treaty and other favours shown to 'Alī Qulī, persuaded him to make a surprise attack on 'Alī Qulī. The emperor agreed and assigned Jaunpur, Ghazipur and Banaras to Mun'īm Khān and ordered him to follow the royal camp.[73] It is possible that Akbar wanted to create misunderstanding between Mun'īm Khān and 'Alī Qulī because the territories assigned to Mun'īm Khān were in the *jāgīr* of 'Alī Qulī. But subsequent events clearly indicate that Mun'īm Khān remained steadfast in his earlier attitude and did his best to save 'Alī Qulī from being captured at Mahmudabad.[74] During this campaign Awaz Khān and some other notable Afghān chiefs joined the imperial army, and 'Alī Qulī had to recross the Ganges and shut himself in the fort of Chillupar.[75] Bahādur Khān and Sikandar Khān marched to Jaunpur and after releasing 'Alī Qulī's mother joined him in Bihar.[76] Meanwhile Akbar marched to Jaunpur and proclaimed his determination to remain there till the rebellion was crushed. 'Alī Qulī once again decided to seek the help of Mun'īm Khān and despatched Muḥammad Mirāk Riẓvī. Mun'īm Khān instead of directly involving himself, requested Mīr Murtaza Sharif, 'Abdullah Sultanpuri and Shaikh 'Abdun Nabi who were highly respected by the emperor to persuade him to pardon the rebels.[77] The emperor agreed to be persuaded and returned to the

[71] *Tazkira-i Humāyūn*, 293-4; *Akbarnāma*, II, 261-2.

[72] *Akbarnāma*, II, 265; *Ṭabaqāt*, II, 192; *Tārikh-i Alfi*, 621b. Akbar left Jaunpur on 24 January 1556 for Banaras, 'Alī Qulī crossed the Ganges and occupied Ghazipur and Muhmudabad that very day.

[73] *Tazkira-i Humāyūn*, 294-5.

[74] *Tazkira-i Humāyūn*, 295; *Akbarnāma*, II, 265; *Ṭabaqāt*, II, 192. Akbar left Banaras on 2 February 1566 to deal with 'Alī Qulī who was encamped at Mahmudabad. Mun'īm Khān accompanied the emperor. The plan to surprise 'Alī Qulī at Mahmudabad was frustrated by Mun'īm Khān. *Darbar-i Akbarī*, 216 refers to Mun'īm Khan's secret message to 'Alī Qulī (source unknown).

[75] *Ṭabaqāt-i Akbarī*, 88; *Tārikh-i Alfi*, 221a; *Tazkira-i Humāyūn*, 295-6; *Akbarnāma*, II, 266-7. Chillupar, the same as Barharganj *pargana* headquarters on the left bank of Ghagra, district Gorakhpur.

[76] *Akbarnāma*, II, 267-8; *Tārikh-i Alfi*, 621a.

[77] *Akbarnāma*, II, 269; *Ṭabaqāt*, II, 194-5; *Muntākhab*, II, 84. *The Tārikh-i Alfi*, 621ab, states 'The Sayyids, Ulma and the grandees who were in the royal service had been on friendly terms (with the Uzbek officers) and no one wanted that they should be uprooted completely.'

capital. Mun'īm Khān and Muẓaffar Khān followed him there, while Khwāja Jahan, Lashkar Khān and certain other nobles were left to finalize the settlement with the Uzbeks.[78] When Mun'īm Khān reached Kara, he was informed that 'Alī Qulī and Bahādur Khān had crossed the river and were taking the road to Agra. Mun'īm Khān sent them a letter post haste through Baltun Khān, whereat they returned to Jaunpur: apparently, the Uzbeks had been planning to surprise Akbar.[79] Suspicious of Mun'īm Khan's conciliatory attitude to the Uzbeks, Muẓaffar Khān left him at Etawah and hurried to the court, to inform the emperor of the double dealing of many grandees. Many nobles were punished as a result. Mun'īm Khān was not touched; but he learnt to be more circumspect.[80]

When the news of the settlement between the Mughals and Uzbeks was made known to the Afghāns of Bengal, they withdrew their support from the Uzbeks. 'Alī Qulī invaded Bengal, but the Afghāns rallying together in large numbers forced him to agree to a settlement. By this, 'Alī Qulī released Ḥasan Khān Batani, while he gained the territories to the west of Garhi, i.e. the whole of Bihar. A little before this event Junaid Karrānī, Sulaimān Karrānī's brother's son, had joined Akbar's service.[81]

The conflict with the Afghāns probably weakened the position of 'Alī Qulī, losing him valuable allies. In the meantime 'Abdullah Khān Uzbek having been defeated in Malwa sought refuge with him.[82] Āṣaf Khān who had fled from the court too joined him about this time.[83] Mirzā Hakim invaded the Panjab towards the end of 1566, and Akbar had to leave Agra for the Panjab.[84] Taking advantage of his absence, the Mirzās also rebelled and joined 'Alī Qulī. All this was a heaven-sent opportunity for the Uzbeks.[85] Their rebellion followed: 'Alī Qulī

[78] *Nafā'is*, 49b; *Akbarnāma*, II, 268-9; *Ṭabaqāt*, II, 195.

[79] *Tazkira-i Humāyūn*, 297-8.

[80] *Akbarnāma*, II, 270, Lashkar Khān was removed from the office of *Bakhshi*. The royal seal which used to be kept in the custody of Khwāja Jahān was withdrawn, and he was ordered to be exiled to Mecca. The order was later withdrawn. 'The severity used towards these men which was the retribution of their deeds, caused circumspection on the part of Mun'īm Khan' (Abū'l Faẓl).

[81] *Muntakhab*, II, 87, refers to another expedition against the Afghāns which was led by Āṣaf Khān and Bahādur Khān. Bāyazīd, 298, adds that Akbar was encouraging the Afghāns against the Uzbeks.

[82] *Akbarnāma*, II, 271. [83] Ibid., 271-2. [84] Ibid., 274-6.

[85] Ibid., 279-80; *Tārikh-i Alfī*, 268a. Professor Iqtidar Alam Khan believes that they were instigated to rebel by 'Alī Qulī. See *Life of Mun'īm Khān*, 93.

recited the *khutba* in the name of Mirzā Hakīm, despatched his men to invite him to the east and began to occupy imperial territories.[86]

Akbar met the crisis with his usual sense of self-assurance. After arranging the affairs of the Panjab, he came to Agra on 20 April 1567. Leaving behind Mun'īm Khān at Agra, Akbar started against 'Alī Quli[87] (on 6 May 1567). Mun'īm Khān was probably deliberately left at Agra because of the belief that he favoured reconciliation with the rebels.

The Uzbeks were now left alone to face Akbar. Āṣaf Khān and the Mirzās left them soon after having joined them; and the Afghāns also withdrew. Moreover, within the Mughal nobility there was no group left to plead their case.

A decisive battle was fought near Jhusi. 'Alī Qulī was killed and Bahādur Khān made prisoner. Akbar wanted to spare his life; but under the pressure of his nobles he had to execute him. Sikandar Khān and Sulaimān Uzbek fled the field and took shelter with the Afghāns. Ibrāhīm was arrested; but at Mun'īm Khan's intercession, he was pardoned.[88] Since nothing is said about his subsequent career, it is not known if he was retaken into service.

On his return from Patna to Jaunpur Mun'īm Khān received a letter from Sikandar Khān with a request to intercede on his behalf. He wrote that he could no longer trust the Afghāns for they had killed Sulaimān Uzbek who held a *jāgīr* near Bhagalpur. They had come to believe that after obtaining familiarity of Bengal, the Uzbeks would ask him to conquer Bengal.[89] Mun'īm Khān despatched this letter along with his own recommendation to the emperor. Akbar thereupon pardoned Sikandar Khān and permitted him to join imperial service. After sometime Sikandar Khān, Yūsuf Muhammad, Sulaimān Uzbek's son, and certain other Uzbek nobles came to Jaunpur and along with

[86] *Tārikh-i Akbarī*, 89; *Akbarnāma*, II, 284-5; *Muntakhab*, II, 90-1; *Ṭabaqāt*, 201-2. Before the revolt actually started the Uzbek officers met at Sarharpur in March 1567 (*pargana* in *sarkār* Jaunpur, *A'in*, (tr.), I, 174). 'Alī Qulī proposed that they should invade Bengal and establish themselves there but this was opposed by Sikandar Khān. They finally decided upon attacking imperial territories. They not only occupied the regions extending from Awadh to Shergarh, but even crossed the Ganges near Qananj. An army under Bahādur Khān struck at Kara Manikpur and besieged Majnūn Khān Qaqshal and Āṣaf Khān (*Tārikh-i Alfī*, 628ab; *Akbarnāma*; II, 285-9).

[87] *Akbarnāma*, II, 290; *Ṭabaqāt*, II, 209; *Muntakhab*, I, 94.

[88] *Nafā'is*, 50b, 51a; *Tārikh-i Akbarī*, 107-10; *Akbarnāma*, II, 298; *Tārikh-i Alfī*, 63b; *Ṭabaqāt*, II, 213; *Muntākhab*, II, 101.

[89] *Tazkira-i Humāyūn*, 304-5.

Mun'īm Khān proceeded to the court. Sikandar Khān was assigned Lucknow and *pargana* Saran in *sarkār* Manikpur where he died after some time (1572). Yūsuf Muhammad was imprisoned in Agra.[90]

Yūsuf Muhammad, Sulaimān Uzbek's son, who was imprisoned at Agra escaped to Gorakhpur and took shelter with Raja Sansar Chand. He also captured the fort of Gorakhpur. Mun'īm Khān despatched an army against him. Worsted in battle, he fled to the Afghāns.[91] We have no information about him or any other Uzbek noble of 'Alī Qulī's clan thereafter. Thus, Akbar finally succeeded in eliminating from his nobility this powerful and dangerous clan.

It may be added that the elimination of the Uzbeks from Mughal service under Akbar was not an incidental circumstance; it was the outcome of a deliberate policy to contain the power of individual clans within the nobility. But the fate of the Uzbek clan does not mean that clan groups of nobles were sought to be destroyed as such. Indeed, other clans were not only retained but new groups were also admitted though on new conditions, with great limitations put upon their power. The Uzbeks had to be destroyed because they simply could not accept these terms.

90 Ibid., 307.

91 *Akbarnāma*, III, 21-2. Yūsuf Muḥammad joined Lodi (an Afghān chief?) near Zamania.

CHAPTER IV

The Family of Raja Bharmal Kachhwaha

Raja Bharmal Kachhwaha was the first Rajput chief to join Mughal service under Akbar and establish matrimonial relations with the Mughal ruling house. Along with him, a number of Kachhwaha chiefs, including his sons and grandsons, entered Mughal service. They played an important role in the expansion of the Mughal empire. Akbar gave them ranks, *jāgīrs* and important administrative posts. The Kachhwahas remained the most favoured and trusted nobles from amongst the Rajputs under Akbar. The house continued to enjoy an important position during Jahāngīr's reign as well, though initially it suffered a setback on account of Man Singh's role in the accession crisis at the time of Akbar's death.

Amber was a small state in the north-eastern plains of Rajputana. The dominant chiefs of the region were of the Kachhwaha clan.[1] Besides Amber, places like Deosa, Neota, Luni, and Sambhar, were also apparently under their control.[2] They had perhaps also established their power in the localities of Lambi Jhari and Amarsar.[3] Abū'l Faẓl says they formed a large body of people; but their numbers were not matched by the size of the territory they held. They had not yet consolidated their authority fully in the whole of Dhundhar; besides, their possessions were subject to perpetual encroachments from the

[1] For the history of Kachhwaha chiefs before Akbar, See Rajiv Narain Prasad, *Raja Man Singh of Amber*, Calcutta, 1966, 1-20; Kunwar Refaqat Alī K͟hān, *Kachhwahas under Akbar and Jahāngīr*, New Delhi, 1976, 1-6; Ahsan Raza K͟hān, *Chieftains in the Mughal Empire during the Reign of Akbar*, Indian Institute of Advanced Study, Simla, 1977, 102-3.

[2] *Akbarnāma*, II, 156, Abū'l Faẓl says that Bharmal was the chief of the area. Deosa was held by his brother Rupsi. Neota was under Ram Das Kachhwaha who might or might not have owed allegiance to the Kachhwahas of Amber. Sambhar was held by Rai Lunkaram the chief of Shaikhawat sept of the Kachhwahas. Shaikhawats also held Bairath and Rewari in the north. *Akbarnāma*, III, 577. See *Ma'āṣir-ul Umarā*, II, 116.

[3] Tod, II, 316. Also see S.P. Gupta, *The Agrarian System of Eastern Rajasthan* (c.1650-c.1750) Manohar, Delhi, 1987, 1-2, 5-7.

more powerful Rathors,[4] and the Muslim officers posted at Ajmer and Nagor.

Prithviraj ascended the throne in 1503; he seems to have accepted the suzerainty of the Rana of Mewar.[5] He was succeeded by Puran Mal. According to the *Akbarnāma*, Puran Mal joined Mughal service under Humāyūn, but there is no information about the circumstances in which he joined and the status he enjoyed. He is said to have been killed in battle while fighting in the army of Hindal against the Mirzās.[6] After the death of Puran Mal, disputed succession and internal turmoil greatly weakened the position of the Kachhwahas.

Stability was restored after the accession of Bharmal on 25 June 1547.[7] His brother Askaran contested his claims, and fleeing to Delhi sought the help of Hājī Khān Afghān, the governor of Mewat, Ajmer and Nagor. Hājī Khān marched to Amber with a big army; Bharmal entered into negotiations and ultimately a compromise was effected. Bharmal was recognized as the ruler of Amber and Askaran was given the territory of Narwar.[8]

After Humāyūn's return to India and his death, the situation completely changed. Hājī Khān was expelled by the Mughals from Rajputana. After the death of Humāyūn, he attacked Narnaul which was under Majnūn Khān Qāqshāl.[9] Bharmal acted shrewdly at this juncture; he took possession of the fort and sent Majnūn Khān to the court and later on handed over the fort to Tardi Beg, when he came to chastize Hājī Khān.[10] Because of this, Majnūn Khān Qāqshāl commended Bharmal's 'support and great loyalty' to Akbar. The emperor thereupon invited him to the court.[11] But soon after Bharmal was again faced with a great crisis. Suja, Puran Mal's son, who had not been reconciled to Bharmal's accession, sought the help of Mirzā Sharafuddīn, the Mughal governor of Ajmer and Nagor, in order to secure his father's *gaddi*. Under the pressure of the joint forces of the Mirzā and Suja, Bharmal thought it expedient to come to terms. He promised to pay a fixed tribute and allow his son Jagannath as well as

[4] Nainsi, *Pargana ri Vigat*, I, 43-5; Tod, II, 19-20.

[5] *Vir Vinod*, II, 1272-3.

[6] *Akbarnāma*, iii, 606; also see *Vir Vinod*, 11. Prasad, however, believes that Puran Mal was murdered by the conspiracy of Bhim Singh, one of his brothers. Cf. *Raja Man Singh of Amber*, 4-6.

[7] *Nainsi Khyat*, 11, 13.

[8] *Vir Vinod*, 11, 1275.

[9] *Akbarnāma*, II, 20.

[10] Ibid., *Vir Vinod*, II, 1276-7.

[11] *Akbarnāma*, 45.

Raj Singh (Askaran's son) and Khanjar (Jagmal's son) to be kept as hostages by the Mirzā.[12] Bharmal's position now was by no means enviable; but it improved rather unexpectedly owing to a sudden development.

After the overthrow of Bairam Khān, the senior Tūrānī nobles started behaving arrogantly. The Tūrāni's also rebelled frequently. This made it imperative for the young emperor to secure some indigenous support.[13] Although certain Afghān chiefs had surrendered to the Mughals, they could not be safely relied upon, especially when other Afghān chiefs were still defying Mughal authority. The only alternative was to explore the possibility of obtaining support from the Rajputs and Indian Muslims. Thus, admission of these elements into Mughal service became an important part of Akbar's policy.[14]

Bharmal had already been introduced to Akbar by Majnūn Khān Qāqshāl. The Raja with his clansmen visited Agra in 1557 at the invitation of the emperor. While they were present at the court, their steadfastness in facing an intoxicated elephant made a great impression on Akbar. He is reported to have said, 'we will look after you'.[15] This incident took place during the period of regency, when Akbar practically had no say in the running of government. Quite possibly it had no immediate sequel. The real developments came in 1562.

During Akbar's visit to Ajmer in 1562, which was his first journey into Rajasthan, Jaimal and his father Rupsi, chief of the area, came to pay homage at Deosa. On the following day, Chaghtāī Khān presented

[12] *Akbarnāma*, II, 155; *Vir Vinod*, II, 1276-7. Prasad's account is confusing in this context. Cf. *Raja Man Singh of Amber*, 6.

[13] Iqtidar Alam Khān 'The Nobility of Akbar and the Development of his Reli-gious Policy 1560-80', *JRAS*, 1968, 29-32. See, also Afzal Ḥasain, 'Growth of Irānī Elements in Akbar's Nobility', *Indian History Congress*, 1975, 166-79.

[14] According to the author of *Ma'āṣir-i Rahimī*, II, 59. Bairam Khān had already taken the initiative in establishing friendly relations with the Rajputs. The *Zakhirat-u'l Khwānīn* records an interesting conversation between Humāyūn and Shāh Tahmāsp of Iran. Shāh Tahmāsp: 'Among Indians which class commands the obedience of big tribes, possesses princely grandeur and is brave?' Humāyūn: 'The Afghāns and the Rajputs'. Shāh Tahmāsp: 'Are they friendly with each other?' Humāyūn 'No'. Shāh Tahmāsp said, 'You cannot win the friendship of the Afghāns; deprive them of military service and force them to become merchants and artisans. Establish close relations with the Rajputs and promote them, for it is not possible to rule India without controlling the *zamīndārs*' (*Z.K.* I, 103-4).

[15] *Akbarnāma*, II, 45.

Bharmal before Akbar at Sangner. Akbar received him very kindly and after the formal meeting, upon the suggestion of Chaghtāī Khān, Bharmal offered his eldest daughter in marriage to Akbar. Akbar readily accepted the proposal and gave leave to Chaghtāī Khān and Bharmal to make arrangements for the marriage. The marriage was solemnized on his return journey, at Sambhar in March 1562. The Kachhwahas immediately reaped the reward. The hostages Raj Singh and Jagannath were released; and Bhagwan Das and Man Singh, son and grandson of Bharmal, were taken into imperial service.[16]

The admission of the Kachhwahas into the nobility was motivated by self interest and political consideration. But Akbar also perhaps saw in the matrimonial alliance, a relationship by which he might be able to invoke the loyalty of the favoured clan by appealing to ties of kinship. Indeed, later events were to show that the 'political' marriages helped to secure very firm loyalty on the part of the Kachhwahas. Moreover, the alliance became a model for settlement with other Rajput clans.

We have prepared a detailed chart of offices (including central ministers and governors of *ṣūbas*) held by the members of the Kachhawahas. A geneological chart shows all the known members of the family who entered Mughal service during our period.[17]

There were three main septs of the Kachhwaha clan, the Rajawats to which Bharmal[18] and his family belonged; the Shaikhawat of Rai Lankaran and the Udawat, the least important sept, from which Ram Das came.

At the time of joining Mughal service the Kachhwahas worked as one clan and they continued to do so till the last days of Akbar's reign. The differences between the sub-clans arose at the time of Akbar's serious illness. The Rajawats led by Man Singh put forward the claim of Khusrau, while Ram Das the Udawat chief, in effect supported Salīm.

After the admission of the Kachhawahas into Mughal service, Raja Bhagwan Das and Man Singh came to the court along with Akbar.[19]

[16] *Akbarnāma*, II, 154-8; *Muntakhab*, II, 49-50; *Ṭabaqāt*, II, 155; *Ma'āṣir-i Rahimī*, I, 694-5; *Vir Vinod*, II, 1276. Shyamal Das writes that Bhagwan Das was in the employment of the Maharanas of Mewar before joining Mughal service.

[17] See Appendix B–IV and Family Chart No.4 and 'Provincial Governors under Akbar, *Indian History Congress,* 1970, 269-77.

[18] *Z.K.*, I, 103, Farid Bhakkari had wrongly identified Raja Bharmal as *Shaikhawat.*

[19] *Akbarnāma*, II, 158.

Bhagwan Das served Akbar in suppressing the refractory peasants of Paronkh (1562),[20] in the campaign against Khān-i Zamān (1566-7),[21] in the Chittor expedition (1568),[22] and in the siege of Ranthambor (1569).[23] In 1570 he was deputed to arrange the marriage of the emperor to the daughter of Rawal Har Rao, the chief of Jaisalmer.[24]

The Kachhwahas' real opportunity to show their mettle came in the first Gujarat campaign. A large number of the Kachhwahas of the family of Bharmal accompanied Akbar: Bhagwan Das, Man Singh, Madhao Singh, Jagannath, Jagmal, Khangar, Rupsi and Bhupat. Bhupat a brother of Bhagwan Das was killed in the battle of Sarnal.[25] In the second Gujarat campaign (August 1573) too, Bhagwan Das accompanied Akbar[26] and Man Singh was ordered to gather the Kachhawaha *jāgīrdārs* and join the emperor in Gujarat.[27] Man Singh joined Muẓaffar Khān near Ujjain in September 1573. But as Akbar had defeated Muẓaffar Shāh, they were ordered to return. Man Singh thereupon returned to his *jāgīr*.[28]

When Akbar had proceeded on his first campaign of Gujarat, Raja Bharmal was given custody of the capital. Badāūnī says he was appointed *Wazīr-i Mutlaq*, but no other source mentions this appointment.[29] Bharmal, however, was given sufficient powers to take action on his own. He sent an army under his nephew Khangar to the Panjab to check possible trouble from Ibrāhīm Ḥasain Mirzā; and another army was despatched to help Mun'īm Khān in the eastern region. Bharmal himself died at Agra in 1574, to be succeeded as chief of his clan by Bhagwan Das.[30]

[20] Ibid., 165.

[21] Ibid., 265, 291. During the expedition he was given charge of the imperial camp twice once at Banaras and later at Shaikhan, near Manikpur.

[22] Ibid., 320. Bhagwan Das described the practice of *jauhar* to Akbar during this campaign.

[23] Though no direct evidence of his presence in the campaign is available, the presence of his 'servants' implies that he was also present. See *Akbarnāma*, II, 338.

[24] Ibid., 339.

[25] For the details of the Gujarat campaign, see *Akbarnāma*, III, 4, 6, 10-18, 31, 43-56; *Mir'āt-i Aḥmadi*, 91-100; *Ṭabaqāt*, II, 239-52.

[26] *Akbarnāma*, III, 43. Bhagwan Das was incharge of the *ḥarem*.

[27] Ibid., 43, 67, 68. This is the first reference to the *jāgīr* of Man Singh but the place of assignment is not mentioned. Apparently Amber was recognized as the *jāgīr* of the Kachhwahas.

[28] *Akbarnāma*, III, 19.

[29] *Muntakhab*, II, 151; *Akbarnāma*, III, 19 mentions that he had charge of the administration of the capital.

[30] *Akbarnāma*, III, 35, 44.

After the conquest of Gujarat, Bhagwan Das was appointed leader of an expedition against Rana Pratap.[31] He proceeded with an army by way of Idar, stormed the fortress of Bhadhnagar and took Rawaliya, the chief of the area into captivity.[32] Raja Narain Das Rathor of Idar also offered submission.[33] When he reached Gogunda, Rana Pratap sent his son Amar to the imperial court as a mark of submission and promised allegiance to Akbar.[34] In October 1573 Bhagwan Das returned to the court with Amar and Rawaliya. This campaign was followed by another one in April 1573 under Man Singh, Lashkar K͟hān and Shāh Qulī. Bhagwan Das returned to the court in June the same year.[35] The following year Bhagwan Das, Man Singh and Madhao Singh accompanied the emperor in his campaign in the eastern provinces.[36] But no details of their activities are furnished.

The services rendered during the Gujarat campaign and in the following year in Rajputana and the eastern region substantially raised the status of the Kachhwahas at the court. In the subsequent years, they were given important administrative responsibilities. From 1576 to 1578, Bhagwan Ḍas and Man Singh along with their clansmen were deputed to subdue Rana Pratap.[37] Thereafter they were transferred to the Panjab, where the Kachhwahas were assigned *jāgīrs*.[38] Man Singh was separately given a *jāgīr* in Sialkot; and Bhagwan Das, Jagannath and Jagmal were deputed to help Sa'id K͟hān who was appointed governor of the Panjab.[39] In 1581 Bhagwan Das was appointed co-governor of the Panjab; and after the transfer of Sa'id K͟hān he was given independent charge of the *ṣūba*. During the same period Man Singh was given independent charge of the frontier (Indus region — 1581-5);[40] after the death of Mirzā Ḥakīm, he was made governor of Kabul in 1585.[41] Bhagwan Das and Man Singh remained in charge of the Panjab and Kabul till 1587, when Man Singh was removed from Kabul, and Bhagwan Das's *jāgīrs* were transferred to Bihar. Man Singh was also transferred to Bihar; and he left Agra for that province in December 1587.

[31] *Akbarnāma*, II, 64. [32] Ibid., 66. [33] Ibid. [34] Ibid.

[35] Ibid., 87. [36] Ibid.

[37] For the details of the activities of Bhagwan Das, Man Singh and other Kachhwahas in the Mewar campaign, see *Akbarnāma*, III, 166, 175, 185, 190-3, 195-6, 216-18; *Muntak͟hab*, II, 224, 228, 235, 239; *Ṭabaqāt*, II, 323, 326-8; *Vir Vinod*, II, 150-3.

[38] *Akbarnāma*, III, 243. [39] Ibid., 262.

[40] Ibid., 372, 377; *Muntak͟hab*, II, 295; *Ṭabaqāt*, II, 362. Nizāmuddīn, however, says that Kabul was entrusted jointly to Bhagwan Das, Sa'id K͟hān and Man Singh.

[41] *Akbarnāma*, III, 336-7, 353, 372, 377, 466-9, 470-3, 486-7.

During these years (1578-87), the Kachhwahas enjoyed great prestige. In 1586 when Akbar reorganized his administration in order to ensure efficiency and better management, he ordered that two officers should be appointed in each *ṣūba*. Kachhwaha nobles were now appointed co-governors in four *ṣūbas,* viz., Ajmer, Agra, Lahore and Kabul.[42] Incidentally, the Kachhwahas held the maximum number of appointments and their provinces were contiguous. Besides, they were also given other duties. In 1583 Akbar introduced some administrative reforms. Raja Askaran along with Sharif Khān was deputed to look after the 'property of deceased persons and conveyance of it to the heirs'.[43] Another department for the maintenance of armour and security of the roads was made over to Jagannath and Qulij Khān.[44] Besides, the numerical strength of the family combined with the total *manṣabs* held by them was also higher than other important families of Akbar's reign. Table 4.1[45] shows the relative strength of the three important family-groups both numerically and in total *manṣabs*, in 1595.

The continuance of matrimonial relations with the imperial family naturally further raised the position of the Kachhwahas.[46]

This would mean that the Kachhwahas emerged as a very powerful and favoured group. But in spite of the high favour they enjoyed, it seemed that Akbar still kept a vigilant eye on them and was quick to express disapproval whenever he found fault. For example, during the Mewar campaign (1576-8), although Man Singh achieved a great victory at Haldighati, Akbar was not satisfied with his performance and he was censured.[47] Similarly, Bhagwan Das was also reprimanded

Table 4.1

	Manṣab	Total No. of nobles
The family of Bharmal	15,300	11
The family of Shamsuddīn	12,000	8
The family of Bairam Khān	10,000	7

[42] Ibid., III, 511-12. Cf. Afzal Husain, 'Provincial Governors under Akbar', *Proceedings of Indian History Congress*, 1970, 269-77.

[43] Ibid., II, 404-5. [44] Ibid. [45] For reference, see Appendix A–III.

[46] Afzal Husain, 'Marriages among Mughal Nobles as an Index of Status and Aristo-cratic Integration', *Proceedings of the Indian History Congress*, 1972, 304-12.

[47] *Akbarnāma*, III, 176, 185. Abū'l Faẓl says that Akbar was displeased with Man Singh due to wrong reports made against him. But Nizāmuddīn and Badauni make no such statements, *Tabqat*, II, 326; *Muntakhab*, II, 235, 239.

because of his inactivity against Rana Pratap.[48] In 1577, when Shāhbāz Khān Kamboh was appointed the supreme com-mander of the Mewar expedition, he sent back both Bhagwan Das and Man Singh on the ground that as 'they were *zamīndārs* there might be delay in inflicting retribution on that vain disturber (Pratap)'.[49] Akbar did not react adversely to this surprisingly bold action of the commander. Similarly, in 1585, Bhagwan Das had also to suffer, when Akbar disapproved of the settlement which he had concluded on his own with Yūsuf Shāh of Kashmir; Akbar had the Kashmiri ruler arrested and declined to ratify the treaty.[50] This naturally shook the confidence of Bhagwan Das, and in the same year when he was appointed governor of Kabul, he laid down certain conditions with regard to his authority before he would assume charge of the province. According to Abū'l Faẓl, 'Bhagwan Das propounded certain improper desires and the Emperor surmising madness restrained him from going.'[51] Akbar thereupon appointed his son Daniyal as governor of Kabul. But soon after when a penitent Bhagwan Das withdrew his conditions, Akbar reappointed him.[52] However, after reaching Sarai Khairabad across the Indus, Bhagwan Das attempted suicide.[53] Badāunī says that this was because of Bhagwan Das's sense of humiliation over the Kashmir affair.[54] He was removed to Attock and royal physicians were sent for his treat-ment. Bhagwan Das returned to Lahore after his recovery and looked after the royal ḥarem.[55] He died in 1589 at Lahore.[56]

Man Singh was also removed from the *ṣūba* of Kabul and the command of subduing the Roshanias upon allegations that the Rajputs had behaved badly with the local people, and that Man Singh did not look closely into 'the case of the oppressed'. The other charge against him was his lack of action in crushing the Roshanias.[57]

Apart from these actions which he took to keep the Kachhwahas under his control, Akbar, did not follow a uniform policy towards

[48] In October 1576, Bhagwan Das, Man Singh and Quṭbuddīn were sent in the vanguard of imperial forces under Akbar. Bhagwan Das and Quṭbuddīn were censured because of their failure to capture the Rana. See, *Akbarnāma*, III, 190-3, 195; *Ṭabaqāt*, II, 326-8; *Muntakhab*, II, 242.

[49] *Akbarnāma*, III, 218; *Ṭabaqāt*, II, 340-1.

[50] *Akbarnāma*, III, 481, 488; *Muntakhab*, II, 352.

[51] *Akbarnāma*, III, 491.

[52] Ibid., III, 491.

[53] Ibid., 492.

[54] *Muntakhab*, II, 352.

[55] *Akbarnāma*, III, 492, 525, 537. On 26 April 1589 when Akbar paid a visit to Kashmir, Lahore was given over to the charge of Bhagwan Das, Qulij Khān and Todar Mal.

[56] Ibid., III, 570.

[57] Ibid., 517-18, 520-1, 525.

them in the matter of promotions. After the marriage of Bharmal's daughter to Akbar, in subsequent years a large number of the Kachhwahas were indeed admitted to Mughal service. But a close study of the careers of the leading members of the family shows that promotions in ranks and the assignment of important official duties were conferred on Bharmal, his sons and grandsons. Rupsi, Jagmal and Askaran, the Bharmal's brothers, were given *manṣabs* but with the exception of Askaran none of the two received a rank or any important administrative appointment. Rupsi's son Jaimal and grandson Udai Singh were also not given promotions in service;[58] ultimately his family went into oblivion. Similarly, Jagmal's family and the nephews of Bharmal, viz., Mohan Das, Surdas and Tilkusi, were also neglected. Even from amongst the sons of Bharmal, only Bhagwan Das and Jagannath were given high ranks and important official duties. Bhupat, Salahadi and Banka remained insignificant throughout their life.[59] With a little difference, we see a similar policy followed with regard to the family of Shamsuddīn Atka; his brothers were retained in service but were not given independent charges; and after their death, their sons were given minor ranks. Hence it appears that Akbar, from the very beginning, wanted to restrict the extent of influence of particular families at higher levels. The admission of a large number of nobles from the Kachhwaha clan was a matter of political and military convenience; but places near the top could only be offered to a very few members of the clan.

Moreover, like the Atkas, the Kachhwahas were also dispersed all over the empire. Until the Gujarat campaign all the Kachhwahas were posted together; but after that Jaimal, Khangar and Raja Askaran

[58] Rupsi was present in 1572-3 in the Gujarat campaign. After that he stayed at his *jāgīr* in Deosa. The *A'in*'s list includes him among the nobles of 1,000, but according to Nizāmuddīn his *manṣab* was 1,500. *Akbarnāma*, II, 156, III, 49-50, 163; *Ṭabaqāt*, II, Jagmal was present in the Gujarat campaign, whereafter no other appointment is mentioned. He attained the rank of 1,000. *Akbarnāma*, II, 196; *Ma'āṣir-ul Umarā*, I, 127; *A'in 165*.

Rupsi's son Jaimal was present in the Gujarat campaign. Afterwards he was sent with Ṣafdar Khān against Duda, Rai Surjan's son. 1583 he died at chausa on his way to Bengal. His rank is not mentioned (*Akbarnāma*, II, 162, III, 49-50, 184, 402).

Udai Singh, Jaimal's son: Apparently remained in the service of Rai Lonkaran.

[59] Jagmal's son Khangar: He was sent by Bharmal with a big force towards Delhi to check the Mirzās in 1573. In 1576 he served with Man Singh against Rana Pratap. He was also despatched to serve under Shahbāz Khān Kamboh in Orissa and Bengal. Abū'l Faẓl does not give his rank but Nizāmuddīn puts him among the nobles of 2,000. *Akbarnāma*, III, 35, 166, 410, 439-40; *Ṭabaqāt*, II.

were not posted together with Bhagwan Das and Man Singh.[60] On the other hand, Bhagwan Das, his brother Jagannath and their sons remained apparently together until their transfer to the Panjab, where they were given *jāgīrs*. Subsequently Akbar started dispersing them as well. Man Singh was given a separate *jāgīr* in Sialkot, and sometimes afterwards he was also given an independent charge of the Indus region. Jagannath served Prince Murād in Kabul and then was given independent command of the Mewar campaign in 1584. Thereafter, he usually served independently or with other Mughal nobles. Similarly Madhao Singh also served with other Mughal nobles.

Although because of their high *manṣabs* these Kachhwaha nobles received extensive *jāgīrs* outside Rajasthan, their 'home *zamindari*' or *waṭan*, was really quite small, comprising Amber and one or two other *parganas*. They could not, therefore, on their own, compete with the other great ruling families of Rajasthan. Thus their dependence on imperial will must have always been considerable. Moreover, the Kachhwaha clan was far from being a homogeneous one. Past family rivalries continued even after they joined Mughal service; and because of the rise of certain members of the family a section of the Kachhwaha nobles grew jealous of them and even showed their resentment before the emperor. As early as 1572 during the Gujarat campaign, Rupsi misbehaved with Akbar and the matter would have taken a serious turn, but for Bhagwan Das who intervened and secured a pardon for him.[61] On another occasion when Akbar fell down from his horse while playing polo and it was rumoured that he was dead, certain Kachhwaha officers rose and expelled the imperial officers.[62] Again in 1578 while the assignment of *jāgīrs* to the Kachhwaha family in the Panjab was being considered, Achla, Mohan Das, Sur Das and Tilkusi, the son of Bhagwan Das' brother, rebelled and fled to their home Baoli in *sarkār* Ranthambor. There is no evidence of the exact cause of their flight, but it appears they might have quarreled over their share of *jāgīrs* with Bhagwan Das, who was supposed to be the head of the family. Dastam Khān, the Mughal officer posted in the area, out of respect for the Kachhwahas, tried to put down the trouble

[60] Askaran in 1577 was sent with Ṣādiq Khān against Madhukar. In 1579 he went with Todar Mal to Bihar. In 1585 he was despatched to Malwa with Mirzā 'Azīz Koka. In 1586 he was appointed co-governor of Ajmer. In 1587 he was sent against Madhukar (*Akbarnāma*, III, 229-30, 261, 287, 307, 372, 457, 464, 511, 526).

[61] *Akbarnāma*, III, 49-50.

[62] Ibid., III, 321.

peaceably. In the meantime Adam Tajband brought orders from the court that if they did not submit through persuasion, the fugitives were to be punished. In the encounter that took place with the rebels Achla and the three brothers were killed; one of them fatally wounded Dastam Khān, before he died.[63]

After the death of Bhagwan Das in 1589, Man Singh was given the title of Raja (and the territory of Amber) and promoted to the rank of 5,000.[64] During his stay in Bihar he brought to submission Puran Mal, Sangram and Anant Chauras, the refractory chiefs of the area. He also conquered Orissa in 1592.[65] Man Singh was given the charge of Bengal in 1594, as the *atāliq* of Prince Khusrau.[66] In 1599 while still holding the charge of Bengal, he was required to accompany Prince Salīm in an expedition against Mewar.[67] At his request his eldest son Jagat Singh was made deputy governor of Bengal. Jagat Singh died before he could take up the charge, and so his young son Maha Singh was appointed in his place; and Pratap Singh, his uncle, was made his guardian. They, however, failed to control the Afghāns,[68] and Man Singh had to return to Bengal.[69] In the last years of Akbar's reign he was summoned to the court. He reached Agra in August 1605 and was promoted to the rank of 7,000/6,000.[70]

Thus by the time of Akbar's death, the Kachhwahas not only remained one of the leading families, but also retained their position as the family group with the largest number of *manṣabs*.[71] Besides, by the marriage of Khusrau to the daughter of Mirzā 'Azīz Koka, the families of both the highest nobles of Akbar seem to have entered

[63] Ibid., 326-7. [64] Ibid., III, 537.

[65] For details of Man Singh's activities in Bihar, see *Akbarnāma*, III, 579-81, 611-13, 615, 631-2.

[66] Ibid., III, 650. [67] Ibid., 575. [68] Ibid., 763.

[69] For Man Singh's activities in Bengal, see *Akbarnāma*, III, 770, 784, 787-8; *Takmila*, III, 808, 821, 824, 827.

[70] *Iqbālnāma*, 510; *Takmila*, III, 838-9.

[71] These Kachhwaha nobles of Bharmal's family were alive at the death of Akbar:

Man Singh	7,000/6,000
Jagannath	5,000
Raj Singh	4,000
Madhao Singh	3,000/2,000
Sakat Singh	1,600/300
Maha Singh	2,000/300
Bhao Singh	1,000/500
Pratap Singh	1,000
Salhadi	700/400

(for reference see Appendix A-III).

into an alliance; since Khusrau was the son of Man Singh's sister. Both Man Singh and 'Azīz Koka accordingly attempted to secure Khusrau's succession, and the failure of this attempt led to partial eclipse in the fortunes of the Kachhwahas under Jahāngīr.[72]

Upon his accession Jahāngīr entered into a commitment to confirm all of his father's nobles in their ranks and offices.[73] Man Singh was accordingly retained as governor of Bengal and the overall position of Kachhwahas in terms of *manṣabs* held by them was not materially altered. As a matter of fact after the accession, certain Kachhwaha nobles were given promotion and there was a substantial increase in their *sawār* rank (from 25,300/9,500 to 25,300/18,500).[74]

Khusrau's rebellion, however, revived Jahāngīr's suspicions, and Man Singh was removed from the governorship of Bengal in 1606, and no other charge was given to him.[75] He left Bengal as desired by the emperor but stayed at Rohtas despite successive orders of recall.[76] He came back to the court only after Rohtas was assigned to Kishwar Khān, in 1608.[77] In the same year he was appointed to the Deccan to serve under 'Abdur Rahīm Khān Khanān. It was for the first time since 1586 that Man Singh was deputed to serve under the command of another noble. Owing, however, to the high status enjoyed by 'Abdur Rahīm Khān Khanān,[78] such a subordinate appointment might not but have been regarded by Man Singh as necessarily humiliating.

[72] For the details of this attempt, see Conclusion.

[73] *Tuzuk*, 4-5. For details see Conclusion.

[74] The names of Kachhwaha nobles were promoted.
1. Jagannath 5,000/3,000
2. Raj Singh 4,000/3,000
3. Bhao Singh 2,000/1,000
4. Karam Chand 2,000/1,500 (for reference, see Appendix A–V).

[75] *Tuzuk*, 37; *Iqbālnāma*, 19; *Tārikh-i Khān Jahāni*, II, 669-73. Cf. R.P. Tripathi, *Rise and Fall of Mughal Empire*, 368 where it is wrongly stated that Man Singh was transferred to Bihar. During the same period Jahāngīr Qulī Khān was appointed Governor of Bihar. Also see, 'The Family of Nur Jahan', 90-4.

[76] *Tuzuk*, 65.

[77] *Tuzuk*, 65; *Bahāristān-i Ghaibī*, I, 144-5, 157-9. Inayat Ali Zaidi relying on the authority of Hawkins, who had placed him among the nobles of 5,000, writes that Man Singh's *manṣab* was reduced around 1608 when he came to the court. But Hawkin's evidence regarding *manṣabs* is very unreliable (Inayat Ali Zaidi, 'The Political Role of Kachhwahas Nobles during Jahāngīr's Reign', *Indian History Congress*, 1975, 181).

[78] *Z.K.*, I, 31, 'Abdur Raḥīm's children always addressed Man Singh as *Dadaji* (grandfather). When Man Singh entered the imperial service at the age of eleven, he was asked to look after and play with the child who later on became *Khān Khanān*.

The author of the *Nuskha-i Dilkusha* relates a tradition that one day Man Singh asked the Khān Khanān about the slow pace of military progress in the Deccan. The Khān Khanān replied: 'You have come back after concluding the affairs of 'Usmān Afghān in Purab (East) and have been appointed my subordinate. If I end the present war quickly, under what noble would I be deputed to serve.'[79]

Man Singh reached the Deccan in 1609 after about a year of his appointment. His presence made little difference in the Deccan, because of the constant disagreements and lack of cooperation among the Mughal commanders posted there. He died at Ellichpur (Achalpur) in 1614.[80]

This lack of favour shown to Man Singh and the Kachhwahas during the first ten years of Jahāngīr's reign was perhaps responsible for the general belief that he was hostile to the Rajputs. William Hawkins, who lived in Agra between 1609 and 1611, found that

> This king hath diminished his chief captains which were Rasbootes (Rajputs) and Gentiles, and natural Indians and hath preferred Mahmumetans (weak spirited men, void of resolution) in such sort that what this mans father, called Eckbar Padasha got of the Deccan this king Salīm Shāh, beginneth to loose.'[81]

Mirzā 'Azīz Koka also accused Jahāngīr of promoting the Persians and Indian Muslims at the expense of the Chaghtāīs and Rajputs.[82] The author of the *Tārikh-i Khān Jahāni* alleges that Jahāngīr, on account of his anger at Man Singh, even ordered the destruction of the Rajputs, but, upon the intervention of Khān-i Jahān Lodi, the order was withdrawn and Man Singh once again received favour.[83]

Man Singh's son Bhao Singh was preferred by Jahāngīr over Maha Singh, a grandson of Man Singh, whom the latter wished to have as his successor. Such a step would be in line with Jahāngīr's interest in having a member of the family made its head, in whom he could have confidence; and his choice Bhao Singh had been his supporter

[79] Bhim Sen, *Nuskha-i Dilkushā*, B.M., or 23, 8a.

[80] For details of the Deccan campaign, see *Tuzuk*, 70-1, 130; *Tārikh-i Khān Jahāni*, II, 511-17. Also see Chapters VI and IX.

[81] *Early Travels in India*, ed. William Foster, London, 1927, 106-7.

[82] For Mirzā 'Azīz Koka's complaint, see Chapter II.

[83] *Tārikh-i Khān Jahāni*, II, 497-8.

The story might, of course, have been set about by the author to show the sagacity and influence of his patron; but it reinforces the perception that there was consi-derable suspicion in Jahāngīr's mind, at this time, against Man Singh and the Rajputs in general.

throughout. This confidence was expressed in his subsequent action in awarding Bhao Singh the title of Mirzā Raja signifying the special status of the Kachhwahas in their relationship with the imperial family. Yet in terms of actual power, the concessions were not unduly generous. Bhao Singh rose to the rank of 5,000/3,000, but he remained at the court without any appointment till 1619. He was then ordered to go to the Deccan where he died in 1621.[84]

Jagat Singh's son Maha Singh, who held the rank of 2,000 after the accession of Jahāngīr, had not been given any important assignment. But he was now given promotion of 500 *sawār* and the territory of Garha as *inam*. In the following year (1615) he was also given the title of Raja, and raised to the rank of 4,000/3,000 in 1616.[85] This was in partial rectification of his supersession of Maha Singh's claims. In 1616 he was sent to the Deccan, and he died in 1617 in Berar.[86] The other Kachhwaha nobles Raja Jagannath, Madhao Singh and Raj Singh were not given any important administrative duties, though they retained their *manṣabs*.[87]

On Bhao Singh's death, the *tika* was given to Jai Singh, Maha Singh's young son because Bhao Singh had no son. Thus Maha Singh's line was restored. The *pargana* of Amber was assigned to Jai Singh in *jāgīr* as *waṭan*.

Table 4.2

	Total No.	Zāt	Sawār
Rajput nobles at the death of Akbar	17	41,000	10,450
Rajput nobles at the end of 6th regnal year of Jahāngīr	19	51,200	21,300
Rajput nobles at the end of 15th year of Jahāngīr	14	35,500	20,650

[84] For details of Bhao Singh's career, see *Tuzuk*, 10, 66, 81, 140, 218-19.

[85] *Tuzuk*, 130.

[86] See *Tuzuk*, 7-8, 17, 111, 156, 168, 176, 217, 266; *Ma'āṣir-ul Umarā*, II, 173-4. His highest rank was 4,000/3,000.

[87] Raja Jagannath, after being transferred from Mewar where he served under Āṣaf Khān, remained without any assignment till 1609. In that year he along with his son was transferred to the Deccan to serve under Parvez. He died the same year. See, *Tuzuk*, 16, 74, 148, 156; *Vir*

The evidence cited above indicates that there was a general feeling that Jahāngīr had reversed the policy of Akbar not only in respect of the Kachhwahas who had conspired against him, but the Rajputs as a whole. Table 4.2 may help us to understand the correct picture.[88]

The table shows that after the accession of Jahāngīr the position of the Rajputs improved considerably (in absolute terms at any rate). But as a matter of fact the rise in numbers and *manṣabs* was not because of any special favour towards the Rajputs, but because of a general policy under which all those nobles who were Jahāngīr's favourites during his princehood or those who had helped him in the accession crisis were promoted. For example, Bir Singh Deo Bundela was admitted to service and within six years was raised to the rank of 4,000/2,000. Ram Das Kachhwaha was also raised to the rank of 3,000 for the service he had rendered during the accession crisis.

In fact, though the position of the Rajputs in terms of *manṣabs* increased after the accession of Jahāngīr, they ceased to play as important a role in the working of Mughal government, as they had done so far. After Man Singh not a single Rajput noble was appointed governor or given independent command in an important campaign.[89] Most of the Rajput nobles remained posted in the Deccan.

With the Kachhwahas, the effect of a relative withdrawal of imperial favour seemed especially harsh, since unlike the Sesodias of Mewar or Rathors of Marwar, they had no hereditary territories (*waṭan*) against which their chiefs could claim high *manṣabs*. Thus, if a Kachhwaha noble died, his sons could begin with a much lower *manṣab*, as was the case with the nobility in general. Sometimes no additional rank at all was given to them. When Madho Singh and Jagannath died in 1608 and 1609, Jagannath's son Karamchand was given the rank of 2,000/1,500, while Madho Singh's sons were apparently not given any *manṣabs*.[90] Similarly, after the death of Maha Singh and Raj Singh, their sons were admitted to service but were given minor ranks. Maha Singh's son Jai Singh was given the rank of 1,000/500 and Ram Das

Vinod, II, 253. Madhao Singh was not given any appointment. See *Tuzuk*, 17, 55, Asad Beg, 29-30. Raj Singh held the rank of 4000; he served in the Deccan and died there in 1615 (*Tuzuk*, 148).

88 For full reference of the table, see Appendix A-III, V and VI.

89 For details see 'The Family of Nur Jahan', 90-4. Also see Inayat Alī Zaidi, 'The Political Role of Kachhwaha Noble during Jahāngīr's Reign', 180-97.

90 *Tuzuk*, 74. At the time of his death, Jagannath had the rank of 5,000/3,000.

of 1,000/400.[91] After the death of Raja Raj Singh in 1616, Jahāngīr refused to confer the title of 'Raja' on his son Ram Das also. After two years, however, on repeated petitions, the title was given.[92]

The resumption of *jāgīrs* of Abhay Ram, Bijoy Ram and Shyam Ram because of some acts of misbehaviour and the refusal of the Rajput nobles, including the Kachhwahas present at the court, to stand surety for them, indicate that none of them were prepared to help an erring member of their own faction apparently on account of Jahāngīr's hostile attitude. Consequently, when the brothers refused to be disarmed, they were attacked by the imperial soldiery and were killed in the skirmish. The punishment given to them was unusual if we study other such cases even during the reign of Jahāngīr.[93]

As a result of both deliberate measures and foruitous circumstances there seems to have occurred a definite decline in the fortunes of the Kachhwaha nobles. Table 4.3[94] gives the total ranks known to have been held by them in various years.

The seeming increase of *sawār* rank between 1605 and 1612 is misleading. The *sawār* ranks held by a number of Kachhwaha nobles in 1605 are not known, and the actual total of *sawār* for 1605 must have greatly exceeded the figure of 9,500 shown by us.

Despite Jahāngīr's policy of restricting their *manṣabs*, the entire Kachhwaha clan including nobles such as Jai Singh, Girdhar, Ram Das Narwari and Narain Das remained loyal to Jahāngīr during the rebellion of K͟hurram.[95] The only exception was Manrup, Jagannath's grandson, who joined K͟hurram. Ram Das Narwari was present in the battle of Bilochpur on the imperial side and got a promotion of

Table 4.3

	Zāt	*Sawār*
At the death of Akbar 1605	25,300	9,500
At the end of sixth year of	16,000	13,500
Jahāngīr (1612) 1624	10,500	6,900

[91] *Tuzuk*, 29-30, 148, 192; *Ma'āṣir-i Jahangiri*, 38ab; *Tārik͟h-i K͟hān Jahānī*, II, 669-70.

[92] Cf. *Tuzuk*, 138, 164, 181.

[93] *Tuzuk*, 29-30, For detailed discussion on Mughal emperor's attitude towards rebels, see Afzal Ḥusain, 'Elements of Continuity and Stability in the Mughal Nobility Under Akbar and Jahangir', *Studies in History*, Vol. II, No.2 (1980) 21-32.

[94] For reference, see Appendix A-III, V and VI.

[95] *Tuzuk*, 360; *Iqbālnāma*, 201-2.

1,000/1,000.[96] Jai Singh, after being summoned to the court, was promoted to the rank of 3,000/4,000. He was sent along with Parvez and Mahābat Khān to pursue Khurram. Ram Das Narwari, Narain Das and Girdhar went with him.[97]

Jai Singh and other Kachhwahas first served in the imperial army in the Deccan,[98] they were then sent to Allahabad against the rebels.[99] After the defeat of Khurram in Bengal, Jai Singh returned with Mahābat Khān and Parvez to the Deccan. About the same time Mahābat Khan's relations with the court deteriorated, and he was replaced in the Deccan by Khān Jahān Lodi.[100] It seems that Jai Singh was sympathetic to Mahābat Khān and did not fully approve of his removal. Jahāngīr thereupon not only directed him to cooperate with Khān Jahān but even warned him.[101] None of the Kachhwahas came out to support Mahābat Khān during his coup.

When Khurram came to know of these developments he sought to persuade Jai Singh to help him.[102] But Jai Singh remained non-committal. He stayed back in the Deccan engaged in the fighting against Ahmadnagar.[103] The court party also wanted him to remain in the Deccan.[104] For his services, he was promoted to the rank of 4,000/2,500, given the title of 'Raja' and assigned Chatsu in *jāgīr*.

At the time of Jahāngīr's death Jai Singh was still in the Deccan. He left the province for the north along with Khān-i Jahān Lodi and Gaj Singh. He had also received a *farmān* from Dāwar Bakhsh.[105] But with Shāhjahān marching through Gujarat into Rajasthan, Jai Singh separated himself from Khān-i Jahān Lodi and proceeded to Ajmer to join Shāhjahān.[106]

96 *Badshanama*, I, 122-3; *Ma'āṣir-ul Umarā*, I, 516.

97 *Tuzuk*, 359-60; *Iqbālnāma*, 204-5; *Ma'āṣir-i Jahangiri*, 159b, 161b, 162b.

98 Jahāngīr's *farmān* to Jai Singh, State Archives, Bikaner N-2 dated 20 July 1623. I am thankful to Mr Inayat Alī Zaidi who showed me copies of these *farmāns*. Ibid., N-3 Jai Singh was granted a *khilat* and ordered to serve under Parvez and Mahābat Khān.

99 *Iqbālnāma*, 204-5, 222-3, 231-3; *farmān*, N-4; *A Dutch chronicle*, 69-70; *Vir Vinod*, II, 286-7 refers to the battle fought near Jaunpur in which Jai Singh distin-guished himself.

100 For details, see Chapters VI and VIII.

101 Jahāngīr's *farmān* to Jai Singh, Bikaner, Archives, N–7.

102 For Jai Singh's relations with Mahābat Khān, see Chapter VIII.

103 For Khurram's letter to Jai Singh, see Inayat Alī Zaidi, 'The Political Role of Kachhwaha Nobie during Jahāngīr's Reign', *Proceedings of Indian History Congress*, 1975, 166-79.

104 Jahāngīr's *farmān* to Jai Singh. It forbids Jai Singh and Gaj Singh to come to Court.

105 Dāwar Bakhsh's *farmān* to Jai Singh, Bikaner Archives, N–176.

106 *Iqbālnāma*, 300. For details, see Chapter VI.

The Kachhwahas, because of their cooperation and loyalty during the rebellion of Shāhjahān, received promotions;[107] but still none of them was assigned important offices. On the whole, it may be concluded that Mirzā 'Azīz Koka's complaint regarding the eclipse of the Rajputs was not absolutely incorrect. Although Jahāngīr continued to keep in service Kachhwahas and also admitted certain new elements of Rajputs ịnto his nobility, yet their rate of promotion was slow and they were not given important charges.

[107] In 1621 after the death of Bhao Singh who held the rank of 5,000, his successor Jai Singh was given the rank of 3,000/1,400. During 1618 to 1624 these Kachhwaha nobles were promoted:

1. Ram Das 2,000/1,000 2. Chatrasal 1,500/1,000.

3. Narain Das 2,000/2,000 4. Karam Chand 2,000/1,500.

CHAPTER V

The Family of Bārha Sayyids

The Bārha Sayyids were an important group among the Mughal nobility, though it was under 'Sayyid Brothers' who dominated the court of Emperor Farrukh Siyar (1713-9), that they rose to utmost prominence. In our period their repute as warriors seems to have been considerable, but they generally remained *manṣabdars* of moderate or low ranks. None of them was appointed governor or central minister. The contemporary sources notably *Akbarnāma*, *Tuzuk-i Jahāngīrī* and *Zakhīrat-ul Khawānīn*[1] introduce us to a large number of persons belonging to Bārha families.[2] These notices form the main source for the present study.

A brief history of the clan may be helpful. Blochmann, Atkinson and Nevill have given family charts followed by a brief history, though there are certain errors in their chronology.[3] Of use also is the history of the Bilgram Sayyids who also claim to be of the same branch. According to their traditions, the ancestor of the Bārhas, Abū Farah left Medina for Ghaznīn; and from there his four sons came to India with the army of Shihābuddīn Ghauri. These four brothers settled in the Panjab in four different villages called Tihanpur, Chhatrauri, Jajner and Kundli, and their families retained these names when they migrated to localities within the present Muzaffarnagar district of Uttar Pradesh. As to the name Bārha, Jahāngīr explained its origin thus: 'They call twelve *bara* in Hindi.

[1] *Abū'l Faẓl*, ed. Maulvi Abdur Rahīm, Asiatic Society of Bengal, 1887; Jahāngīr, Sayyid Aḥmad Khān, Aligarh, Ghazipur; Fareed Bhakkari, MS. Habib Ganj Collection, Maulana Azad Library, Aligarh, and ed. Dr Syed Moinul Haq, *Pakistan Historical Society*, Karachi.

[2] See Appendix A–IV. Blochmann in his translation of the *Ā'īn-i Akbarī*, I, attempted identifications of all members of the Bārha families by using some of these sources.

[3] *Ā'īn-i Akbarī*, I. Notes on Bārha Sayyids; *Statistical, Descriptive and Historical Account of North Western Provinces of India*, Vol.III, Muzaffarnagar district; *District Gazetteers of United Provinces*, Muzaffarnagar district.

As in the Duab there are twelve villages near each other which are the native country of these Sayyids they have become known as Sayyids of Bārha.'[4]

There was a controversy during the reign of Akbar and Jahāngīr regarding their descent from the Prophet.[5] The question probably came up because the families did not produce any scholars and theologians. The interesting historical question is what they were before entering Mughal nobility. An apparently hostile tradition has been preserved that some of them worked as menial servants in the army of Humāyūn.[6] They, however, appear to have taken to soldiering and developed considerable influence over local Zamīndārs. After the death of one Raja Ram Chand of Sambhalera, Sayyid Ḥasan of the Chhatrauri sept is said to have appropriated his whole estate at the request of the widow.[7] It appears that they enjoyed some position in the service of the Afghāns. From the *Ā'īn* also we do not know whether they possessed *zamīndāri* rights in the villages, as in its listing of Zamīndār castes in the *sarkār* of Saharanpur, it enters Sayyids in some *parganas*, but rather surprisingly the Sayyids of Bārha are not recorded as Zamīndārs anywhere.[8]

Sayyid Maḥmūd Bārha of the Kundliwal sept was the first Bārha Sayyid known to have joined Mughal service. Before that he was in the employment of Sikandar Afghan, whom he deserted during the siege of Mankot, to come over to the Mughals, taking service with Bairam Khān.[9] When Bairam Khān sent a vanguard under the command of Khān-i Zamān to face Hemu, Sayyid Maḥmūd was sent with him.[10] After the victory at Panipat in 1566 he was despatched in the expedition against Ajmer and Nagor against Hājī Khān.[11] In 1558 he was despatched along with Adham Khān against the Bahaduryas of Hatkant. He also served in the expedition against fort Jaitaran in Jodhpur.[12] Later on when the emperor was alienated from Bairam Khān, he joined imperial service and received a *jāgīr* in Delhi.[13]

[4] *Tuzuk*, 336. Also see *Z.K.*, I, 181.

[5] *Tuzuk*, 362, *Z.K..*, I, 182.

[6] Nevill, 162.

[7] Ibid., 168.

[8] *Ā'īn-i Akbarī*, I (tr.), see account of 12 *ṣūbas*.

[9] *Muntakhab-ut Tawārikh*, II, 18; *Ma'āṣir-ul Umarā*, II, 375-7.

[10] *Akbarnāma*, II, 33.

[11] *Muntakhab-ut Tawārikh*, 46, 66; *Ma'āṣir-ul Umarā*, II, 375-7.

[12] *Muntakhab-ut Tawārikh*, II, 78; *Akbarnāma*, II, 78; *Ma'āṣir-ul Umarā*, II, 375-7.

[13] *Ma'āṣir-ul Umarā*, II, 375-7.

When Akbar took over the reins of government personally and was faced with opposition in his nobility, he seems to have turned to the Rajputs and the Indian Muslims to counter the old nobility.[14] The rise of the Bārha Sayyids, who were admitted in large numbers after the overthrow of Bairam Khān, would seem to support this view.

Akbar introduced many other Shaikhzāda (Indian Muslim) families,[15] but no other clan equalled the Bārhas except the families of Shaikh Mubārak and Shaikh Salīm Chishtī who had special relations with the emperor. However, even these two families did not have as many *manṣabdars* as the Bārha Sayyids.[16]

In the siege of Chittor which was personally supervised by the emperor, the Sayyids of Bārha fought bravely. Sayyid Jamāluddīn, Sayyid Aḥmad Khān Bārha's son was killed when a mine exploded.[17]

In the Gujarat campaign, Sayyid Maḥmūd Bārha, Sayyid Aḥmad Khān, Sayyid Qāsim and Sayyid Hāshim were despatched to accompany the advance guard of Khān-i Kalān. After reaching Pattan the charge of the contingent was given to Mirzā Khān under the guardianship of Sayyid Aḥmad Khān.[18] After the occupation of Ahmadabad, Akbar decided to expel the Mirzās from Gujarat. An army was sent under Man Singh, Sayyid Maḥmūd Bārha and others for the conquest of Surat, which was under the occupation of the Mirzās. But owing to the approach of Ibrāhīm Ḥasain Mirzā from Broach, the army was recalled, and as Akbar hurried forward to face the Mirzā, he was joined by Sayyid Maḥmūd and others raising the strength of the army to 200 *sawārs*. A fierce battle was fought at Sarnal in which Ibrāhīm was defeated and put to flight.[19]

[14] Cf. Iqtidar Alam Khan, 'The Nobility of Akbar and the Development of his Religious Policy', *JRAS, 1968*, 29-30.

[15] For example, the Shaikhzadās of Nagor. Akbar also established matrimonial relations with the Shaikhzadās of Delhi and Agra (see *Muntakhab-ut Tawārikh*, II, 61-2). Cf. Iqtidar Alam Khan 'The Nobility of Akbar and Development of his Religious Policy'. The Sayyids of Amroha were also admitted into service by Akbar and a number of them were given *manṣabs*. But they had no relationship with the Bārha Sayyids. For a detailed history of the Amroha Sayyids, see Jalal Aḥmad Naqvi, *Tārikh-i Amroha* (Urdu), I, Hyderabad Deccan, 1934.

[16] For the account of the family of Shaikh Salīm Chishtī, see Chapter VI. For the total number of Bārha nobles in Akbar's reign, see Appendix A–IV.

[17] *Akbarnāma*, II, 317; *Ma'āṣir-ul Umarā*, II, 379.

[18] *Akbarnāma*, II, 372, III, 61; *Muntakhab-ut Tawārikh*, II, 139-40, writes that he was given the *jāgīr* of Pattan. *Ma'āṣir-ul Umarā*, II, 378-9, 408-10.

[19] *Akbarnāma*, III, 11-16; *Muntakhab-ut Tawārikh*, II, 141.

After the victory at Sarnal the emperor along with Sayyid Maḥmūd and other Bārha Sayyids marched to Surat.[20] While the operations were in progress, the Mirzās tried to create commotion near Pattan and Ibrāhīm Ḥasain attempted to surprise Agra. Akbar despatched Sayyid Maḥmūd Bārha, Shāh Qulī Maḥram and Bhagwan Das to intercept the rebels.[21]

While the emperor was in Surat, Muḥammad Ḥusain Mirzā, Shāh Mirzā and the Faulādi Afghāns attacked Pattan and besieged Sayyid Aḥmad Bārha there. Mirzā 'Azīz Koka rushed to his help and the Mirzās raised the siege. After the defeat of the Mirzās, Khān-i 'Ālam along with Sayyid Qāsim Bārha was deputed to pursue Muḥammad Ḥusain Mirzā who had fled to the Deccan.[22]

After the completion of the conquest of Gujarat, Sayyid Maḥmūd returned to the court along with Akbar, but Sayyid Aḥmad, Sayyid Qāsim and Sayyid Hāshim were left in Gujarat.

When next year Akbar personally proceeded by forced marches towards Ahmadabad to face a fresh rebellion, a strong advance guard was formed under Man Singh, Bhagwan Das, Sayyid Maḥmūd and other Bārha Sayyids.[23] In the battle fought with Muḥammad Ḥusain Mirzā, the Bārha Sayyids were in the centre under the command of Mirzā Khān. The centre was responsible for the victory; and in the battle Sayyid Maḥmūd Bārha and Rai Singh distinguished themselves.[24]

In the same year after the reconquest of Gujarat, Sayyid Maḥmūd, along with the Amroha Sayyids, was despatched against the rebel Madhukar, Sayyid Maḥmūd behaved courageously and brought the country to order. Shortly afterwards he died.[25]

In 1575 a contingent of the Bārha Sayyids was despatched under Ṣādiq Khān to Basantpur in the foothills of Kumaon to crush rebels. The rebels had previously defeated an imperial army under Ḥusain Khān.[26]

In the same year Sayyid Aḥmad and Sayyid Hāshim along with a contingent of Bārha Sayyids were sent against Maldeo's son Chandrasen who had strengthened the fort of Siwana. The Bārhas fought bravely and inflicted losses on the rebels, but the

[20] *Akbarnāma*, III, 19. [21] Ibid., 23.
[22] *Muntakhab-ut Tawārikh*, II, 147-9; *Ma'āṣir-ul Umarā*, II, 378-9.
[23] *Akbarnāma*, II, 41-3; *Muntakhab-ut Tawārikh*, II, 164-70.
[24] *Akbarnāma*, III, 47-9. [25] Ibid., 77. [26] Ibid., 143-4.

fort of Siwana was captured in 1576 under the command of Shāhbāz Khān Kamboh.[27]

In 1576 Man Singh was sent against Rana Pratap of Mewar. He was accompanied by Sayyid Qāsim, Sayyid Hāshim, Sayyid Rāju and a number of other Bārha Sayyids. Some of the Bārha Sayyids under the command of Sayyid Hāshim numbering about 80 were in the vanguard, and Sayyid Aḥmad commanded the right wing. There was severe fighting and the Sayyids reputedly threw the valour of the Rajputs into the shade. Badāūnī remarks, 'if the Sayyids had not held their ground firmly... the affairs would have turned out a disgraceful defeat'.[28]

After the victory Akbar took steps to isolate the Rana. Sayyid Hāshim and Rai Singh were deputed to bring to submission Sulṭān Deora of Sirohi and Tāj Khān of Jalor. Realizing the futility of resistance they agreed to submit. Hāshim and Rai Singh were posted at Nadot (Nadol), a historic place in the Aravallis to keep watch on the chiefs of those territories and to block the road to the Rana's territory.[29]

Later on in 1577 another army under the command of Shāhbāz Khān was sent against Rana Pratap. Man Singh, Raja Bhagwan Das, Sayyid Rāju, Sayyid Qāsim and Sayyid Hāshim were ordered to accompany him.[30]

In 1580 Sayyid Hāshim and Sayyid Qāsim were ordered to march against Chandrasen, who had again rebelled. After a fight they expelled him from the imperial territory.[31]

It appears that until 1584 Sayyid Hāshim and Sayyid Qāsim remained at Ajmer serving in imperial armies. They were also granted *jāgīrs* in the *ṣūba*.[32] However, in 1584, they were appointed to Gujarat with 'Abdur Raḥīm Khān-i Khānān , who was called upon to deal with the rebellion of Muẓaffar Gujarati.[33] The vanguard of the army was commanded by the Bārha Sayyids. In the battle fought at

[27] *Akbarnāma*, III, 159, 176-8. The author of the *Ma'āṣir-ul Umarā*, II, 378-9, believes that Sayyid Aḥmad died in 1572-3, which is not correct because he was with Man Singh in the campaign against Rana Pratap in 1576. See *Akbarnāma*, III, 166-7.

[28] Ibid., 166-7, 174-6; *Muntakhab-ut Tawārikh*, II, 227-8, 230-3; *Ma'āṣir-ul Umarā*, II, 403-4.

[29] *Akbarnāma*, III, 189-90; *Ma'āṣir-ul Umarā*, II, 409-10.

[30] *Akbarnāma*, III, 218-19; *Ma'āṣir-ul Umarā*, II, 409-10.

[31] *Akbarnāma*, III, 318-19; *Ma'āṣir-ul Umarā*, II, 409-10.

[32] *Ma'āṣir-ul Umarā*, II, 409-10.

[33] *Akbarnāma*, III, 409-10, 413-14; *Ma'āṣir-ul Umarā*, II, 409-10.

Sarkhij, Sayyid Hāshim was killed and Sayyid Qāsim was severely wounded. Abdur Raḥim Khān Khanān achieved victory, but Muẓaffar escaped.[34]

After some time Muẓaffar again revolted. 'Abdur Raḥīm Khān Khanān himself proceeded towards Cambay leaving Sayyid Qāsim and other Bārhas to defend Pattan; he also left Sayyid Lād and Sayyid Bahādur along with some other Bārhas in the village of Hadala.[35]

While the Gujarat rebels were hard pressed by 'Abdur Rahīm Khān Khanān, Raja Jagannath was despatched against Rana Pratap in the same year along with Sayyid Rāju. The Sayyid was left at Mandalgarh, while Jagannath proceeded towards the Rana's headquarters. The Rana escaped and raided the imperial territories. Sayyid Rāju marched forward to pursue him but the Rana fled towards Chittor. Jagannath and Rāju some time later made a surprise attack on the Rana's residence, and narrowly missed capturing him.[36]

In 1585 when 'Abdur Raḥīm Khān Khanān came to the court, he left Qulij Khān to defend Ahmadabad and Sayyid Qāsim was appointed commander of the forces of the province. During the absence of 'Abdur Raḥīm Khān Khanān, Muẓaffar once again invaded the territories of Junagarh with the help of the Jam, the ruler of little Kutch (Jamnagar). He gained some initial success, but Sayyid Qāsim and Nizāmuddīn took immediate action, plundered the town of Rajkot and beat back Muẓaffar.[37]

In the meantime while 'Abdur Raḥīm Khān Khanān was returning from the court he forced the Raja of Sirohi and Ghaznī Khān of Jalor to surrender. In both these engagements he was aided by Sayyid Qāsim and Nizāmuddīn.[38]

During the years 1587 and 1588 the Sayyids of Bārha under Sayyid Qāsim and Nizāmuddīn fought many battles with Muẓaffar and the Jam and achieved much success.[39]

In 1590 Gujarat was assigned to Mirzā 'Azīz Koka. The Sayyids remained there during his tenure of office, and fought in every

[34] *Akbarnāma*, III, 409-10, 413-14; *Ma'āṣir-ul Umarā*, II, 409-10. Two of the other Bārha Sayyids referred to in the campaign were Sayyid Bahādur and Sayyid Lād, *Akbarnāma*, III, 423-4.

[35] *Akbarnāma*, III, 425; *Ma'āṣir-ul Umarā*, II, 409-10; *Muntakhab-ut Tawārikh*, II, 331-2.

[36] *Akbarnāma*, III, 452-4; *Ma'āṣir-ul Umarā*, II, 409-10.

[37] *Akbarnāma*, III, 440, 468; *Ma'āṣir-ul Umarā*, II, 402-3.

[38] *Akbarnāma*, III, 471-2; *Ma'āṣir-ul Umarā*, 409-10.

[39] *Muntakhab-ut Tawārikh*, II, 345; *Ma'āṣir-ul Umarā*, II, 409-10.

battle against Muẓaffar, their place being as usual in the vanguard. Apart from Sayyid Qāsim, Sayyid Bāyazīd, Sayyid Salīm, Sayyid Bahādur and Sayyid Muṣtafa are also referred to during this period.[40]

In the year 1591-2 when 'Abdur Raḥīm Khān Khanān was despatched for the conquest of Thatta, the Sayyids of Bārha also accompanied him, for Sayyid Bahādur Bārha is said to have served in the flanks. After the conquest of Thatta, when 'Abdur Raḥīm Khān Khanān proceeded to the court, he left Sayyid Bahādur along with Ḥasan 'Alī to guard the country.[41]

When in 1591 Prince Murād was appointed governor of Malwa, Sayyid Rāju was placed under him.[42] When the emperor ordered Murād to return from the expedition against Madhukar, Rāju was left behind to tackle the rebel.[43]

After some time Prince Murād was deputed to the Deccan. Sayyid Rāju, Sayyid Qāsim and other Bārha Sayyids accompanied the prince, under 'Abdur Raḥīm Khān Khanān.[44] Owing to misunderstanding among the Mughal commanders, dissension arose in the camp, and this weakened the Mughal army when it besieged the fort of Ahmadnagar.[45] The enemy attacked the Mughal forces but retreated without achieving much success. In the battle Sayyid Rāju and Sayyid Ālam were killed. The emperor assigned the *jāgīr* of Sayyid Rāju to his sons.[46] In the meantime, Suhail Khān who had come with a big army to help Chand Bibi, challenged the Mughals. In the subsequent battle fought at Ashti, the Mughals suffered an initial reverse, finally, Khān Khanān defeated Suhail Khān with the help of Daulat Khān Lodī, Sayyid Qāsim and the Bārha Sayyids.[47]

After the death of Prince Murād, command of the Deccan forces was given to Prince Dāniyāl in 1599. In the same year Sayyid Qāsim was killed while fighting the Deccanis.[48]

[40] *Akbarnāma*, III, 524, 530-1; *Ma'āṣir-ul Umarā*, 409-10.

[41] *Akbarnāma*, III, 593-5, 597; *Ṭabaqāt*, II, 411, 413-14.

[42] *Akbarnāma*, III, 608-9, 633-4.

[43] Ibid., III, 598-600; *Ma'āṣir-ul Umarā*, II, 402-3.

[44] *Ma'āṣir-ul Umarā*, II, 402-3.

[45] *Akbarnāma*, III, 698-9; *Ma'āṣir-ul Umarā*, II, 403-4, 409-10, writes that Rāju was seconded to the Deccan command.

[46] *Ma'āṣir-ul Umarā*, II, 400-3; *Akbarnāma*, III, 698-701.

[47] *Akbarnāma*, III, 699-700; *Ma'āṣir-ul Umarā*, II, 402-3.

[48] *Z.K.*., I, 43-5; *Ma'āṣir-ul Umarā*, II, 402-3.

An interesting account of Khān Khanān's battle with Suhail Khān is given in these works. The details of the war show the great valour shown by the Bārha Sayyids and Daulat Khān Lodī.

In 1600 Shaikh Farīd Bukhārī along with a big army which included a contingent of Bārha Sayyids was sent to besiege Asirgarh.[49]

After 1600, there are no references to Bārha nobles in my sources until the last days of Akbar when the emperor was on his death bed. It appears that during this period Shaikh Farīd Bukhārī was their principal patron in the higher nobility.[50] It has been already seen that they had served under him earlier. During the last days of Akbar a conspiracy was planned by Mirzā 'Azīz Koka and Man Singh to arrest Salīm and enthrone his son Khusrau. But Shaikh Farīd collected his Bārha soldiers and went to offer allegiance to Prince Salīm.[51] The great support rendered by the Bārhas was generously rewarded by Jahāngīr after his accession. Sayyid 'Alī Aṣghar who was in personal service of the prince was promoted to the rank of 3,000 and given the title of Saif Khān.[52]

In the first regnal year (1605) Prince Khusrau rebelled. An army under the command of Shaikh Farīd along with a contingent of Bārha Sayyids under Saif Khān and Sayyid Jalāl was sent against him. The battle was unusually severe and the Bārha and Bukhārī Sayyids had to bear the brunt of the fight. The Bārhas, as usual, were in the vanguard and at one stage about 50 or 60 of them had to face some 1,500 Badakhshis. Fortunately Sayyid Kamāl Bukhārī came to their rescue; even then Sayyid Jalāl was killed and Saif Khān severely wounded. Saif Khān was promoted to the rank of 2,000/1,000.[53] Later on during the fourth regnal year (1609) Saif Khān was assigned the *faujdāri* of Hisar and received a further promotion to the rank of 2,500/1,350.[54]

In the fifth regnal year (1610) certain Bārha nobles such as Adam Bārha and Sayyid 'Alī, both from Gujarat were favoured.

Next year Sayyid Ādam was killed while fighting the Afghān leader 'Usmān, in Bengal.[55]

In 1613 Khurram was sent against the Rana of Mewar. It would appear that Saif Khān was also deputed with him, because, at his

[49] *Akbarnāma*, III, 757. [50] Ibid., 767.

[51] *Halat-i Asad Beg*, 52, 53; *Akbarnāma*, III, 797-8. Also see Chapter II.

[52] *Tuzuk*, 13-14; *Ma'āṣir-ul Umarā*, II, 410-11; but there is no reference of *manṣab* being given to him at this stage.

[53] *Tuzuk*, 40; *Ma'āṣir-ul Umarā*, II, 410-11.

[54] *Tuzuk*, 75; *Ma'āṣir-ul Umarā*, II, 410-11.

[55] *Tuzuk*, 86-7, 166, 209-10. Sayyid 'Alī was promoted to the rank 1,500/700.

request, the *manṣab* of Saif Khān was increased to 3,000/1,500. Hizabr Khān Bārha was also deputed to the same expedition.[56]

In 1615 Saif Khān Bārha, Sayyid 'Alī Bārha and 'Abdullah Bārha were raised to the ranks of 3,000/1,000/, 1,500/1,000 and 700/450 respectively. In the following year (1616) Sayyid Dilāwar's son, Sayyid Qāsim, was also promoted to the rank of 800/450.[57]

In 1616 news of the death of Saif Khān was conveyed to the emperor. He died in the Deccan, which suggests that he had been transferred there from Ajmer along with Prince Khurram when the latter was appointed viceroy of the Deccan. His two minor sons, 'Alī Muḥammad and Bahādur were given ranks of 600/400 and 400/200, and his nephew Sayyid 'Alī Bārha was also promoted to the rank of 2,000/1,500. In the same manner Sayyid Qāsim Bārha was also promoted to the rank of 1,000/600.[58]

In 1617 Sayyid 'Abdullah came from the Deccan with the news of the peace reached with the Deccanis. He was given a *jāgīr* worth 2,000,000 *dams* in return for communicating this joyful news to the emperor, and received the title of Saif Khān.[59]

While the emperor was in Gujarat in 1618, he promoted certain Bārha nobles who were serving in that province. Sayyid Hizabr Khān was promoted to the rank of 1,000/400; Sayyid Bāyazīd and others were also rewarded in the like manner.[60] In the same year Ṣafi Bārha, and his brethren were killed in the Kangra campaign against Surajmal.[61]

'Izzat Khān, who was serving in Bangash at the request of Mahābat Khān, had his *manṣab* increased to 1,500/800. In the same year his brother 'Abdul Wahāb Bārha was given the title of Dilér Khān and his *manṣab* was increased to 1,000/500, in reward for his service in Gujarat. He was appointed *faujdār* of Baroda.[62]

During the emperor's visit to Kashmir in 1620, news of the death of 'Izzat Khān was received from Bangash. He had been deputed by Mahābat Khān to go to the hill country and ravage the crops of the

[56] *Tuzuk*, 127; *Ma'āṣir-ul Umarā*, II, 410-11, 415-16, mentions the appointment against the Rana.

[57] *Tuzuk*, 148, 146, 138, 159.

[58] Ibid., 159, 163. Si-sad for *zāt* rank of 'Alī Muḥammad should really read *Shash-sad*; and this has been assumed in our text. *Ma'āṣir-ul Umarā*, II, 410-11 does not mention about *manṣab* being given to his son.

[59] *Tuzuk*, 188-9.

[60] Ibid., 228-30.

[61] Ibid., 254-5.

[62] Ibid., II, 40, 73; *Ma'āṣir-ul Umarā*, II, 493-4.

Afghāns. The Afghāns entrapped him and assaulting from all sides killed him and his brothers. Jahāngīr had a great regard for 'Izzat Khān and his family. Therefore, both *manṣab* and *jāgīr* were given to his minor son, 'so that those left behind should not be scattered about, and others might have increased hope'. At the same time Dilér Khān, a brother of 'Izzat Khān, was also promoted to the rank of 1,000/800.[63]

In the same year Hizabr Khān was deputed with Khān-i Jahān Lodī to Multan. He was promoted to the rank of 1,500/600 and ordered to proceed along with his sons Sayyid 'Alī and 'Abdul Ḥādī.[64]

In 1622 Khurram was ordered to march to Qandhar with all his troops. But the prince preferred to remain in Mandu till the rainy season. Jahāngīr thereupon ordered the prince to despatch immediately all great *amirs*, the Bārha and Bukhārī Sayyids to court.[65] It is not known whether Khurram complied with the orders, but certain Bārha nobles were with him when he openly rebelled. Sayyid Khān Jahān and Sayyid Shujā'at Khān, who were in the personal service of the prince, are referred to in all our sources.[66] But at the same time many of the Bārha nobles remained loyal to the emperor. When the imperial armies were deputed to fight the rebels, in the battle of Bilochpur, the Bārha Sayyids were placed under the command of 'Abdullah Khān Fīroz Jang. Although 'Abdullah Khān deserted in the midst of the battle, the Bārhas remained firm and loyal and many of them were killed. After the battle, Sayyid Bahwa was promoted to the rank of 2,000/1,500.[67]

When an army was appointed to pursue the rebels under Parvez and Mahābat Khān, along with others, Hizabr Khān was also deputed with them.[68]

Hereafter we have very little information regarding the activities of the Bārhas. However, in the rebel camp, Shujā'at Khān and Khān-i Jahān accompanied the prince in all his marches. When the prince proceeded towards Bengal, Sayyids Khān-i Jahān fought a battle with Ibrāhīm Khān Fateh Jang and defeated him; the Sayyid remained

[63] *Tuzuk*, II, 307-8.

[64] Ibid., 191, 196.

[65] Ibid., 345.

[66] *Z.K.*, 118b, 119b. A brief biography of Sayyid Khān-i Jahān and Sayyid Ja'far Shujā'at Khān has been given by the author. *Ma'āṣir-ul Umarā*, I, 758-9; II, 423-4.

[67] *Tuzuk*, 357-8; *Ma'āṣir-ul Umarā*, I, 493-4.

[68] *Tuzuk*, 360-1; *Ma'āṣir-ul Umarā*, II, 415-16.

loyal to Khurram throughout.[69] But Shujā'at Khān left the prince after his defeat at the battle of Tons; and when he came to know that the prince wished to proceed to Iran, he went home.[70]

Khurram after being defeated fled towards the Deccan. As Bhim was killed at Bilochpur, he made over the *ṣūba* of Gujarat to 'Abdullah Khān who, in turn, appointed his servant Wafadar to take charge. The officers of Gujarat under Mirzā Safi and Dilér Khān Bārha expelled Wafadar. When 'Abdullah Khān came to know of it he rushed to defend Ahmadabad, but he was also defeated by Ṣafi (later Saif Khān)[71] and Dilér Khān Bārha. For his meritorious service Dilér Khān was promoted to the rank of 2,000/1,200.[72] It was at this time that Jahāngīr remarked on their bravery and quoted Azīz Koka as saying that 'the Sayyids of Bārha were the averters of clamity for the Mughāl dominion', and added that such was in reality the case.[73]

In 1623, while the imperial armies were in Ahmadabad under Parvez and Mahābat Khān, a strange event took place, in which the Bārha Sayyids and the Rajputs came to blows. One of the brothers of Sayyid Kabīr Bārha had some grievance against a cutler whose shop was near Raja Girdhar's lodging. This minor event turned into an armed affray between the Rajputs and the Sayyids. Sayyid Kabīr also came to his kinsmen's help. Raja Girdhar and his Rajputs closed doors to protect themselves. The Sayyids set fire to the door, entered the house and killed Girdhar and his 26 servants. Some Sayyids were also killed. When the Rajputs came to know of it, they armed themselves and so did the Bārhas. The Rajputs assembled in a plain outside the citadel. Mahābat Khān having been informed of it, rushed to the place and soothed the Rajputs. He took some of the chief men of the Rajputs and went to the house of Khān-i 'Ālam. Parvez also reached Khān-i 'Alam's house. Mahābat Khān promised to conduct an inquiry into the matter. The crisis was averted for the moment, but the Rajputs could not be pacified until Sayyid Kabīr was arrested and later on executed.[74]

The progress of events suggests that the Bārhas had some sympathy for Khurram. When Jahāngīr died, Dilér Khān who was

[69] *Z.K.*, 118b; *Ma'āṣir-ul Umarā*, I, 758; II, 423-4.

[70] *Z.K.*, 118b; *Ma'āṣir-ul Umarā*, I, 758; II, 423-4.

[71] He was an Irānī officer.

[72] *Tuzuk*, 362-4, 366.

[73] Ibid., 269.

[74] *Tuzuk*, 274-5.

in Gujarat was the first to come forward and render homage to Shāhjahān.[75] Hizabr Khān was with Āṣaf Khān at the time of Jahāngīr's death, and fought against Shahryār.[76] It appears that Shāhjahān also had great regard for them. After his accession no less than seven persons of the Bārha families were promoted. Sayyid Shujā'at Khān who had deserted him was recalled from his home town and granted *a manṣab* of 4,000/400, 2,000 *du aspa sih aspa*.[77]

[75] *Ma'āṣir-ul Umarā*, I, 493-4.

[76] *Ma'āṣir-ul Umarā*, II, 415-16.

[77] The *Bādshāhnāma* mentions the *manṣabdars* of the Bārha family for the first ten years of Shahjahan's reign.

Sayyid Khān-i Jahān	5,000/5,000 *du aspa sih aspa*
Shujā'at Khān	4,000/4,000, 2,000 *du aspa sih aspa*
Sayyid Dilér Khān	4,000/3,000
Hizabr Khān	3,000/1,000
Sayyid 'Ālam Bārha	2,000/800
Sayyid Makhan Bārha	900/500.

CHAPTER VI

The Family of Shaikh Salīm Chishtī

The rise of the family of Shaikh Salīm Chishtī of Fatehpur-Sikri goes back to Akbar's time, though its members attained really large *manṣabs* only during the reign of Jahāngīr. It may be useful to consult the family chart (in Appendix B), which has been compiled from the scattered references to its members in various contemporary sources.[1]

Shaikh Salīm Chishtī was the son of Shaikh Bahāuddīn, a reputed descendant of Shaikh Farīd Ganj-i Shakar. The family originally belonged to Delhi where Shaikh Salīm was born in 1479. He visited various Muslim countries after which he settled at Sikri, about 30 km from Agra. Another branch of the family settled at Badaun. But the two branches continued to have close links, and contemporary historians considered them as one. The father of Quṭbuddīn Khān, a foster brother of Jahāngīr, and a grandson of Shaikh Salīm, belonged to the Badaun branch.[2]

Shaikh Salīm Chishtī enjoyed great reputation as a mystic and attracted Akbar's attention. As is well known, Akbar sent his wives to Sikri to give birth to sons under the protection of the Shaikh. The first son born at Sikri was Salīm (the later Jahāngīr).[3] The Shaikh died in 1570. Since Akbar had great regard for the Shaikh's family, the Shaikh's sons, grandsons and sons-in-law received offices. The Shaikh's own daughter served as a foster mother to Prince Salīm, so that her son Quṭbuddīn Khān was recognized as Salīm's foster brother (*koka*).

[1] In the course of my study, I came across an excellent Urdu history of the family, *Nawab Farīd* by Sultan Haider Josh, printed at Nizami Press, Badaun in 1917, which heavily draws on family traditions said to be preserved in MS. The genealogy reconstructed by me from contemporary sources is confirmed by this work. But the chart prepared by me is much fuller. Josh's work also throws light on many other aspects of the history of the family.

[2] *Akbarnāma*, II, 343-4; *Muntakhab*, II, 12; *Akhbār-ul Akhyār*, 176-7. Cf. *Nawab Farīd*, 10-2.

[3] *Akbarnāma*, II, 343-5.

Shaikh Aḥmad, a son of Shaikh Salīm, is the first person known to have joined service under Akbar. In 1573 when Akbar marched to Gujarat he was left along with his cousin, Shaikh Ibrāhīm and other officers at the capital.[4] He also acted as guardian *(atāliq)* of Prince Salīm. Shaikh Aḥmad died in 1577 at Ajmer, holding the rank of 500.[5] About this time, Shaikh Ibrāhīm, his cousin, was appointed to the *thanedari* of Ladlai in *ṣūba* Ajmer.[6] In the following year (1578) he was given charge of 'the *ṣūba* of capital' (*iyalat-i Ṣūba-i darul khilafa*).[7] It appears that he continued to hold this position till 1581 because when Akbar marched into the Panjab against Mirzā Ḥakīm, and Prince Dāniyāl was left at the capital, Shaikh Ibrāhīm was among the officers left to assist the prince.[8] Conditions became complicated with the arrival at Fatehpur Sikri of Shāhbāz Khān Kamboh who for about ten months took the reins of administration in his hands and started assigning *Khālṣa* lands in *jāgīrs* without seeking the permission of the emperor.[9] From a letter of Abū'l Fatḥ it emerges that Shaikh Ibrāhīm remained at Fatehpur and at least in the view of Abū'l Fatḥ's brother administered Fatehpur Sikri very competently. Shaikh Ibrāhīm also refused to accept Shāhbāz Khān's assignment of *pargana* Mahawana in *jāgīr* to him without the orders of the emperor and only acted as *Karorī* of the area.[10]

In 1582 Ibrāhīm was despatched to Bengal to help Mirzā Azīz Koka; he remained there till 1584.[11] He was thereupon appointed governor of Agra along with Raja Askaran in 1586 when two governors were appointed in each *ṣūba*. Shaikh Ibrāhīm held this office till his death in 1591.[12]

In the closing years of Akbar's reign, Shaikh Bāyazīd (later Mu'aẓẓam Khān) a grandson of Shaikh Salīm, was granted a *manṣab* of 2,000.[13] Prince Salīm patronized Shaikh Khūbu (later Quṭbuddīn Khān), his foster brother, and Shaikh Kabīr (later Shujā'at Khān). Both of them were his close associates at Allahabad.[14]

[4] *Akbarnāma*, III, 43. [5] Ibid., 212. [6] Ibid., 220.

[7] Ibid., 236-7. [8] Ibid., 337. [9] Muntakhab, II, 296.

[10] Abū'l Fateh Gilani, *Ruqqat-i Ḥakīm Abul Fatḥ Gilani*, ed. Dr. Mohd. Bashir Aḥmad, Idarh-i Tahqiqat Pakistan, Danishgah Panjab, Lahore, 1967, 37-8. See Afzal Husain, 'The letters of Ḥakīm 'Abul Fateh Gilani — An unexplored source of Akbar's reign', *Indian History Congress*, 1984, 189-97.

[11] *Akbarnāma*, III, 384, 389, 398, 435-6.

[12] Ibid., III, 511-12, 596. In *Z.K.*, I, 219, Shaikh Ibrāhīm is described as son-in-law and sister's son of Shaikh Salīm Chishtī.

[13] *Tuzuk*, 13. [14] Ibid., 12-13.

The later developments in the fortunes of this family may be viewed in the context of the political crisis that ensued with the illness and death of Akbar. The mistrust that this generated in Jahāngīr towards the old (Akbarshāhī) section of nobles forced him to encourage a new group of nobles thought to be completely faithful to him. As a result, those persons, many of whom had been personal servants of his, when a prince, were given rapid promotions. Owing to its members' personal attachment to Jahāngīr, Shaikh Salīm's family benefited from the new policy. At the death of Akbar the family held *manṣabs* totalling 3,200 *zāt*.[15] But soon after his accession, Shaikh Bāyazīd was given the title of Mu'aẓẓam Khān and was promoted from 2,000 to the rank of 3,000. He was also made governor of Delhi in 1606.[16] Shaikh 'Alāuddin 'Islām Khān and Shaikh Kabīr 'Shujā'at Khān were also promoted to the ranks of 2,000 and 1,000 respectively.[17] Quṭbuddīn Khān was given the very high rank of 5,000/5,000 and appointed governor of Bengal and Orissa.[18] His son, Shaikh Ibrāhīm was given the rank of 1,000/300.[19] As a result of these promotions, the total number of *manṣabs* held in the family came to 12,500 *zāt* and 6,000 *sawār* in 1606.[20]

Quṭbuddīn Khān's term as governor of Bengal proved to be very brief. In the second regnal year he was ordered to send Sher Afgan to the court as 'it was not right to leave such a mischievous person there'. Quṭbuddīn Khān immediately proceeded to Burdwan, which was Sher Afgan's *jāgīr* and summoned him to an interview. As he entered the camp, Quṭbuddīn Khān ordered him surrounded. Sher Afgan grew suspicious and when Quṭbuddīn advanced to explain the matter, he drew his sword and struck down the governor. Upon this a struggle started in which Aiba (Amba) Khān Kashmiri, a relation

[15] Shaikh Bāyazīd 2,000 *zāt*; Shaikh Khūbu 500 *zāt* Shaikh Kabīr 500 *zāt*; and Shaikh 'Alāuddīn 200 *zāt*.

[16] *Tuzuk*, 32, 37; *Z.K.* (MS) 94ab; *Ma'āṣir-ul Umarā* III, 365-6.

[17] *Tuzuk*, 12-13; *Iqbālnāma*, 24, 38; *Z.K.* (MS), 79a-80a.

[18] *Tuzuk*, 55, 81; *Ma'āṣir-ul Umarā*, I, 483-4.

[19] *Tuzuk*, 36; *Z.K.*. (MS), 76a.

[20] The following nobles were promoted:

(i) Mu'aẓẓam Khān 3,000 (*Tuzuk*, 32)
(ii) Quṭbuddīn Khān 5,000/5,000 (Ibid., 37, 68)
(iii) Islām Khān 2000 (Ibid., 13)
(iv) Shuja-at Khān 1,500/700 (Ibid., 54)
(v) Kishwar Khān 1,000/300 (Ibid., 36).

of Quṭbuddīn Khān, and Sher Afgan were cut to pieces. Quṭbuddīn Khān succumbed to his injuries shortly afterwards.[21] A detailed description of the incident is provided by an eye-witness Haidar Malik in his *Tārikh-i Kashmir*. He says that Quṭbuddīn Khān had previously told his officers that Sher Afghan had to be either killed or arrested.[22]

European travellers apparently conveying a view that gained popular currency, held Jahāngīr responsible for the murder of Sher Afgan. Beni Prasad relying upon the silence of the Persian histories rejects the travellers' suspicions and rules out any conspiracy against Sher Afgan.[23] But Haidar Malik's narrative suggests that Sher Afgan's suspicions were not unjustified though the subsequent career of his wife, Nūr Jahān, was bound to inject romantic elements into later narratives of the episode.

Jahāngīr's great regard for Quṭbuddīn Khān comes out from the terms in which he describes his death:

> What can I say of this unpleasantness. How grieved and troubled I became: Quṭbuddīn Khān was to me in place of a dear son, a kind brother and congenial friend.... After the departure of the late King (Akbar) and the death of that honoured one, no two misfortunes had happened to me like the death of the mother of Quṭbuddīn and his own martyrdom.[24]

Quṭbuddīn Khān's family was summoned to the court after his death and his two minor sons, Shaikh Fatḥuddīn and Shaikh Farīd, were kept under the care of the ladies of the ḥarem. Kishwar Khān (Shaikh Ibrāhīm), another son of his, was given charge of the fort of Rohtas.[25]

In 1607, Islām Khān, Shaikh Salīm's grandson, was appointed governor of Bihar in place of Jahāngīr Qulī Khān, who was transferred to Bengal after the death of Quṭbuddīn Khān. He was also promoted to the rank of 4,000/3,000. Upon the death of Jahāngīr Qulī in 1608, Islām Khān was made governor of Bengal and *atāliq*

[21] *Tuzuk* 54-5; *Iqbālnāma*, 24-5.

[22] Haidar Malik, *Tārikh-i Kashmir,* India office, 1100 Ethe 1/510.

[23] *History of Jahāngīr*, 166-8. Later Persian histories also held Jahāngīr responsible for the murder of Sher Afgan Cf. Khafi Khān, I, 265-7; Sujan Rai Bhandari, *Khūlāṣat-ul Tawārikh* (Delhi edn) 446-7.

[24] *Tuzuk*, 55.

[25] Ibid., 60; *Nawab Farıd*, 68-9, gives the information about the arrival of Quṭbuddin's family to the court.

of Prince Jahāndār, son of Emperor Jahāngīr.[26] Jahāngīr writes that when he was appointed to this duty 'most of the servants of the state made remarks on his youth and want of experience'.[27] But not only did Jahāngīr ignore such criticism, he promoted the young man to 5,000/5,000 in the following year.[28]

Sulṭān Haider, a modern scion of the family, gives a different version of the circumstances that led to Islām Khān's appointment as governor of Bengal. According to him, the family of Shaikh Salīm had become quite powerful after the accession of Jahāngīr, and Islām Khān had raised a contingent of 20,000 Shaikhzāda retainers under him. The growing power of the family became a great obstacle to the power of Nūr Jahān's family. Nūr Jahān, therefore, conspired to get him appointed as governor of Bengal. Although it was an important appointment, the main purpose behind this move was to send him away from the court. Moreover, as the Afghāns were still offering great resistance to the imperial forces, the strength of the family was expected to suffer in the struggle against them. Sulṭān Haider adds that Nūr Jahān actually succeeded in her mission: although Islām Khān defeated Usmān Khān Afghān, in the course of his wars against him (Usmān) a large number of his relations and Shaikhzadās were killed. Consequently the influence and power of the family declined. He further says that the members of the family came to know of Nūr Jahān's conspiracy when Shaikh Fatḥuddīn, son of Quṭbuddīn Khān, suddenly died in the harem. They complained that Shaikh Fatḥuddīn was poisoned at the instance of Nūr Jahān and pleaded that Shaikh Farīd, the other son, who was still in the ḥarem might be permitted to go to Badaun. Jahāngīr refused to permit him to go to Badaun, but he was taken out from the ḥarem and given into the care of I'timad Khān, brother of Nūr Jahān.[29]

This information is not corroborated by any other contemporary or near contemporary sources except for the fact that Islām Khān has indeed been credited with possessing 20,000 retainers under him.[30] While it may be accepted that the appointment of Islām Khān to Bengal was partly due to the military contingent he had been able to raise, the alleged conspiracy of Nūr Jahān to send him off

[26] *Tuzuk*, 8, 68; *Iqbālnāma*, 38; *Z.K.* (MS), 79a-80a.
[27] *Tuzuk*, 68-9, *Iqbālnāma*, 64. [28] *Tuzuk*, 74. [29] *Nawab Farīd*, 67-9.
[30] *Z.K.*, II, 191-3.

to Bengal can hardly be true since she did not marry Jahāngīr till 1611, and her family until then was hardly in a position to wield any influence. The *Tuzuk* and *Iqbālnāma-i Jahāngīrī* give very little information about his activities in Bengal;[31] but the author of *Bahāristān-i Ghaibī*, Mirzā Nāthan who served under Islām Khān gives ample information to prove that during his tenure of office in Bengal he behaved very autocratically, and his relations with the court were not very friendly. Mirzā Nāthan speaks of Islām Khān's arrogant conduct towards the officers posted in Bengal, and specifically mentions his hostility towards Ihtimām Khān and Bahādur Qalmāq.[32] Thus, it is possible that there is a kernel of truth in the story reported by Haider, though as often happens in such traditions, the name of Nūr Jahān has been inserted to represent court circles' hostile to the family.

Islām Khān became so powerful that he came to enjoy full control over the governor of Orissa also. When Shujā'at Khān was sent to help him, he appointed him governor of Orissa in place of Raja Kalyan, without the prior permission of the imperial court.[33] He also gave orders that no one should be allowed to enter Bengal from 'Hindustan' or leave it without his permission. He rigorously enforced this order and an imperial officer Shaikh Ḥusain, who was on way to meet the governor, was detained by Shaikh Aḥmad at Akbarnagar (Rajmahal).[34] Similarly, Raja Kalyan the governor of Orissa who was proceeding to the court was detained at Akbarnagar. When these incidents were reported to the emperor, Shaikh Aḥmad's *manṣab* and *jāgīr* were confiscated and he was summoned to the court; but Islām Khān refused to send him back.[35]

Islām Khān also assumed certain royal prerogatives. Mirzā Nāthan says,

> He prepared a high platform higher than the height of two men and constructed a small house on it. It was named *jharokhā*, the great officers who could not attend to pay respect at *chauki*, were ordered to depute one of their sons or near relations in their place and they were ordered to pass their nights at the royal guard house. The other officers were directed to make their obeisance standing at the *qur* (standard).[36]

[31] Cf. *Tuzuk*, 101-5, *Iqbālnāma*, 60-3.

[32] *Bahāristān-i Ghaibī*, I, 72, 115-17.

[33] Ibid., I, 160, 219. [34] Ibid., I, 132-3. [35] Ibid., 144-5.

[36] Ibid., 120.

Shaikh Ḥusain, an imperial officer, who had come to him from the court, was also not spared and was forced to offer *kornish*.[37]

Regarding Islām Khān's war with Usmān Afghān, Mirzā Nāthan states that for a long time no progress was made and nobles at the court questioned Islām Khān's competence. When Jahāngīr wrote to Islām Khān in this connection, he asked that Shujā'at Khān along with his brothers and relations be sent to his help. Jahāngīr agreed and Shujā'at Khān who was serving in the Deccan was summoned and sent to Bengal, along with his brothers.[38] Kishwar Khān from Rohtas and Qāsim Khān, brother of Islām Khān, from Monghyr, were also ordered to proceed to his help. Mukarram Khān along with his brothers and Shaikh Achhey, a relation of Islām Khān, also accompanied Shujā'at Khān.[39] Islām Khān appointed Shujā'at Khān as governor of Orissa; Shujā'at Khān despatched his son Shaikh Quṭub as his deputy to Orissa and himself joined the campaign against Usmān.[40]

According to Mirzā Nāthan Jahāngīr now seems to have set up Shujā'at Khān to subvert Islām Khān's power. Shujā'at Khān was not only given the title of Rustam-i Zamān and promoted to the rank of 6,000/6,000 *du aspa sih aspa* but appointed governor of Bengal in place of Islām Khān. Islām Khān was given the option of remaining in Bengal under Shujā'at Khān or coming back to the court.[41] About this time Shaikh Husain arrived at the court and informed the emperor of Islām Khān's high handedness, and presumption. On this, an ordinance containing 17 points of admonition was issued to the *ṣūbedars* and particularly to Islām Khān, to be observed without the slightest deviation.[42] Islām Khān's *manṣab* was also reduced to 3,000/3,000 from 5,000/5,000, on the charge that he had not accompanied Shujā'at Khān against Usmān and had instead sent Kishwar Khān, Quṭbuddīn's son, who died in the campaign. But despite these punishments, Islām Khān continued to be governor and to sit in the *jharokhā*.[43]

These details from *Bahāristān-i Ghaibī*, are not fully corroborated by either the *Tuzuk-i Jahāngīrī* or the *Iqbālnāma-i Jahāngīrī*;[44]

[37] Ibid., 132-3. [38] Ibid., I, 157-9. [39] Ibid., 158-9.
[40] Ibid., 160, 219. [41] Ibid., 211. [42] Ibid., I, 213-14.
[43] Ibid., 214-15.
[44] Cf. *Tuzuk*, 101-4, and *Iqbālnāma*, 60-3, where the campaign against Usmān has been discussed.

but a close examination supports the view that Nāthan's account contains much truth. Although the *Tuzuk-i Jahāngīrī* states that Islām Khān overthrew Usmān Afghān, it also records the fact that Islām Khān had not led the campaign and the victory was achieved by Shujā'at Khān, who was given the title of *Rustam-i Zamān* though the rank assigned to him now was only 3,000/2,500 and not 6,000/ 6,000 *du aspa sih aspa*, as reported by Nāthan.[45] According to the *Tuzuk* it was, Islām Khān who was promoted to the rank of 6,000/ 6,000.[46]

The text of the ordinance containing prohibitions of presumptuous practices is reproduced in the *Tuzuk* as a *dastural-'amal*; it was a general order for the governors of 'frontier provinces' whereas Nāthan refers to Islām Khān as its particular recipient and adds details of regulations not found in the order quoted in the *Tuzuk*.

The appointment of Shujā'at Khān as governor of Bengal, and the curtailment of Islām Khān's *manṣab* and his dismissal from the governorship are not corroborated at all by the *Tuzuk*. However, the sudden accidental death of Shujā'at Khān is intriguing;[47] and one may think that it was this which prevented Jahāngīr's order for the dismissal of Islām Khān from taking effect.

Islām Khān too died in the following year.[48] Upon his death Jahāngīr ordered that till the appointment of a new governor, the seniormost officer of Bengal should take over the administration of the *ṣūba*; if an officer of that status was not present, the governor of Bihar should take charge. Accordingly, Ẓafar Khān, the governor of Bihar, proceeded to Bengal, but Islām Khān's son Hushang, did not allow him to take charge of the *ṣūba* on the plea that he had not received the imperial order. Shortly afterwards, Qāsim Khān, brother of Islām Khān, was appointed governor and promoted to the rank of 5,000/4,000.[49]

Hushang appears to have been unhappy with this appointment and left Bengal without the permission of the new governor. Qāsim Khān sent his son, Shaikh Farīd, to detain him, but he avoided Farīd and proceeded to the court. Qāsim Khān took into his custody a number of Hushang's servants and tortured them. He also seized

[45] *Tuzuk*, 102-4. [46] Ibid. [47] Ibid., 110-11.

[48] *Bahāristān-i Ghaibī*, I, 218-19; *Tuzuk*, 125-6; *Iqbālnāma*, 72.

[49] *Bahāristān-i Ghaibī*, I, 258; *Tuzuk*, 136 states that he was given rank of 4,000/ 4,000.

Rs.20,000 belonging to Islām Khān. When the Emperor came to know of Hushang's departure from Bengal, he ordered him to stay there. But Hushang paid no heed and continued his journey. When he reached the court 'the Emperor in consideration of the prestigeof the family of Shaikh Salīm did not take exception to this wrong action and granted him an interview'.[50] In 1615, Hushang was raised to the rank of 1,500/700 and made *faujdār* of Fatehpur.[51]

Qāsim Khān also behaved in the same manner as his brother. He completely sealed the frontiers of the *ṣūba*; even the reports of the *waqi'a-navis* were not permitted to go without his approval and scrutiny. He was also accused of misbehaving with his subordinates.[52] On account of this he was reprimanded but pardoned 'in consideration of the services of the Chishtī family' and advised to behave with all the officers of the state according to their status in a friendly manner. But he did not improve his behaviour, and so was dismissed and summoned to the court.[53]

Qāsim Khān started from Bengal along with all the elephants, pieces of artillery, and the fleet of boats that he had at his command. Certain chiefs of Bengal and imperial *manṣabdars* also accompanied him. When Ibrāhīm Khān who was appointed governor of Bengal came to know of this, he wrote to him to surrender the animals and equipment. Qāsim Khān declined to do so, and a battle was fought, in which Qāsim Khān was badly defeated. He killed his wives fearing their humiliation, and started for the court. After his arrival he was not given any assignment for several years.[54]

In the year, when Qāsim Khān was dismissed from Bengal, Mukarram Khān of the Chishtī family was appointed governor of Orissa and promoted to the rank of 3,000/2,000. But in 1619, he was also removed and not given any appointment.[55]

[50] *Bahāristān-i Ghaibī*, I, 268-9.

[51] *Tuzuk*, 145; *Z.K.* (MS), 94b.

[52] *Bahāristān-i Ghaibī*, I, 269-70.

[53] *Tuzuk*, 185, mentions the dismissal without giving any specific reasons but it also refers obliquely to his bad conduct. Jahāngīr writes, 'As for a long time no good has been heard of the affairs of Bengal and of the conduct of Qāsim Khān, it entered my mind to send to the *ṣūba* of Bengal Ibrāhīm Khān Fatḥ-i Jang.... I sent for Qāsim Khān to court' (R.B.I, 373). Mirzā Nāthan has cited several acts of misbehaviour, particularly his hostility towards Mirzā Ḥusain Beg, the *Diwān* of Bengal, and his brothers, Raja Parakshit Narayan, the Raja of Kuch, and Mukhlis Khān (*Bahāristān-i Ghaibī*, I, 286-7, 290-3, 310-14).

[54] Ibid., I, 436-7. No other source gives these details.

[55] *Tuzuk*, 220, 223; also see, 'The Family of Nūr Jahān during Jahāngīr's Reign — a Political Study', 90-4.

Thus by 1619 the position of the family both in terms of *manṣabs* and numerical strength had declined considerably. Table 6.1. (based on the *Tuzuk*) shows the fortunes of the family at different years during the reign of Jahāngīr.[56]

The ascent of the family of Shaikh Salīm itself, no doubt, lends some substance to Mirzā Azīz's charge that Jahāngīr tended to favour Indian Muslims. Initially starting from 3500 *zāt* this Shaikhzāda family was raised to 15,500/12,000 in 1612. But it may be remembered that the promotions were given primarily on account of Jahāngīr's close association with the family of Shaikh Salīm from the time of his birth, and not necessarily because of any deliberate policy of encouraging Indian Muslims. While promoting Islām Khān to the rank of 2,000 he writes. 'He had grown up with me from his child-hood and may be a year younger than I.'[57] Similarly, about Shujā'at Khān he says, 'I had honoured him with the title of Shujā'at Khān when I was prince, on account of his manliness and bravery. I now selected him for the rank of 1000.'[58] Quṭbuddīn Khān and other members of the family were also promoted on the same grounds.

The decline in the fortunes of the family is rather difficult to explain, although it is possible that it went into shade partly as a result of the increasing prominence of Nūr Jahān's family with which, owing to the fatal incident between Quṭbuddīn and Sher Afgan, relations were unlikely to have been friendly. The author of *Nawab Farīd* writes that Āṣaf Khān married his second daughter Shahpara Begum to Shaikh Farīd, Quṭbuddīn's son in 1618-19; but despite this relations remained strained between Nūr Jahān and this family.[59] But there is no known contemporary authority for this particular marriage.

Table 6.1

Year	*Zāt*	*Sawār*
1605	3,200	-
1606	12,500	6,000
1612	15,500	12,000
1619	5,000	3,500
1622	8,000	7,000

[56] For reference, see Appendix A–V and VI.

[57] *Tuzuk*, 13.

[58] *Tuzuk*, 12.

[59] *Nawab Farīd*, 71-2.

Certain high ranking nobles of Shaikh Salīms's family died during this period, and after their death, in accordance with custom their sons were not given the same high ranks as were held by their fathers.[60] In course of time, therefore, the family became increasingly less prominent. But Jahāngīr always kept them in high regard because of his respect for Shaikh Salīm. In 1619 when he promoted Ikrām to the rank of 2,000/1,500 and posted him to the *faujdāri* of Mewat, he took care to say, he 'is the son of Islām Khān who was grandson of the venerable asylum of pardon Shaikh Salīm, whose excellency of person and approved disposition and connection in blessing with this illustrious family have been described in these pages with the pen of sincerity'.[61]

Although by 1621, the family was much reduced in power, none of its members joined Shāhjahān during his rebellion. On the contrary in the crucial period Qāsim Khān was appointed governor of Allahabad, and Mukarram Khān, of Delhi.[62] Thereafter Mukarram Khān and Ikrām Khān were despatched to the Deccan to pursue Shāhjahān under Parvez.[63] At the end of Jahāngīr's reign, Ikrām Khān was given charge of Asirgarh, and Mukarram Khān was appointed governor of Bengal. But Mukarram Khān died before taking charge of the *ṣūba*.[64]

During the accession crisis following the death of Jahāngīr, Shaikh Farīd, who was serving under Āṣaf Khān, (supposedly his father-in-law according to family tradition), came out openly to support the candidature of Shāhjahān. But the attitude of other members of the family is not known to us. Shaikh Farīd was promoted to the rank of 1,500/600 after the accession of the Shāhjahān.[65] Yet the family's political fortunes were now eclipsed. The total number of *manṣabs* held by the family henceforth never exceeded 6,000/4,300.[66]

[60] After the death of Quṭbuddīn who held the rank of 5,000/5,000, his son could not rise above the rank of 2,000/2,000. Similarly, Islām Khān's son's highest rank was 2,000/1,500, although Islām Khān held the rank of 6,000/6,000 at his death.

[61] *Tuzuk*, 278. [62] Ibid., 220. [63] Ibid., 351-2.

[64] *Iqbālnāma*, 286. [65] *Bādshahnāma*, I, 184; *Nawab Farīd*, 87.

[66] Here is a list of persons who held *manṣabs* in Shāhjahān's reign:

(i) Shaikh Farīd son of Quṭbuddīn Khān -2500/1500 (*Bādshahnāma*, I, 229)
(ii) Ikrām Khān 2,000/100 (Ibid., 229)
(iii) Shaikh Allah Diya 1,000/700 (Ibid., 302)
(iv) Shaikh Quṭub 500/200 (Ibid., 329)

CHAPTER VII

The Family of Daulat Khān Lodī

The Lodī clan, which gave Delhi the Lodī dynasty, and to which this family also belonged, occupied a part of Roh (the hilly country south of Peshawar). Nuṣrat Khān, son of Malik Aḥmad Lodī, came to India during the reign of Sikandar Lodī. He joined Daulat Khān, the governor of Lahore, and married his niece. Nuṣrat Khān's brothers, Bahār Khān and Daulat Khān, also came to Lahore and were admitted to the service of Daulat Khān Lodī. The three brothers were given two *parganas*, Lali Khakhar and Lakhi Jungali in *jāgīr* by Daulat Khān Lodī. Sometimes afterwards Daulat Khān, the brother of Nuṣrat Khān, was given the title of Sher Khān Lodī.[1]

At the time of the conquest of India by Bābur, Daulat Khān (Sher Khān Lodī), along with his brothers and clansmen, fled to Bihar and entered the service of Sulṭān Maḥmūd, son of Sulṭān Sikandar Lodī, who had proclaimed himself king there.[2] Daulat Khān was granted some villages in *jāgīr* from the assignments of Sher Khān Sur, the *jāgīrdār* of Sahasram.[3] After the defeat of the Afghāns in the battle near Jaunpur, Daulat Khān who was seriously injured, escaped with his brother Nuṣrat Khān and left the profession of soldiery like many other Afghāns.[4] In 1539 when Sher Shāh Sur defeated Humāyūn at Chausa, Daulat Khān joined Sher Shāh's service with his brothers and became one of his trusted officers.[5] He was despatched as a guardian of Qutb Khān, Sher Shāh's son, to occupy certain Mughal possessions. But the chiefs proved false to their promise and both Qutb Khān and Daulat Khān were killed.[6] Sher Shāh paid tribute to

[1] For more details regarding the ancestry of Daulat Khān Sher Khān Lodī, see *Tārikh-i Khān Jahāni*, II, 442-6. Sikandar Lodī added two more *parganas* in their *jāgīr* when they went to court to pay their homage.

[2] *Tārikh-i Khān Jahāni*, II, 449-50.

[3] Ibid., 450.

[4] Ibid., 451.

[5] Ibid.

[6] Ibid., 451-2. The Mughāl officer who joined the Zamīndārs against Daulat Khān was Ulugh Khān.

Daulat Khān's services and summoned his four sons Maḥmūd Khān, Umar Khān, Qāsim Khān and Kamāl Khān. He gave them the *parganas* of Kampila, Patiyali, Saketa and Bhongaon in the Doab in *jāgīr*. Umar Khān remained at the court while the other brothers were sent to look after the *jāgīr*.[7]

During this period 'Ālam Khān Lodī, a prominent noble of Gujarat, came to the court of Sher Shāh. He was treated generously by Sher Shāh and his daughter was married to Umar Khān Lodī. Daulat Khān Lodī, father of Khāṇ Jahān, was the offspring of this marriage.[8]

The family's fortunes went into eclipse once again after the death of Islām Shāh, as they refused to accept the overlordship of Mubariz Khān, who had now seized the throne. 'Umar Khān was imprisoned at Chunar from where he escaped to Arail. His other brothers, however, remained in prison. When the Mughal armies marched towards Delhi after Humāyūn's conquest of Panjab, 'Umar Khān's brothers Maḥmūd Khān, Qāsim Khān and Kamāl Khān were brought out from prison and sent under Hemu to fight the Mughals. In the subsequent battle at Panipat, both Maḥmūd Khān and Qāsim Khān were killed. 'Umar Khān, hearing of these events, fled to Gujarat.[9] There his brother-in-law Mian Tātār Khān ('Ālam Khān II) introduced him to Sher Khān Faulādi. Not much is known about his life in Gujarat except that he also served for some time under Hājī Khān who gave him a village near Ahmadabad for his maintenance. There too he got Daulat Khān married to the daughter of Haybat Khān Bihlam, a noble of Gujarat.[10]

When the Mughals invaded Gujarat, 'Umar Khān was in the service of Muḥammad Khān (Sher Khān Fauladi's son). He was killed along with his master fighting against the Mughals. Daulat Khān who was also present in the battle, fled to Surat along with his clansmen.[11] Shortly afterwards when Shāh Abū Turāb joined Mughāl service, Daulat Khān was also invited by him and introduced to Mirzā 'Azīz Koka who took him in service and assigned

[7] Ibid., 453.

[8] Ibid., 454-6. Daulat Khān Lodī was born at Gwalior during the last days of Islām Shāh (1550).

[9] Ibid.

[10] Ibid., 459-60. There are no references to Umar Khān or his son, Daulat Khān, in *Mi'rat-i Sikandarī* and *Mir'āt-i Aḥmadi*.

[11] *Tarikh-i Khān Jahāni*, II, 462-3. There is no reference to Umar Khān and Daulat Khān in the accounts of the conquest of Gujarat either in *Akbarnāma*, III, 9-16 or in *Mi'rat-i Aḥmadi*.

him half of the *pargana* of Jhalawar in *jāgīr*.[12] However, Abū Turāb does not mention Daulat Khān in his memoirs at all.[13]

Daulat Khān came to the court along with Mirzā Azīz Koka in 1575. He was introduced to Akbar, who is said to have given him his own shawl.[14] But soon afterwards Azīz Koka was dismissed, and at the request of 'Abdur Rahīm, Mirzā Azīz entrusted Daulat Khān to him. Mirzā Azīz is said to have valued Daulat Khān so highly that he counselled 'Abdur Raḥīm to 'take care of this man, if you want to rise high and get your father's title'.[15] The author of *Zakhīrat-ul Khawānīn* also says that Akbar took personal interest in Daulat Khān's training; and he was given the rank of 1,000.[16] But this is a patent exaggeration, since the *Āʾīn-i Akbarī* assigns him a *manṣab* of 300 only.[17] Daulat Khān remained in the service of 'Abdur Raḥīm during the later part of his career, except for brief period of three years when his services were transferred to Prince Daniyal. As a soldier he distinguished himself in various campaigns, particularly in the battles fought against Muẓaffar Shāh of Gujarat and Mirzā Jānī Beg of Sind. After the victory over Mirzā Jānī Beg he was promoted to the rank of 2,000 and appointed deputy governor.[18] Later on, in the Deccan campaign also, he played an important role along with his two sons, Pīr Khān and Muḥammad Khān in defeating Suhail Khān.[19]

Prince Daniyal who was appointed viceroy of the Deccan in 1599, asked 'Abdur Raḥīm to transfer Daulat Khān to him as 'he had no brave man like him in the retinue'. Daniyal promoted Daulat Khān to the rank of 3,000 and granted him in *jāgīr* six *parganas*, including Kavi, from *sarkār* Gujarat, Dawalgaon and Khalgaon, Nakalur from Bhatta and others.[20] Daulat Khān died in 1602 while in the service of Prince Daniyal.[21]

12 *Tārikh-i Khān Jahāni*, II, 462-3. *Z.K.*, II, 69-70 mentions that Daulat Khān in his youth was in the employment of Mirzā Azīz Koka in Gujarat, but makes no reference to the grant of the *pargana* of Jhalawar. *Akbarnāma*, III, 785 briefly mentions that Daulat Khān was in the service of Mirzā Azīz Koka.

13 Mīr Abū Turāb Walī, *Tārikh-i Gujarat*, ed. Denson Ross, Asiatic Society of Bengal, 1909, 52-4.

14 *Tārikh-i Khān Jahāni*, II, 463. 15 *Z.K.*, II, 70. 16 Ibid.

17 *Āʾīn*, 164.

18 *Akbarnāma*, III, 454-5, 608-10, *Tārikh-i Khān Jahāni*, II, 474-6; *Z.K.*, I, 32-7. For his activities in Gujarat and Sind, see also Chapter I. The promotion in rank has been referred to by Farīd Bhakkari and Ni'amatullah only.

19 *Akbarnāma*, III, 700, 763; *Tārikh-i Khān Jahāni*, II, 474-6; *Z.K.*, I, 40-2.

20 *Tārikh-i Khān Jahāni*, II, 478-9; Ni'amatullāh adds that Dāniyāl gave him the title of *masnad-i Alī* and office of *Wakīl*. Abū'l Faẓl states that 'Dāniyāl made him his own servant and had advanced him to the rank of 2,000' (*Akbarnāma*, III, 785).

21 *Akbarnāma*, III, 785; *Tārikh-i Khān Jahāni*, II, 482-3.

There is some discrepancy regarding Daulat Khān's position in the accounts of the main chroniclers of Akbar's reign, where he is hardly mentioned, and those of the later *Tārikh-i Khān Jahāni* and the *Zakhīrat-ul Khawānīn*, which claim that he enjoyed considerable status. The author of the *Zakhirat-ul Khawānīn* reports an incident of gross misbehaviour on the part of Daulat Khān towards 'Abū'l Faẓl, which affected the relations between Abū'l Faẓl and 'Abdur Raḥīm for some time. We are further told that 'Abdur Raḥīm had 10,000 Afghān soldiers under him in the Deccan, and all of them were loyal to Daulat Khān.[22] An earlier incident of a similar nature is reported as early as in 1578 during the Mewar campaign where Daulat Khān had a brush with Shāhbāz Khān.[23] On the other hand, Daulat Khān is said to have maintained intimate relations with Man Singh.[24]

Daulat Khān was assigned certain duties directly by Akbar. In 1586 when Bhagwan Das allegedly lost his balance of mind, Daulat Khān was employed by the emperor to conduct Ḥakīm Ḥasan and Mahadeo to Attock for his treatment.[25] In 1594 when Akbar appointed certain officers to check the exactions of unauthorized tolls at ferries, Daulat Khān was given the task of ensuring compliance with the imperial ban from Lahore to Bengal.[26] These tasks did not, however, apparently mean that he had left 'Abdur Raḥīm's service, though they do show that Daulat Khān had attracted Akbar's attention.

It is a reflection of his high status that Prince Dāniyāl designated him his 'son'.[27] The low rank as recorded in the *Ā'īn* possibly is more reflective of Mughal apprehensions about the Afghāns. Daulat Khān's impulsive behaviour could also have been a hurdle in his promotion. Akbar is even said to have remarked at the time of Daulat Khān's death, 'Today Sher Khān Sur is dead'.[28]

Daulat Khān left two sons and one daughter. Both the sons had been unhappy with their father and fled to Bengal where Man Singh was the governor. But they could not stay there because the day they reached Gaur, they killed two nephews of Raja Man Singh. When they reached Man Singh after the incident, he gave them 3,000 rupees and a few horses although he had already come to know of the death

[22] *Z.K.*, II, 71.

[23] Ibid., I, 154.

[24] *Tārikh-i Khān Jahāni*, II, 472-3; *Z.K.*, II, 72-3.

[25] *Akbarnāma*, III, 492.

[26] Ibid., 670.

[27] *Z.K.*, II, 70. It is interesting that Daulat Khān's son Khān Jahān was designated as his 'son' by Daniyal and then by Jahāngīr.

[28] *Z.K.*, II, 70.

of his nephews. He ordered them to return to their father because he thought that the Rajputs might take revenge against them.[29]

After their return they entered the service first of 'Abdur Raḥīm Khān Khanān and later on of Prince Dāniyāl. Muḥammad Khān, the eldest son, was deeply religious and spent his time in the company of divines, but he remained a great favourite of the prince. Shortly afterwards he went half-mad and was killed by a group of Kolis and Bhils (near Burhanpur). He was survived by two sons Mian Mummrez Khān and Bahādur Khān, who remained in the service of their uncle.[30]

The second son, Pīr Khān was also very close to the prince who too used to call him 'son'. After the death of Prince Daniyal, he joined the service of 'Abdur Raḥīm Khān Khanān.[31]

A little after the accession of Jahāngīr, Pīr Muḥammad (Pīrā) gained great eminence, being raised to the rank of 5,000/5,000 and granted the title of Khān-i Jahān. The case of Khān-i Jahān's admission and subsequent promotion in service was slightly different from that of other Jahāngīrī nobles who were promoted after the accession. If we examine the list of nobles who were admitted and promoted to higher ranks it would appear that almost all of them were either in his personal service when he was a prince or helped him to secure the throne at the time of Akbar's illness and death. Khān-i Jahān Lodī, on the other hand, had apparently no contact with him until after Akbar's death. Hence, his induction into the highest echelons of Mughal aristocracy may be treated as a case of Jahāngīr's attempt to conciliate the Afghāns. We come across certain other Afghān nobles who were raised to high ranks by him.[32] The author of the *Tārikh-i Khān Jahāni* highlights this point when he wrote:

[29] *Tārikh-i Khān Jahāni*, II, 484-5; *Z.K.*, II, 72-3.

[30] *Tārikh-i Khān Jahāni*, II, 484-5; *Z.K.*, II, 73; *Takmila*, III, 802-3.

[31] *Tārikh-i Khān Jahāni*, II, 489-90; *Z.K.*, II, 72-3.

[32] Besides Khān-i Jahān the following Afghāns were also promoted to higher ranks and given important assignments in the early years of Jahāngīr.

(i) Dilāwar Khān Kakar, given *manṣab* of 1,500, and charge of Lahore, 1606 (*Tuzuk*, 23; *Iqbālnāma*, 7).

(ii) Sher Khān, *manṣab* of 3500, and charge of Peshawar and the Khaibar pass, 1607-8 (*Tuzuk*, 7, 49, 60).

(iii) Ghaznīn Khān Jalori, *manṣab* of 2,000/700, 1610 (*Tuzuk*, 85).

(iv) Mangali Khān, *manṣab* of 1,500/800 (*Tuzuk*, 146).

(v) Mubārak Khān Sarwānī, *manṣab* of 1,000/300 and *faujdār* of Hissar, 1607 (*Tuzuk*, 65, 76).

(vi) Tāj Khān held the charge of Thatta (*Tuzuk*, 131).

> He (Jahāngīr) gave so much attention to them (the Afghāns) that they gave up their hostile attitude and bound themselves in submission and attachment to him even at the sacrifice of their lives. By their distinguished service they raised themselves to the ranks of great nobles and became worthy of being admitted to the Emperor's company.[33]

This was perhaps made possible by the fact that the suspicion of the Afghāns which had haunted the Mughals earlier, might now have been moderated considerably after the firm foundation laid by Akbar for Mughal rule.

The author of the *Tārikh-i Khān Jahāni* asserts that even before his accession Jahāngīr had wished to take Pīr Muḥammad into his service, but Dāniyāl did not permit this.[34] After Dāniyāl's death and at the time of Jahāngīr's accession, Pīr Muḥammad was in the Deccan serving under 'Abdur Raḥīm Khān Khanān. Mirzā Alī Akbar who came to Jahāngīr's court from the Deccan after his accession highly praised him and Jahāngīr summoned him to the court through Muqarrab Khān. In April 1607, he came in the escort of the sons of Dāniyāl and presented himself before Jahāngīr at Lahore. He was immediately given the rank of 3,000/1,500 and the title of Ṣalābat Khān, along with the designation of *farzand* (son)[35] In the same year his title was changed to the much more exalted one of Khān-i Jahān, and the next year he was promoted to the rank of 5,000/5,000. He also became one of the most influential nobles at the court. Jahāngīr himself states: 'I promoted him beyond his fellows and equals. Today in my government there is none of greater influence than Khān Jahān, so much so that on his representation I pass over faults that are not pardoned at the intercession of any other servant of the court.'[36] These remarks were not made in any fit of excitement. The great influence that Khān-i Jahān came to enjoy with Jahāngīr is also attested to by other contemporary and near contemporary works like the *Iqbālnāma-i Jahāngīrī* and the *Zakhīrat-ul Khwānīn*. For example, in the second regnal year while the court was returning from Kabul, a conspiracy against Jahāngīr had been detected and a number of conspirators executed. According to Mu'tamid Khān, Āṣaf Khān's son Nuruddīn

[33] *Tārikh-i Khān Jahāni*, II, 489.

[34] Ibid., II, 486-92; Also see *Tuzuk*, 42-3.

[35] *Tuzuk*, 42-3; *Iqbālnāma*, 30-1; *Z.K.*, II, 74. *Tārikh-i Khān Jahāni*, II, 492 mentions that after reaching Lahore he received the rank of 2,000.

[36] *Tuzuk*, 66.

would also have been executed, but for Khān-i Jahān's intercession.[37] Similarly, in the same year, he is said to have intervened and saved Mirzā Azīz from being executed.[38] Ni'amatullah states that Khān-i Jahān also saved Man Singh and other Rajputs from being exiled from the empire.[39] Farīd Bhakkari writes that Jahāngīr was so pleased with him that he even wished him to marry into the Mughal royal family, to be given the title of *sulṭān* and assigned a place in the *ghuslkhanā*. But Khān-i Jahān politely refused, submitting that these two privileges were reserved for princes alone.[40]

Khān-i Jahān's rise was certainly remarkable in that before 1610 he had made no contribution to any military campaign nor acted in any important administrative capacity. Hence, apart from the personal charm of his manners his rise can be explained only in the context of Jahāngīr's attempts to conciliate and reassure the Afghāns by promoting one whom he thought to be of a very high status amongst them. While discussing the ancestry of Khān-i Jahān, Jahāngīr identifies him as the nephew of Daulat Khān Lodī, governor (*ḥākim*) of Lahore, who sent his son Dilāwar Khān to Bābur to invite him to conquer India, adding that Daulat Khān and his son Dilāwar Khān served loyally under Bābur and Humāyūn. But in the light of the ancestry given in the *Tārikh-i Khān Jahāni*, Jahāngīr's version is not correct. Jahāngīr might indeed have given this picture to justify his promotion.[41]

The information contained in the *Tārikh-i Khān Jahāni* and *Zakhīrat-ul Khwānīn*, indicates that the Mughal nobility was sharply divided on the question of admission and promotions being given to Afghān nobles. It is significant that the faction which was particularly hostile to them was led by Sharīf Khān, Jahāngīr's great favourite and principal adviser in the early years of his reign. Those favouring the Afghāns included Mirzā Azīz Koka an old Akbarshāhī noble and a great critic of Jahāngīr's policy towards the nobility. It is said that Jahāngīr, after his accession, had been persuaded to issue orders for expelling the Afghāns from the empire, but that Mirzā Azīz Koka protested on the ground that there were a large number of Afghāns throughout the country and the implementation of the order would lead to a great disturbance. Jahāngīr accepted Mirzā Azīz Koka's

37 *Iqbālnāma*, 27-8.

38 See Chapter II.

39 See Chapter IV. Khān-i Jahān also secured pardon for Dulip Rai. See *Tuzuk*, 70.

40 *Z.K.*, II, 74-5.

41 *Tuzuk*, 42-3.

arguments and the order was withdrawn.[42] There is no reference in the *Tuzuk*, however, to this entire matter.

Khān-i Jahān Lodī left the court for the first time in 1610 when he was despatched to the Deccan. Incidentally, this was his first appointment to any administrative duty. The circumstances in which he was sent to the Deccan again testify to the great confidence that Jahāngīr had come to place in him. Owing to the successive failures of Parvez, 'Abdur Raḥīm Khān Khanān and other commanders in the Deccan, which was crowned by the loss of Ahmadnagar, Jahāngīr decided to proceed to the Deccan in person. But at this point Khān-i Jahān offered his services and Jahāngīr agreed to send him practically as a substitute for himself. Jahāngīr speaks of his own unwillingness to let Khān-i Jahān be away from the court; but perhaps he expected good service from him notably in view of his long experience of the Deccan.[43]

Khān-i Jahān left for the Deccan on 22 June 1610 travelling via Ujjain and Mandu and reaching Burhanpur in April. After staying for seven days at Burhanpur he started for Malkapur to join Parvez. In the meantime Ambar's Marathas (*bargis*) attacked him and it was only with great difficulty that he maintained his ground. When 'Abdur Raḥīm came to know of his arrival, he despatched his sons Mirzā Iraj and Mirzā Darāb to support him. After some time 'Abdur Raḥīm along with Āṣaf Khān and other nobles also came and met him; and in their company Khān-i Jahān presented himself before the prince.[44] Soon after his arrival, an offensive was launched against Malik Ambar. But the Mughals failed to make any headway, on account of the rainy season, shortage of supplies and mutual jealousies.[45] Thereupon they agreed to a proposal of Malik Ambar on the condition that all the *parganas* from Balaghat to Ahmadnagar which had been under the Mughals during the time of Dāniyāl, be restored to them.[46]

This could hardly be regarded as an achievement and the Mughal commanders began to accuse one another of treason. Jahāngīr records

[42] *Tārikh-i Khān Jahāni*, II, 494; *Z.K.*, I, 98-9, II, 186-7.

[43] *Tuzuk*, 77-8; *Tārikh-i Khān Jahāni*, II, 505; *Z.K.*, II, 75. For his old association with 'Abdur Raḥīm Khān Khanān, see supra.

[44] *Tārikh-i Khān Jahāni*, II, 505-9; *Z.K.*, II, 75-6.

[45] *Tārikh-i Khān Jahāni*, II, 505-9. *Tuzuk*, 107; *Iqbālnāma*, 43-4; *Ma'āṣir-i Jahāngīrī*, 56b.

[46] *Tuzuk*, 107. But the details of the terms of the treaty are given only in *Tārikh-i Khān Jahāni*, II, 510-11. *Z.K.*, II, 76 fails to mention this campaign.

that Khān-i Jahān wrote to him that 'all this mischief and confusion had arisen through the treachery of the Khān Khanān'; he asked for the latter's withdrawal and his own elevation to his position with a posting of 30,000 troopers. He pledged himself, in the space of two years, to not only free the territories previously held by the Mughals, but also seize Qandhar and other forts and even annex Bijapur.[47] Jahāngīr accepted Khān-i Jahān's version of the episode, and 'Abdur Raḥīm was summoned to court; Khān-i Jahān was also given the command of the Deccan, and the responsibility of civil and revenue administration.[48] It is interesting that the *Tārikh-i Khān Jahāni* seeks to cloak Khān-i Jahān's intrigue against Khān-i Khanān and his own unrealistic pledges, by giving a different version. The reasons it gives for the defeat of the Mughals are just the rainy season and shortage of supplies.[49] As regards the alleged treachery of the Khān-i Khanān, Ni'amatullah's account presents Khān-i Jahān as his consistent defender. Ni'amatullah indeed asserts that Khān-i Jahān contested the suspicions against 'Abdur Raḥīm that he was in league with Malik Ambar who had given him several *parganas* including Jalna and that he stood surety for the conduct of 'Abdur Raḥīm. Jahāngīr accepted his representation and Khān-i Khanān once again returned to favour and was reappointed to the Deccan.[50] Besides this Ni'amatullah also claims that Khān-i Jahān was actually responsible for clearing the misunderstanding and securing pardon for the other two old *Akbarshāhī* nobles, Mirzā Azīz Koka and Man Singh.[51]

These two contradictory statements bring before us Khān-i Jahān's dual personality; and perhaps neither of the two versions can be rejected altogether. We have already seen that Khān-i Jahān's position among the new nobles was not quite secure apparently on account of his Afghān descent and his meteoric rise.[52] Besides, Jahāngīr who showered great favours on him did not give high ranks either to his sons or any other relations.[53] Khān-i Jahān himself was unwilling to rally the Afghāns under himself for fear of rousing suspicions.[54] As a

[47] *Tuzuk*, 86; *Iqbālnāma*, 45; Mutamid Khān has copied *Tuzuk*'s account. Also see *Ma'āṣir-i Jahāngīrī*, 56b.

[48] *Tuzuk*, 86, 107; *Iqbālnāma*; 45; *Tārikh-i Khān Jahāni*, II, 510-11, gives more details of the campaign.

[49] *Tārikh-i Khān Jahāni*, II, 509.

[50] *Tārikh-i Khān Jahāni*, II, 497-8; Cf. *Tuzuk*, 86-7.

[51] *Tārikh-i Khān Jahāni*, II, 495, 500. See also Chapter II.

[52] See supra.

[53] See Appendix A–V and VI for list of nobles of Jahāngīr.

[54] See supra.

result he was shrewd enough to realize the value of friends within the nobility. So he continued to have good relations with the old *Akbarshāhī* nobles; his secret demand that Khān-i Khanān, be recalled from the Deccan was, therefore, not in any irresoluble contradiction to his plea that the old noble should not be further humiliated.

Khān-i Jahān failed to achieve any measure of success in the Deccan. His own biographer makes only vague observations such as saying that during his term he enjoyed popularity among the people and those commanders who had lost their *jāgīrs* got them back.[55] But somehow Jahāngīr does not seem to have believed that the Deccan could be left fully in his hands. Mirzā Azīz Koka was appointed commander-in-chief in his place in 1611 and Jahāngīr planned a 'grand offensive' to dictate terms to Malik Ambar. During this campaign Khān-i Jahān seems to have been the effective commander, but the Mughals once again were defeated because of the lack of cooperation with the army marching from Gujarat under 'Abdullah Khān.[56] 'Abdullah Khān was directed to move into the Deccan via Nasik and Trimbak and Khān-i Jahān, Man Singh and Sharīf Khān were to march from Berar. The commanders of the two armies were ordered to inform each other about their movements and regulate their marches and halts in such a way that they could attack Malik Ambar simultaneously. But such coordination apparently failed owing to the impetuosity of 'Abdullah Khān.

After the disaster Man Singh and Sharīf Khān Amīr-ul Umarā advised Khān-i Jahān to return to Malkapur as the enemy was in a much better position both in men and material and there was no likelihood of the Mughals getting relief or reinforcements.[57] But Khān-i Jahān Lodī resisted their suggestion. Thereupon Man Singh and Sharīf Khān held a meeting of the commanders and decided to abandon the campaign and return to Malkapur where Mirzā Azīz Koka and Prince Parvez were staying. They also wrote to Mirzā Azīz Koka informing him of the position of the imperial army and the attitude of Khān-i Jahān Lodī. They took full responsibility of their action in the event the emperor or the prince disagreed with their decision. Similarly they informed Khān-i Jahān Lodī of their decision. He once

[55] *Tārikh-i Khān Jahāni*, II, 511-12.

[56] *Tārikh-i Khān Jahāni*, II, 513-17; *Tuzuk*, 107; *Iqbālnāma*, 65-6; *Z.K.*, II, 75-7. For details of the Mughāl defeat and collapse of the 'grand offensive', see Chapter VIII.

[57] *Tārikh-i Khān Jahāni*, II, 516-17; *Tuzuk*, 86, 107, make no reference to this discussion.

again refused to return to Malkapur unless he was compelled to do so.[58] It appears that Mirzā Azīz Koka, who had come to know of the collapse of the 'grand offensive', decided that the campaign had to be called off. However, about the same time that Man Singh's communication reached Malkapur, an agreement at the instance of 'Ādil Shāh and Malik Ambar was reached; and with this truce Mirzā Azīz Koka asked the Mughal forces to return to Malkapur. Khān-i Jahān had thereupon no option but to return.[59] He was now posted to Berar by Parvez. When Jahāngīr came to know of this not only did he confirm him in that position, but added a few more *mahals* to his *jāgīr*.[60] About the same time Jahāngīr sent him a *pundnāma* (letter of counsels) as a mark of special favour.[61]

As Mirzā Azīz Koka had also failed in the Deccan, it was suggested by Khwāja Abū'l Ḥasan and other nobles that 'Abdur Raḥīm Khān-i Khanān should once again be given the command there.[62] Jahāngīr accepted this advice and sent a *farmān* to Khān-i Jahān that since the affairs of the Deccan were in the hands of 'Abdur Raḥīm, he should come to court. He was also warned that if he continued to stay, no letter from the emperor would in future be sent to him.[63] On receiving this *farmān*, Khān-i Jahān consulted his *Wakīl*, Rai Bhagwan Das, who advised him to seek the opinion of Prince Parvez and 'Abdur Raḥīm under whom he was presently working. As a reason for the delay it could be submitted that since the *kharīf* crop was ripe, his going to the court at this juncture would cause great inconvenience to the peasantry; and it was thus necessary for his departure to be postponed by at least a month.

Khān-i Jahān informed 'Abdur Raḥīm about the imperial *farmān* and sought his advice. 'Abdur Raḥīm asked him to stay till the conclusion of the campaign and wrote to the emperor requesting that Khān-i Jahān be allowed to remain in the Deccan till the final conquest. The emperor agreed, but Khān-i Jahān was transferred to Thalner with the task of expelling rebel Kols and Bhils and checking the flight of Bahādur Shāh of Gujarat to the Deccan. He was assigned a few *parganas* in *tankhwāh jāgīr* in exchange of *jāgīrs* vacated in Berar.[64]

[58] *Tārikh-i Khān Jahāni*, II, 517-19. No other source has reported these details.

[59] Ibid., 519.

[60] Ibid., 520.

[61] Ibid. *Pundnāma* or *Nasihatnāma-i Jahāngīrī*, consists of Jahāngīr's maxims and regulations pertaining to private and public life. See ibid., 701-3.

[62] *Tuzuk*, 108; *Iqbālnāma*, 67.

[63] *Tārikh-i Khān Jahāni*, II, 527-8.

[64] Ibid., II, 529-30; *Z.K.*, II, 77, briefly mentions that after the defeat, Khān-i Jahān was transferred to the *Thānedāri of Thalner*.

Khān-i Jahān remained at Thalner for about one year and seven months. Afterwards on the request of Parvez, he was posted to Burhanpur which he reached in March 1614.[65] During the time he was in Burhanpur, Jahāngīr despatched several *farmāns* asking him to come to the court. Jahāngīr said that as he often thought of him (Khān-i Jahān), Nūr Jahān had suggested that he be brought to court where he could give first-hand information about the situation in the Deccan.[66]

A *farmān* to this effect was despatched to Burhanpur with the approval of Nūr Jahān as well as of Mahābat Khān and other important nobles of the court. Upon the arrival of this *farmān*, Prince Parvez and 'Abdur Raḥīm wrote to the emperor that Khān-i Jahān's services were still required in the Deccan. The emperor rejected their appeal and ordered Khān-i Jahān to come to the court without further delay to report on the Deccan affairs. Khān-i Jahān left Burhanpur on 22 June 1615 and reached Ajmer where Jahāngīr was then holding court, in 22 days.[67]

The details of the activity of Khān-i Jahān after the failure of the 'grand offensive' in 1612 are furnished in the *Tārikh-i Khān Jahāni*. Its author quite naturally makes no reference to Jahāngīr's unhappiness with the author's patron on account of his failures. Jahāngīr himself does not mention Khān-i Jahān during the intervening years (1612-15). In the account of the tenth year of his reign (1615) he simply says, 'As I had a great desire to see my *farzand* Khān-i Jahān Lodī and for the purpose of enquiring into important matters connected with the Deccan, it was necessary for him to come at once, I sent for him.'[68] But the information contained in the *Zakhīrat-ul Khwānīn*, though very brief, is clear and is corroborated by the facts stated in the *Tārikh-i Khān Jahāni*. The *Zakhīrat-ul Khwānīn* says that after the failure of the campaign the nobles involved in it were demoted, transferred and censured. He specifically mentions 'Abdullah Khān, Mirzā Azīz Koka and Khān-i Jahān among those who fell from grace. About Khān-i Jahān he writes that he was demoted to the *thānedāri* of Thalner from the *ṣūbedāri* of the Deccan.[69] Ni'amatullah also records the transfer,

[65] *Tārikh-i Khān Jahāni*, II, 530-1.

[66] Ibid., 531-2. No other source has referred to these details. It is a very early (1615) reference to Nūr Jahān's political influence.

[67] *Tārikh-i Khān Jahāni*, II, 532-3; *Tuzuk*, 145-6, briefly mention that he summoned Khān-i Jahān to court to discuss about the Deccan problem.

[68] *Tuzuk*, 145-6.

[69] *Z.K.*, II, 77.

first to Elichpur and thereafter to Thalner. From his account it is also evident that Khān-i Jahān sought to avoid going to the court.[70] He himself writes that as Khān-i Jahān delayed in reaching the court, certain nobles sought to denigrate him in the eyes of Jahāngīr by saying that he was reluctant to return to court as he had not discharged his duties faithfully.[71] But there must have been also some other reason for his anxiety to stay in the Deccan, for if Jahāngīr was annoyed with him, going to the court would have been one means of mollifying the emperor. Indeed when Khān-i Jahān arrived at the court, he was warmly received with the usual favours.[72] It is possible then that the main reason of his wishing to stay away from the court was to avoid giving his opinion about the Deccan affairs. He might have come to the conclusion that Nūr Jahān, Mahābat Khān and a section of the nobles were trying to discredit both Prince Parvez and 'Abdur Raḥīm and have them transferred so as to clear the way for Khurram. As Khān-i Jahān had been serving in the Deccan, they might have expected an adverse report about Parvez and 'Abdur Raḥīm Khān Khanān. But Khān-i Jahān who himself had failed when he was appointed as the supreme commander, appears to have been in a dilemma, as his relations with 'Abdur Raḥīm were very old and cordial. He might also have been convinced during his long stay in the Deccan that the charges against 'Abdur Raḥīm of accepting bribes from the Deccanis were baseless. Besides, he may also have developed cordial relations with Prince Parvez.

Some of these inferences that we have drawn are corroborated by the discussion that took place at the court after the arrival of Khān-i Jahān Lodī from Burhanpur.

Khān-i Jahān Lodī reached Ajmer in 1615.[73] Ni'amatullah gives an interesting account of a meeting that was convened by the emperor to discuss the Deccan problem. Jahāngīr asked Khān-i Jahān four questions; firstly he asked him to give reasons for his retreat from Balaghat; secondly, why the reinforcement did not reach 'Abdullah Khān; thirdly, what was the opinion of the nobles, especially that of Man Singh and Amīr-ul Umarā Sharīf Khān, in connection with the retreat of the army from Burhanpur; and lastly, what was the actual

70 See infra.

71 *Tārikh-i Khān Jahāni*, II, 529.

72 *Tuzuk*, 146-7. On his arrival, Khān-i Jahān was presented a *khilat*, elephant and other valuables.

73 *Tuzuk*, 146; *Tārikh-i Khān Jahāni*, II, 534.

state of affairs in the Deccan and the nature of 'Abdur Raḥīm Khān Khānān's conduct and activities. One of the nobles present criticized 'Abdur Raḥīm and asserted that as long as he was there affairs in the Deccan would not be settled. Khān-i Jahān strongly refuted these allegations and said that the Deccanis were much too strong to be quickly and easily suppressed. Jahāngīr complained that ten years had passed by and a large amount of money had been spent without any sign of progress. He added that whoever come from there (the Deccan) reported that the delay was because of 'Abdur Raḥīm Khān Khanān. If effort had been made by him in right earnest, the campaign would have succeeded. At this stage Khurram offered to go to the Deccan himself. Khān-i Jahān intervened and said that Parvez was the heir to the throne; he and his *atālīq* 'Abdur Raḥīm Khān Khanān were making utmost efforts to conquer the Deccan. He submitted that Khurram's appointment to the Deccan would cause dissension. Ni'amatullah says that upon this plain speaking by Khān-i Jahān, the nobles present in the meeting were stunned and said nothing. The emperor also remained silent; the nobles took leave from him and the meeting came to an end.[74] No other source has reported this discussion, but as Jahāngīr writes that Khān-i Jahān was summoned to discuss the Deccan problem, some discussion must have taken place after his arrival and the later events tend to confirm Ni'amatullah's account; Parvez was transferred and Khurram took over the command.[75] It is also of some interest that Roe corroborates Ni'amatullah. He states (12 June 1616):

> There is resolution taken that Sulṭān Khurram shall go to the Deccan wars. Prince Parvez is called home who (it is reported) wrote to his father that if he would send his elder brother (Khusrau) he would obey, but to dishonour by employing this, he would first fall on him and after finish the war. All the captains as Khān-i Jahān, Khān-i Khanān and Mahābat Khān refuse to stay if this tyrant came to command'.[76]

Soon after, Khān-i Jahān was again sent back to the Deccan in the company of Mahābat Khān. At the time of his departure he was given a *khilat*, horse, elephant and sword; and Shāhbāz Khān Lodī (probably some kinsman) was, at his request, promoted to the rank of 2,000/1,000.[77]

[74] *Tārikh-i Khān Jahāni*, II, 536-40.

[75] *Tuzuk*, 161, 164-5. Khurram was despatched to the Deccan in 1616.

[76] *The Embassy of Sir T. Roe*, II, 278-80.

[77] *Tuzuk*, 147.

In 1616, Khurram was despatched to the Deccan, despite Khān-i Jahān's advice; and Parvez was transferred to Allahabad.[78] We have no information about what Khān-i Jahān did in the Deccan under Khurram; but apparently the two were reconciled, for on that prince's recommendation, Khān-i Jahān was promoted to the rank of 6,000/6,000.[79] Khān-i Jahān returned to the court on 12 October 1617 along with Khurram.[80]

After his return from the Deccan, Khān-i Jahān was not given any important assignment for the next three years. He was appointed *faujdār* of Agra and remained with the emperor.[81] In 1619, when he accompanied Jahāngīr to Kashmir, the *faujdāri* of Agra was given to Amanat Khān. On his return to Lahore in November 1620, Jahāngīr appointed Khān-i Jahān governor of Multan with the additional charge of the defence of Qandhar.[82] In the light of the above facts and a close examination of the evidence contained in the *Intekhāb-i Jahāngīrshāhī*, it seems that Khān-i Jahān's relative eclipse might also have been the result of the excessive influence enjoyed by I'timad-ud daulah's family.[83]

During his governorship of Multan, Qandhar fell to the Safavids. Khān-i Jahān informed the emperor about this while the latter was in Kashmir. Jahāngīr left Kashmir and issued a *farmān* to Khān-i Jahān asking him not to start in the direction of Qandhar before the arrival of the imperial army.[84] However, Asālat Khān (Khān-i Jahān's son) was promoted to the rank of 2,000/1,000;[85] sometimes later Khān-i Jahān came to the court apparently to discuss the loss of Qandhar; but after staying for some time he returned to Multan.[86] Farīd Bhakkari says that on this occasion, when he went to the court peopie believed his life would not be spared.[87] Without discussing the reasons for this rumour, he further says that after the fall of Qandhar, many Afghān tribes from near Qandhar came to Khān-i Jahān in Multan and offered to serve in his army in large numbers till they had 'conquered Isfahan', provided he promised to pay them five *tankas* per day per horseman and two *tankas* for a foot soldier. Khān-i Jahān refused the assistance

[78] Ibid., 164-5. [79] Ibid., 184. [80] Ibid., 195.

[81] Ibid., 267; *Ma'āṣir-i Jahāngīrī*, 124b.

[82] *Tuzuk*, 267, 323; *Iqbālnāma*, 176-7; *Ma'āṣir-i Jahāngīrī*, 141a; *Z.K.*, II, 77-8.

[83] For a detailed discussion of the information contained in *Intekhāb-i Jahāngīrshāhī*, see Chapter IX.

[84] *Tuzuk*, 344-5; *Iqbālnāma*, 191-2; *Z.K.*, II, 78-9. [85] *Tuzuk*, 352.

[86] Ibid., 348, 351-2; *Ma'āṣir-i Jahāngīrī*, 156b; *Z.K.*, II, 79.

[87] *Z.K.*, II, 79.

of his fellow tribesmen saying that if the king came to know of this kind of agreement, he would never allow him to remain alive.[88] Presumably Khān-i Jahān was hinting at the suspicions that would be inevitably engendered if Afghāns gathered around him.

It is surprising why Jahāngīr ordered Khān-i Jahān not to proceed to defend Qandhar although much preparation had been made, and many nobles from the Deccan were despatched to Multan to help him.[89] Perhaps Jahāngīr thought that a much larger army would be needed to make any impression on a fort like Qandhar.

Meanwhile Khurram openly revolted and refused to move to Qandhar, to which he was being posted. Khān-i Jahān was summoned urgently to the court. Owing to ill health his departure was delayed. Jahāngīr however thought the delay was deliberate and was reported to have said 'If at this time Sher Shāh were living, he would in spite of all his enmity have come to us; and yet you have not come.'[90]

Anxious to mass troops against Khurram, Jahāngīr sent Mui'z-ul Mulk to summon Khān-i Jahān to the court (1623). Mui'z-ul Mulk returned with a letter from Khān-i Jahān in which he spoke of his own serious illness. He had sent his son Asālat Khān with 1000 horse to serve under the emperor and expressed regrets at being deprived of the honour of meeting him. Jahāngīr after receiving this letter, writes: 'As his apology was evidently sincere, I accepted it.'[91]

Khān-i Jahān came to the court in the nineteenth year (1524). After his arrival he was given charge of the defence of the Agra Fort and the *Thānedāri* of Fathpur Sikri. But when the emperor proceeded to Kashmir the same year, Khān-i Jahān Lodī also accompanied him.[92] On the emperor's return to Lahore, Khān-i Jahān was appointed governor of Gujarat, on the death of Mirzā 'Azīz Koka. But it is significant that Dāwar Bakhsh, the nominal governor of Gujarat was now summoned to the court, probably to leave a free hand to Khān-i Jahān.[93] Sometime afterwards (September 1625) he was made *atāliq* of

[88] Ibid.

[89] *Tuzuk*, 344-5. Jahāngīr despatched Khwāja Abul Ḥasan the *Diwān* and Ṣādiq Khān *Bakhshī* in advance to Lahore to make arrangements and summoned armies from Bengal, Gujarat and Bihar. Bahādur Khān Uzbek was deputed to go as auxiliary to the army of Qandhar. *Iqbālnāma*, 191-2; *English Factories in India*, 1622-3, 99, 112.

[90] *Z.K.*, II, 80.

[91] *Tuzuk*, 360; *Ma'āṣir-i Jahāngīrī*, 168b, 170b-1a; *Z.K.*, II, 60.

[92] *Tuzuk*, 373, 375-6; *Z.K.*, II, 80.

[93] *Iqbālnāma*, 230-1; *Ma'āṣir-i Jahāngīrī*, 148b, 185a; *Z.K.*, II, 280.

Sulṭān Parvez in place of Mahābat Khān, who was transferred to Bengal. Parvez refused to relieve Mahābat Khān and accept Khān-i Jahān as his *atāliq*, but ultimately when another firmly worded *farmān* was sent to him, he agreed. After Parvez's death in October 1626 Khān-i Jahān was appointed viceroy of the Deccan in his own right.[94]

We have very little information in our sources about the Deccan during the closing years of Jahāngīr's reign. However, serious allegations come to be made about Khān-i Jahān's conduct in the Deccan, and these need some consideration.

Mutamid Khān in *Iqbālnāma-i Jahāngīrī* and Kamgar Husaini in *Ma'āṣir-i Jahāngīrī* say that Khān-i Jahān sold the whole of Balaghat for a sum of 3 lac *huns*.[95] The other allegation relates to his hostile attitude towards Shāhjahān after the death of Jahāngīr. The information contained in the *Anfaul Akhbar*[96] and a close study of even Mutamid Khān's own account discount this allegation.

First of all it must be made clear that *Iqbālnāma-i Jahāngīrī*, *Ma'āṣir-i Jahāngīrī* and *Bādshahnāma* were written during the reign of Shāhjahān and come under the category of official histories. Therefore, whatever they wrote, it was in close conformity with the bias current at the court. On account of Shāhjahān's hostility towards Khān-i Jahān, they have not credited any success to Khān-i Jahān. Even Muḥammad Amīn the author of *Anfaul Akhbār* who wrote the account of Jahāngīr's reign also (including Khān Jahān's activities in the closing years) had to go over his text and we can see the alterations he has made in it in the manuscript. However, his corrections are made in such a manner that one can read both the versions, the earlier as well as the later.[97] As far as we can judge the facts are as follows:

The rebellion of Khurram created utter confusion in the Deccan. Mahābat Khān reaching there tried to retrieve the Mughal position

94 *Iqbalnāma*, 245, 248; *Ma'āsir-i Jahāngīrī*, 187b; *A Dutch Chronicle*, 74.

95 *Iqbālnāma*, 383-4, 399; *Ahwāl-i Shahzādqi-i Shāhjahān Padshah*, 77-8; *Ma'āṣir-i Jahāngīrī*, 216b. Modern historians Beni Prasad and B.P. Saksena have also accepted their version. Cf. Beni Prasad, *History of Jahāngīr*, 389-90, and P.B. Saksena, *History of Shāhjahān of Delhi*, 130. R.A. Alvi on the basis of some new information available in *Anfaul Akhbār* has seriously doubted the authenticity of Mutamid Khān's version, but has not offered an explanation. Cf. R.A. Alvi, 'Evidence on the Last Years of Jahāngīr's Reign in the *Anfaul Akhbar*', Indian History Congress, 1975 (cyclostyled copy).

96 Muḥammad Amīn bin Daulat Muḥammad al-Husaini, *Anfaul Akhbār*, Asafiya Library, No.974, 42/18/9. British Museum No. Oriental 1661.

97 He changed the version of the Qandhar campaign, particularly Khurram's role in it, the

and entered into an alliance with 'Ādil Shāh against Malik Ambar.[98] But after his departure to Bengal, Malik Ambar inflicted a crushing defeat on the combined forces at Bhatodi (10 miles from Ahmadnagar), and laid siege to Ahmadnagar. He left his men to pursue the siege and himself proceeded towards Balaghat and occupied the entire territory.[99] He also besieged the fort of Burhanpur. While the siege operations were in progress, Khurram once again appeared in the Deccan after being expelled from Bihar and Bengal and joined Malik Ambar in pressing the siege. But they were forced to raise the siege on the approach of Mahābat Khān and the arrival of reinforcements.[100] The Mughals recovered the territories of Balaghat that had been lost to Malik Ambar. About this time Mahābat Khān was transferred and Khān-i Jahān took over as *atāliq* of Parvez.[101] We have no information in our sources to suggest that Khān-i Jahān was able to recover Balaghat from the Niẓām Shāhis during the period that he was *atāliq* of Parvez.

In October 1626 Parvez died and Khān-i Jahān was appointed viceroy of the Deccan.[102] From October 1626 to the death of Jahāngīr (28 October 1627) when he was viceroy of the Deccan, two major events in the Deccan are described in our sources. In the first reference it is mentioned that after the death of Malik Ambar in May 1626 Ya'qub Khān Ḥabshī, being dissatisfied with the handling of the affairs of the state by the young Niẓām Shāh and other nobles, opened negotiations with Sarbuland Rai on behalf of himself and Fatḥ Khān (Malik Amber's son), offering allegiance to the Mughal emperor. Khān-i Jahān accepted the offer and wrote to Ya'qub Khān in warm terms. He directed the *amirs* to receive them with hospitality and respect and bring them to Burhanpur. But we are not informed about the outcome of these negotiations.[103]

rebellion of Khurram, and the account of the Deccan in the last years of Jahāngīr's reign (1624-6). For details see *Anfaul Akhbār* (Asafiya), 220, 222-3, 229-30, 235.

98 For details, see Chapter IX.

99 *Anfaul Akhbār* (Asafiya), 225-7, (B.M.) 235. See also *Iqbālnāma*, 235-8; and *Ma'āṣir-i Jahāngīrī*, 183-4b.

100 *Iqbālnāma*, 237-8, 243-4, *Ma'āṣir-i Jahāngīrī*, 183b-4a. But Muḥammad Amīn does not say that Shāhjahān had also joined hands with Malik Ambar. Cf. *Anfa-ul Akhbār* (Asafiya), 227-8, 231-2.

101 *Iqbālnāma*, 245, 248; *Anfaul Akhbār*, 216-17.

102 *Iqbālnāma*, 273, 279-80; *Anfaul Akhbar (B.M.)*, 239b.

103 *Iqbālnāma*, 280. See also *Anfaul Akhbār* (Asafiya), 235, (B.M.) 239b, where the name of Fatḥ Khān, and the details of the communication that took place between Ya'qūb Khān, Sarbuland Rai and Khān-i Jahān are not, however, mentioned. *A Dutch Chronicle*, 85-6.

Next we hear that Fatḥ Khān and other officers were despatched by Niẓām Shāh to create disturbance in the imperial territories. They captured most of the *thānās* of Balaghat and Jauhar Khān Ḥabshī another Niẓām Shāhi officer with a large force besieged the fort of Ahmadnagar.[104] Sipahdār Khān the *qiladār* of Ahmadnagar vigorously defended the fort and forced him to retreat. Soon afterwards, however, Jauhar Khān reappeared with a strong force of *bargis*. At this juncture, Khān-i Jahān Lodī after leaving Lashkar Khān to protect Burhanpur marched into Balaghat, and proceeded towards Daulatabad, the Niẓām Shāhi capital. He defeated the Niẓām Shāhis and, forcing them to take refuge in Daulatabad, laid waste the surrounding areas. Nizamul Mulk realizing his weakness opened negotiations with Khān-i Jahān. Ultimately, it was agreed that whatever territories the two sides held before this war, they would continue to hold. After concluding this treaty Khān-i Jahān returned to Balaghat.[105]

The information contained in the *Iqbālnāma-i Jahāngīrī* is identical about this campaign from the beginning to the arrival of Khān-i Jahān at Khirki.[106] Thereafter the version diverges. Instead of mentioning the treaty that the *Anfaul Akhbār* describes, Mutamid Khān alleges that Ḥamīd Khān Ḥabshī approached Khān-i Jahān and by stratagem succeeded in getting the whole of Balaghat vacated upon payment of three lac *huns*. Khān-i Jahān thereupon issued orders to his officers to hand over Balaghat to the Niẓām Shāhis. All the officers, obeying his orders vacated their posts, but Sipahdār Khān, the *qiladār* of Ahmadnagar refused demanding a royal *farmān* to this effect.[107]

Quite clearly the events or alleged events that Mutamid Khān records, are wrongly ascribed by him to the settlement made with the Nizām Shāhis immediately after Khān-i Jahān's successful campaign of 1626-7. For one thing, Muḥammad Amīn would hardly have missed the opportunity of praising his patron Sipahdār Khān,[108] had his refusal

[104] *Anfaul Akhbār*, (B.M.) 239b-40a; the name of Fatḥ Khān is mentioned by Mutamid Khān. Cf. *Iqbālnāma*, 282.

[105] *Anfaul Akhbār* (Asafiya), 267-8, (B.M.), 239b-40b; *A Dutch Chronicle*, 87, states that Abdullah Khān who was with Khān-i Jahān at this time entered into secret correspondence with the Niẓām Shāhis and planned the destruction of Khān-i Jahān's army.

[106] *Iqbālnāma*, 282-3; Cf. *Anfaul Akhbār*, 239b.

[107] *Iqbālnāma*, 282-4, but *Anfaul Akhbār*, 239b-40b makes no reference to this deal of Khān-i Jahān with the Niẓām Shāhis.

[108] Muḥammad Amīn was in the service of Sipahdār Khān (later Khanjar Khān) the commandant of the fort of Ahmadnagar.

to surrender Ahmadnagar occurred before he finished his work, which was just before Jahāngīr's death. But it is Lahori's account, which is decisive. He says that the surrender of Balaghat by Khān-i Jahān took place after the death of Jahāngīr and before the formal accession of Shāhjahān, a period during which, according to the official chronicler, Khān-i Jahān had fallen prey to perverse counsel and improper ambitions. It was then that he handed over the Mughal posts in Balaghat, especially the fort of Bir, to the Nizām Shāhis. It is curious that Lahori does not mention the alleged bribe of three lac *huns*. Nor does he mention Sipahdār Khān's action in refusing to surrender Ahmadnagar.[109]

From all this one can draw the following inferences:

(1) Khān-i Jahān seized large areas, including Bir and other areas in Balaghat, besides Ahmadnagar, as a result of his successful campaign in 1626-7.

(2) Upon hearing the news of the death of Jahāngīr and Shāhjahān's march northwards from Nasik, Khān-i Jahān became anxious to leave the Deccan with as many troops as possible to take the side of Dāwar Bakhsh, who had then been proclaimed king at Lahore, for he seems to have taken (as will be seen later) his accession seriously.

(3) It was not possible to withdraw forces from the Deccan without concessions to the Nizām Shāhis, which Khān-i Jahān made now.

(4) The concession seems to have involved largely the cession of territory in Balaghat regained by Khān-i Jahān in 1626-7. It did not probably involve Ahmadnagar at all, which since 1616 had never been lost. Khān-i Jahān probably never personally received three lac of *huns*, an immense amount for those days; this was probably promised, and that also, quite possibly, to Dāwar Bakhsh. This might therefore explain Lahori's silence over the matter.

Khān-i Jahān was still viceroy of the Deccan when Jahāngīr died. Mutamid Khān and other official historians of Shāhjahān's reign state that Dāwar Bakhsh, Khurram's son, was raised to the throne only as a sacrificial lamb in order to secure the succession of Shāhjahān.[110] It is said that Āṣaf Khān despatched his personal servant Banarsi with full

[109] *Bādshahnāma*, I, 85-6.

[110] *Iqbālnāma*, 293-4, Mutamid Khān specifically used the word. *Bādshahnāma*, I, 69-70, 72. Banarsi Prasad Saksena also accepts the version of Mutamid Khān. See *History of Shāhjahān*, 57.

details to Shāhjahān then at Nasik to come immediately to the court. Shāhjahān, thereafter despatched Jān Niṣār Khān with a *farmān* to Khān-i Jahān, conferring on him the *Ṣubahdāri* of the Deccan. Jān Niṣār Khān was also asked to ascertain his views about his accession and also to seek his permission to go through Burhanpur. Khān-i Jahān refused to acknowledge the *farmān* and also to allow Shāhjahān to pass through Burhanpur.[111] In fact, according to an English report Khān-i Jahān declared for Dāwar Bakhsh, proclaiming him emperor even in his *jāgīrs* in Gujarat.[112] Khān-i Jahān also seized Malwa, when Mahābat Khān was despatched towards that region by Shāhjahān. Mutamid Khān therefore suggests that Khān-i Jahān's act was rebellious, because he was supporting Dāwar Bakhsh against Shāhjahān who was the real successor.[113]

There is no denying the fact that Khān-i Jahān was supporting Dāwar Bakhsh. But it would be difficult to prove, as asserted by Mu'tamid Khān and other official historians, that Khān-i Jahān's action was particularly hostile to Shāhjahān. As a matter of fact even if Dāwar Bakhsh was really raised to the throne to destroy other rivals, the plot had to remain a closely guarded secret almost confined to Āṣaf Khān alone. It is even not fully established that Āṣaf Khān considered Dāwar Bakhsh only as a stopgap arrangement from the very beginning. Shāhjahān had to urge Āṣaf Khān, while proceeding from Gujarat to Agra, that it would be very well if in these troubled days, Dāwar Bakhsh, his brothers and the sons of Daniyal were eliminated (from this world) and he was saved from worry.[114] From the reports which must have been received by Khān-i Jahān and other nobles in the Deccan, it would have appeared that Dāwar Bakhsh had received the support of all the important nobles including Nūr Jahān. Conversely, during this period, Shāhjahān's position was very weak. His supporters had deserted him and until he reached Gujarat, he had a very small following.[115] Hence, in these circumstances Khān-i Jahān,

[111] *Iqbālnāma*, 294, 297-300. Mutamid Khān adds that Daryā Khān Rohilla who had lately joined Khān-i Jahān after deserting Shāhjahān, and Afẓal Khān, *Diwān* of the Deccan, who was a brother of Shaharyar's *Diwān* were responsible for Khān-i Jahān's hostile attitude towards Shāhjahān. Regarding the seizure of Malwa, Farīd Bhakkari states that he took this action because his family was residing there. Cf. *Z.K.*, II, 81-2. It might be that he wanted to control the route to the capital which lay through Malwa. See also *Bādshahnāma*, I, 76.

[112] *English Factories Records*, 262.

[113] *Iqbālnāma*, 299-300.

[114] *Iqbālnāma*, 303.

[115] Shāhjahān even thought of going to Persia to obtain the help of his friend, Shāh Abbas. In

who no doubt was not very happy with Shāhjahān, particularly from his action in raising Mahābat Khān to a very high position by giving him the rank of *Khān Khanān*, decided to support Dāwar Bakhsh who seemed to have the backing of all the leading nobles at the court.[116] Raja Gaj Singh, Raja Jai Singh and other nobles also accompanied Khān-i Jahān up to Mandu and apparently until then supported Dāwar Bakhsh.[117] Shāhjahān's position considerably improved when he reached Gujarat, and after that many nobles who were with Khān-i Jahān left him.

What is really intriguing is the attitude that Khān-i Jahān maintained now when most nobles joined Shāhjahān. One obvious reason could have been an increased misunderstanding between him and Shāhjahān, aggravated by the dominant position of Mahābat Khān.

Another aspect is of more significance as well. In a *farmān* issued to Raja Jai Singh, Dāwar Bakhsh assumed the title of Sher Shāh.[118] The assumption of this title by a Mughal prince suggested a deliberate attempt to appeal to Afghān sentiment, while also seeking to arouse popular support by taking the title of a reputedly benevolent ruler.[119] This may then have made Khān-i Jahān expect a greater role in a sovereign so publicly committed to the Afghān tradition.

After the accession of Shāhjahān, Khān-i Jahān Lodī sent his *Wakīl* to the court with letters of apologies, assuring him of obedience and loyalty. Shāhjahān accepted his representation and confirmed him in the governorship of the Deccan.[120] But in the same year he was replaced by Mahābat Khān on the charge that he was reluctant to recover the territories lost to the Deccanis.[121] About the same time Khān-i Jahān came to know that Mahābat Khān had advised the emperor to seize

---

the same year he fell ill. A number of his servants like Abdullah Khān Fīroz Jung and Daryā Khān Rohilla left him. For more details, see *Iqbālnāma*, 273-4, 280-2; *Z.K.*, II.

116 *Z.K.*, II, 81-2. At the time of the arrival of Jān Niṣār Khān with a *farmān* of Shāhjahān, Shāhjahān's undue favour to Mahābat Khān was particularly mentioned as a grievance among Khān-i Jahān's counsellors.

117 *Iqbālnāma*, 300.

118 State Archive, Bikaner, Old Serial No.176, New S.N.21. *Tārikh-i Ālam Ara-i Abbasi*, 750.

119 *Gowaliornāma*, 19a. No less a person than Mirzā Azīz Koka in 1613 had written in a letter to Jahāngīr that 'Sher Shāh Afghān was not an angel (*malak*) but a king (*malik*). In six years he gave such stability to the structure that the foundation still survives.' There are guarded admissions in Abū'l Fazl also to this effect.

120 *Bādshahnāma*, I, 199; *Z.K.*, II, 82-3; *Ma'āṣir-ul Umarā*, III, 719-20.

121 *Bādshahnāma*, I, 273.

his family and treasure in Malwa. Upon this he took precautionary measures and started towards Malwa. Although this proved to be a mere rumour, his servants were convinced that Khān's days were numbered and many of them fled to the court.[122]

Khān-i Jahān came to the court in 1629 after suppressing the rebellion of Jujhar Singh Bundela. He was disappointed at the reception accorded to him on his arrival, as no noble came forward to welcome him.[123] Besides, Shāhjahān reprimanded him for coming to the court at the head of a big force (7,000 horses). He was ordered to keep only a limited number of troops and his *du aspa sih aspa* rank was curtailed. His *jāgīr* in Ujjain and Malwa was resumed. About the same time Fāzil Khān, the *Bakhshī* of the Deccan, warned him to remain vigilant and keep his retainers with him as the emperor was looking for an opportunity to arrest him.[124] Certain other incidents also took place that shook his confidence.[125] He might have come to the conclusion that Shāhjahān who had already executed royal princes on the eve of his accession would not pardon him for his role in the issue of succession.

Therefore according to Farīd Bhakkari, Khān-i Jahān decided to resign from imperial service. He prepared a list of the imperial treasures, horses, elephants and armoury that he had under him and came to Āṣaf Khān. Āṣaf Khān became quite concerned and said that all nobles would resign if things went like this. However, he advised Khān-i Jahān to restrain his emotions and promised to intervene in the matter. But it appears that Āṣaf Khān's efforts also failed and Khān-i Jahān's entire property was confiscated.[126]

Shāhjahān also attempted to create dissension in the camp of Khān-i Jahān. He summoned Khān-i Jahān's sons and other relations, promoted them to higher ranks and assigned fresh *manṣabs* to those who had no rank. Bahādur Khān, Khān-i Jahān's brother's son, was promoted to the rank of 3,500. He and Khān-i Jahān's other relations

[122] *Z.K.*, II, 84-5.

[123] *Bādshahnāma*, I, 352; *Z.K.*, II, 87. The latter says that Shāhjahān removed Mahābat Khān to Delhi, because the latter on account of the high military rank or the title of Khān Khanān would not bow to Khān-i Jahān.

[124] *Z.K.*, II, 88.

[125] *Bādshahnāma*, I, 373; *Z.K.*, II, 91. One night Mirzā Lashkari, son of Mukhlis Khān, said in jest to the sons of Khān-i Jahān that they and their father would soon be thrown into prison. Khān-i Jahān was much dismayed on hearing this and retired to his house.

[126] *Z.K.*, II, 91-2; Khafi Khān, I, 412.

were given *jāgīrs* in Gujarat and were ordered to go there. Many of the personal servants of Khān-i Jahān were given *manṣabs* and *jāgīrs*.[127]

On account of these steps taken by the emperor a large number of Khān-i Jahān's followers left his service.[128] Khān-i Jahān naturally started feeling even more insecure and one night fled along with his family and followers.[129] He was hotly pursued by the imperial army and after a long and bitter rebellion defeated and killed along with his four sons in 1631.[130]

If we go through the details of the rebellion of Khān-i Jahān, it is clear that Shāhjahān failed in his attempt to isolate him from his relations and followers. Almost all the Afghān nobles and chiefs collected under him.[131] We have also some evidence to show that Khān-i Jahān had close links with Afghāns of the frontier region.[132]

Khān-i Jahān's end also destroyed his family. None of his surviving sons Muẓaffar (he came to the court leaving his father while the rebellion was in full swing), Farīd, Jān-i Jahān, Aḥmad and Ālam were given any *manṣab* by Shāhjahān. The author of the *Ma'āṣir-ul Umarā* writes, 'Up to the present day none of his descendants have reached an eminent position.'[133]

[127] *Z.K.*, II, 92-3.

[128] Ibid., II, 93-5. Lodī Khān Niyāzi, Qāẓi Khān Barki, Niṣār Khān Panni, Muẓaffar Khān Ghilzai were among those who left Khān-i Jahān and went to their home.

[129] *Bādshahnāma*, I, 275; *Z.K.*, II, 99-101.

[130] *Bādshahnāma*, I, 349-51; *Z.K.*, II. Also see Banarsi Prasad *History of Shāhjahān of Delhi*, 71, 77-9, 81-2.

[131] *Bādshahnāma*, I, 277-8; *Z.K.*, II, 87-8; *Ma'āṣir-ul Umarā*, III, 720-2.

[132] See supra.

[133] *Ma'āṣir-ul Umarā*, III, 732.

CHAPTER VIII

The Family of 'Abdullah Khān Fīroz Jang

Khwāja 'Abdullah, better known by his title 'Abdullah Khān Fīroz Jang, was born in 1575 at Hissar in Transoxiana.[1] He was a descendant of Khwāja 'Ubaidullah Nasīruddīn Ahrār, one of the greatest mystics of the Naqshbandi order.[2] The Timuride rulers showed great reverence to the saint, and Bābur's father 'Umar Shaikh Mirzā had become his disciple. Bābur himself out of a belief that it would relieve him of his illness, put to verse that saint's *Walidiya-i Risala*.[3] After the establishment of Mughal rule in India a number of Khwāja Ahrar's descendants came to this country, relying upon the Mughal emperor's attachment to the saint.[4] As a mark of exceptional favour, the Mughal rulers even married their daughters to certain members of Khwāja Ahrār's family. The first marriage that took place was of a sister of Akbar to Mirzā Sharafuddīn Ḥusain Ahrāri. Later on Mirzā Hakim's sister was married to Khwāja Ḥasan Naqshbandi, another descendant of Khwāja Ahrār.[5] Both these officers rose to high positions; Mirzā Sharafuddīn held the charge of Ajmer and Nagaur and rebelled in 1562-3; Khwāja Ḥasan became *Wakīl* of Mirzā Ḥakīm.[6]

'Abdullah Khān along with his two brothers Mirzā Yādgār and Mirzā Barkhurdār came likewise to India, in search of employment in 1592.[7] But we have no information about his early career or even about his family proper. We know only that Amīr Sayyid 'Āshiq, a great scholar and mystic of Samarqand was his great grandfather.[8]

[1] *Bādshahnāma*, II, 402, mentions that the death of 'Abdullah Khān occurred in the year 1645 when he was 70 years. Therefore, it can be inferred that 'Abdullah Khān must have been born about year 1575. For a biography of 'Abdullah Khān, see *Z.K.*, II, 172-85.

[2] *Z.K.*, II, 172-3.

[3] *Bāburnāma* tr. Baveridge, I, 36 and 62.

[4] For more details of such immigrants, see *Bāburnāma*, Beveridge, II, 631; *Akbarnāma*, II, 127; *Muntakhab-ut Tawārikh*, III, 150.

[5] *Akbarnāma*, II, 127-8, 142-3. Also see, 'Marriages among Mughal Nobles as Index of Status and Aristocratic Integration', *Proceedings of Indian History Congress*, 1972, 304-12.

[6] *Akbarnāma*, II, 129.

[7] *Ma'āṣir-i Jahāngīrī*, 12a; *Z.K.*, II, 172-4.

[8] Ibid., 12a, For a detailed biography of Amīr Sayyid Ashiq, see *Habib us Siyar*, IV, 35-6.

On reaching Akbar's court, 'Abdullah Khān and his brothers entered imperial service. Shortly afterwards 'Abdullah Khān was despatched to the Deccan to serve under Bashir Khwāja who was closely related to him. He rendered valuable service, but was not given a high rank consonant with his lineage and close link to the ruling family.[9] Accordingly in 1595 he joined Prince Salīm as an *ahdi*.[10] It was during this period that Salīm rebelled and established himself at Allahabad. As he was one of his early associates 'Abdullah Khān was given a rank of 1,000 and title of *Khān*. But soon after his relations with Sharīf Khān, the *Wakīl* of the prince, became strained.[11] This led to 'Abdullah Khān deserting Salim in 1603, when he rejoined Akbar's service. Through Khwāja Yādgār who remained at the court and was held in great esteem by Akbar, 'Abdullah Khān was warmly received and given the rank of 1,000 and the title of *Ṣafdar Khān*.[12] In 1604 he was given the *jāgīr* of Kalpi, and his brothers were sent with him.[13]

At the time of Akbar's death, 'Abdullah Khān was at Kalpi and apparently took no part in the accession crisis. But soon after Jahāngīr's accession, he came to the court and was confirmed in the rank of 1,000. Jahāngīr, however, made no secret of his indignation about his earlier defection. The imperial diarist notes:

> In the commencement of his service he was an *ahdi* and had risen to the rank of 1,000, but without reason had gone to my father's service.... Although I considered it best for my prosperity that my attendant and people should go into his (Akbar's) service, yet this occurred without my leave, and I was rather annoyed at it. But the fact is that he is a manly and zealous man; if he had not committed this fault, he would have been a faultless hero (jawan).[14]

Apparently on this account, 'Abdullah Khān was not given promotion in rank immediately after Jahāngīr's accession. But shortly afterwards, in the same year, he was promoted to the rank of 2,500/500 and sent back to Kalpi.[15] While he was in Kalpi, he defeated and captured Ram Chand Bundela, Raja Madhukar's son. In 1606 when he came to the court along with Ram Chand, he was promoted to the

[9] *Ma'āṣir-i Jahāngīrī* 12a, *Takmila*, III, 823. However, we are not aware of the exact relationship of Bashir Khwāja and 'Abdullah Khān.

[10] *Takmila*, III 823, *Tuzuk*, 11-12.

[11] *Ma'āṣir-i Jahāngīrī*, 14a; *Tuzuk*, 11-12. [12] Ibid., 18a. [13] Ibid.

[14] *Tuzuk*, 11-12.

[15] Ibid., 34; *Ma'āṣir-i Jahāngīrī*, 37a, however, mentions that he was promoted to the rank of 2,500/2,500.

rank of 3,000/2,000 married to the daughter of Mirzā Sulaiman and appointed governor of Malwa.[16] During the governorship of Malwa he was again promoted to the rank of 3,000/2,500 when he foiled the conspiracy of Mirzā Badiuzzaman, Mirzā Shahrukh's son, who wanted to defect to Rana Amar Singh along with his supporters.[17]

'Abdullah Khān was transferred from Malwa and given the command of the Mewar campaign in 1609. This was a major assignment because two earlier campaigns organized during Jahāngīr's reign had failed to effect much. He achieved some important victories initially, and to encourage him, Jahāngīr promoted him to the rank of 5,000/5,000 and gave him the title of *Fīroz Jang*.[18] But these successes were short lived, as at Rampur, near Kumbhalgarh, he was defeated by the armies of Mukund Das and Kunwar Bhim.[19]

After this defeat, Abdullah Khān was transferred as governor of Gujarat, to cooperate in the grand campaign against Niẓām Shāh. Important officers like Raja Ram Das, Khān-i 'Ālam, 'Alī Mardan Bahādur, Ẓafar Khān and Sayyid Saif Khān were deputed to serve under him.[20] Two thousand of 'Abdullah Khān's *sawār* rank was converted into *du aspa sih aspa*.[21] He was ordered to march via Nasik and Trimbak in close cooperation of the other army under the command of Mirzā 'Azīz Koka which was to march through Berar and surprise Malik Ambar. The plan was indeed an ingenious one; nevertheless, its success depended entirely on the extent the commanders of the two armies cooperated with each other. But as the campaign progressed, both 'Abdullah Khān and Khān-i Jahān (who was the effective commander of the other army) attempted to conquer Daulatabad single-handedly. 'Abdullah Khān marched on to Daulatabad without informing or learning of the progress of the other army under Khān-i Jahān, Sharīf Khān and Man Singh. Khān-i Jahān and other officers, on the pretext that he had not informed them of his movements, seem to have deliberately moved slowly. When the Niẓām Shāhī leader Malik Ambar came to know of this lack of

[16] Ibid., 39; *Ma'āṣir-i Jahāngīrī*, 39a-40a, states that he was promoted to the rank of 4,000/4,000.

[17] *Tuzuk*, 66.

[18] *Tuzuk*, 74-5; *Ma'āṣir-i Jahāngīrī*, 51-2; *Z.K.*, II, 173; *Vir Vinod*, V, 224-5.

[19] *Vir Vinod*, II, 226. The Persian chroniclers have not mentioned this defeat.

[20] *Tuzuk*, 97, 107; *Iqbālnāma*, 57; *Mir'āt-i Aḥmadi*, 189 mentions that he was also promoted to the rank of 6,000/6,000.

[21] *Tuzuk*, 97; *Iqbālnāma*, 58; *Ma'āṣir-i Jahāngīrī*, 84b.

coordination among his opponents, he marched boldly to face 'Abdullah Khān. 'Abdullah Khān was outnumbered and compelled to retreat.[22] The author of the *Iqbālnāma-i Jahāngīrī* and Jahāngīr in his memoirs held 'Abdullah Khān solely responsible for the collapse of the grand offensive.[23] The author of *Ma'āṣir-ul Umarā* gives an interesting account of Jahāngīr's reaction to the flight of 'Abdullah Khān, calling him *Gurez Jung* (Fugitive from Battle) instead of *Fīroz Jang* (Victorious in Battle).[24]

After the collapse of the grand campaign, 'Abdullah Khān returned to Gujarat. Shortly afterwards he was ordered to join Khurram in his campaign against the Rana of Mewar.[25]

The description of the career of 'Abdullah Khān indicates that he was given rapid promotions and important duties as part of Jahāngīr's endeavour to raise his own nobles to counter the Akbarshahis. This was naturally resented by the Akbarshāhī nobles, particularly when the Jahāngīrī nobles did not prove very successful. In a letter addressed to Jahāngīr, Mirzā 'Azīz Koka strongly condemned his policies in this regard and particularly mentioned rapid promotions and important duties given to 'Abdullah Khān even after his successive failures.[26]

It seems that this letter had some effect, because 'Abdullah Khān's fortune started declining thereafter. In 1616 on the complaint of 'Abid Khān the *waqia Navis* of Gujarat, his *manṣab* and *jāgīr* were confiscated and he was summoned to the court leaving his brother Mirzā Yādgār as his deputy. When he reached Ajmer, where Jahāngīr was encamped, he was refused an interview. It appears that 'Abdullah Khān approached Khurram, and at his intercession, his *manṣab* and *jāgīr* were restored. However, he was transferred from the governorship of Gujarat and deputed to accompany Khurram to the Deccan.[27]

[22] *Ma'āṣir-i Jahāngīrī*, 84b. For more details, see Chapters II and VII.

[23] *Iqbālnāma*, 65-7; *Tuzuk*. 107-8. But Kamgar Husaini who was cousin of 'Abdullah Khān says that Man Singh's unhelpful attitude was the real cause of 'Abdullah Khān's defeat. Cf. *Ma'āṣir-i Jahāngīrī*, 84b.

[24] *Ma'āṣir-ul Umarā*, I, 99.

[25] *Tuzuk*, 232-3; *Z.K.*, II, 176-82; *A Dutch Chronicle*, 47; *Vir Vinod* II, 230-3, give details of the campaign.

[26] For details of the letter of 'Azīz Koka to Jahāngīr, see Chapter II and Appendix C–III.

[27] *Tuzuk*, 162-4; *Ma'āṣir-i Jahāngīrī*, 121b. Kamgar Husaini states that 'Abdullah Khān was reappointed governor of Gujarat, but this is not correct because in the same year, in his place, Muqarrab Khān was made governor of Gujarat. Also see *The Embassy of Sir Thomas Roe*, 278-9.

He returned to the court with Khurram in 1617 and was despatched to his *jāgīr* of Kalpi along with his brothers.[28] While he was at Kalpi in 1618, 'Abdullah Khān was again punished on a complaint of 'Abid Khān. 'Abid Khān stated that as governor of Gujarat. 'Abdullah Khān had ordered his garden to be cut down. 'Abid Khān further complained that 'Abdullah Khān had ordered a man to be killed in a drinking party. Upon receiving these complaints Jahāngīr ordered 1,000 of his *du aspa sih aspa* to be converted into ordinary *sawār* rank and for the difference of pay which came to 700,000 *dāms,* to be deducted from his *jāgīr*.[29]

'Abdullah Khān was not given any important duty between 1617 and 1621 and apparently remained at Kalpi. It is quite significant that the period coincides with the one during which I'timād-ud dullah's family became extremely influential and the fortunes of a number of other important nobles declined.[30] Later events indicate that 'Abdullah Khān was also not on good terms with Nūr Jahān, and might have suffered because of her influence.[31] It seems that 'Abdullah Khān came close to Khurram, who had helped him when he was in distress. He had also served in Mewar and in the Deccan campaign under Khurram;[32] and in 1621 when Khurram was again despatched to the Deccan, 'Abdullah Khān along with his brothers accompanied him.[33] But after some time, suddenly without taking Khurram's permission he returned to Kalpi. When the matter was reported to the emperor, he ordered resumption of his *jāgīr*, and I'timād Rai was ordered to conduct him to Burhanpur. Once again Khurram came to his rescue. Upon his request 'Abdullah Khān was not only pardoned, but promoted to the rank of 6,000.[34] He returned to Kalpi shortly afterwards.[35]

'Abdullah Khān was summoned to the court in the same year and given command of the Qandhar campaign when Khurram set impossible conditions for taking that command. He presented himself near Lahore, but the campaign was given up, in view of Khurram's rebellion.[36] 'Abdullah Khān accompanied the emperor and was given

[28] *Tuzuk*, 196. [29] Ibid., 208. [30] See Chapters VII and IX.

[31] *Ma'āṣir-i Jahāngīrī*, 161a. [32] See supra.

[33] *Tuzuk*, 330-1; *Iqbālnāma*, 181; De Laet, 199, and *A Dutch Chronicle*, 55, mix up the two Deccan campaigns led by Khurram.

[34] *Tuzuk*, 334, 336; *Iqbālnāma*, 186; *A Dutch Chronicle*, 55.

[35] 'Abdullah Khān was summoned from Kalpi, when Khurram refused to take up the Qandhar campaign, see *Tuzuk*, 338-9, *Ma'āṣir-i Jahāngīrī*, 157a.

[36] *Tuzuk*, 343-4;

command of the van of the army sent against Khurram. But 'Abdullah Khān deserted the imperial army in the middle of the battle of Bilochpur and joined Khurram.[37]

At this stage it seems important to discuss the nature of Khurram's rebellion and the extent of 'Abdullah Khān's involvement in it. The *Dutch chronicle* of Jahāngīr's reign gives an interesting account of the situation:

> Not much remained to be done now as he thought. In five or six years he had amassed much wealth in Gujarat and Burhanpur, his father was far away in Lahore and he was in correspondence with all the dignatories of his father such as 'Āṣaf Khān, 'Abdullah Khān, Khān-i Khana and his sons, Lashkar Khān and Bir Singh Deo Bundela and many others.[38]

He further adds that Khurram collected those nobles who were with him and

> made them promise an oath that they would be true to him. He wanted to revolt against his father, and expected that they would not only be not disloyal to him, but gird him with the sword of his father the king. All of them promised this on oath. After this 'Abdullah Khān went to Kalpi with Shāhjahān's permission.[39]

It would seem that the discontent which was brewing among a section of Jahāngīrī nobles since the rise of I'timad-ul daulah's family led some of them to lend ears to Khurram's overtures even if they did not ultimately join him. 'Abdullah Khān who was also one of those nobles 'whose heart was full of grievances on account of indifferent attitude of the Emperor and ill treatment by Nūr Jahan'[40] became a secret supporter of Khurram, deserting to his side at a crucial moment.

However, 'Abdullah Khān's attitude is rather intriguing; specially his sudden departure from the Deccan without informing Khurram. It might be that 'Abdullah Khān at first feared to get involved to Khurram's plans, when their success seemed very uncertain. But when after his return to Kalpi, the emperor punished him, while Khurram came to his rescue;[41] his attitude might have changed. When he rejoined Khurram in the Deccan he became a party to the conspiracy and returned a second time to Kalpi with some definite understanding as mentioned by the Dutch chronicler.[42] This is corroborated by the Persian sources

37 Ibid., 357-8; *Iqbālnāma*, 202-3; *Ma'āṣir-i Jahāngīrī*, 161a; *A Dutch Chronicle*, 59.

38 *A Dutch Chronicle*, 57.

39 Ibid., 55.

40 *Ma'āṣir-i Jahāngīrī*, 161a.

41 See supra.

42 Ibid.

also if we closely examine the details of the battle of Bilochpur. For example, when 'Abdullah Khān fled to Khurram's army he was warmly received as most of the commanders knew his real affiliations. The author of *Ma'āṣir-i Jahāngīrī*, a nephew of 'Abdullah Khān, accepts that 'Abdullah Khān had made this arrangement with Khurram much before.[43]

Despite 'Abdullah Khān's defection, Jahāngīr's troops were victorious at Bilochpur, partly owing to the sudden death of Raja Bikarmajit and the cool strategy of Mahābat Khān.[44] After the defeat,[45] Khurram fled to Mandu. He appointed 'Abdullah Khān, as his governor of Ahmadabad in place of Raja Bikramajit. 'Abdullah Khān, however, accompanied Khurram and despatched Wafadar Khān as his deputy to Ahmadabad.[46]

Shortly after taking over the charge of the *ṣūba*, Wafadar Khān was defeated and taken prisoner by Mirzā Safi, Syed Dilér Khān, Nahar Khān and other imperial officers posted in the *ṣūba* of Gujarat.[47]

When 'Abdullah Khān came to know of this, he immediately started for Ahmadabad without making proper arrangement. He headed a small force of 5,000 horses. Certain officers of 'Abdullah Khān like Muhtasib Khān and Sharza Khān also deserted to the imperialists. Thus 'Abdullah Khān was badly handicapped in the battle which ensued at Kankaria Talao near Ahmadabad. He himself was wounded and 3,000 of his soldiers were killed.[48]

'Abdullah Khān fled from the battlefield and in three days reached Bharoch. Himmat Khān's son who was in charge of the fort refused entry, but gave him 500 *mahmudis*. From there he went to Surat and stayed for two months. After collecting men and material he rejoined Khurram at Burhanpur.[49] Khurram had arrived from Asir shortly before, hotly pursued by the imperial army under Parvez and Mahābat Khān. As the river bank was fortified by the rebels it became difficult for

[43] Jahāngīr in his memoirs states, 'I was ignorant of the fact that he ('Abdullah Khān) was in league with Bidaulat (Khurram) and the real object of the evil natured one was to send news from my army to his.' *Tuzuk*, 365.

[44] *Ma'āṣir-i Jahāngīrī*, 161a.

[45] *Tuzuk*, 357-8; *Iqbālnāma*, 201-2. For Mahābat Khān's role, see Chapter IX.

[46] *Tuzuk*, 361; *Ma'āṣir-i Jahāngīrī*, 162a; *A Dutch Chronicle*, 61.

[47] *Tuzuk*, 361-5; *Iqbālnāma*, 207; *Mir'āt-i Aḥmadi*, I, 167-98.

[48] For details of 'Abdullah Khān's defeat, see *Tuzuk*, 361-5; *Iqbālnāma*, 207-8; *Mir'āt-i Aḥmadi*, I, 197-8; *Z.K.*, II, 180-2; *A Dutch Chronicle*, 61-4; *Factory Records*, 240-1.

[49] *Tuzuk*, 365; *Ma'āṣir-i Jahāngīrī*, 165; De Laet, 211.

Mahābat Khān to cross the Narbada.[50] Therefore, he resorted to diplomacy and won over 'Abdur Rahīm Khān Khanan. The author of *Ma'āṣir-i Jahāngīrī* writes that Khān Khanan persuaded Khurram to start negotiations with Parvez and offered his own services. But 'Abdullah Khān who was aware of the secret understanding between Mahābat Khān and Khān Khanan opposed this suggestion and said that Khān Khanan's aims was to join the imperialists.[51] *The Dutch Chronicle* not only confirms this but adds that, 'Khān Khanān, who had also bribed Bairam Beg, wrote him that he was coming back after making a settlement with Parvez and his aim now was to arrest Khurram and hand him over to Parvez.'[52] But 'Abdullah Khān came to know of it through his informers; he immediately informed the prince and advised him to flee. Khurram acting on the advice crossed the Tapti and entered the Golkunda kingdom.[53] During this period a large number of his servants left him.

In these circumstances Khurram decided to march into Orissa and Bengal. Aḥmad Beg Khān the governor of Orissa fled to Burdwan and from there to Bengal.[54] Orissa was thus occupied without any resistance. The *ṣūba* was made over to Muḥammad Taqi who was also given the rank of 5,000/5,000 and 'Abdullah Khān was appointed *Sipah Salar* of Khurram's army.[55] 'Abdullah Khān wrote a letter to Muḥammad Ṣālih the *faujdār* of Burdwan to surrender the fort, but Ṣālih refused. Khurram and 'Abdullah Khān marched from Cuttack to Burdwan via Midnapore and despatched Daryā Khān, Raja Bhim, Sayyid Jafar Bārha, Bahādur Khān and Khwāja Sabir, 'Abdullah Khān's son-in-law, to besiege the fort. Ṣālih thereupon surrendered and Burdwan was given to the charge of Khān-i Dauran Bairam Beg.[56]

Ibrāhīm Khān, the governor of Bengal, refused all overtures from Khurram. But he was defeated and killed in a battle with Khurram's troops. This victory was considered a great military achievement of

[50] *Tuzuk*, 365; *Ma'āṣir-i Jahāngīrī*, 166b. See also Chapters I and IX.

[51] *Ma'āṣir-i Jahāngīrī*, 167a. Jahāngīr, however, mentions that Bidaulat (Khurram) himself through Sarbuland Rai opened negotiations with Parvez. *Tuzuk*, 279; *Iqbālnāma*, 211; *A Dutch Chronicle*, 65-6.

[52] *A Dutch Chronicle*, 66; De Laet, 212 also corroborates it.

[53] *Ma'āṣir-i Jahāngīrī*, 167a; *Tuzuk*, 279-201; and *Iqbālnāma*, 210-1, however, does not mention 'Abdullah Khān's role.

[54] *Tuzuk*, 382; *Ma'āṣir-i Jahāngīrī*, 167a. *Bahāristān-i Ghaibī*, II, 688-9, gives more details about Khurram's campaign in Orissa, Bengal, Bihar and Allahabad.

[55] *Bahāristān-i Ghaibī*, II, 688-9.

[56] Ibid., II, 689-90; *Iqbālnāma*, 217-18; *Ma'āṣir-i Jahāngīrī*, 168a.

'Abdullah Khān. Khurram ordered a portrait of 'Abdullah Khān riding on a lion with a naked sword in his right hand and the severed head of Ibrāhīm Khān Fateh Jang in the left hand to be painted on a standard. 'Abdullah Khān was promoted by Khurram to the rank of 7,000/7,000 *du aspa sih aspa* and given a cash reward of three lacs of rupees.[57]

After making necessary arrangements in Bengal, Khurram despatched Raja Bhim to Patna in advance and followed him in the company of 'Abdullah Khān. Mukhlis Khān the governor of Bihar fled to Allahabad.[58] 'Abdullah Khān was given Hajipur and its vicinity along with Darbhanga for his *jāgīr*.[59]

Khurram despatched two separate detachments from Bihar into the *ṣūba* of Allahabad. 'Abdullah Khān and Raja Bhim were sent to Jaunpur and Daryā Khān to Manikpur to check the advance of the imperial army. On the approach of 'Abdullah Khān Jahāngīr Qulī Khān fled to Allahabad, and Jaunpur fell into the hands of 'Abdullah Khān.[60] Thereupon Khurram himself started towards Jaunpur and ordered 'Abdullah Khān to march on to Allahabad.

'Abdullah Khān laid siege of the fort of Allahabad in September 1624. Khurram tried to win over Mirzā Rustam by conciliatory methods, but it did not produce any effect. 'Abdullah Khān vigorously pressed the siege, and as a result, Zabardast Khān Deccani, Siyādat Khān and many other nobles came out of the fort and joined him.[61] But in the meantime Daryā Khān, defeated at Manikpur by the imperialist army under Parvez and Mahābat Khān, fled to Jaunpur and misunderstanding arose between Raja Bhim and 'Abdullah Khān.[62] The former withdrew from Arayal without informing 'Abdullah Khān. Therefore 'Abdullah Khān too raised the siege and joined Khurram at Banaras along with Raja Bhim and Daryā Khān. Khurram now pitched his camp at Bahadurpur, and also withdrew his forces from Chunar, under Wazīr Khān, though the fort seemed about to fall.

57 *Iqbālnāma*, 218-20; *Ma'āṣir-i Jahāngīrī*,, 172a-3b; *Riyaz-us Salatin*, 189-90. *Bahāristān-i Ghaibī*, II, 690-4 is more detailed.

58 *Bahāristān-i Ghaibī*, II, 701-2.

59 *Iqbālnāma*, 222; *Ma'āṣir-i Jahāngīrī*, 174a; *Bahāristān-i Ghaibī*, II, 711-12.

60 *Bhāristān-i Ghaibī*, II, 718, 721; *Iqbālnāma*, 223.

61 *Ma'āṣir-i Jahāngīrī*, 174; *Iqbālnāma*, 223-4; *Bahāristān-i Ghaibī*, II, 726-31; *A Dutch Chronicle*, 68.

62 *Bahāristān-i Ghaibī*, II, 732-8; *Ma'āṣir-i Jahāngīrī*, 178ab, and *A Dutch Chronicle*, 68, refer to the misunderstanding between Raja and 'Abdullah Khān.

He also summoned from Bengal 'Manmil, Durjisuz and all other *firangis* along with their fleets'; these men arrived in very short time.[63]

While these preparations were made at the camp in Bahadurpur, Bairam Beg who was left to defend the river at Jhusi was defeated and killed by Mahābat Khān.[64] The defeat affected the morale of Khurram's army adversely; a number of officers started deserting him.[65] He now consulted 'Abdullah Khān and Raja Bhim about his future plans. 'Abdullah Khān advised him to avoid a pitched battle with the imperial army as it was superior in number. He thought it would be more practical if they proceeded to Delhi via Awadh and surprised it because the royal army with the heavy baggage would not be able to intercept them. But Raja Bhim not only openly opposed this proposal but threatened to withdraw with his followers if Khurram did not decide upon a straight battle.[66] Khurram succumbed to the pressure of Raja Bhim and ordered his armies to form in battle order near the fort of Kantit. In the battle that was fought on 20 October 1624, Khurram was completely defeated. A large number of his troops perished along with Raja Bhim.[67] According to the author of the *Bahāristān-i Ghaibī*, Khurram was defeated partly because of the treachery of 'Abdullah Khān who fled from the battlefield and partly because of slackness on the part of Daryā Khān and the Rajputs who also did not give proper support to Raja Bhim.[68]

After the defeat Khurram proceeded to Rohtas and despatched 'Abdullah Khān and Daryā Khān to Patna. He also summoned Darāb Khān with the forces that he had under his command in the Decca.[69] In the meantime Mahābat Khān crossed the river Son. When this news was conveyed to Khurram, he decided to flee to Bengal, as he had lost confidence in his nobles.[70] In Bengal also he did not get the support of his officers. Darāb Khān the governor of the *ṣūba* was himself besieged by the local chiefs. Therefore, after 24 days stay in Bengal, Khurram decided to return to the Deccan. But before returning a large number of deserters including Aram Bakhsh, Darāb Khān's son, were killed by 'Abdullah Khān.[71]

[63] *Bahāristān-i Ghaibī*, II, 732, 736-7. [64] Ibid., 738. [65] Ibid., 749-50.

[66] *Iqbālnāma*, 232; *Z.K.*, (MS), 77a. But *Bahāristān-i Ghaibī*, II, 753-62 does not mention it.

[67] *Iqbālnāma*, 232; *Z.K.*, (MS) 77ab; *Bahāristān-i Ghaibī*, II, 753-62.

[68] *Bahāristān-i Ghaibī*, II, 760-1. Also see Chapter IX.

[69] *Iqbālnāma*, 238; *Bahāristān-i Ghaibī*, II, 763.

[70] *Bahāristān-i Ghaibī*, II, 771-2.

[71] *Iqbālnāma*, 238; *Bahāristān-i Ghaibī*, II, 763.

On his arrival in the Deccan, Khurram was warmly received by Malik Ambar. He was provided with a big army and Yaqut Khān Ḥabshī accompanied him to besiege Burhanpur. But they had to raise the siege because of the differences among commanders and the news of the arrival of Parvez and Mahābat Khān.[72] When Khurram left Burhanpur, 'Abdullah Khān deserted him and became a religious recluse at the village of Indur (Telengana).[73] It seems that 'Abdullah Khān decided to leave Khurram when he realized that his condition was hopeless. Although, he pretended to have left the world, he started writing letters of repentence to Parvez and Khān-i Jahān Lodī. On the promise that he would intercede on his behalf 'Abdullah Khān came and joined Khān-i Jahān Lodī. He was pardoned but it is not known whether he was given any rank by Jahāngīr.[74]

'Abdullah Khān accompanied Khān-i Jahān when he proceeded on an expedition against the Niẓāmshāhis. While they were marching, a letter written to 'Abdullah Khān by his son-in-law Khwaja Sabri's father, Khwaja Hissari, who was in the service of the Niẓām Shāhis, was intercepted. The contents of the letter indicated that he was planning to join the service of the Niẓām Shāhis. In another letter written to Malik Ambar which was also intercepted, he informed them that Khān-i Jahān had a small force and if they attacked him at this time, Khān-i Jahān would be defeated.[75]

'Abdullah Khān was thereupon arrested and handed over to Ikrām Khān, Islām Khān Chisti's son, to be confined in the fort of Asir.[76] During this period several *farmāns* on behalf of Mahābat Khān were sent to Khān-i Jahān with orders to blind 'Abdullah Khān. But Khān-i Jahān refused on the plea that 'Abdullah Khān had surrendered upon promise of safety. However, he promised to bring him to the court on his next visit.[77]

At the time of the accession of Shāhjahān, 'Abdullah Khān was in prison in the fort of Gwalior. But on 27 March 1627 at the request of a distinguished member of the Naqshbandi order, Abdur Rahīm Khawaja, the ambassador of Imam Qulī the ruler of Turan, he was pardoned. 'Abdullah Khān was given the rank of 5,000/5,000 and Rs.50,000 in *inam* and *sarkār* Kanauj in *jāgīr*.[78] His son-in-law Khwāja

[72] Ibid., 238-9.

[73] Ibid., 243-4; *Ma'āṣir-i Jahāngīrī*, 187a; *Z.K.*, II, 183.

[74] *Z.K.*, II, 183.

[75] *Z.K.*, 183-4; *A Dutch Chronicle*, 75-6.

[76] Ibid.

[77] *Ma'āṣir-ul Umarā*, I, 102.

[78] *Bādshahnāma*, I, 193-5; *Tā'rīkh-i Shahjahani*, 7a.

Sābir (the future Khān-i Dauran) who had joined Malik Ambar after 'Abdullah Khān had left Khurram, was also readmitted into service and given the rank of 3,000/2,000.[79] Khwāja Kamgar Ghairat Khān a nephew of 'Abdullah Khān was given the rank of 1,000/400.[80]

During the reign of Shāhjahān also 'Abdullah Khān continued to be one of the leading nobles of the empire. However, on a number of occasions he was punished for certain lapses. After suppressing the rebellion of Khān-i Jahān Lodī he was raised to the rank of 6,000/6,000 and appointed governor of Bihar in 1632.[81] In 1640 he was removed from the governorship and deputed to subdue the rebels Champat Bundela and Pirthvi Raj. He was given *sarkār* Islamabad (Mathura) in *jāgīr*.[82] During the campaign against the rebels he showed little interest and was even accused of helping Champat to escape. Therefore, he was dismissed from service.[83] But in the tenth regnal year he was pardoned and appointed governor of Allahabad.[84] In the same year he was again dismissed from service, on the charge of negligence of duty and disobedience and given a subsistance allowance of Rs.100,000.[85] In 1643 'AbdullahKhān was once again pardoned and his rank was restored; however, no administrative charge was given.[86] He died on 7 December 1644, at the age of 70 years.[87]

The study of 'Abdullah Khān's career indicates that even the nobles who were shifting in their loyalties, could maintain their position if they were related to some eminent families of mystics or had qualities of leadership. 'Abdullah Khān was a descendant of Khwāja Ubaidullah Nasīruddīn Ahrar, a famous Naqshbandi saint and was a gifted commander.[88] The author of *Zakhīrat-ul Khwānīn* writes that he looked after his soldiers very well. Although the soldiers did not get more than three or four months' salary yet compared to the payments made by other nobles, the salary paid by 'Abdullah Khān was equal to one year's salary. He further says that whenever he was engaged in an important expedition he used to march 60 to 70 km a day. He kept trustworthy soldiers as rear guards and if any one lagged behind, his head was cut off.[89]

However, his relations were not recruited into service in any numbers. His brother Sardār Khān who attained the rank of 3,000/

[79] Ibid., 266-7; *Ma'āṣir-ul Umarā*. I, 750.
[80] Ibid., 319-20.
[81] *Bādshahnāma*, I, 354, 426.
[82] Ibid., II, 137.
[83] Ibid., I, 195.
[84] Ibid., II, 307.
[85] Ibid., 332.
[86] Ibid., 348.
[87] Ibid., 402.
[88] See, supra.
[89] *Z.K.*, II, 184-5.

2,500 seldom held an independent charge. He served under 'Abdullah Khān and died in 1624.[90] Mirzā Walī, Khwāja Ḥasan Naqshbandi's son, who was married to the daughter of Daniyal also could not rise to a higher rank (he held the rank of 2,000/1,000).[91] 'Abdullah Khān's two sons Mirzā Khān and Abdul Rasul were also not given *manṣabs* during Jahāngīr's reign. Mirzā Khān was arrested and put to death by Jahāngīr after 'Abdullah Khān joined Khurram in the battle of Bilochpur.[92] 'Abdul Rasul was alive during Shāhjahān's reign and also served in the Deccan, but his rank is not known[93] so that it is likely that it was less than 500 *zāt*. It is significant that in his life-time many of 'Abdullah Khān's servants after leaving his and joining imperial service, 'rose to the rank of 5,000 and 4,000'.[94] However, during the reign of Shāhjahān his son-in-law Khān-i Dauran attained the rank of 7,000/7,000, 5,000 *du aspa sih aspa* and held the governorship of the Deccan.[95] Ghairat Khān, Sardar Khān's son, was also promoted to the rank of 3,000/2,000 and appointed governor of Delhi in 1638.[96]

[90] *Tuzuk*, 76, 117, 158-9; *Ma'āṣir-i Jahāngīrī*, 141b, 153a, 155a.

[91] *Tuzuk*, 283, 344.

[92] *A Dutch Chronicle*, 65.

[93] *Ma'āṣir-i Jahāngīrī*, I, 101-2.

[94] These nobles are mentioned in *Zakhīrat-ul Khwānīn* as those previously in the service of 'Abdullah Khān.
(i) Ṣafdar Khān (*Z.K.*, III, 40), (ii) Yūsuf Mohd. Khān (*Z.K.*, III, 42), (iii) Shadi Khān Uzbeg (*Z.K.*, III, 59), (iv) Umar Khān Tūrānī (*Z.K.*, III, 7), (v) Yaulam Khān Uzbeg (*Z.K.*, III, 90), (vi) Nazar Bahādur Uzbeg (*Z.K.*, III, 90).

[95] *Bādshahnāma*, II, 376-7.

[96] Ibid., I, 352, 398, II, 198, 225, 338.

CHAPTER IX

The Family of Mahābat Khān

Mahābat Khān became one of the most powerful and influential nobles of Jahāngīr, although he did not possess a large clan or following within the nobility. His rise to a high position immediately after Jahāngīr's accession was the result of his earlier service with Jahāngīr. Later in the reign his relations were strained with both the imperial factions, the Tūrānīs and the Irānīs (although he was himself of Irānī descent). But he was still called upon to suppress the rebellion of Khurram. Subsequently, when his dominant position excited jealousy at court, he carried out a *coup d'etat* and even obtained control of the person of the emperor for some time.

During the last years of Jahāngīr at least, Mahābat Khān seems to have enjoyed the support of many Rajputs and Indian Muslims (particularly Afghāns). He himself said that his strength lay in the Rajputs. Of his 6,000 retainers, 4,000 were Rajputs and the remainder consisted of Sayyids, Shaikhs, Mughals and Afghāns.[1] According to the author of the *Fatḥ Nāma-i Nūrjahān Begum*, Mahābat Khān recruited only Rajputs and Afghāns and claimed that ten Rajputs could overwhelm a hundred Mughals.[2] But except for a very vague statement that he had the cooperation of the Sisodia Rajputs, it is difficult to discover which particular clans of Rajputs were specially attached to him. Besides, no important Rajput noble has been specially mentioned among his associates, except Sarbuland Rai of Bundi.[3] His links with the Afghāns may be explained by the fact that Kabul was his native place. Mahābat Khān's relations with Indian Muslims were of

[1] *Z.K.*, II, 132. Kami Shirazi, *Fatḥ Nāma-i Nūrjahān Begum*, Bibliotheque Nationale, Paris, MS, iii, 187-8, 506, fol. 22b, however does not count Sayyids, Shaikhs and Mughāls among his retainers.

[2] *Fatḥ Nāma-i Nūrjahān Begum*, 27a.

[3] Mahābat Khān made Sarbuland Rai (Rao Ratan Hara) incharge of the Deccan while proceeding to east against Khurram. See *Iqbālnāma*, 224; *Z.K.*, II, 125-6. *Z.K.*, II, 132, says that the Rana of Mewar helped him when he was dismissed from the governorship of Bengal and was going to the court.

a special nature too: he took a wife from a family of the Khānzadas of Mewat. This was a rather uncommon act for a noble of Irānian origin.

However, we do not come across any prominent Afghān or Indian Muslim nobles among his friends and allies.

It is a matter of enquiry why Mahābat Khān became hostile to the Tūrānīs and the Irānīs and friendly to the Rajputs and Indian Muslims. About the Tūrānīs it might be suggested that as he was an Irānī, the hostility was of a factional nature. His equally unfriendly attitude towards the Irānīs, might have possibly grown out of suspicions against the family of I'timad-ud daulah, which by now had become the nucleus of the Iranian nobility.

Mahābat Khān's father Ghaiyūr Beg was a Rizvi Sayyid of Shirāz. He came to Kabul in his youth and entered Mirzā Hakim's service. After the death of that prince, Ghaiyūr Beg came to India and joined Akbar's service;[4] but he did not rise to a high position and apparently failed to get a *manṣab*. His son Zamān Beg thereupon had to enter the service of Prince Salīm as no more than an *ahadi* or cavalry trooper. Salīm was highly impressed by his loyalty and devotion, and gave him the rank of 500 and the office of the *Bakhshī* of *Shagird Pesha*.[5] Zamān Beg remained loyal to the prince even during the period he was at Allahabad defying his father, when many of his other followers had left him. Upon Salīm's instructions he killed Raja Ujjainia who had come to meet the prince at the head of a large force.[6]

After the accession of Jahāngīr, Mahābat Khān was raised to the rank of 1,500, along with other nobles who had been the prince's supporters at the accession crisis or were his personal servants.[7] When Khusrau rebelled, Mahābat Khān was deputed with Shaikh Farīd Bukhārī in his pursuit. It was even decided that if Khusrau resolved on going to Kabul, the emperor himself would follow him and if the prince fled to Badakhshan the emperor would return to India leaving

[4] *Tuzuk*, 10, gives the name of Zamān Beg's father. See also *Ma'āṣir-i Jahāngīrī*, 28b; *Z.K.*, II, 116-7. Although the author of *Zakhīrat-ul Khawānīn* had not discussed the circumstances which led Ghaiyūr Beg to migrate from Shirāz, the religious persecution in Iran might have been an important reason because Mahābat Khān was a Sunni in his early life. See Afzal Hasain, 'Growth of Irānī Elements in Akbar's Nobility', *Proceedings of Indian History Congress*, 1975; 166-79.

[5] *Tuzuk*, 10.

[6] *Z.K.*, II, 117. Manucci believes that this was the main reason of the rise of Mahābat Khān (Niccolao Manucci, *Storia do Mogor*, ed. and tr. William Irvin, London, 1907, Vol.I, 166-7).

[7] *Tuzuk*, 10.

Mahābat Khān at Kabul to defend it from the joint forces of Khusrau and the Uzbeks.[8]

During the campaign against Khusrau, differences arose among the nobles. Mahābat Khān and Sharīf Khān Amīr-ul Umarā complained that Shaikh Farīd was deliberately marching slowly, allowing Khusrau time to escape. Jahāngīr accepted their version and Shaikh Farīd was reprimanded.[9] This incident may be treated as a reflection of the tension between the old Akbarshāhī nobility of which Shaikh Farīd was the representative, and the Jahāngīrī nobles.

After the defeat of Khusrau, he was handed over to the custody of Mahābat Khān and this was, of course, a mark of the emperor's great confidence in him.[10] Mahābat Khān was also promoted twice in the same year, raising him to the rank of 2,500/1,300.[11] The *pargana* of Mahaban was given to him in *jāgīr*.[12] About this time a conspiracy against Jahāngīr was hatched by some supporters of Khusrau. According to one early report, a younger brother of Mahābat Khān was involved. When the conspiracy was detected Mahābat Khān's brother was among those to be hanged. When Mahābat Khān reached the spot, his brother was still alive and was groaning. Jahāngīr told him that if he wanted his brother's life to be spared, he could himself take him down from the gallows. But Mahābat Khān went to his brother, took out his sword and cut off his head. The author of *Tārikh-i Khān Jahāni* writes that after this incident Mahābat Khān became a great confidant of the emperor.[13]

The first important assignment given to Mahābat Khān was the campaign against the Rana of Mewar in 1608. He was promoted to the rank of 3,000/2,500, and 1,2000 troops and important commanders like Bir Singh Deo Bundela, Ẓafar Khān, Shujā'at Khān, Narain Das, Mangali Khān and Hizabr Khān were despatched with him.[14] Significantly most of these men belonged to the categoryof Jahāngīrī nobles. The campaign, however, was not very successful and Mahābat Khān was summoned to the court in 1609. Jahāngīr does not record the failure of the campaign, and only says rather vaguely that Mahābat Khān was called to the court to arrange certain matters.[15]

[8] *Tuzuk*, 30-1. Jahāngīr anticipated an alliance between Khusrau and the Uzbeks.

[9] *Tuzuk*, 31; *Iqbālnāma*, 9-10.

[10] *A Dutch Chronicle*, 39.

[11] *Tuzuk*, 37.

[12] Ibid.

[13] *Tārikh-i Khān Jahāni*, II, 691-2. But *Tuzuk*, 58-9, and *Iqbālnāma*, 27-9, do not mention this incident, though they mention the conspiracy.

[14] *Tuzuk*, 69-70; *Iqbālnāma*, 34; *A Dutch Chronicle*, 43-4. Also see Chapter VIII.

[15] *Tuzuk*, 74; *The Dutch Chronicle*, 44, mentions that Mahābat Khān conquered a very small

Soon after his return from Mewar, Mahābat Khān was despatched to the Deccan to bring 'Abdur Raḥīm Khān Khanān, who had been relieved of the Deccan command at the suggestion of Khān-i Jahān Lodī. He was also asked to find out the strength of the forces of the *manṣabdars* stationed in the Deccan. Mahābat Khān returned to the court along with 'Abdur Raḥīm Khān Khanān in 1610.[16]

In 1610, as the Deccan campaign under Khān-i Jahān too failed to achieve any success, Jahāngīr appointed Mirzā 'Azīz Koka as the supreme commander in his place. Mahābat Khān was promoted to the rank of 4,000/3,500 and ordered to conduct Mirzā 'Azīz Koka and the army appointed with him to Burhanpur. He was also asked to enquire into the circumstances leading to the defeat of the imperial forces. After that he was to return to court. Mahābat Khān reached Agra in the last month of 1611.[17]

During the next two years Mahābat Khān was not given an important duty, and he remained at the court. He was given a promotion during the new year's celebration of the seventh regnal year and assigned in *jāgīr* the territory previously held in (ordinary) *jāgīr* and *watan* by Raja Jagman who had failed in his duty in the Deccan in 1613.[18] In 1614 Mahābat Khān was sent to Udaipur to bring to the court Mirzā 'Azīz Koka who had been dismissed from service on account of his alleged treachery in the Mewar campaign.[19] Mahābat Khān returned to Ajmer, along with Mirzā 'Azīz and his son Mirzā 'Abdullah.[20] When he reached Ajmer, he was asked to take custody of the person of Aḥmad Beg Khān who had been imprisoned at the complaint of Qulich Khān; the prisoner was to be confined in the fort of Ranthambor which was in Mahābat Khān's *jāgīr*.[21]

In 1615 Mahābat Khān was appointed to serve in the Deccan and posted there along with Khān-i Jahān Lodī. At this juncture 1,700 of his *sawār* rank were converted into *du aspa sih aspa*.[22] We have no information

portion of the country of the Rana. But the author of *Ma'āṣir-i Jahāngīrī*, 48ab clearly states that as Mahābat Khān did not perform this service successfully, 'Abdullah Khān was given the command. *Z.K.*, III, 117; *Vir Vinod*, V, 224-5. For more details, also see Chapter VIII.

[16] *Tuzuk*, 86; *Iqbālnāma*; *Ma'āṣir-i Jahāngīrī*, 57a.

[17] *Tuzuk*, 88-9.

[18] *Tuzuk*, 106. There is some confusion in the noting of *manṣabs*. In the account of 1611, while mentioning Mahābat Khān's promotion by 1,000/1,000, his *manṣab* is recorded as 4,000/3,500, although the previous rank held by him was 2,500/1,300. In 1,613 after a promotion of 500 *sawār* his rank is again recorded as 4,000/3,500.

[19] See Chapter II for details.

[20] *Tuzuk*, 126-7; *Iqbālnāma*, 74.

[21] *Tuzuk*, 136.

[22] Ibid., 148; *Z.K.*, II, 117, but does not mention the *du aspa sih aspa* rank being given to him. *The*

about his activities in the Deccan during the period that he was apparently posted there. The next reference about him in the *Tuzuk* relates to the year 1617. Jahāngīr writes that Mahābat Khān had been given a special *du aspa sih aspa* rank (involving additional cavalry and corresponding pay) on condition of service in the Deccan. Since he did not perform this service, the rank was withdrawn and his *jāgīrs* correspondingly reduced.[22]

The information contained in the *Iqbālnāma-i Jahāngīrī* for the same period is slightly different, but it helps us to understand the causes of the resumption of his *du aspa sih aspa* rank. Mu'tamid Khān says that when Khurram was appointed to the Deccan, and Parvez transferred to Allahabad, Mahābat Khān was despatched to Burhanpur to conduct Parvez to Allahabad after collecting the revenues.[24] Mu'tamid Khān does not mention that Mahābat Khān was already serving in the Deccan. Apparently, upon his return from Allahabad, he fell into some disfavour with Khurram, leading to the withdrawal of the special rank.

Mahābat Khān was among those who returned with Khurram to the court in 1617. He was now appointed governor of Kabul.[25] The author of *Zakhīrat-ul Khawānīn*, writes that this appointment, removing him from the court, was on account of the influence of Khurram and the family of I'timad-ud-daulah with whom his relations were strained. Mahābat Khān is said to have been so resentful at this appointment that he toyed with the idea of fleeing to Iran, after he had reached Kabul. 'But his son Khānazād Khān cleverly managed to scare away his men and he had to give up the idea.'[26] From the *Tuzuk* it is also evident that Mahābat Khān was no longer in much favour. Indeed, much time passed before he could come to the court again. In the account of the fourteenth regnal year while permitting Mahābat Khān to come to the court Jahāngīr writes, 'As Mahābat Khān had been prevented from the good fortune of coming before me for a long time I ordered at his request that if he was satisfied with the order of affairs and was not troubled with regard to any occurrence, he should leave

---

Dutch Chronicle, 47, states that after the collapse of the 'grand offensive', Jahāngīr appointed Mahābat Khān as 'governor-general of Burhanpur and Barar'. Also see De Laet, 188-9.

[23] *Tuzuk*, 190.

[24] *Iqbālnāma*, 92, but he gives reference to neither the assignment of the *du aspa sih aspa* rank nor its withdrawal.

[25] *Tuzuk*, 196; *Z.K.*, II, 117.

[26] *Z.K.*, II, 117.

his force at their posts (*thānās*) and come to court unattended.'[27] It is interesting to note that Khān-i Jahān Lodī was also summoned to court in 1617; and that he remained there without any important duty being given to him until his posting to Multan in 1620.[28]

An anecdote in the *Intekhāb-i Jahāngīr Shāhi*, a source of doubtful authenticity, recounts that Nūr Jahān had attained a dominant influence over the affairs of the empire, and that Mahābat Khān in the presence of Khān-i Jahān Lodī and Khān-i Ālam complained to the emperor about this state of affairs. He also pleaded for the release of Khusrau from confinement, and the entrusting of his person to a trusty noble. Both Khān-i Jahān Lodī and Khān-i Ālam agreed with these sentiments. Jahāngīr, therefore, the next day entrusted Khusrau to Khān-i Jahān Lodī, with permission to the prince to pay his respects at the court. An order for a proper treatment of his eyes was also issued. For a few days after the representation of Mahābat Khān, Jahāngīr remained reserved in his demeanour towards the empress; but when Mahābat Khān left the court at Pakli, the emperor again fell under her control.[29]

From the information available in our sources, it appears that the anecdote has some factual basis. The event could have occurred in 1619-20. During this period Jahāngīr proceeded to Kashmir, accompanied by Khān-i Jahān Lodī and Khān-i Ālam. Mahābat Khān also came to the court from Kabul and accompanied him up to Pakli.[30] Khusrau was indeed released and permitted to come to pay his respects at this time,[31] and from a statement in the *Iqbālnāma-i Jahāngīrī*, it transpires that Khusrau, Khān-i Jahān Lodī and Khān-i Ālam rode one stage behind the emperor during the march to Kashmir. Possibly Khān-i Jahān Lodī might have been entrusted with the custody of Khusrau's

[27] *Tuzuk*, 287-8; *Iqbālnāma*, 134. [28] Cf. Chapter V.

[29] *Intekhāb-i Jahāngīr Shāhi* B.M. Or. 1648, 320-2; Elliot and Dowson, Vol.VI, 451-2; Nurul Ḥasan, 'The Theory of Nūrjahān Junta — a critical examination', *Indian History Congress*, 1958, 325-5. He does not consider the information reliable on the ground of the 'extreme unlikelihood of a noble complaining to Jahāngīr about Nūrjahān in 1620'. But we have the example of Mirzā 'Azīz Koka who criticized Jahāngīr in no less harsh terms. See Chapter II.

[30] *Tuzuk*, 287-9; *Iqbālnāma*, 134-5.

[31] *Tuzuk*, 280, while Jahāngīr was at Brindaban in 1619, Khusrau was released from confinement and permitted to come to the court (*Iqbālnāma*, 129-30). According to Mu'tamid Khān, Mirzā 'Azīz Koka asked Jadrup Gosain to pray for Khusrau's release, *Tawārikh-i Jahāngīr Shāhi*, 40ab. Walī Sarhindis writing in 1619 praises the sons of the emperor, starting with Khusrau. His account certainly goes against the possibility of Khusrau being in confinement at that time.

person.[32] Mahābat Khān was in fact given permission to go to Kabul from Pakli, just as is recorded in the *Intekhāb-i Jahāngīr Shāhī*.[33]

In the light of the evidence of *Intekhāb-i Jahāngīr Shāhī* and other information discussed earlier, it is quite clear that the family of I'timad-ud daulah had become very influential around 1616 and 1617. As the family had matrimonial relations with Khurram, it might have utilized the opportunity of the reverses of the Mughal forces in the Deccan under Parvez to further build up Khurram's position.[34] As a result of the appointment of Khurram in the Deccan, the career of Parvez and certain nobles was adversely affected. Although after the transfer of Parvez to Allahabad, Mahābat Khān, Khān-i Jahān Lodī and 'Abdur Raḥīm Khān Khanān served under Khurram, the relations of Mahābat Khān and Khān-i Jahān Lodī remained strained.[35] 'Abdur Raḥīm Khān Khanān who had nominally served under Parvez appears to have changed sides and became now a partisan of Khurram;[36] but Mahābat Khān and Khān-i Jahān Lodī were summoned to court shortly afterwards. The reason for their recall might have been Khurram's suspicions towards them because Khān-i Jahān Lodī had openly criticized his appointment in the Deccan in place of Parvez.[37] Regarding Mahābat Khān, although there is no reference to show at this stage that he favoured Parvez, his hostility to I'timad-ud daudlah's family may be assumed from the attitude he was openly to adopt later on. He could then well have pleaded for the release of Khusrau as suggested by the *Intekhāb-i Jahāngīr Shāhī*.

This, however, need not mean that the Mughal court was divided into two groups, 'the adherents of the Nūr Jahān Junta and their opponents' as concluded by Beni Prasad.[38] There is no denying that the family of I'timad-ud daulah had become quite influential, and as a result of its machinations, Mahābat Khān and Khān-i Jahān Lodī were sent to distant provinces, and Mahābat Khān was not given promotion in rank for a very long time.[39] But there is no evidence that

[32] *Iqbālnāma*, 128, 138. [33] Ibid., 121, 135, 137.

[34] For the campaigns in the Deccan under Parvez, see Chapters I and V.

[35] See supra. [36] See Chapters I and V. [37] For details see Chapter V.

[38] *History of Jahāngīr*, 177-9.

[39] Nurul Ḥasan in his 'The Theory of Nūrjahān Junta', 329-30 has tried to explain that Mahābat Khān was not treated unfavourably. But as a matter of fact his *manṣab* was not raised beyond 4,000/3,500 after 1621. He was given 1,700 *du aspa sih aspa* at the time of his appointment to the Deccan, but the rank was withdrawn on the charge that he did not perform this service. In 1617 he was sent to Kabul. Mahābat Khān was so unhappy on this appointment that he wanted to go to Iran. See supra for more details.

the critics of I'timad-ud daulah's family were united among themselves so as to form a group. For example, Mahābat Khān, Khān-i Jahān Lodī and 'Abdullah Khān were themselves greatly hostile to each other.[40] On the other hand, the family of I'timad-ud daulah itself from 1620 onwards was divided, Nūr Jahān and 'Āṣaf Khān pulling in apparently different directions.[41] As a matter of fact we hardly come across a family group with permanent loyalties; their attitude and the attitude of even individual nobles was determined from the point of view of their own personal interests.

During the period of Mahābat Khān's governorship of Kabul, he was supposedly not on good terms with the 'court party'; yet his son Amānullah got considerable promotions. In 1618 he was promoted to the rank of 1,000/300 and in the following year to the rank of 1,500/800. In 1620, when Mahābat Khān returned to Kabul from his visit to the court, Amānullah was promoted to the rank of 2,000/1,500.[42] These promotions are quite significant because during the same period Mahābat Khān himself was not given any increase in rank.

It is not known what Mahābāt Khān's attitude towards Prince Shaharyār was, but his relations with Nūr Jahān seem to have improved. In 1622 when Mahābat Khān came to the court he was very warmly received and styled *Rukn-us Saltanat*. Mahābat Khān brought with him a physician called Ḥakīm Mumina for undertaking a treatment of the emperor. Mu'tamid Khān writes that when the emperor started recovering, Mahābat Khān was given leave to go to Kabul. During the same period his son Amānullah was further promoted to the rank of 2,000/1,800.[43]

When Khurram rebelled in 1622, Mahābat Khān, whose attitude to Khurram must have hardened particularly after the murder of Khusrau, was summoned to the court. It is significant that the summons should have been sent by Nūr Jahān, at, it was said, Mahābat Khān's own insistence.[44] This would have been very unlikely if Mahābat Khān had any reservations about the empress herself. However, before coming to the court, he wrote that he would come only after 'Āṣaf Khān who was in league with Khurram was transferred to Bengal and Mu'tamid Khān, another partisan of the prince, was punished.[45] Being

[40] See Chapters V and VIII. [41] See infra. [42] *Tuzuk*, 248, 274, 344.
[43] *Tuzuk*, 343-4; *Iqbālnāma*, 191-2. [44] *Iqbālnāma*, 195; *Bādshahnāma*, II, 24.
[45] *Iqbālnāma*, 195; *Ma'āṣir-i Jahāngīrī*, 156ab; *Ahwāl-i Shahzadgi-i Shāhjahān Padshah*, 18b-19b.

assured of these conditions, Mahābat Khān came to the court. Immediately after reaching the court, he brought to the notice of the emperor the existence of a party of nobles in treacherous correspondence with the rebel prince, its alleged ring-leaders being Muhtarim Khān, Mu'tamid Khān and certain others.[46] Mu'tamid Khān adds that Mahābat Khān suggested that Mu'tamid Khān be despatched to Kabul where his agents would have him done away with. 'Āṣaf Khān was also despatched to Agra, and if European accounts are to be believed, he was held in custody by the king.[47] Mahābat Khān was promoted to the rank of 6,000/5,000 and given command of the army against Khurram. His son Amānullah was promoted to the rank of 3,000/1,800.[48]

A battle between the imperial army and the rebels was fought at Bilochpur.[49] The author of the *Ma'āṣir-i Jahāngīrī* writes that when Mahābat Khān noticed that the rebel forces were in a commanding position he took recourse to stratagem and through deceitful words convinced Qāẓi Abdul 'Azīz that if Khurram accepted the royal order and turned back towards the Deccan, he would undertake the confirmation of his *jāgīrs* and send the *sanads* of those *mahals* stamped with the *Uzuk* seal. When this message was communicated to Khurram through Qāẓi Abdul 'Azīz, he grasped the opportunity of reconciliation now provided, and turned towards the Deccan. But when Khurram crossed Ghati Chanda, Mahābat Khān threw the proposal overboard and persuaded the emperor to proceed to Ajmer and depute an army under the command of Parvez and himself as his *atāliq* to pursue the rebels.[50] But Kamgar Husaini is alone in giving this story, which, on the face of it, is quite improbable. The battle of Bilochpur was a hard fought battle, though it is true that Khurram kept away from it.

After marching from Bilochpur, Khurram took shelter in the fort of Mandu. When Parvez and Mahābat Khān, approached the fort he came out to fight. But the rebels were demoralized on account of dissension encouraged by Mahābat Khān and the defeat of 'Abdullah Khān Fīroz Jang in Gujarat.[51] Having no alternative left, Khurram

[46] *Iqbālnāma*, 199; *Ma'āṣir-i Jahāngīrī*, 158b. Others who were involved were Khalīl Beg Zulqadar and Nuruddin Qulī. According to Kamgar Husaini, Mu'tamid Khān was sent to Thatta. See *English Factory Records*, 1622-3, 197.

[47] *Iqbālnāma*, 195, 197, 199; *Ma'āṣir-i Jahāngīrī*, 157b; Deela Valle, 121.

[48] *Tuzuk*, 347-8; *Ma'āṣir-i Jahāngīrī*, 156ab states that the command was given to Prince Shaharyār.

[49] *Tuzuk*, 357-8; *Iqbālnāma*, 202; *A Dutch Chronicle*, 59. For details, see Chapter VIII.

[50] *Ma'āṣir-i Jahāngīrī*, 161ab. But *Tuzuk*, 356-9 and *Iqbālnāma*, 204, do not mention any understanding whatsoever.

[51] Barqandaz Khān with the entire artillery deserted Khurram, and he was followed by

opened negotiations with Parvez and Mahābat Khān. But Parvez and Mahābat Khān demanded that he first send 'Abdur Rahīm Khān Khanān to the imperial side. Khurram had no faith in 'Abdur Rahīm Khān Khanān as he was already in correspondence with Mahābat Khān but was forced to give him up under the circumstances. No sooner had 'Abdur Rahīm Khān Khanān left Khurram's camp than some imperialists, taking advantage of the lack of vigilance of the enemy, owing to the peace moves, crossed the river and fell upon the rebels. 'Abdur Rahīm Khān Khanān and a number of other nobles who were wavering in their loyalty now joined Parvez. Khurram fled to Golkunda and from there made his way to Orissa and Bengal.[52]

After the departure of the rebels, Mahābat Khān started making arrangements for the settlement of the Deccan affairs. Malik Ambar offered his submission and requested that the Deccan affairs be given to his charge. His main motive behind this move was to attack 'Ādil Shāh with the help of the Mughals. But Mahābat Khān preferred an alliance with 'Ādil Shāh who also accepted the suzerainty of the Mughals and despatched his *Wakil* Mullā Muḥammad Lari with 5,000 horses to serve the imperial army posted in the Deccan.[53]

While these negotiations were in progress, a *farmān* was issued ordering Parvez and Mahābat Khān to proceed to Allahabad to check the progress of Khurram's troops in the east, if the governor of Bengal and Bihar failed to counter them. On receiving this order, Mahābat Khān appointed Sarbuland Rai (Rao Ratan Hara), one of his confidants, to take charge of the Deccan and himself proceeded to the north along with Parvez.[54]

In the meantime Khurram had marched through Orissa, Bengal and Bihar and laid siege to the fort of Allahabad. But when they came to know of the approach of Mahābat Khān, Khurram's troops raised the siege, and a decisive battle was fought on the bank of the Tons. Khurram was again defeated and fled to Bengal and from there to the Deccan. After this victory Mahābat Khān received the title of *Khān Khanān* was promoted to the rank of 7,000/7,000 *du aspa sih aspa* and made governor of Bengal.[55] When he reached

---

Muḥammad Bakhsh, Rustam Khān and others. 'Abdur Rahīm Khān Khanān also opened negotiations with Mahābat Khān and one of his letters written to him was intercepted by Khurram men. 'Abdur Raḥīm and his sons were then made prisoners. *Iqbālnāma*, 209-10: *Ma'āṣir-i Jahāngīrī*, 194ab and Chapter VIII.

[52] For details, see Chapter VIII.

[53] *Iqbālnāma*, 223-5; *Z.K.*, I, 119-21; *Anfaul Akhbār* (Asafiya), 223-8.

[54] *Iqbālnāma*, 224-8; *Anfaul Akhbār* (Asafiya), 229-30; *Z.K.*, II, 118-20.

[55] *Iqbālnāma*, 232-3, *Ma'āṣir-i Jahāngīrī*, 180a records the promotion in his rank. he adds that Bengal was given to Mahābat Khān and his son in *jāgīr* in lieu of their salary. *Z.K.*, II, 122-4.

Bengal, Darāb Khān, 'Abdur Rahīm Khān Khanān's son, who had been appointed governor of Bengal by Khurram but presently was in the custody of the Zamīndār, was produced before him. On the orders of the emperor, he was executed. Mahābat Khān, in a particular act of malice, sent the head of Darāb Khān to 'Abdur Raḥīm Khān Khanān who was then in his custody.[56]

During the absence of Parvez and Mahābat Khān the situation in the Deccan again became alarming. Malik Ambar showing great zeal and energy gained the greatest victory of his life; he was successful in defeating the combined forces of the 'Ādil Shāhis and the Mughals at Bhatodi. He occupied the whole of Balaghat and laid siege to Ahmadnagar and Burhanpur. With the arrival of Khurram, the situation worsened.[57] Hence, Jahāngīr issued a *farmān* to Parvez and Mahābat Khan to proceed immediately to the relief of the Mughal forces in the Deccan. At the request of Mahābat Khān, his son Amānullah, now titled Khānazād Khān, was also summoned from Kabul and despatched to help his father.[58]

When Mahābat Khān along with Parvez reached Sarangpur on his way to the Deccan, Fidāi Khān arrived with an imperial *farmān*, with the order of Mahābat Khān's transfer to Bengal and Khān-i Jahān's appointment as the *atāliq* of Parvez. But Parvez did not agree to this arrangement. He refused to relieve Mahābat Khān and accept Khān-i Jahān as his substitute. On this, another *farmān* was issued which required Parvez to obey the imperial orders, adding that if Mahābat Khān was not willing to go to Bengal, he should come to the court leaving Khānazād Khān as his deputy in Bengal. Mahābat Khān was charged with appropriating a huge amount of money at the time of the transfer of *jāgīrs* of the imperial servants and of withholding elephants which were captured in Bengal.[59] Shortly afterwards Arab Dast Ghaib was despatched to bring him to the court.[60]

[56] For details see Chapter VIII.

[57] *Iqbālnāma*, 234-8; *Z.K.*, II, 125-9. See also Chapter VII.

[58] *Iqbālnāma*, 239; *Z.K.*, II, 130. *A Dutch Chronicle*, 71 states that Khānazād Khān was also promoted to the rank of 5,000 at this juncture.

[59] *Iqbālnāma*, 245-8; *Ma'āṣir-i Jahāngīrī*, 187b; *Z.K.*, II, 131. *A Dutch Chronicle*, 74 gives an altogether different version of this event.

Mahābat Khān suspected that Khān Khanān (who was summoned to court from his custody) was trying to bring about his ruin and misunder-standing arose between Mahābat Khān and the followers of Sulṭān Parvez which led the prince acting on bad advice to ask the king to recall Mahābat Khān. The King did so at the instigation of Nūr Jahān, her brother 'Āṣaf Khān, Khān Khanān and other Chaghtāī enemies (of Mahābat Khān). But this is not corroborated by any other source.

[60] *Iqbālnāma*, 248; *Z.K.*, II, 131.

Mahābat Khān left Burhanpur to make his way to the court. Parvez accompanied him up to Sarai Bahari. Mahābat Khān wanted to take with him some of the *manṣabdars* and trusted servants of the prince, but Fāzil Khān, the *Diwān* of the Deccan, demurred saying that as he had incurred imperial displeasure and was ordered to come alone, it would be advisable if no one accompanied him. Mahābat Khān agreed but said that as this plan of separating him (from Parvez) was actually aimed against the prince, grave consequences would follow.[61]

It is quite interesting to note that Mahābat Khān was summoned to the court and the plan subsequently to arrest him was made jointly by Nūr Jahān and 'Āṣaf Khān though during the years 1620-2 both had been in different camps.[62] After the murder of Khusrau and the rebellion of Khurram, Nūr Jahān's efforts were directed in raising Shaharyār to the status of the heir to the throne. As already discussed in the beginning, Jahāngīr appears to have made no objections to this and even gave Shaharyār promotions in rank and important military commands, because he was not satisfied with the performance of Parvez.[63] But it seems that Mahābat Khān was opposed to Shaharyār, and it had been at his suggestion that Parvez was initially given the command against Khurram.[64] When Nūr Jahān realized that the rebels were completely under control, and the need for a military commander like Mahābat Khān receded, she planned to isolate Parvez. For this the best course, as seen by Mahābat Khān himself, was to separate Mahābat Khān from Parvez.[65] Although 'Āṣaf Khān was considered a partisan of Khurram, yet because throughout the rebellion he had remained loyal, he again became a favourite with the emperor, and at the request of Nūr Jahān he was not sent to Bengal. The common point which might have facilitated an understanding between Nūr Jahān and 'Āṣaf Khān appears to have been their fear of and hostility to the rise of Parvez and Mahābat Khān; for 'Āṣaf Khān it was hardly possible at this time to support Khurram directly.

On the transfer of Mahābat Khān, the reactions of many nobles are not known, but from a *farmān* of Jahāngīr issued to Mirzā Raja Jai Singh, it transpires that the Raja was not very happy with Mahābat Khān's removal from the Deccan, and was tardy in extending cooperation to Khān-i Jahān Lodī. Both Jahāngīr and Nūr Jahān tried

61 *Z.K.*, II, 131; Cf. *A Dutch Chronicle*, 74.

62 See supra.

63 See supra.

64 See supra.

65 *Z.K.*, II, 131.

to persuade him to help Khān-i Jahān and even threatened him with dire consequences including dismissal from imperial service if he failed to extend full obedience to orders.[66]

After reaching Ranthambor, Mahābat Khān began to take precautionary measures and collected a large number of retainers. Rana Kohi (apparently the Rana of Mewar) also came to see him and supplied him with 1,000 fully armed troops. When Mahābat Khān started from Ranthambor he had 6,000 retainers of whom 4,000 were Rajputs and 2,000 Indian Muslims, including Afghāns.[67]

While Mahābat Khān was at Ranthambor, Arab Dast Ghaib reached there with 1,000 soldiers to conduct him to the court. On his arrival, Mahābat Khān sent him a message saying that he was aware of his mission and as he was himself going to the court, he should not say anything to him in company. Arab Dast Ghaib considered it advisable to remain silent.[68]

Mahābat Khān reached Lahore at a time when the emperor was proceeding to Kabul. 'Āṣaf Khān informed him that he would not be allowed to pay his respects until he had cleared the demands made on him by the office of the imperial *Diwān* and had explained his conduct in Bengal in appropriating the revenues of certain *Jāgīrs*. About the same time the matter regarding the marriage of his daughter to Khwāja Barkhurdār without the permission of the emperor was also brought up. Jahāngīr showed much annoyance and ordered Barkhurdār to be brought to the court, where he was humiliated and imprisoned. Fidāi Khān was asked to get back from him whatever was given to him by Mahābat Khān, and deposit it in the imperial treasury.[69] Shortly after this incident Mahābat Khān's daughter was summoned to the court. Mahābat Khān thereupon appealed to his Rajput allies saying that the honour of his daughter was in danger.[70] He also entertained the fear that 'Āṣaf Khān had made a plan to take him prisoner. 'Āṣaf Khān had so arranged that on the day when the imperial encampment was on the banks of Jhelum, after the whole army and the camp had crossed the river and the emperor was left alone with his guards on this side of the river Mahābat Khān would come to pay his respects.

[66] See Chapter IV.

[67] *Z.K.*, II, 132-3; *Iqbālnāma*, 252, also mentions that Mahābat Khān had four to five thousand Rajput retainers with him at the time when he reached Lahore.

[68] *Z.K.*, II, 132; *Iqbālnāma*, 248, mentions only the appointment of Arab Dast Ghaib.

[69] *Iqbālnāma*, 252-3; *Z.K.*, II, 132-3, provides more details.

[70] *Z.K.*, II, 134. No other source refers to this incident.

The emperor would take him by hand and put him into the royal boat; the bridge would then be broken, and Mahābat Khān's men would be unable to accompany him. Mahābat Khān, therefore, despatched Aḥmad Khān Afghān with 1,000 horses to protect the bridge while reporting to the court that Aḥmad was going to join the imperial army. When the royal camp reached Shahabad, Jagpat Khān came to Mahābat Khān to demand the royal elephants. In the course of discussion, Mahābat Khān was convinced that the court party was determined to ruin his family.[71] Therefore, when the imperial army had crossed the river, Mahābat Khān overpowered the royal guards and took Jahāngīr into his custody. Now it was his men who destroyed the bridge, thus making any effective resistance against him impossible.[72]

Mu'tamid Khān writes that after taking possession of the emperor, Mahābat Khān said to him that he had done so in order to escape 'Āṣaf Khān's hostility. He added that if the emperor considered this act a crime, he might order Mahābat Khān executed.[73] In the meantime his Rajput retainers surrounded the imperial camp from all sides, and Mahābat Khān struck Muqarrab Khān with a stick when he protested against his rude behaviour, saying that 'when my wives and daughters were apportioned, you said nothing?'[74]

When the imperial camp came to know that the emperor was taken captive, an attempt was made to rescue him, but it failed. 'Āṣaf Khān fled to the fort of Attock and Nūr Jahān joined Jahāngīr.[75] Mahābat Khān took command of the government and despatched an army under his son Bahram, Jujhar Rajput and Shāh Alī to besiege Attock. On a promise of security of life, 'Āṣaf Khān surrendered, and was taken into custody by Mahābat Khān when the camp crossed the Indus at Attock on the way to Kabul.[76] During this period Mahābat Khān put to death some persons whom he considered as to be 'Āṣaf Khān's friends and associates, like Abdul Khāliq, Khwāja Shamsuddīn's brother's son Muḥammad Taqi Bakhshī and Mullā Muḥammad Thattavi.[77] On the other hand, he made an attempt to gain the support of Mirzā Raja Jai Singh. Soon after taking Jahāngīr

[71] *Z.K.*, II, 134-5. No other source refers to this conspiracy but a close study of *Iqbālnāma-i Jahāngīrī*, corroborates many points. Cf. *Iqbālnāma*, 253-6.

[72] *Iqbālnāma*, 257-79; *Z.K.*, II, 134-5.

[73] *Iqbālnāma*, 263-4; *Z.K.*, II, 137.

[74] *Z.K.*, II, 135-6.

[75] *Iqbālnāma*, 260-6; *Z.K.*, II, 137-40.

[76] *Iqbālnāma*, 266-7.

[77] Ibid., 267-8.

prisoner on 21 March 1627, he had a *farmān* issued to Jai Singh in which the emperor recorded the favourable reports made by Mahābat Khān regarding Jai Singh's role in the Deccan.[78] But such friendly gestures did not result in any positive response from the Rajput chiefs who seem to have withheld any open commitment to his coup. It appears that Mahābat Khān could not rally the support of other sections of the Mughal nobles also, apparently on account of his hostility towards the Irānī and the Tūrānī nobility, and because of the dominance of his Rajput and Afghān retainers.

Besides, Mahābat Khān appears to have himself remained in a confused state of mind. Although he took the bold step of arresting the emperor, he could not think of removing Jahāngīr — or even Nūr Jahān — from the nominal pinnacle of power. He continued to hope that he could operate through Jahāngīr and win allies among the nobles letting all remain at their posts. As a result he could not offer much power or wealth to his own men, who thereby became desperate and started behaving cruelly. The tyranny of Mahābat Khān's Rajput retainers which led to a skirmish near Kabul between them and the *ahdis* in which many Rajputs were killed further weakened his position.[79] Taking advantage of this situation the emperor strengthened his position by enlisting the support of a large number of nobles. On his way back to Lahore, when the imperial camp was near Rohtas, Jahāngīr sent orders to Mahābat Khān to go a stage ahead, as he was holding a review of the Begum's troops.[80] Mahābat Khān who realized the weak position in which he was now placed took to flight taking with him as hostages, 'Āṣaf Khān, his son Abū Ṭālib, Prince Daniyal's sons Tahmures and Hushang, and Lashkari, Mukhlis Khān's son. Afẓal Khān was despatched from the court after him, commanding him to release the hostages at once, and to proceed to Thatta to block the path of Khurram, who, informed of the developments at the court, had re-entered the empire from the south. Mahābat Khān was warned that if he delayed sending 'Āṣaf Khān to the court, an army should be sent after him. After an exchange of letters, Mahābat Khān released 'Āṣaf Khān and the other hostages; Abū Ṭālib was released a little later.[81]

[78] See Chapter IV.

[79] *Iqbālnāma*, 270-1. Six hundred to seven hundred Rajputs were killed in this skirmish, *English Factories* (1624-9), 152. The number of Mahābat Khān's soldiers slain in the conflict was estimated at 2,000. *Z.K.*, II, 141.

[80] *Iqbālnāma*, 275-6.

[81] *Iqbālnāma*, 277-8.

Mahābat Khān fled through Jaisalmer. Reaching Pokhran, a dependency of Jaisalmer, he stayed for sometime. He demanded the chief's daughter in marriage for his son. It had not been reported whether the marriage took place, but the chief of Pokhran and Rawal Kalyan Jaisalmeri (who was related to the chief of Pokhran) came to him and presented him with elephants, horses and other valuables. They also requested him to pass the rainy season in their territory.[82] After the rainy season he went to the Raṇa of Mewar, but the Rana did not show him much courtesy. Thereafter he fled into the territory of the Bhils between Mewar and Gujarat, and 12,000 Bhils are said to have come to his banner. He stayed for sometime in their mountainous home. During these hard days many of his Rajput retainers left his service, and only 2,000 of them remained.[83] About the same time Khānazād Khān, his son, having been dismissed from the governorship of Bengal, came to the court, where he was graciously received. He tried to bring about a reconciliation between the court and Mahābat Khān, but could not succeed because of the hostile attitude of Nūr Jahān and 'Āṣaf Khān.[84]

Mahābat Khān, reduced in men and material and hotly pursued by the imperial army had no choice but to open negotiations with Khurram,[85] so far his inveterate enemy. His letters reached the prince when the latter was on his way back to the Deccan having come to know of the death of Parvez. Mahābat Khān offered complete reconciliation and alliance with Khurram if he promised full pardon for his past conduct. Himself in straitened circumstances, Khurram responded favourably, and Mahābat Khān presented himself before Khurram (hereafter Shāhjahān) at Junair with 2,000 horses. Shortly after his arrival there, Jahāngīr died.[86]

On receiving a communication from 'Āṣaf Khān about the development at the court, Shāhjahān sent a *farmān* to Khān-i Jahān confirming him in the viceroyalty of the Deccan.[87] But Khān-i Jahān declined to offer his allegiance.[88] The author of the *Zakhīrat-ul Khawānīn* represents Daryā Khān and Fāzil Khān as having advised Khān-i

[82] *Z.K.*, II, 141. [83] Ibid., II, 141-2.

[84] *English Factories*, 4 January 1628, 204; *Iqbālnāma*, 286, refers only to the dismissal of Khānazād Khān and the appointment of Mukarram Khān in his place.

[85] *English Factories*, 204; *Iqbālnāma*, 286, refers to a huge treasure brought from Bengal for Mahābat Khān being captured by the imperial forces.

[86] *Z.K.*, II, 142; *Iqbālnāma*, 289. For details see Chapter VI. *English Factories*, 204-5.

[87] *Bādshahnāma*, I, 75; *Iqbālnāma*, 294.

[88] See Chapter VI. For the details of Khān Jahān's attitude towards Shāhjahān.

Jahān against joining Shāhjahān on the ground of the favour shown by the latter to Mahābat Khān. They pointed out that 'Shāhjahān had given him (Mahābat Khān) the title of *Sipahsalār* (Khān Khanān) which had been conferred on you by the late King'.[89]

Shāhjahān proceeded towards Agra through Gujarat after Khān-i Jahān's refusal to permit him to march through Burhanpur.[90] The author of the *Zakhīrat-ul Khawānīn* states that during this time Mahābat Khān combined in himself the offices of *Wakil, Vazīr, Munshi, Mīr Manzil, Bavarchi,* and *Safarchi*.[91] He also asserts that the Rana of Mewar and other imperial officers joined Shāhjahān through the efforts of Mahābat Khān.[92]

But Mahābat Khān's fear of 'Āṣaf Khān remained. When upon reaching Ajmer, Shāhjahān went to offer prayers in the *dargah* of Muinuddin Chishtī, Mahābat Khān is reported to have solicited him to swear by the Quran, making the great Khwāja a witness, that his offences were forgiven in accordance with pact previously undertaken, 'because tomorrow 'Āṣaf Khān the head of the family of I'timad-uddaula with whom you have very close relationship would come and order my execution as he is thirsty for my blood'. Otherwise, he said, he might be permitted to go to Mecca. Shāhjahān assured him of his protection. He was also assigned Ajmer and its neighbourhood in *jāgīr* (*tuyul*).[93]

Later events were to show that Mahābat Khān's suspicions of 'Āṣaf Khān's intentions towards him were not totally misplaced.

After reaching Agra, along with other nobles Mahābat Khān was promoted to the rank of 7,000/7,000 *du aspa sih aspa*, and was presented four lacs of rupees in cash.[94] Khānazād Khān, who had closely associated himself with 'Āṣaf Khān during the succession crisis, was promoted to the rank of 5,000/5,000 and given the title of Khān-i Zamān.[95] He was also appointed governor of Malwa. Mahābat Khān's second son Mirzā Lahrāsp was given the rank of 2,000/1,000.[96] Dilér Himmat, Afrasiyāb and Bahrawar, seem to have received only minor ranks.[97]

[89] *Z.K.*, II, 81-2, *Iqbālnāma*, 298, however, refers only to the title of *Khān Khanān* being conferred on Khān-i Jahān after the death of Abdul Rahīm Khān Khanān.

[90] See Chapter VII.

[91] *Z.K.*, II, 142.

[92] Ibid., *Bādshahnāma*, I, 79-80. Lahori writes that when Shāhjahān entered the territory of Mewar, Rana Karna came and offered him obedience. He was confirmed to the rank of 5,000/5,000.

[93] *Z.K.*, II, 143-4; *Bādshahnāma*, I, 81-2. Lahori refers to Shāhjahān's visit to the *dargah* but makes no reference to this incident.

[94] *Bādshahnāma*, I, 116-17.

[95] Ibid., I, 158; *Z.K.*, II, 263-4.

[96] Bādshahnāma, *Z.K.*, III, 95-6, mention 1,000/1,000.

[97] *Z.K.*, III, 95-7, where brief notices of Mirzā Lahrāsp, Dilér Himmat, Mirzā Gurshop, Bihroz and Afrasiyāb are to be found.

Shortly afterwards Mahābat Khān was appointed governor of the Deccan, and Khān-i Zamān (the former Khānazād Khān) who was governor of Malwa, was ordered to proceed to take charge of the *ṣūba* as his deputy.[98]

These events show that Mahābat Khān and his sons were generously rewarded, through high promotions in rank and important appointments. But apparently 'Āṣaf Khān was still hostile to him, because the order of posting to the Deccan was countermanded, and Irādat Khān was appointed to the Deccan before Khān-i Zamān could reach there. Khān-i Zamān was summoned to the court and given the *jāgīr* of Sambhal,[99] and Mahābat Khān was given the governorship of Delhi instead of the much more prestigious viceroyalty of the Deccan.[100] The fort of Ranthambor which had been in his *jāgīr* from the time of Jahāngīr was also taken from him and given to Husaini Chela now styled Qiledār Khān.[101]

From 1628 to 1632 Mahābat Khān and his son Khān-i Zamān remained at the court and their services were utilized in suppressing the rebellion of Jujhar Singh Bundela and Khān-i Jahān Lodī. Khān-i Zamān also accompanied Shāhjahān to the Deccan.[102] It appears that until 1632, the family, though it received promotions in rank, was not given important assignments, because of the great influence enjoyed by 'Āṣaf Khān. But as the problems in the Deccan could not be tackled by A'ẓam Khān (the former Irādat Khān), and 'Āṣaf Khān declined the offer of the viceroyalty of the Deccan, Mahābat Khān had to be given charge of the *ṣūba* in 1632.[103] It also appears that the influence of 'Āṣaf Khān also declined somewhat after his abortive campaign against Bijapur. Mahābat Khān proceeded to the Deccan from Agra along with his sons and grandsons to take up the command.[104] He remained in charge of the Deccan until his death in 1634.

98 *Bādshahnāma*, I, 199.
99 *Ibid.*, 256, 269.
100 Ibid., 255.
101 Ibid., I, 287.
102 Ibid.
103 Ibid., 242.
104 Bādshahnāma., 428.

Conclusion

The study of the different family groups of nobles shows that Akbar succeeded in giving a new structure to the Mughal nobility, which continued largely under Jahāngīr also.

When Akbar ascended the throne he had to face a serious crisis in the nobility. The period of regency and the rivalries for the office of *Wakīl* (1556-60 to 1560-2) witnessed a grim struggle between Bairam Khān and his associates and the rest of the nobility and later on between the groups of Maham Anaga and Shamsuddīn Atka. On both these occasions Akbar himself used one of the groups to overthrow or control the other and ultimately succeeded in getting the reins of government in his hands.[1]

But this period provided Akbar with an opportunity to study the internal problems and tensions in the Mughal nobility and made him conscious of the fact that for the consolidation of his empire a disciplined ruling class faithful only to the ruler was a necessity. Therefore, soon after taking the reins of government in his hands, he introduced administrative reforms that would reduce the powers of the clans of nobles,[2] and strengthen the central authority. These attempts were resisted by the old Tūrānī nobility because these reforms affected them directly.[3]

The effects of these reforms were far reaching. Akbar succeeded in breaking the strength of the important Tūrānī factions, including the clan-cum-family groups of nobles. In their place he raised to high ranks younger elements both among Tūrānīs and Irānīs. Further, he also introduced in substantial numbers indigenous elements, both Indian Muslims and Rajput chiefs. Important offices were now given

[1] See especially Chapters I, II and III.

[2] Chapter II. Also see *Life of Munim Khan,* xvii-xix, for a discussion on the nature of these reforms and their effects on the clan-cum-family groups of nobles.

[3] See Chapter III.

largely to these new groups. Along with individual nobles, certain clan-cum-family groups which served him faithfully during the critical years of 1562-5, were raised to high ranks and came to enjoy very important positions.[4]

Akbar once again had to face the pressures of the entrenched groups of nobles after his triumph over the Uzbek nobles in the 1560s. Undoubtedly there was a marked difference between the old clan-cum-family groups and the ones raised by Akbar.[5] The new family groups were the creations of Akbar whereas the old ones had been in the service of the Mughals for the last several generations, and had played an important role in the conquest of India. However, Akbar remained vigilant towards these new groups also and took measures through which he could keep in check the growth of clannish tendencies in his nobility. One such measure was the transfer of his officers from one place to another in quick succession.[6] In this connection Abū'l Fazḷ's remarks at the time of the transfer of the Atka clan from the Panjab are worth quoting:

> It is not hidden from the hearts of the far-seeing and clear sighted that the spiritual garland-twiners of sovereignty (i.e. kings) resemble gardeners. As gardeners adorn gardens with trees and move them from one place to another, and reject many, and irrigate others and labour to rear them to a proper size, and extirpate bad trees and lop off evil branches, and remove trees that are too large and graft some upon others and gather their various fruits and flowers and enjoy their shade when necessary and do other things which are established in the science of horticulture, so do just and far seeing kings, take care of the affairs of the servants by instructing, educating and punishing them and thereby light the lamp of wisdom and uprear the standard of guidance.[7]

He also declared it a state policy not to give contiguous *jāgīrs* to members of the same family or clan group.[8] Another important step

[4] See Chapters I, II, IV and V.

[5] See Chapter III for an idea of the working of the old clan group and Chapters I (II section), II, IV and V for the new groups raised by Akbar.

[6] Cf. also Afzal Husain, 'Provincial Governors under Akbar', *Indian History Congress*, 1970, 269-77.

[7] *Akbarnāma*, II, 332, Beveridge's translation is slightly confusing and has been modified by refering to the original.

[8] Abū'l Fazḷ in this connection writes :

> Whenever a large body is gathered together of one mind and speech, and show much push and energy, it is proper to disperse them, firstly for their own good and secondly for the welfare of the community. Even if no improper act in consequence of the aggregation be seen or suspected

which shattered the tribal and clannish tendencies among his nobles was the appointment of a junior member of the family at the head of his elders, who were also senior in service. These steps were resented by the nobles but Abū'l Fazl, the official historian of Akbar, strongly justifies these appointments. His observation with reference to Mirzā 'Azīz Koka's appointment as governor of Gujarat is an example.

> Though the Khān-i Kalān and Quṭbuddīn Muḥammad Khān were the uncles of the Khān A'ẓam and were old, yet the far-sightedness of the Shahinshāh put them in subordinate position, for in the code of just sovereignty, weight is given to wisdom and not to years and reliance is placed upon abundance of loyalty and not upon age. Far-sightedness is the pillar, not bodily bulk. Intellect is the substantive thing, not the largeness of the visible body. The foundation of appointments is talents and virtues and the qualities of ancestors are not regarded.[9]

Apart from making use of these new devices, Akbar did not hesitate to punish the highest officials of his realm for their lapses or refusal to implement imperial orders. Members of the most prominent families were so punished as seen from my account of some such families.[10] To keep the nobles in check Akbar also raised a parallel bureaucracy which comprised persons rising from lower ranks with no social or ethnic group to support them. Some such persons (e.g. Muẓaffar Khān, Todar Mal, Khwāja Shāh Mansur, Shāhbāz Khān Kamboh), held important central offices.[11]

By adopting these measures Akbar was able to efficiently run his government, and prevent any serious crisis in his nobility for a very long time.

However, in 1580-1 the Mughal empire was faced with a very critical situation on account of the rebellion of the Qāqshāls, a close knit clan group of nobles. But as soon as Akbar was able to finally subdue this rebellion, he took further steps to weaken the power of the family groups. The study of the family of Bharmal Kachhwaha, the family

---

such dispersion is the material of union, for security cannot be guaranteed where there is damage from the man-throwing wine of the world, and the weak-headed drinkers of the cup of intoxication. Especially when strife-mongers and table bearers abound. Negligence is implanted in the human constitution.

Akbarnāma, II, 332 (Beveridge's translation, modified).

9 *Akbarnāma*, III, 33.

10 See Chapters II and VI.

11 A.J. Qaisar, 'Shāhbāz Khān Kamboh', *Medieval India — A Miscellany*, I, 48-73. For the career of Muẓaffar Khān, Todar Mal and Khwāja Shāh Mansur, see *Ma'āṣir-ul Umarā* I, 653-9, III, 221-7.

of Shamsuddīn Atka and the family of Bairam K͟hān indicates Akbar's discriminatory attitude towards certain members of these families. He gave promotions and important assignments only to the sons of those nobles with whom he had personal relations. For example, after the death of Ḥusain Qulī K͟hān-i Jahān and Ismaīl Qulī their sons were given only minor ranks with no further promotions.[12] Similarly, the sons of Quṭbuddīn K͟hān, Mīr Muḥammad and Sharīf K͟hān were not given high *manṣabs* or important assignments.[13] For the Kachhwahas (Rajawat) also the same policy was adopted. Bharmal's brothers who also joined service, in due course of time, lost their position in the Mughal hierarchy. High *manṣabs* and important charges were given only to the brothers and sons of Bhagwan Das.[14] In this connection it may be added that an important reason which hampered the rise of the Bārha Sayyids seems to have been their deep-rooted clannish tendencies.[15]

We have seen in the preceding pages how Akbar was able to build up an efficient and loyal bureaucracy by effecting some basic changes in the Mughal polity (especially in the conditions of service of his nobles). But he failed to provide any solution to the problem of succession; and as a result the nobility tended to divide into factions supporting rival princes. Expectations from a potential successor could also weaken the rigid bonds of loyalty to the reigning monarch. We know that when Mirzā Ḥakīm was alive, on two occasions he was declared king by rebel nobles.[16] Subsequently, as Akbar's own sons grew to maturity, the nobles tended to attach themselves to one or the other of the princes. For example, 'Abdur Raḥīm K͟hān-i K͟hanān was considered a supporter of Prince Salīm and Ṣādiq Muḥammad K͟hān of Prince Murād.[17]

The problem relating to the crisis of succession arose once again at the time of Akbar's serious illness when physicians gave up all hopes for his recovery. The Mughal nobility was sharply divided on this issue. Although Salīm was now the only son of Akbar who, had survived certain leading nobles of the empire like Mirzā 'Azīz Koka and Raja Man Singh were apparently not sure whether they

12 See Chapter I. 13 See Chapter II. 14 For more details, see Chapter IV.

15 See Chapter V.

16 See Chapter III. During the rebellion of Qāqshāls (1580-1) also *k͟hutba* was read in the name of Mirzā Ḥakīm. Cf. *Ma'āṣir-ul Umarā*, III, 207-11.

17 Chapter I (III section).

would be able to maintain their pre-eminent position in the event of his accession. So they decided to raise to throne a prince of their own choice. As there was no other son of Akbar available, they decided to enthrone Khusrau the eldest son of Salīm. A meeting to put forward the claim of Khusrau and to nominate him as heir in which Mirzā 'Aziz Koka, Qulich Khān, Man Singh, Sa'id Khān and Shaikh Farīd Bukhārī, took part, was held — according to one account, in the presence of Akbar. Sa'id Khān and Qulich Khān vehemently opposed the move and with the crucial support of Shaikh Farīd foiled the attempt to supersede Salīm. Mirzā 'Azīz now decided to abandon the court, and with the help of Shaikh Farīd opened negotiations with Salīm and promised to surrender if he agreed to assign Bengal up to Chausa to Khusrau and pardon all those nobles who had supported him. Salīm agreed to these conditions and Man Singh and Mirzā 'Azīz Koka along with Khusrau presented themselves before him. They were given dresses of honour and confirmed to their old assignments. It is quite interesting to note that these developments took place when the emperor was alive. Ni'amatullah states that in the meeting Akbar made no comments but when Salīm came to see him, he informed him of the conspiracy hatched to arrest him. He asked Salīm not to visit him again and designated him his heir. These events clearly show the anxiety among the nobles about their future careers, which forced them to take important decisions about the imperial succession, on their own.[18]

Jahāngīr honoured most of his commitments and in respect of the eleventh article of his 'twelve regulations' issued immediately after his accession, he says, 'I gave a general order that the *ranks* and *jāgīrs* held by my father's servants will remain unchanged. Later the *manṣabs* were increased according to each one's circumstances by not less than 20 per cent to 300 or 400 per cent.'[19]

The order seems to have been enforced in practice: the *manṣabs* of Man Singh and Mirzā 'Azīz Koka were not curtailed after the

[18] *Risala-i Tārīkh Asad Beg Qazwīnī*. Rotograph, B.M., fols. 52-3; *Tārīkh-i Khān Jahāni*, II, 654-660, Ni'amatullah gives more details and also mentions that Qulich Khān was one of the main supporters of Salīm. Shaikh Farid's role has also been highlighted by him. Jahāngīr in his memoirs also mentions that on the day of his accession he forgave the offences of Akbar's nobles. See *Tuzuk* 6-7.

[19] *Tuzuk*, 4-5; Roger's translation is modified. At another place in the same year he said, 'I left all those who were in possession of posts, both inside and outside, in the position which they had with my father.' *Tuzuk*, 7 (R.B., I, 14).

accession. Later on action was taken against 'Azīz Koka, but this was for other reasons.[20]

However, Jahāngīr could not place absolute reliance on the old Akbarshāhī nobility, particularly when Khusrau rebelled soon after his accession.[21] Hence he raised a new nobility on whom he could have complete confidence. So, he promoted to a higher rank, 'Abdullah Khān Fīroz Jang, Khān-i Jahān Lodī, Mahābat Khān, Quṭbuddīn Khān, Bir Singh Deo Bundela[22] and others. Although as I have already mentioned, the *manṣabs* of old nobles were not curtailed, younger officers were raised to equal ranks by means of extraordinary promotions. This naturally created rivalry and suspicion between the 'Akbarshāhī' and 'Jahāngīrshāhī' nobles. As a result of these differences among nobles the emperor's hold on the nobility weakened considerably. The regulations issued at the end of sixth year of Jahāngīr's reign bear testimony to this.[23] On the other hand, the campaigns against the Mewar rulers and the Deccan states also ran into difficulties owing to dissensions among the nobles. Certain important nobles, both old Akbarshāhī and the new ones, lost favour with the emperor.[24] In the meantime after the marriage of Nūr Jahān to

[20] See Chapter II.

[21] Jahāngīr writes in the first year of his reign: 'Though on the day of my accession I had forgiven all offences and determined with myself that I would exact no retribution for past deeds, yet on account of the suspicion that had been aroused in my mind about them I considered the 'Amīr-ul Umarā my guardian and protector.' *Tuzuk,* 9.

[22] See Chapters VI, VIII and IX. For Bir Singh Deo Bundela, see K.K. Trivedi, 'Rajput Clans in the Mughāl Nobility — The Bundela Case', presented to the *Indian History Congress*, held at Bhubaneswar (1977).

[23] At the end of sixth year of his reign, Jahāngīr issued the following regulations as he came to know that 'some nobles on the borders practice things which are of no concern to them and do not observe *Tura* and regulations (*Zawabit*)':

The first thing is this that they should not sit in the *jharokhā* and should not trouble their officers and captains of the auxiliaries with keeping guards or saluting them, and should not have elephant fights, and should not inflict the punishment of blinding and should not cut off ears and noses and should not force Islām on any one, and should not confer titles on their servants and should not force the musicians to observe *chauki* in the manner which is customary in (royal) *darbars*, and should not beat drums when they go out, and when they give a horse or elephant to any one, whether to the King's attendants or to their own servants, they should not place reins or elephants' goads on their backs and make them perform obedience. In going in procession they should not take with them on foot in their retinue the royal attendants. If they write anything to them, they should not put a seal on it. The regulations which have been styled the rules of Jahāngīr (*Ain-i Jahāngīrī*) are now in force.

Tuzuk, 100; Roger's translation has been slightly modified.

[24] See Chapters I, II, VII and IX for details.

Jahāngīr, the family of I'timād-ud daulah rose to occupy a unique position.

Regarding the rise of the family of I'timād-uddaulah and the extent of its influence a good deal of work has already been done.[25] It may be added that the family was not a newcomer and had been enjoying an important position from the time of Akbar. Khwāja Ghayāṣuddīn Alī Āṣaf Khān, Āqā Mullā's son, had become an important noble at the Mughal court as early as 1573. He was given the title of Āṣaf Khān and held the offices of *Diwān* and *Mīr Bakhshī*.[26] Another member of the family Jafar Beg Āṣaf Khān who arrived at the court of Akbar in 1577 also held the office of *Mīr Bakhshī* and rank of 4,000. Certain other relations of Jafar Beg also came during the reign of Akbar and received *manṣabs*. After his accession, Jahāngīr himself promoted Ja'far Beg Āṣaf Khān to the rank of 5,000 and made him the guardian of Parvez who was despatched to the Mewar campaign.[27] Other members of the family Ghayāṣ Beg, Āqā Mullā and Irādat Khān were also promoted after the accession.[28] The earlier importance of the family, however, does not mean that Nūr Jahān's marriage to Jahāngīr did not play a key role in its further rise. Indeed before 1611, the family had come under some cloud. The marriage restored imperial confidence in the family and cleared the way for I'timād-uddaula's appointment as *Wakil*. The almost meteoric rise of this family was accompanied by a decline in the fortunes of other important nobles and high families.

I have examined the extent of the influence enjoyed by Nūr Jahān. Between 1617 and 1619 Nūr Jahān had gained sufficient influence to affect the career of certain families and nobles. In this context I have also examined the information contained in the *Intekhāb-i Jahāngīr Shāhi*. A close scrutiny of the evidence shows that its account is corroborated by other contemporary sources. Besides it also emerges from my study that at one stage (1620) the interests of Nūr Jahān and Āṣaf Khān were at variance; Āṣaf Khān supported the cause of his son-in-law Khurram and the energies of Nūr Jahān were at work

[25] Beni Prasad, *History of Jahāngīr*, 171-180; Hodivala, 'Numismatic Supplement', *JASB*, 1929, 59-68; S.N. Hasan, 'The Theory of Nūrjahān Junta', *Proceedings of Indian History Congress*, 1958, 324-5; Irfan Habib, 'The Family of Nūrjahān During Jahāngīr's Reign, a Political Study', *Medieval India — A Miscellany*, I, 74-95.

[26] *Akbarnāma*, III, 228, 264; Badāūnī, 170. He was one of those nobles who actively co-operated in the implementation of branding regulations. He died in 1581.

[27] *Tuzuk*, 7; *Iqbālnāma*, 22.

[28] *Tuzuk*, 9; *Iqbālnāma*, 19.

to promote the cause of her son-in-law Shaharyār. Thereafter they ceased to work in unison as their interests clashed.[29]

The setback that occurred in the fortunes of the families of Shaikh Salīm Chishtī, Mahābat Khān, 'Abdullah Khān and Khān-i Jahān Lodī was not only because of the hostile attitude of Nūr Jahān's family clique as suggested by some contemporary historians or modern scholars. If we study more closely the political developments at the court of Jahāngīr after his accession it would appear reasonable to hold that the decline of the other families was only indirectly due to the elevation of I'timād-uddaulah's family. The *manṣabs* of the above mentioned nobles and their family members in service were not curtailed; only further promotion was stayed or slowed down. Apparently this step was taken because of limited resources. In the early years of Jahangir's reign, because of political compulsions, high *manṣabs* were given to a large number of newcomers, while the old nobles were confirmed in their *manṣabs* and some of them were also promoted. To meet the additional burden, since no new territory was gained, the extent of *khāliṣa* (emperor's own dominion) must have been reduced.[30] But there was a limit to this also. After the sixth year of his reign, the rate of promotion in *manṣab* slowed down. After Nūr Jahān's marriage a large number of her relations were admitted and given promotions to higher ranks; this naturally must have curtailed further the extent to which other families could be given promotions.

The subsequent events of the reign of Jahāngīr revolve round the activities of the royal princes. With their changing fortunes there were new alignments and realignments of the groups of nobles and there were sharp divisions of nobles at the court.[31] The main cause behind these divisions was the lack of confidence among them about their future careers. They were certain that if the prince of their own choice did not succeed, they would be eclipsed. The rebellions of Khurram, Mahābat Khān's coup and the civil war after the death of Jahāngīr were the result of these apprehensions. Shāhjahān's accession confirmed the apprehension of some who had supported

[29] See specially Chapter IX.

[30] 'During the reign of Jahāngīr the *khāliṣa* is said to have suffered considerable reduction till its *jama* fell to even below five percent of that of the whole Empire.' Qazwini (Add. 20734, 444-5, or 173 fols. 221a-b) says it was reduced to 28 *karor 'dāms*. The total *jama* of the Empire about 1627-9 was 630 *karor dāms (Majalisu-s Salatin*, fol.115a-b) cited in, Irfan Habib, *The Agrarian System of Mughāl India*, 272.

[31] See Chapters VII, VIII and IX.

the other side.[32] We notice that promotions to higher ranks and all important appointments were given to those who were his favourites and those who supported his cause. Although like Jahāngīr, Shāhjahān also pardoned almost all those who were in the opposite camp, yet as all important posts were filled by his own favourites, and all surviving princes were executed on the eve of the accession, certain important nobles rebelled and the career of many other nobles and families declined rapidly.[33]

The racial composition of the nobility also underwent a great change in our period on account of political compulsion and the measures adopted by Akbar to check the recalcitrant nobility. Akbar gave a fair degree of representation to not only Irānīs but also to local elements — the Rajputs and Indian Muslims — to counter the old nobility. However, attempts made in recent years to analyse the racial composition of Akbar's nobility, and the rise of one or the other ethnic group explained in relation to various politico-religious pressures in the empire is very difficult to explain in the light of the studies of prominent family groups of almost every important ethnic group present in the nobility. For example, the progress of any of these family groups: Shamsuddīn Atka, Bairam Khān, Bharmal Kachhwaha and Bārha Sayyid, was affected neither by religious tensions nor by political pressures. They continued to enjoy a preeminent position as long as they remained loyal to the emperor. The temporary setback which these families experienced was usually the outcome of their own political conduct.[34]

The accession of Jahāngīr brought no significant change in the composition of the nobility, except for the inclusion of Afghāns in the ruling class. One of the important reasons for their admission into the nobility no doubt, was to take into confidence the Afghāns, who had been relegated to a lower position by Akbar. This restoration of the Afghāns to favour became possible only because certain Afghāns had served the Mughals since a long time, although in minor capacities. A few Afghāns had also been in the personal service of Jahāngīr during his princehood.[35]

In or about 1613, Mirzā 'Azīz Koka in a letter addressed to the emperor, accused him of promoting the Shaikhzadās and Khurāsanīs

[32] See Chapters VII and IX for details. [33] See specially Chapters II, VII and IX.

[34] See Chapters I, II, IV and V. Cf. Iqtidar Alam Khan, 'The Nobility under Akbar and the Development of his Religious Policy 1560-80', *JRAS*, 1968, 30-5.

[35] For details see Chapter VII.

at the expense of the Tūrānīs and Rajputs. But a close scrutiny of facts suggests the need for scepticism with regard to this allegation. Table 10.1[36] shows that the charge of undue favour shown to Khurāsanīs and Shaikhzadās is not really borne out.

But there must have been some reason which prompted the Mirzā to write such a harsh letter and bewail the importance being given to the upstart elements.

We have seen that during the reign of Akbar a few family groups, like the family of Shamsuddīn Atka and Raja Bharmal Kachhwaha, enjoyed a distinct position at the court. When Akbar was seriously ill and the question of succession arose, 'Azīz Koka and Man Singh (representing the two families) to retain their predominant position at the court conspired to enthrone Khusrau who was closely related to them through matrimonial relations. But as the conspiracy failed, and Jahāngīr raised a new nobility to counter the old Akbarshāhī nobles who were involved in the effort to supersede him, Mirzā 'Azīz Koka saw only ruin for the Tūrānīs and Rajputs. A similar question was raised by him during the reign of Akbar, when promotions were given to Abul Faẓl, Faizi, Qulich Khān and others. Hence the main reason behind this complaint was the rise of a new nobility, and not a change in the emperor's 'racial' policy.[37]

However, the Rajput nobility suffered a setback, not because their numerical strength declined or their total *manṣabs* fell sharply,[38] but

Table 10.1

	Total no. of *manṣabdars*		Tūrānī	Irāni	Rajput	Indian Muslims
1575-95	500 & above	184	64 37.78%	47 25.54%	30 16.30%	34 18.48%
At the death of Akbar	500 & above	95	30 31.58%	21 22.26%	17 17.89%	5 5.26%
During six years of Jahāngīr	1000 & above	91	30 32.97%	21 23%	19 20%	16 17.59%

[36] For reference see 'The Nobility under Akbar and the Development of his Religious Policy 1560-80', 35, and Appendix A–III and V.

[37] See Chapter II for more details.

[38] See Appendix A–III and V for the list of nobles who were alive at the death of Akbar and

because they were not given charge of *ṣūbas* and independent commands. Moreover, after the death of Man Singh the rank of 7,000/7,000 was also not given to any Rajput noble. However, it does not mean that Jahāngīr became hostile to the Rajputs in general. Other clans of Rajputs were given high ranks, but as the Kachhwahas (Rajawat) lost the pre-eminent position which they had enjoyed for the last four decades, it appeared as if the whole Rajput nobility had lost its importance. Even during the reign of Akbar, governorships and independent commands were given generally to the Kachhwahas (Rajawat) only.[39] As regards the promotions to the rank of 7,000/7,000, only I'timād-uddaulah was given this rank before the rebellion of Khurram and Mahābat Khān; Khān-i Jahān Lodī was granted this rank after the revolt of Khurram.[40]

---

during the first six years of Jahāngīr's reign, and of the *manṣabs* held at the end of fifteenth regnal year of Jahāngīr.

[39] See Chapter IV.

[40] Jahāngīr's comments at the time of Sharīf Khān's promotion to the rank of 5,000 in the first year of his reign are quite significant. He writes, 'I promoted him to the rank of 5,000/5,000 and the lofty title of *Amīr-ul Umarā* to which no title of my servant is superior. Though his position might have warranted a higher rank, he himself represented to me that until some notable service on his part had become perceptible to me he would not accept a higher rank than that mentioned (5,000).' *Tuzuk*, 6.

APPENDIX A

List of Nobles

I. LIST OF BĀBUR'S NOBLES

1.	Araish Khān (Indian)	(*Bāburnāma*, 403, 505, *T.U.*, 136).
2.	Aḥmad Parvanchi	(*T.U.*, 12a, *Bāburnāma*, 408, 472).
3.	'Abdul Shakoor Mughal	(*T.U.*, 16b).
4.	'Alī Khān Shaikhzāda of Farmal (Indian)	(*Bāburnāma*, 520-7, 567; *T.U.*, 14b).
5.	Arghun Sulṭān brother of Muḥammad Alī Jang	(*Bāburnāma* 461; *T.U.*, 12a)
6.	Aḥmad Shāh s/o Sulṭān Nasiruddīn (Indian)	(*Bāburnāma*, 593, 596).
7.	Aḥmad Yūsuf Oghlu	(*Bāburnāma*, 550).
8.	Aulia Khān Sarwānī (Indian)	(*Bāburnāma*, 677; *T.U.*, 14a)
9.	Khwāja Asadullah Jandar Khwafī (Irānī)	(*Bāburnāma*, 543, 546)
10.	'Ālam Khān Kalpiwal (Indian)	(*Bāburnāma* 544, 590, 682; *T.U.*, 15a)
11.	'Ādil Sulṭān s/o Mahdī Sulṭān	(*Bāburnāma*, 567; *T.U.*, 11b)
12.	'Abul Fatḥ Turkmān	(*Bāburnāma*, 540; *T.U.*,16a)
13.	Amīr 'Abdullah Kitabdar	(*Bāburnāma*, 471-2).
14.	Amīr 'Abdul Azīz Mīr Akhuar	(*Bāburnāma*, 567; *T.U.*, 11b)
15.	Mīr 'Abul Baqā	(*T.U.*, 14a)
16.	'Abul Muḥammad Nezabāz	(*Bāburnāma*, 473, 582; *T.U.*, 16b).
17.	Aḥmad Qāsim Kabuli	(*T.U.*, 14b.)
18.	Sulṭān 'Alāuddīn 'Ālam Khān son of Sulṭān Bahlol (Indian)	(*Bāburnāma*, 439-42, 444, 505).
19.	Ustad 'Alī Qulī	(*Bāburnāma*, 469).
20.	'Alāwal Khān Nurkhani (Indian)	(*T.U.*, 13b; *Bāburnāma*, 677, 888).
21.	Mirzā Khān Yār Khān	(*T.U.*, 16b).
22.	Bābā Sulṭān Qashqa	(*Bāburnāma*, 405, 442;)
23.	Bāqī Saqāval	(*T.U.*, 12a; *Bāburnāma*, 676).
24.	Bikhub Sulṭān Uzbek Shaibānī	(*Bāburnāma*, 442,
25.	Shaikh Bhikhari (Indian)	(*T.U.* 17a).
26.	Chin Timūr Sulṭān Chaghtāī,	(*Bāburnāma*, 472).
27.	Amīr Darvesh Muḥammad Sarban	(*Bāburnāma*, 472).
28.	Dilāwar Khān Khān Khanān(Indian) son of Daulat Khān Lodī	(*Bāburnāma*, 461, 567; *T.U.*, 12a).
29.	Malik Dād Karrāni (Indian)	(*Bāburnāma*, 540, 557).
30.	Darwesh 'Alī son of Yūsuf 'Alī	(*Bāburnāma*, 567).
31.	Dost Muḥammad Beg Mughal son of Bābā Qaqshqa	(*Bāburnāma*, 539).
32.	Mīr Faqir 'Alī	(*T.U.*, 14b).
33.	Fatḥ Khān Sarwānī Khān-i Jahān (Indian)	(*T.U.*, 13a; *Bāburnāma*, 534).

34.	Fīroz Khān Sārang Khānī (Indian)	(*Bāburnāma*, 527).
35.	Shaikh Ghuran (Indian)	(*Bāburnāma*, 529).
36.	Ḥusain Khān Daryā Khānī (Indian)	(*T.U.*, 17a).
37.	Hindu Beg Quchin	(*Bāburnāma*, 472).
38.	Ḥu sain 'Alī Turkmān,	(*T.U.*, 14a).
39.	Husāmuddīn 'Alī Barlās son of Nizāmuddīn Khalifa	(*Bāburnāma*, 601).
40.	Khwāja Ḥusain Beg brother of Uzun Ḥasan	(*Bāburnāma*, 458, 549; *T.U.*, 17a).
41.	Sayyid Mīr Hama (Irānī)	(*Bāburnāma*, 456, 549; *T.U.*, 17a).
42.	Ḥusain Āqā Sīstānī (Irānī)	(*Bāburnāma*, 566).
43.	Muṣtafa Rumi Tawachi (Irānī)	(*Bāburnāma*, 471, 550).
44.	Mīr Mughal son of Abul Wahāb Shaghwal	(*Bāburnāma*, 658, 673-4).
45.	Muḥammad Zamān Mirzā	(*Babarnama*, 606, 631) (*T.U.*, 16a).
46.	Maḥmūd Khān son of Fateḥ Khān Sarwānī (Indian)	(*T.U.*, 14a).
47.	Shaikh Muḥammad (Indian)	(*T.U.*, 17a).
48.	Sayyid Mashādī (Irānī)	(*Bāburnāma*, 688).
49.	Momin Atka	(*T.U.*, 13a).
50.	Mujāhid Khān Multānī (Indian)	(*Bāburnāma*, 404; *T.U.*, 16a).
51.	Muḥammad Sulṭān Mirzā son of Wais Mirzā	(*Bāburnāma*, 468, 472).
52.	Muḥammad Alī Jang Jang	(*Bāburnāma*, 472; *T.U.*, 11b).
53.	Sayyid Mahdī Khwāja son of Musā Khwāja	(*Bāburnāma*, 472, 475).
54.	Muhib 'Alī Khān Barlās son of Niẓāmuddīn Khalifa	(*Bāburnāma*, 472).
55.	Sulṭān Muḥammad Bakhshi (Indian)	(*Bāburnāma*, 460; *T.U.*, 13a).
56.	Muḥammadi Kokaltāsh	(*Bāburnāma*, 472; *T.U.*, 11b).
57.	Malik Sharaf	(*T.U.*, 14a).
58.	Sulṭān Muḥammad Duldai	(*Bāburnāma*, 472).
59.	Maḥmūd Khān Lohāni (Indian)	(*Bāburnāma*, 527; *T.U.*, 14b).
60.	Shāh Muḥammad son of Bābā Qashqa	(*Bāburnāma*).
61.	Sayyid Niẓāmuddīn Khalifa	(*Bāburnāma*, 473).
62.	Niẓām Khān brother of 'Ālam Khān of Biana (Indian)	(*T.U.*, 15b; *Bāburnāma*, 567).
63.	Mirzā Nuruddīn son-in-law of Bābur	(*T.U.*, 14b).
64.	Pīr Qulī Sīstānī (Irānī)	(*Bāburnāma*, 472, 566).
65.	Khwāja Pahalwān Bakhshī	(*T.U.*, 166).
66.	Amīr Qarā Quzi	(*Bāburnāma*, 473).
67.	Isma'īl Jilwani (Indian)	(*Bāburnāma*, 404, 677; *T.U.*, 14a).
68.	Isma'īl Beg	(*T.U.*, 14b).
69.	Amīr Jānī Beg Atka	(*Bāburnāma*, 460).
70.	Sulṭān Jalāluddīn son of Ḥusain Shāh (Indian)	(*Bāburnāma*, 651-2).
71.	Sulṭān Junaid Barlās	(*Bāburnāma*, 466, 471).

72. Jamāl Khān son of Sulṭān 'Alāuddīn (Indian) (*Bāburnāma*, 567).
73. Ja'far Khwāja son of Mahdī Khwāja (*Bāburnāma*, 579, 562; *T.U.*, 17a).
74. Shaikh Jamāl Farmali (Indian) (*Bāburnāma*, 551; *T.U.*, 16b).
75. Khalifa Kuki son of Bābā Qashqa (*Bāburnāma*, 551).
76. Kichak Khwāja brother of Khwāja Kalān Beg (*Bāburnāma*, 661; *T.U.*, 14a).
77. Khwāja Kalān Beg son of Maulana Muḥammad Sardār (*Bāburnāma*, 438, 631; *T.U.*, 12a).
78. Kitta Beg Kohbar Chaghtāī (*Bāburnāma*; *T.U.*, 12a).
79. Khusrau Kokaltash (*Bāburnāma*, 472).
80. Khalīl Akhta Beg (*T.U.*, 17a).
81. Kamāl Khān son of Sulṭān 'Alāuddīn (Indian) (*Bāburnāma*, 567; *T.U.*, 13b).
82. Lāl Walī (*Bāburnāma, 43a*).
83. Lashkar Khān Janjua (Indian) (*T.U.*, 18a).
84. Muḥammad Qāsim Mughal (*Bāburnāma*, 599).
85. Qutlu Qadam Qarāwal (*Bāburnāma*, *T.U.*, 11b).
86. Qismati Mirzā (*Bāburnāma*, 474).
87. Qāsim Ḥusain Sulṭān (*Bāburnāma*, 550).
88. Qawwam Beg son of Urdu Shāh (*Bāburnāma*, 550, 556; *T.U.*, 13b).
89. Quchak Beg brother of Tardi Beg (*T.U.*, 16a).
90. Khawāja Raḥīm Dāḍ paternal nephew of Mahdī Khwāja (*Bāburnāma*, 539-40).
91. Rafi'uddīn Safavī (Irānī) (*Bāburnāma*, 539, 606).
92. Rustam Turkistāni (*Bāburnāma*, 568; *T.U.*, 17a).
93. Shāh Mīr Ḥusain Qarlāq (*Bāburnāma*, 463, 422; *T.U.*, 12a).
94. Shāh Manṣūr Barlās (*Bāburnāma*, 465-6).
95. Tengri Bardi (*Bāburnāma*, 472).
96. Tradika (*T.U.*, 12a).
97. Tāj Khān Sārang Khanī (Indian) (*Bāburnāma*, 657).
98. Timur Sulṭān Uzbek (*T.U.*, 17b).
99. Tukhta Beg Sulṭān Chaghtāī (*Bāburnāma*, 647).
100. Walī Khazin Qarquzi (*T.U.*, 16b).
101. Yādgār Nasīr Mirzā (*T.U.*, 17b).
102. Amīr Yūnus 'Alī son of Bābā 'Alī (*Bāburnāma*, 398, 472).
103. Shaikh Zain Khwafi (Irānī) (*Bāburnāma*, 476; *T.U.*, 11a).
104. Qāẓī Jia (Indian) (*Bāburnāma*, 546).
105. Muḥammad Zaitun (Indian) (*T.U.*, 15b).
106. Ḥusain Āqā Sīstānī (Irānī) (*Bāburnāma*, 566).
107. Mullā Apaq (*Bāburnāma*, 598).
108. Mīr Bardi Beg (*Bāburnāma*, 590).
109. Tardi Beg (*T.U.*, 11a).
110. Ṣadār Khān (Indian) (*T.U.*, 13a).
111. Sulaimān (*T.U.*, 13a).
112. Arohi Sarwānī (Indian) (*T.U.*, 14a).
113. Sher Afgan brother of Quch Beg (*T.U.*, 15a).
114. Rahīm Dād (Indian) (*T.U.*, 15a).
115. Tātār Khān (Indian) (*T.U.*, 17a).
116. Sulṭān Jalāluddīn Sharqī (Indian) (*T.U.*, 18b).

II. LIST OF NOBLES WHO ACCOMPANIED HUMĀYŪN TO IRAN FROM *AKBARNĀMA*, I, 221-2

1. Bairam Khān
2. Khwajā Mu'azzam
3. Aqil Sulṭān Uzbek
4. Ḥājī Muḥammad Koki
5. Roshan Koka
6. Ḥasan Beg brother of Maḥram Koka
7. Khwajā Maqsud of Hirat
8. Khwajā Ghāzī Tabrezi
9. Khwajā Amīnuddīn Harvī
10. Bābā Dost Bakhshī
11. Darwesh Muḥammad Bangali Harvī
12. Ḥasan 'Alī Ishq Āqā
13. 'Alī Dost Barbegi son of Ḥasan 'Alī Ishq Āqā
14. Ibrāhīm Ishq Āqā
15. Yūsuf Choli a descendant of Shaikh Aḥmad Yasvi
16. Shaikh Bahlol
17. Maulana Nūruddīn
18. Muḥammad Qāsim Mauji
19. Ḥaider Muḥammad Akhta Begi
20. Sayyid Muḥammad Pakna
21. Sayyid Muḥammad Qulī Harvī
22. Hāfiz Sulṭān Muḥammad Rakhna

23-4 Mirzā Beg Biloch of Khurāsan and his son

25. Khwajā Ambar Nazir
26. 'Ārif Tushkachin Mamluko

III. *MANṢAB* HELD AT THE DEATH OF AKBAR

	Name	*Racial group*	*Manṣab*	*Source*
1.	Mirzā 'Azīz Koka	(T)	7000/	*Iqbālnāma*, 510
2.	Raja Man Singh	(R)	7000/6000	*Iqbālnāma, Takmila*; III, 839.
3.	Mirzā Shāhrukh	(T)	7000/6000	*Iqbālnāma*, 506; *Tuzuk*, 11.
4.	'Abdur Raḥīm Khān Khanān	(I)	5000/5000	*M.R.* II, 497, 501.
5.	Qulich Khān	(T)	5000/5000	*Iqbālnāma*, 494; Takmila, 621.
6.	Sa'īd Khān Chaghta	(T)	5000	*Ā'īn*, 25.
7.	Mirzā Rustam Ṣafavī	(T)	5000	*Ā'īn*, 9.
8.	Shāh Beg Khān	(T)	5000	*Iqbālnāma*, 469; *Takmila*, 815.
9.	Mirzā Ghāzī Beg Tarkhan	(T)	5000	*Tuzuk*, 33.
10.	Raja Jagannath	(R)	5000	*Tuzuk*, 7; *Takmila*, 787.
11.	Rai Rayan Bikarmajit		5000	*Iqbālnāma*, 500; *Takmila*, 627.
12.	Shaikh Farīd Bukhārī	(Ind. Muslim)	4000	*Iqbālnāma*, 505; *Tuzuk*, 9.

	Name	Racial group	Manṣab	Source
13.	Rai Singh	(R)	4000	*Iqbālnāma*, 510; *Takmila*, 839.
14.	Raja Raj Singh	(R)	4000/3000	*Iqbālnāma*, 510; *Tuzuk*, 83.
15.	Āṣaf Khān	(I)	4000/2000	*Iqbālnāma*, 565; *Takmila*, 834 (*Tuzuk*, 7, 2500 only)
16.	Rai Durga Sisodia	(R)	4000	*Tuzuk*, 63.
17.	Pāyanda Khān Mughal	(T)	3500	*Iqbālnāma*, 505; *Takmila*, 834.
18.	Madhao Singh	(R)	3000/2000	*Iqbālnāma*, 494; *Tuzuk*, 7.
19.	Rawal Sal Darbari	(R)	3000/1250	*Tuzuk*, 7.
20.	Ḥakīm Alī Gilānī	(I)	3000/200	*Iqbālnāma*, 508.
21.	Makhṣus Khān	(I)	3000/1500	*Iqbālnāma*, 505.
22.	Pratap Zamīndār of Baglana		3000	*Takmila*, 770.
23.	Mirzā Shamsuddīn Khān	(T)	2500/2000	*Iqbālnāma*, 505.
24.	Takhta Beg Kabulī	(T)	2500	A.N. III 853.
25.	Shaikh 'Abdur Raḥmān	(Ind. Muslim)	2000	*Tuzuk*, 8.
26.	Shaikh Bāyazīd	(Ind. Muslim)	2000	*Iqbālnāma*, 505; *Tuzuk*, 14.
27.	Maha Singh	(R)	2000	*Tuzuk*, 8; *Takmila*, 839.
28.	Zāhid Khān son of Ṣādiq Khān	(I)	2000	*Tuzuk*, 8.
29.	Yūsuf son of Ḥusain Khān Tukaria	(T)	2000	*Iqbālnāma*, 509; *Takmila*, 836-7.
30.	Qarā Khān Turkmān	(I)	2000	*Tuzuk*, 8.
31.	Wazīr Beg Jamīl		2000	Ibid.
32.	Mīran Ṣadar Jahān	(Ind. Muslim)	2000	Ibid., 9.
33.	Tāj Khān	(T)	2000	Ibid., 13.
34.	Tardī Khān	(T)	2000/500	*Iqbālnāma*, 567; *Takmila*, 627.
35.	Ram Das Kachhwaha	(R)	2000/1200	*Iqbālnāma*, 508; *Tuzuk*, 9.
36.	Mīr Murtaẓā	(I)	2000/2000	*Iqbālnāma*, 498; *Takmila*, 825.
37.	Mirzā Khurram	(T)	2000	*Tuzuk*, 9.
38.	Shaikh Daulat Bakhtiyār	(Ind. Muslim)	2000	*Iqbālnāma*, 483; *Takmila*, 808.
39.	Mīr Bāpus Aghur	(T)	2000	*Ain*, 73.
40.	Samānjī Khān	(T)	2000	Ibid., 100.
41.	Mihtar Khān		2000	Ibid., 102.
42.	Lālā Beg Bāz Bahādur	(T)	1500	*Tuzuk*, 9.
43.	Hāshim Khān son of Qāsim Khān	(T)	1500	*Tuzuk*, 36; *Takmila*, 805.
44.	Raḥmat Khān *Faujdār*.		1500/300	*Iqbālnāma*, 507; *Takmila*, 836.
45.	Mirzā Shādmān	(T)	1500/1500	*Iqbālnāma*, 498.
46.	Mirzā 'Abdullah son of Khān-i A'ẓam	(T)	1500/700	Ibid., 498.
47.	Muḥammad Qulī Turkmān	(T)	1500/600	Ibid., 480.
48.	Jalāl Khān Gakhar	(Ind. Muslim)	1500	*Ain*, 170.
49.	Raja Basu	(R)	1500	*Tuzuk*, 23.
50.	Khwāja 'Abdullah	(T)	1000	*Iqbālnāma*, 497; *Tuzuk*, 34.
51.	Faridun Barlas	(T)	1000/500	*Iqbālnāma*, 510 (*Takmila*, 839 has 1500)
52.	Abedin Khwāja	(T)	1000/500	*Iqbālnāma*, 508; *Takmila*, 834.
53.	Khwāja Fatḥullah	(I)	1000	*Iqbālnāma*, 497; *Takmila*, 824.

	Name	*Racial group*	*Manṣab*	*Source*
54.	Ḥakīm Muẓaffar	(I)	1000/200	*Iqbālnāma*, 508 (*Takmila*, 836-7 gives 1200)
55.	Pratap Singh	(R)	1000/500	*Iqbālnāma*, 507; *Takmila*, 836-7.
56.	Sakat Singh	(R)	1000/20	*Iqbālnāma*, 508 (*Takmila*, 836-7 gives the rank of 1600).
57.	Ḥamza Beg		1000/500	*Iqbālnāma*, 508.
58.	Bhao Singh	(R)	1000/500	*Iqbālnāma*, 508 (*Takmila*, 836-7 gives 700).
59.	Mīr Sharīf Kolābī	(I)	1000/500	*Iqbālnāma*, 510.
60.	Raja Shayam Singh Tonvar	(R)	1000	Ibid., 504.
61.	Raja Jagatman Chauhan	(R)	1000	Ibid.
62.	Ashraf Khān	(I)	1000/500	Ibid.
63.	Kalyan Das son of Todar Mal		1000	Ibid., 505.
64.	Iftikhār Beg		1000	Ibid., *Tuzuk*, 85 (1500).
65.	Mirzā Anwār	(T)	1000	Ibid., 481.
66.	Raja Bhoj	(R)	1000	Ibid.
67.	Mīr Jamāluddīn Inju	(I)	900	*Tuzuk*., 21.
68.	Mīr Sharīf Amulī	(I)	900	Ibid., 22.
69.	Naqīb Khān	(I)	900	Ibid.
70.	Mirzā Khurram	(T)	800	Ibid., 74.
71.	Chin Qulij	(T)	800	Ibid., 53.
72.	Ẓafar Khān	(I)	700	Ibid., 66.
73.	Abul Qāsīm Namakīn	(I)	700	Ibid., 13.
74.	Aḥmad Beg Khān	(T)	700	Ibid., 35.
75.	Ṣadar Jahān	(Ind. Muslim)	700	Ibid., 13.
76.	Ghayāṣ Beg	(I)	700	Ibid.
77.	Salhadi	(R)	700	*Takmila*, 837.
78.	Ẓaīn-ul Mulk	(I)	700	Ibid., 822.
79.	Mīr Gadāi son of Mīr Abū Turāb	(I)	700	*Takmila*., 825.
80.	Qāẓi 'Iazatullah	(I)	700	*Takmila*., 834.
81.	Bābu Mangalī	(Afghān)	700	Ibid.
82.	Ḥakīm 'Alī Gilānī	(I)	700	A.N. III 836.
83.	Amīnuddīn	(I)	500	*Takmila*., 837.
84.	Shaikh Kabīr	(Ind. Muslim)	500	Ibid.
85.	Mirzā Walī	(T)	500	Ibid.
86.	Ram Chand son of Madhukar	(R)	500	*Tuzuk*, 39.
87.	Dalpat Bundela	(R)	500	Ibid., 111.
88.	Ismaīl Qulī son of Shāh Qulī Maḥram	(I)	500	*Takmila*, 836.
89.	Abul Bi Uzbek	(T)	500	Ibid., *Tuzuk*, 70.
90.	Mīr Abul Wahāb		500	*Tuzuk*, 35.
91.	Shaikh Ruknuddīn		500	Ibid., 64.
92.	Qamar Khān	(I)	500	*Ā'īn*, I, 128.
93.	Muḥammad Khān Niyāzī		500	*Takmila*, 836.
94.	Ḥakīm Ainul Mulk Shīrāzī	(I)	500	Ibid., 805.
95.	Khwāja Jahān	(I)	1500	*Tuzuk*, 93.

IV. *MANṢABS* HELD BY BĀRHA SAYYIDS

(The first list is compiled from the list of *manṣabdars* holding rank of 200 and above, given in the *Ā'īn*. This and list in the *Ṭabaqāt-i Akbarī* relate to the years 1594-5.

The second list is entirely based on the *Tuzuk-i Jahāngīrī*, and comes up to 1622).

1. *MANṢABS* OF BĀRHA SAYYIDS UNDER AKBAR, C.1594-5

	Ā'īn	*Ṭabaqāt*
1. Sayyid Maḥmūd	2000	4000
2. Sayyid Aḥmad Khān	2000	3000
3. Sayyid Qāsim	1500	2000
4. Sayyid Hāshim	1000	2000
5. Sayyid Rāju	1000	1000
6. Sayyid Chhajjū	500	-
7. Sayyid Jamāluddīn	500	-
8. Sayyid Lād	200	-
9. Sayyid Bāyazīd	300	-

2. *MANṢABS* OF BĀRHA SAYYIDS UNDER JAHĀNGĪR .

	Tuzuk
1. 'Alī Asghar Saif Khān	3000/2500
2. Sayyid 'Alī Bārha	2000/1500
3. Sayyid Dilēr Khān	2000/1200
4. Sayyid Qāsim s/o Dilāwar Khān	1000/600
5. Izzat Khān	1000/800
6. Sayyid 'Abdullah Bārha	700/450
7. Sayyid Hizabr Khān	1500/600
8. Sayyid Bahwa	2000/1000
9. 'Alī Muḥammad	300/400
10. Bahādur	400/200
11. Sayyid Bāyazīd	2000/700
12. Sayyid 'Ālam Bārha	1500/60

V. *MANṢABS* HELD DURING SIX YEARS OF JAHĀNGĪR

Name	Racial group	*Manṣab under Akbar*	*Manṣab under Jahāngīr*	*Sources and remarks*
1. Mohammad Sharīf	(I)		5000/5000	*Tuzuk*, 6 died in 7th r.y *Tuzuk*, 113
2. Jafar Beg Āṣaf Khān	(I)	4000	5000	Ibid., 7 died in 7th r.y. Ibid, 108.
3. Raja Jagannath	(R)	5000	5000	Ibid., date of death not exactly known.
4. Madhao Singh	(R)	3000/2000	3000	Ibid., No further reference in the *Tuzuk*.
5. Rawal Sal Darbari	(R)	3000/1250	3000	Ibid.
6. Shaikh Ruknuddīn Afghān	(Afghān)		3500	Ibid., died in 2nd r.y. *Tuzuk*, 64.
7. Shaikh 'Abdur Rahmān	(Ind. Muslim)	2000	2000	*Tuzuk*, 8. Promoted to the rank of 2,000/2,000 in 2nd r.y. *Tuzuk*, 51, 57; died in 3rd r.y.
8. Maha Singh	(R)	2000	2000	Ibid., 8. Promotion after 6th r.y. *Tuzuk*, 108.
9. Zāhid Khān s/o Ṣādiq Khān	(I)	2000	2000	Ibid., Promotion after 6th r.y. *Tuzuk*, 108.
10. Wazīr Beg Jamīl		2000	2000	Ibid.
11. Qarā Khān Turkmān	(T)	2000	2000	Ibid.
12. Shaikh Farīd Bukhārī	(Ind. Muslim)	4000/2000	5000	Ibid., 9,5000/5,000 in 4th r.y. *Tuzuk*, 78.
13. Ram Das Kachhwaha	(R)	2000	3000	Ibid.
14. Lālā Beg Bāz Bahādur	(T)	1500	4000	Ibid.
15. Keso Das Maru	(R)	300	1500, 1500/1500	*Tuzuk*, 9,37
16. Mirān Ṣadr Jahān	(Ind. Muslim)	2000	4000	Ibid., 9. 5000/5000 in 3rd r.y. *Tuzuk*, 66
17. Ghayas Beg	(I)	700	1500	1500/250 in 3rd r.y. & 2000/500 in 6th r.y., *Tuzuk*, 67, 97.
18. Mirzā Bairam	(T)	2000	2500	Ibid., 10.
19. Mirzā Sulṭān	(T)	1000		Ibid., 2000/1000 in 2nd r.y., uzuk, 57.
20. Bhao Singh	(R)	1000/500	1500	Ibid., 2000/1000 in 3rd r.y., *Tuzuk*, 66.
21. Zamāna Beg Mahābat Khān	(I)	1500	2000/1300	*Tuzuk*, 10,36 3000/2500

Name	Racial group	Manṣab under Akbar	Manṣab under Jahāngīr	Sources and remarks
				in 3rd r.y. and 4000/ 3500 in 4th r.y., *Tuzuk*, 70, 89.
22. Bir Singh Deo Bundela	(R)		3000	Ibid, 10. 4000/2000 in 6th r.y., *Tuzuk*, 100.
23. Mirzā 'Alī Akbarshāhī	(T)		4000	Ibid., 11 died in 11th r.y. *Tuzuk*, 163.
24. Khwāja 'Abdullah	(T)	1000	1000, 2500/1500	Ibid., 10,36 3500/2000 in 3rd r.y. and 5000/2000 in 4th r.y., *Tuzuk*, 66, 75.
25. 'Abdul Nabi Uzbek	(T)	500	1500	Ibid., 12, promotion after 8th r.y. *Tuzuk*, 109.
26. Ghayāṣuddīn 'Alī Naqīb Khān	(I)	900	1500	Ibid., 12 died in 9th r.y. *Tuzuk*, 129.
27. Shaikh Kabīr Shujā'at Khān	(Ind. Muslim)	500	1000, 1500/700	Ibid., 12, 39 1500/1500 in 2nd r.y. and 2000/1500 in 6th r.y., *Tuzuk*, 54, 93.
28. Tāsh Beg Qurchi Khān Tāj Khān	(T)	2000	3000	Ibid., 13 3000/2000 in 5th r.y., *Tuzuk*, 86.
29. Abūl Qāsim Namakīn	(I)	700	1500	*Tuzuk*, 13
30. Shaikh 'Alāuddīn	(Ind. Muslim)		2000	Ibid., 4000/3000 in 3rd r.y. and 5000/5000 in 4th r.y., *Tuzuk*, 68, 76.
31. 'Alī Asghar Bārha Saif Khān	(Ind. Muslim)		3000 (2000/1000)	Ibid.,14,35. 2500/1350 in 4th r.y. *Tuzuk*, 75.
32. Faridūn Barlās	(T)	1500	2000/500	Ibid., 14 1500/1300 in 3rd r.y. and 2500/2000 in 4th r.y. *Tuzuk*, 68, 75.
33. Shaikh Bāyazīd (Muaẓẓam Khān)	(Ind. Muslim)	2000	3000	Ibid., 4000/2000 in 3rd r.y., *Tuzuk*, 66.
34. Mīr Jamāluddīn Injū	(I)	900	3000	Ibid., 21.
35. Mir Sharīf Āmulī	(I)	900	2500	Ibid., 22.
36. Dilāwar Khān Afghān	(Afghan)		1500, 2000/1400	Ibid., 23,36.
37. Qayām Khān			1000/1000	Ibid., 36.
38. Shyam Singh	(R)	1000	1500/1200	Ibid., 37.

Name	*Racial group*	*Manṣab under Akbar*	*Manṣab under Jahāngīr*	*Sources and remarks*
39. Abul Ḥasan	(I)		1000/500	Ibid., 1500 in 3rd r.y. *Tuzuk*, 66.
40. Shāh Beg Khān	(I)	500	5000	Ibid., 23
41. Raja Basu		1500	3500	Ibid.
42. Āqā Mullā	(I)	200	1000/300	Ibid., 28
43. 'Abedin Khwāja	(T)	1000/500	1000/1000	Ibid.
44. Mirzā Ghazi Tarkhān	(I)	5000/5000	5000/5000	Ibid., 33
45. Ḥakīm Fatḥullah	(I)	1000	1000/300	Ibid., 34.
46. Sa'dullah Khān	(T)		2000/1000	Ibid.
47. Aḥmad Beg Khān	(T)	700	2000/1500	Ibid., 35, 2500/1500 in 5th r.y., *Tuzuk*, 82.
48. Shaikh Ibrāhīm Kishwar Khān	(Ind. Muslim)		1000/300	*Tuzuk*, 36 1500/700 in 5th r.y., *Tuzuk*, 80.
49. Hāshim Khān son of Qāsim Khān	(T)	1500	2500/1500	Ibid., 3000/2000 in 2nd r.y., *Tuzuk*, 60.
50. Bāz Bahādur Qalmāq	(T)		1000/1000	Ibid., 37
51. Bahādur Khān Qūrbegi	(T)	400	1500/800	Ibid., 38.
52. Ṣalābat Khān Khān-i Jahān Lodī	(Afghan)		3000/1500	Ibid., 42, 5000/5000 *Tuzuk*, 66
53. Chin Qulij son of Qulij Khān	(T)	800	800/500	Ibid., 53. 1300/800 in 5th r.y., *Tuzuk*, 96.
54. Rana Shankar son of Udai Singh	(R)	200	2500/1000	Ibid., 54.
55. Rai Manohar	(R)	400	1000/1000	Ibid.
56. Irādat Khān s/o Āṣaf Khān	(I)		1000/500	Ibid., 55.
57. Kishan Chand s/o Mota Raja	(I)		1000/200	Ibid., 63.
58. Mīr Khalīl son of Ghayāṣuddīn Mīr Mirān	(I)		1000/200	Ibid., 63.
59. Ẓafar Khān	(I)	700 (3rd r.y.)	2000/1000	Ibid., 68. 2500/1000 in 4th r.y., *Tuzuk*, 76.
60. Pāyanda Khān Mughal	(T)	3500	2000	Ibid., 68.
61. Ihtimām Khān			1000/300	Ibid., 68.
62. Shamsuddīn Jahāngīr Qulī	(T)	2500/2000	2000/500	Ibid., 68, 3000/2500 Ibid. 73.
63. Kishan Singh	(R)		2000/1000	Ibid., 72.
64. Ḥakīm 'Alī	(I)	3000	2000	Ibid., 73.
65. Raja Suraj Singh	(R)		3000/2000	Ibid., 74.
66. Mirzā Khurram,	(T)	800 (4th r.y.)	2000/1500	Ibid., 74.
67. Karamchand S/o Jagannath	(R)		2000/1500	Ibid.
68. Raj Singh	(R)	4000/3000	4000/3000	*Tuzuk*, 75.
69. Ghayāṣ Khān ('Ināyat Khān)	(I)		1500/800	Ibid., 75.

Name	Racial group	Manṣab under Akbar	Manṣab under Jahāngīr	Sources and remarks
70. Mubārak Sarwānī	(Afghan)		1000/300	Ibid.
71. Abul Bi Uzbek	(T)		1500	Ibid., 78.
72. Fidāi Khān	(T)		1000/400	Ibid., 77.
73. Khanjar Khān brother of 'Abdullah Khān	(T)		1000/500	Ibid.
74. Mirzā Badi'uzzaman son of Shāhrukh Mirzā	(T)		1000/500	Ibid.
75. Ṣafdar Khān	(T)	1000 (5th r.y.)	1500/700	Ibid., 80.
76. Mu'īzul Mulk		1000	1200/350	Ibid., 83.
77. Qāsim Khān	(T)	1000/500	1500/1000	Ibid., 85. 1500/1250 in 6th r.y., *Tuzuk*, 96.
78. Iftikhar Khān		1500	2000	Ibid., 85.
79. Ghairat (Ghaznīn) Khān Jālorī		1500/500	2000	Ibid., 85.
80. 'Abdus Subhān		200	1000/400	Ibid., 85.
81. Sayyid Alī Bārha	(Ind. Muslim)	1000/500	1500/700	Ibid., 87.
82. Khwāja Jahān		1500/1000	2000/1200 (6th r.y.)	Ibid., 93.
83. 'Abdur Razzāq Ma'murī	(I)	1500	1800/250	Ibid., 95.
84. Qulich Khān	(T)	5000/5000	6000/5000	Ibid., 96.
85. Raja Kalyan	(R)	1500	1700/1000	Ibid., 98.
86. Mirzā Shādmān	(T)	1500/1500	1700/500	Ibid.
87. 'Abdur Rahīm Khān-i Khanān	(I)	5000	5000/5000	*M.R* II, 497, 501
88. Raja Man Singh	(R)	7000	7000/5000	*AN* III, 839.
89. Mirzā Rustam Safavī	(I)	5000	5000/3000	*Z.K.*, 95.
90. Mirzā Azīz Koka	(T)	7000		*Z.K.*, 14, 149.

VI. *MANṢABS* HELD AT THE END OF FIFTEENTH YEAR OF JAHĀNGĪR (BASED ON *TUZUK-I JAHĀNGĪRĪ*)

Name	Racial group	Manṣab	Source
1. I'timādudaulah	(I)	7000/7000	*Tuzuk*, 267.
2. Abdur Raḥīm Khān Khanān	(I)	7000/7000	Ibid., 256.
3. Mirzā 'Azīz Koka	(T)	7000/500	*Tuzuk*, 355.
4. Khān-i Jahān Lodī	(Afghān)	6000/6000	Ibid., 184.
5. Khwāja Abul Ḥasan	(I)	5000/2000	Ibid., 309.
6. Bahādur Khān	(T)	5000/4000	Ibid., 310.
7. Raja Bir Singh Deo	(R)	5000/5000	Ibid., 288.

Name	Racial group	Manṣab	Source
8. Āṣaf Khān	(I)	5000/4000, 4000 2h-3h	Ibid., 223.
9. Mirzā Rustam Safavi	(I)	5000/5000	Ibid.
10. Darāb Khān	(I)	5000/5000	Ibid.
11. Khān-i 'Ālam	(T)	5000/5000	Ibid., 288.
12. I'tibār Khān Khwajasara		5000/3000	Ibid., 184, 344.
13. Mirzā Raja Bhao Singh	(R)	5000/3000	Ibid., 337.
14. Muqarrab Khān	(Ind. Muslim)	5000/5000	Ibid., 338.
15. Kr. Karan son of Rana Amar Singh	(R)	5000/5000	Ibid., 138.
16. Mīr Jamāluddīn Inju	(I)	5000/3500	Ibid., 156, 327.
17. Lashkar Khān son of Khwāja Beg Mirzā	(I)	4000/2500	Ibid., 229, 326.
18. I'tiqad Khān	(I)	4000/1500	Ibid., 306.
19. Mahābat Khān	(I)	4000/3500	Ibid.
20. Raja Barju (Pratab) of Baglana		4000	Ibid., 196, 203.
21. Ẓafar Khān	(I)	4000/2500	Ibid., 343.
22. Ibrāhīm Khān Fatḥ Jaṅg	(I)	4000/4000	Ibid., 155.
23. Qāsim Khān Muhtashim Khān	(Ind. Muslim)	4000/4000	Ibid., 150, 328.
24. Khanjar Khān		3000/3000	Ibid., 315.
25. Ḥasan 'Alī Khān Turkmān	(T)	3000/3000	Ibid., 308.
26. Nawazish Khān son of Said Khān	(T)	3000/2000	Ibid., 309.
27. Raja Gaj Singh son of Suraj Singh	(R)	3000/2000	Ibid., 277.
28. Eldest son of Aḥmad Beg Khān	(I)	3000	Ibid., 233.
29. Yūsuf Khān son of Ḥasain Khān Tukaria	(T)	3000/1500	Ibid., 200.
30. Mukarram Khān son of Mu'aẓẓam Khān	(Ind. Muslim)	3000/2000	Ibid., 215, 359.
31. Uda Ram	(Deccani)	3000/1500	Ibid., 357.
32. Bahādurul Mulk	(Ind. Muslim)	3000/2300	Ibid., 139.
33. Jahāngīr Qulī son of 'Azīz Koka	(T)	3000/2500	Ibid., 136.
34. Rawal Sal Darbari	(R)	3000/1250	Ibid., 7.
35. Ilahdād Afghān	(Afghān)	2500/1200	Ibid., 304.
36. Shujāat Khān Arab	(T)	2500/2000	Ibid., 305.
37. Ṣādiq Khān	(I)	2500/1400	Ibid., 306.
38. Sarbuland Rai	(R)	2500/1500	Ibid., 272.
39. Sarfaraz Khān son of Muṣāhib Beg	(T)	2500/1400	Ibid., 205, 224.
40. Raja Shyam Singh	(R)	2500/1400	Ibid., 138.
41. Bairam s/o Khān-i A'ẓam	(T)	2500	Ibid., 10.
42. 'Abdul 'Azīz Naqshbandi	(T)	2000/1500	Ibid., 320.
43. Amānullah s/o Mahābat Khān	(I)	2000/1300	Ibid., 343-44.

Name	Racial group	Manṣab	Source
44. Mubāriz Khān Afghān	(Afghān)	2000/1700	Ibid., 320.
45. Qāsim Khān		2000/1500	Ibid., 323.
46. Amānat Khān	(I)	2000/400	Ibid., 320.
47. Himmat Khān		2000/1500	Ibid.
48. Mīr Mīrān	(I)	2000/1500	Ibid., 310.
49. Mīr Jumla	(I)	2000/300	Ibid., 304.
50. Tātār Khān		2000/500	Ibid.
51. Sayyid Bāyazīd Bukhārī	(Ind. Muslim)	2000/1500	Ibid., 305.
52. Jān Sipar Khān	(T)	2000/1500	Ibid.
53. Raja Kishan Das	(R)	2000/300	Ibid., 282.
54. Ikrām Khān	(Ind. Muslim)	2000/1500	Ibid., 278.
55. Mukhliṣ Khān	(T)	2000/700	Ibid., 280.
56. Raja Suraj Singh	(R)	2000/2000	Ibid., 269.
57. Mirzā Manuchahar son of Shāhnawāz Khān	(I)	2000/1000	Ibid., 270.
58. Ani Rai Singh	(R)	2000/1000	Ibid., 260.
59. Irādat Khān	(I)	2000/1000	Ibid., 232, 332.
60. Mīr Abū Salih 'Rizvi Khan'	(I)	2000/1200	Ibid., 232.
61. Keshav Das Maru	(R)	2000/1200	Ibid., 193.
62. 'Alī Khān Tatāri		2000/1500	Ibid., 161.
63. Rawal Kalyan Jaisalmari	(R)	2000/1000	Ibid., 163.
64. Balju Qalich Khān	(T)	2000/1200	Ibid., 174.
65. Sayyid 'Alī Bārha	(Ind. Muslim)	2000/1200	Ibid., 159.
66. Raja Nath Mal		2000/1200	Ibid., 145.
67. Wafādar Khān		2000/1200	Ibid., 138.
68. Kishwar Khān	(Ind. Muslim)	2000/2000	Ibid.
69. Iftikhār Khān son of Mirzā Rustam Safavī	(I)	2000/2000	Ibid., 85.
70. Mirzā Khurram, Son of 'Azīz Koka	(T)	2000/1500	Ibid., 74.
71. Karamchand S/o Jagannath	(R)	2000/1500	Ibid.
72. Mirzā Walī	(T)	2000/1000	Ibid., 263, 344.
73. Mirzā Sulṭān	(T)	2000/1000	Ibid., 10.
74. Wazīr Beg Jamīl		2000	Ibid., 8.
75. Qara Khān Turkmān	(T)	2000	Ibid., 8.
76. Abdur Razzāq Mamurī	(I)	1800	Ibid., 95.
77. Muizul Mulk		1800/350	Ibid., 110.
78. Raja Kalyan	(R)	1700/100	Ibid., 98.
79. Mirzā Shādmān	(T)	1700/500	Ibid.
80. Nāhar Khān		1500/1000	Ibid., 236, 365.
81. Raja Sangram of Jammu		1500/1000	Ibid., 314.
82. Alaf Khān Qayam Khān	(Ind. Muslim)	1500/1000	Ibid., 320.
83. Sayyid Hizabr Khān Bārha	(Ind. Muslim)	1500/1000	Ibid., 223.
84. Fidāi Khān		1500/700	Ibid., 309.
85. Man Singh son of Rawal Shankar	(R)	1500/800	Ibid., 310.
86. Mīr Husāmuddīn Injū	(I)	1500/500	Ibid.
87. Mu'tamid Khān	(I)	1500/600	Ibid., 393.

Name	Racial group	Manṣab	Source
88. Debi Chand Gowaliori		1500/500	Ibid., 30.
89. Bāqar Khān	(I)	1500/400	Ibid., 274.
90. Naṣrullah s/o Fatḥullah		1500/400	Ibid., 274.
91. Maktub Khān		1500	Ibid., 236.
92. Mirzā Badi'uzzamān	(T)	1500/1500	Ibid., 230, 344.
93. Qizilbash Khān	(I)	1500/1200	Ibid., 302.
94. Ram Das son of Raja Raj Singh	(R)	1500/700	Ibid., 207.
95. Bahlol Miāna Sarbuland Khān		1500/1200	Ibid., 203, 344.
96. Mirzā Isa Tarkhān	(T)	1500/800	Ibid., 148.
97. Sardār Khān	(T)	1500/800	Ibid., 159, 344.
98. Mubārak Khān Sarwānī	(Afghān)	1500/700	Ibid., 142.
99. Muṣtafa Khān		1500/250	Ibid., 178.
100. Mu'taqid Khān	(T)	1500/350	Ibid., 179.
101. Ṣafdar Khān		1500/700	Ibid., 80, 425, 581.
102. Mirzā Ḥusain Kifāyat Khān		1200/300	Ibid., 218.
103. Tarsūn Bahādur		1200/450	Ibid., 263.
104. Jalāl Khān Kakar	(Ind. Muslim)	1000/600	Ibid., 312.
105. Sardār Afghān	(Afghān)	1000/400	Ibid., 320.
106. Zabardast Khān		1000/500	Ibid., 321.
107. Zāhid Khān son of Shujāat Khān	(T)	1000/500	Ibid., 200, 322.
108. Akbar Qulī Gakhar	(Ind. Muslim)	1000/1000	Ibid., 308.
109. Dilér Khān brother of Izzat Khān Bārha	(Ind. Muslim)	1000/800	Ibid.
110. Sayyid Aḥmad Sadr	(Ind. Muslim)	1000	Ibid.
111. Mirzā Ḥusain son of Mirzā Rustam	(I)	1000/500	Ibid.
112. Bizan s/o Nad Alī	(T)	1000/500	Ibid., 309.
113. Shaikh Farīd son of Quṭbuddīn Khān	(Ind. Muslim)	1000/400	Ibid., 304.
114. Mīrān Jalari	(T)	1000/400	Ibid., 304.
115. Mīr Khān son of Abul Qāsim Namakīn	(I)	1000/800	Ibid., 303.
116. Sayyid Bahwa	(Ind. Muslim)	1000/800	Ibid., 262.
117. Khwāja Abdul Latif Khush Begi		1000/400	Ibid., 288.
118. Ilahyār son of Iftikhār Khān	(I)	1000/500	Ibid., 273.
119. 'Āqil Khān		1000/800	Ibid., 274.
120. Bahlim Khān		1000/500	Ibid., 275.
121. Shāh Muḥammad son of Khān-i Dauran	(T)	1000/800	Ibid., 275.
122. Bābā Khwāja	(T)	1000/600	Ibid., 288.
123. Maqsud Khān	(T)	1000/130	Ibid., 275.
124. Tughrīl son of Shāhnawāz Khān	(I)	1000/500	Ibid., 270.
125. Fāẓil Khān		1000/500	Ibid., 272.
126. Mirzā Ibrāhīm Ḥusain Kāshgharī	(T)	1000/500	Ibid., 272, 344.
127. Sādāt Khān		1000/60	Ibid., 272.
128. Jagat Singh s/o Raja Basu		1000/500	Ibid., 264.

Name	*Racial group*	*Manṣab*	*Source*
129. Muẓaffar son of Burhānul Mulk		1000/500	Ibid., 239.
130. Ibrāhīm Khān (Aqidat Khān)		1000/200	Ibid., 245.
131. Girdhar s/o Raisal	(R)	1000/800	Ibid., 248.
132. Mirzā 'Abdullah	(T)	1000/300	Ibid.
133. Salih nephew of Ja'far Beg Āṣaf Khān	(I)	1000/300	Ibid., 224.
134. Sayyid Niẓām	(Ind. Muslim)	1000/700	Ibid., 230.
135. Alī Qulī Beg Darmān		1000/700	Ibid.
136. Nūruddīn Qulī		1000/600	Ibid., 207, 358.
137. Raja Bhim Narayan		1000/500	Ibid., 203.
138. Jai Singh son of Maha Singh	(R)	1000/500	Ibid., 192.
139. Ḥakīm Beg		1000/200	Ibid., 194.
140. Sikandar Jauharī		1000/300	Ibid., 185.
141. Sayyid Qāsim Bārha	(Ind. Muslim)	1000/600	Ibid., 163.
142. Karam Sen Rathor	(R)	1000/300	Ibid., 143.
143. Khwāja Taqī		1000/180	Ibid., 140.
144. Zorāwar Khān		1000/1000	Ibid., 140.
145. Kishan Chand son of Mota Raja	(R)	1000/500	Ibid., 61.
146. Mīr Khalīlullah son of Mīr Mīrān	(I)	1000/200	Ibid., 63.
147. Bāz Bahādur Qalmāq	(T)	1000/1000	Ibid., 88.
148. Āqā Mullā brother of Āṣaf Khān J'afar Beg	(I)	1000/300	Ibid., 28.
149. Abedin Khwāja	(T)	1000/1000	Ibid.

APPENDIX B

Family Charts

I. FAMILY CHART OF BAIRAM KHĀN

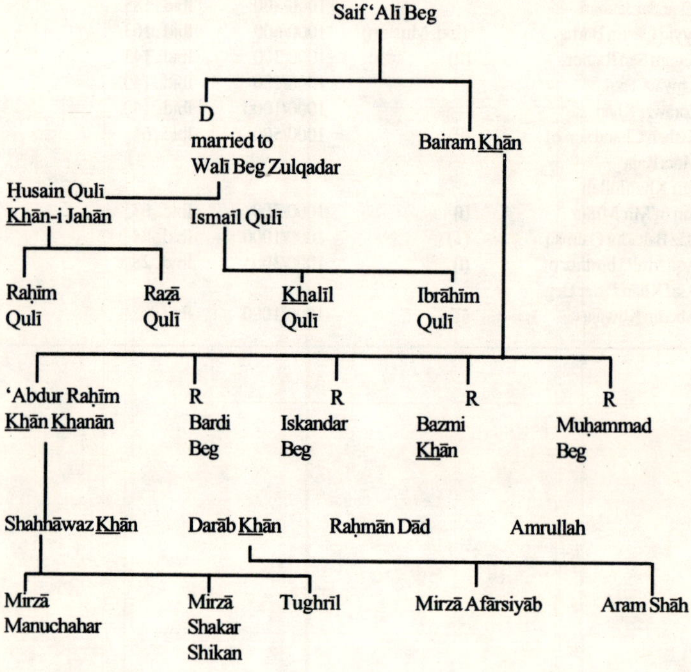

D: Daughter
R: Relation
S: Son

II. FAMILY CHART OF SHAMSUDDĪN ATKA

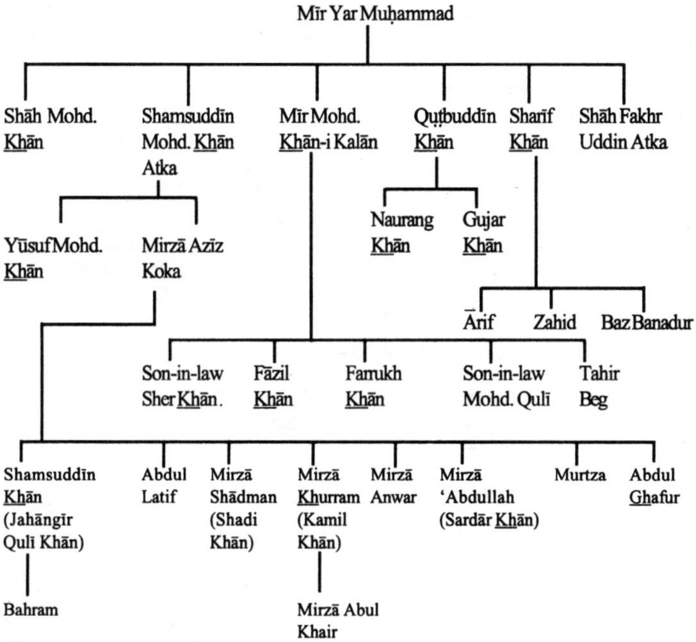

III. FAMILY CHART OF ALĪ QULĪ KHĀN-I ZAMĀN

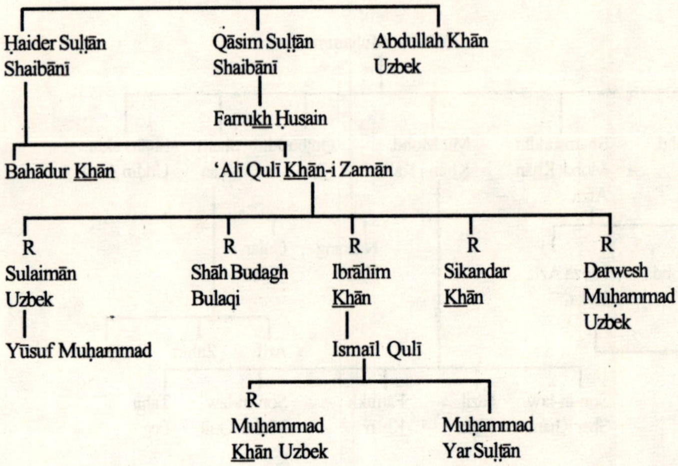

IV. FAMILY CHART OF BHARMAL KACHHWAHA

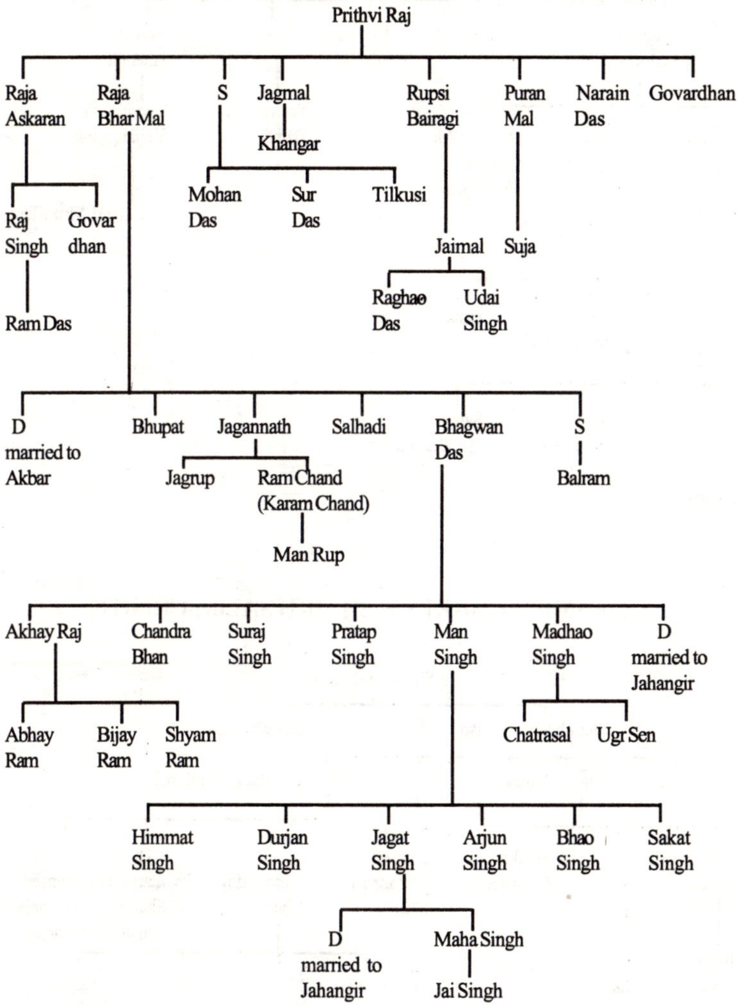

V. FAMILY CHART OF BĀRHA SAYYIDS

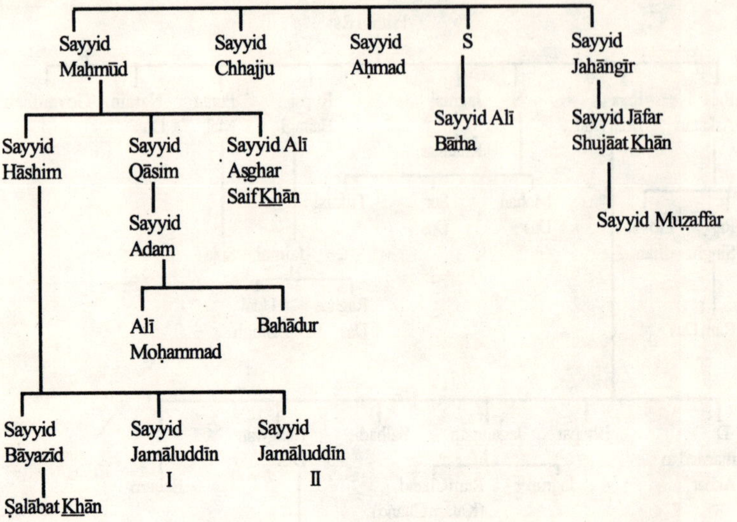

VI. FAMILY CHART OF SHAIKH SALĪM CHISHTĪ

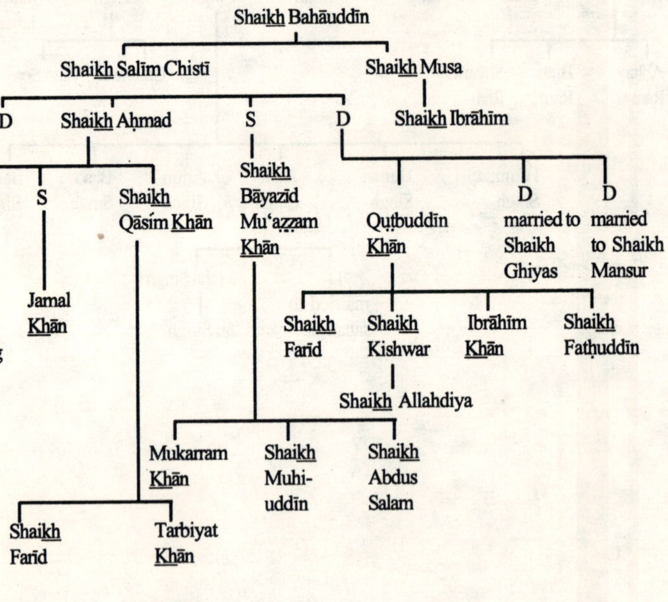

VIA. FAMILY CHART OF RELATIONS OF SHAIKH SALĪM CHISHTĪ

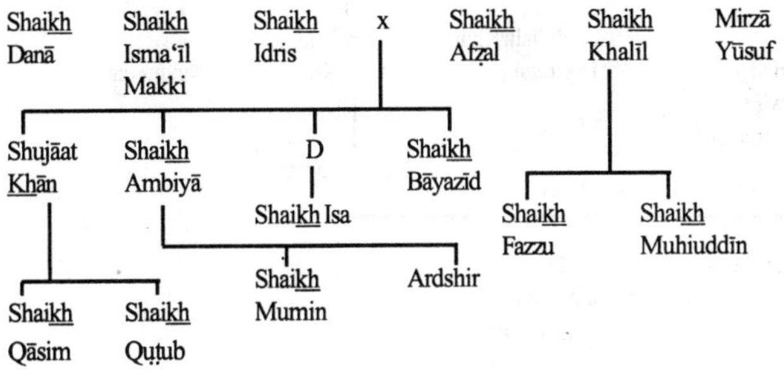

VII. FAMILY CHART OF DAULAT KHĀN LODĪ

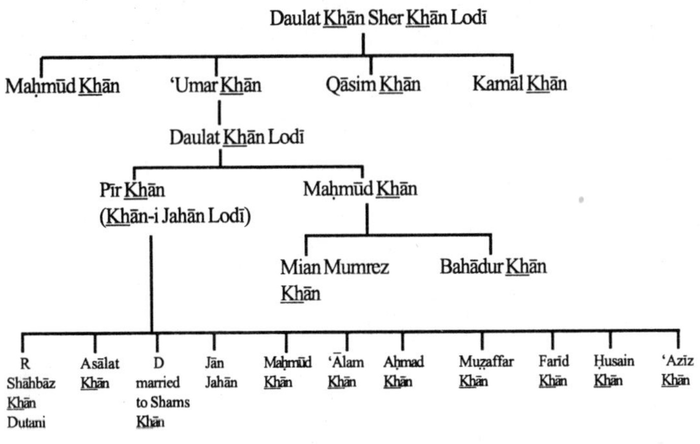

VIII. FAMILY CHART OF ABDULLAH KHĀN FĪROZ JANG

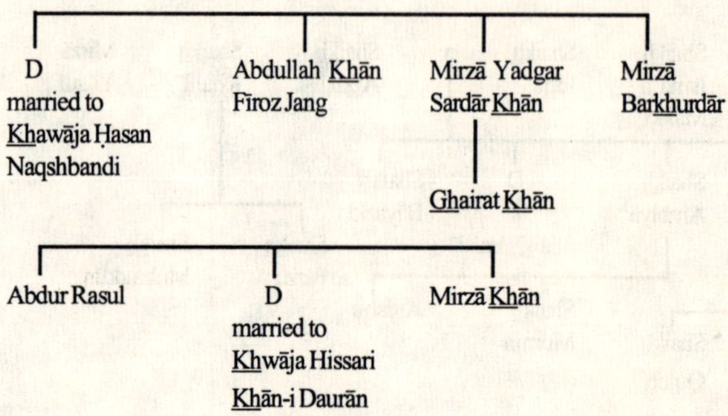

APPENDIX C

Petitions of Khān-i A'ẓam Mirzā 'Aziz Koka

Khān-i A'ẓam's petition (*'Arẓdāsht*) in reply to Akbar's letter

[The letter is appended to a manuscript in Cambridge University Library, King College Collection MS. 194 (fols. 5b - 8b).]

The most humble servant of the Royal Court, high as saturn and the Dwelling Place of the Angels, of the Emperor who holds the insignia of Jamshed, the grandeur of Faridūn, the power of Kaikhusrau; whose court is like Kaikaos', the magnificence like Alexander's, who is the refuge of the world, whose armies are (as numerous) as stars and whose camp is (as vast) as the sky; the shadow of God, 'Azīz Koka makes submission that imperial (exalted) order was issued for the summons of this humble servant. (In compliance) the heart and soul, which are the water and clay in substance (his sons) were sent along with a great many sincere and devoted nobles to the imperial court where the entire world takes refuge and which is the fountain head of generosity and majesty. But as the magistrate of wisdom and the judge of doubt, or rather certainly, had already handed down the judgement (condemning) with pangs of separation and frustration (I had no choice) but stay away with the tormented body holding the neck in the reproaching hands. As he (the petitioner) was convinced that thc whispcrs of the antagonists and the instigations of the enemies have gone home and they have succeeded in turning away the royal temperament from this servant through the means of slanders and calumnies brought to the royal ears, and that, one who is the guide of the world-adorning opinion[1] and other attendants of the court have plotted the destruction of this guiltless one. He felt that for this humble and worthless existence, which has grown in the service of the worthies of that sky-high court so much that he has attained the status of 'A'ẓam Khān and 'Azīz Koka and was honoured

[1] Obviously, Abū'l Faẓl

with the government of Gujarat, it would be only fit in view of these honours to take this body to the Sacred dust of Mecca as it would be ill-mannered and unworthy to consign it to the same dust in the same place along with the infidels of Hindustan who are the creatures of the king's bounties and favours. Therefore, entrusting Gujarat, which is a prosperous province of the empire to the confidants, and removing the dust of anxiety and vexation from the minds of the attendants (lit. sweepers) of that angelic court, and having withdrawn his hand from all claims (*matālabāt*) and removing his feet thence he took out the provisions that he had gathered through his exertions and courage in the battles against the infidels and considering it the most lawful wherewithal undertook his departure. These earnings were sufficient to enlist troops that could buy for him the position of A'ẓam Khāni in the court of the Ottoman ruler (*badshāh-i Rum*) who controls the choicest parts of the inhabited world. But his only ambition is to fix stipends for the deservingly pious people of that land and establish there a *madrasah* in the name of the emperor which may be an object of the attention of the historians till the last day, and busy himself in that *madrasah* in investigations in the religious sciences and contemplation of poetry in the praise of God and encomium of the Prophet and the companions and pray for the ever-increasing dominions. He knew it for certain that his going away would not in any way affect the attendants (lit. sweepers) of that court, rather it would accomplish the objective of the destructors and back-biters, who wish the inexistence of this non-existent as they don't consider this unfortunate one worthy of the status of A'ẓam Khān and the government of Gujarat, and the honour of Azīz Kokagi (foster brotherhood). Out of necessity, he made an offering of all the above-mentioned things to his detractors who could not get these without his being removed while this humble servant might have these things without any need of them and even outside Hindustan. And at last when the breeze of favours and bounties turned to the benefit of others and the sapling of the hopes and rights of this servant was consigned to the blistering wind of disappointment, he makes bold to submit the following to the inhabitants of the august threshold out of the considerations of devotion and foresight. God forbid that those few who are creating in the royal mind an aversion from the religion of the Prophet, (peace be on him) should be deemed friends while this humble servant who only wishes a good name (for the king) in both the worlds should be considered an enemy worthy of expulsion. Now this world is nothing more than a perishable amusement and, therefore, reliance should be put on the flatteries of those who are ever-ready to sell salvation for this world, and, after all, the entire world has not lost its understanding and judgement. There have been rulers who commanded great power and authority but it never occurred to anyone of them to advance a claim for Prophethood and strive to abrogate the religion of Muḥammad. Until and unless there is a miraculous book and some chosen friends like the four friends (of the Prophet) and happenings like the splitting of the moon, the people would never accept. O my God, who are the people who claim to become the four friends: is it Qulich Khān who possesses the inward and outward purity and natural innocence, or is it Ṣādiq Khān who received the honour of *rikabdari* from Bairam Khān, or is it Abū'l Fazl whose virtue and courage is to be equalled with those of Usmān and 'Alī? By God and by the dust of Emperor's feet, there is none except 'Azīz Koka who wants a good name, all others depend on flattery and passing out time; the only one who wants a good name (of the empire) is this servant who till the end did not speak of anything but the goodness. Now here in Sacred Mecca also he would not do anything which detract of the good name (Couplet:)

Anyone who chooses a way opposite to the way of the prophet.
Will never reach the destination.

The difference between the dignitaries of that paradise-like assembly and this humble servant is that the words *'Abul Ghāzi* have been added in his *farmān*. Others have preferred infidels over Muslims and this will remain imprinted on the pages of the days and nights. It is sincerity which is incumbent on this servant and in that he had never lacked.

Benedictions

Khān-i Azam's (*'Arzdāsht*) petition addressed to Emperor Jahāngīr (Maktūbāt-i Khān-i Jahān Muẓaffar Khān wa Gowālior Nāma, fol. 176-190) This collection includes a letter written by Mirzā 'Azīz Koka to Jahāngīr)

The writer says that the responsibility of the business assigned to him against the accursed Rana is really a serious one. Until the completion of this business, the possibility to show his face is remote. He further says that as His Majesty knows the fact well that Arsh Ashiyani Akbar has been anxious to uproot the seeds of this evil monger for fifty years. From the day of His Majesty's accession till date a period of seven years has elapsed — the imperial armies have been campaigning against the accursed Rana without success. Your Majesty! the business cannot be brought to an end in this way. (No doubt), the fortune of his Majesty is stronger, but care should be taken for the real modes to bring this campaign to an end. Your Exalted one! may God preserve you, the well-wishers have taken oaths to tell the false things and not to communicate the truth, and to work in disunity. Your Majesty had cited in the *farmān* that the people of *ṣūba* of Kabul had spoiled the campaign on account of dissension. Your Majesty, whereas the dissension is there under the very imperial throne, the people of the (various) provinces are not much to be blamed. The dissensions at the court strengthen the dissension outside. If the said seed of discard is uprooted from the court, nothing of that sort could take place on the frontiers and in the provinces. This expedition has been assigned to this servant now that his age is seventy-six years, has lost much of his strength, is hard of hearing, failing eye sight with falling teeth. He lacks in strength to mount a horse and do something. By the generosities of Arsh Ashiyani and Your Majesty the servant has no desire left to be fulfilled, therefore he requests for the accord of permission for retiring to a corner and engaging himself in praying for the (prosperity) of the Emperor.

This expedition is for ambitious young men who aspire for the *manṣab* of 5,000, can mount a horse and use sword with determination. The assignment of *manṣab* and *jāgīr* to this servant is sheer wastage while it could have satisfied brave young people. This servant cannot serve any purpose now. May God preserve your Majesty. I accept any of the (following) three alternatives: Firstly, to be allowed to act as attendant to the tomb of Hazrat Arsh Ashiyani and be permitted for *kornish* once a week. Secondly, to retire to a corner in offering five time prayers and recite Quran and thirdly, be allowed to pass the remaining part of life under the (shadow) of your throne as it is no more possible for me to move about in the service of the Master. Moreover, I don't command any army. My old servants have become old and the new do not know the temperaments and attitude. If His Majesty has already decided to assign this campaign to this servant despite his disinclination, he has no option to refuse imperial mandate, nor can dare to do so. A plan for the management of the expedition which was submitted earlier is being put for the imperial consideration. The armies of the *thānās* of Gujarat *ṣūba* should march via Sirohi and the armies of Shahabad also from the same route; Raja Suraj Singh and Ṣafdar Khān should march through Doi(?) and this servant should come through Mandesor so that a four pronged attack may be launched. By God's grace and Emperor's good fortune the accursed (Rana) would be captured or expelled from the country. Adequate money should also be granted so that the campaign may be accomplished. If His Majesty desires to protect the *thānās*, Raja Basu and Ṣafdar Khān were competent enough for the job.

May God preserve the Exalted One, 'Abdullah Khān and Mahābat Khān were appointed to the expedition and an adequate war material was provided for the same. Now probably some decline in the strength of the Rana has been reported to the imperial ears and the letters of Abdullah Khān who stayed without any excuse and endeard in the eyes of His Majesty and pretended that he (Rana) could be overcome in a single onslaught and through these tricks succeeded in getting the charge of the *ṣūba* of Gujarat. But the strength of the accursed (Rana) has not decreased but rather went on increasing day by day. The consequence of the expedition of the Deccan led by Abdullah Khān was that not withstanding his intrepidity he fled from the Deccan and spoiled the whole thing. (In reward) to this matchless bravery the title of Jān Sipar Yakrang Abdullah Khān Fīroz Jang was bestowed on him. He spoiled the expedition against Rana in this way and those to the Deccan in that way and was honoured with high titles.

There can be no praise for the wisdom and farsightedness of the well wishers of the Empire that the affairs of Kabul were entrusted to Qulich Khān who could not take care of himself, whose teeth have fallen, has lost his eye sight, hearing power and was by the time totally invalid and whom they carried about like corpse. As a result of falsehood and dissension Khān Khānān was deprived of the governership of Kabul and Qulich Khān appointed in spite of the facts mentioned above. Then his son who scattered the entire imperial army, left them to be killed and himself fleeing from there came to the court and through sheer lies and concoctions managed to get himself appointed governor of Gujarat and honoured with *alam* and *naqqara*. Though the Kabul affairs were spoiled in this way, the wisdom and farsightedness of the people in His Majesty's service may be imagined that despite such a hopeless performance they enterusted him again for the same duties.

What can be said in this respect. Your Majesty may God preserve, the kings have been applying the sorts of remedies and keeping the opinion of *muhandis* before them have been cited in the historical accounts of Naushervan, Alexander, Kaikhusrau, Kaiqubad and what sort of devices they applied to achieve a business have been recorded and they are suggested to be studied. Specially Sher Khān Afghān was not an angel (*malak*) but a king (*malik*). In six years he gave such stability to the structure (of the kingdom) that foundation still survives. He had made Hindustan flourishing in such a way that the king of Iran and Turan appreciate it, and have a desire to look at it. Hazrat Arsh Ashiyani (Akbar) followed his administrative manual (*zawābit*) for fifty years and did not discontinue them. In the same Hindustan due to the able administration of the well wishers of the court, nothing is left except rabble and jungles. His Majesty Akbar during the fifty years of his reign increased the number of Chaghtāis and Rajputs among nobles for these people are not seditious. They know nothing but loyalty. Since your accession, Your Majesty destroyed both groups and had entrusted your entire business to Khurāsanīs and Shaikhzadās who know nothing but hypocrisy and sedition, and it is because of this that they do not have any faith in anybody who is assigned some duty. It was in this way that when a duty was assigned to this servant and he was sent away, and has yet not reached Burhanpur, orders started coming in that the affairs of the place are in the care of 'son' Khān-i Jahān and therefore the same should be settled in consultation with him.

The servant though he gets old even then he is made happy. And then he is handed over the letter (of monumission) and is made free. What has been done in the darkness of night, let it be done, but the same cannot be done in the light of the day.

Bibliography

A. CONTEMPORARY AND NEAR CONTEMPORARY SOURCES

Yuan-Chao-Pi-shi, *The Secret History of Mongol Dynasty,* tr. Wei Kwei Sun, Aligarh, 1957.

Ghayāsuddīn b Humāmuddīn Khwāndmīr, *Ḥabīb-us Siyar,* Edition Tehran 1271/1855.

Bāburnāma, tr. A.S. Beveridge, London, 1921, and tr. John Leyden and K.W. Eraskin, Oxford University Press, 1921 (I have used both translations).

Khwāndmīr, *Qānūn-i Humāyūnī*, tr. Beni Prasad, Bib. Ind., Calcutta, 1940.

Mirzā Ḥaider Dūghlat, *Tāriḵh-i Rashīdī*, tr. D. Ross, London, 1895-8.

Sidi Ali Reis, *The Travels and Adventures of the Turkish Admiral, Sidi Ali Reis in India, Afghanistan, Central Asia and Persia during the year 1553-56*, tr. A. Vambery, London, 1899.

Mulla 'Ala-ud-daulah Qazwīnī, *Nafā'is-ul Maāṣir*, B.M. Add 22, 831.

'Abbās Khān Sarwānī, *Tārikh-i Sher Shāhī* (*Toḥfa-i Akbar Shāhī*) India Office, 218.

'Ārif Qandhārī, *Tārīkh-i Akbarī*, ed. Sayyid Moinuddin Nadvi, Azhar Ali Dehlavi, Imtiyaz Ali Arshi, Rampur, 1962.

Jauhar Aftābchī, *Taẕkirat-ul Waqi'āt,* B.M. Add 18, 711.

Bāyazīd Bayāt, *Taẕkira-i Humāyūn O Akbar*, ed. Hidayat Husain, Bib. Ind. Calcutta, 1941.

Gulbadan Begum, *Humāyūn Nāma*, ed. & tr. A.S. Beveridge, Royal Asiatic Society of Bengal, 1909.

Abū Turāb Walī, *Tārīkh-i Gujrāt*, ed. Denison Ross, Asiatic Society of Bengal, 1909.

Amīn Aḥmad Rāzī, *Haft Iqlīm*, Tehran.

Aḥmad Thattavi et al., *Tārīkh-i Alfī*, B.M. or 405.

Niẓāmuddīn Aḥmad, *Ṭabaqāt-i Akbarī*, ed. B. Dey, Bib. Ind., Calcutta, 1913-35.

'Abdul Qādir Badāūnī, *Muntakhab-ut Tawārīkh*, ed. Ali Ahmad & Lees, Bib. Ind., Calcutta, 1864-9.

Saiyid 'Alī Ṭabāṭabāī, *Burhān-i Maāsir*, Jamia Delhi, 1936.

Abū'l Faẓl, *Akbarnāma*, ed. Maulavi Abdur Rahim, Asiatic Society of Bengal, 1877.

Ā'īn-i Akbarī, text ed. Saiyid Ahmad Khan, Delhi, 1856, English tr. Vol.I Blochmann, Calcutta, 1927, Vols.II and III, Jarrette, Calcutta, 1949 and 1948.

Mīr Ma'ṣūm, *Tārīkh-i Ma'sūmī*, ed. U.M. Daudpota, Poona, 1838.

Abu'l Fatḥ Gilānī, *Ruqa'āt-i Ḥakīm Abu'l Fatḥ Gīlānī*, ed. Mohd. Bashir Ahmad, *Idarh-i Tahqiqat Pakistan*, Lahore, 1967.

Takmilah-i Akbarnāmā (a detailed account of Akbar's reign from forty-seventh year to the death of Akbar).

Abū'l Faẓl, *Maktūbāt-i 'Allāmī*, compiled by Abdus Samad, Delhi, 1846.

Asad Beg Qazwīnī, *Risāla-i Tārīkh Asad Beg Qazwīnī*, B.M. 999.

Muḥammad Qāsim Hindū Shāh Farishtā, *Gulshan-i Ibrāhīmī*, or *Tārīkh-i Farishta*, Nawal Kishore, Kanpur, A.H. 1290/A.D.1874.

Abū'l Qāsim 'Namakīn, *Munshaāt-i Namakīn*, MS. Aligarh, Maulana Azad Library, Lyton Farsiya 3,26 & 27 A.M.U., Aligarh.

'Abdul Bāqī Nihāvandī, *Ma'aṣir-i Raḥīmī*, ed. Hidayat Hosain, Bib. Ind., Calcutta, 1910-31.

Sikandar b. Manjhū, *Mir'āt-i Sikandarī*, Bombay, 1890.

Ahmad Yādgār, *Tārīkh-i Shāhī*, ed. Hidayat Hosain, Bib. Ind., Calcutta, 1939.

Khwājā Ni'amatullāh, *Tārīkh-i Khān Jahānī o Makhzani Afghānī*, ed. Imam Al-Din, Dacca, 1960.

Aḥmad b. Bahbal, *Maadan-i Akhbār-i Aḥmadī*, India Office, No.814.

Muḥammad Kabīr b. Shaikh Ismā'īl, *Afsāna-i Shāhān,* B.M. Add 11, 633.

Shaikh 'Abdul Haq, *Akhbār-ul Akhyār*, Delhi, 1309 A.H./1891-92 AD.

Iskandar Beg Turkmān, *Tārīkh-i 'Ālam Ārā-i 'Abbāsī*, Tehran, A.H. 1214/ 1799-80 AD.

Jahāngīr, *Tuzuk-i Jahāngīrī*, ed. Saiyid Ahmad, Ghazipur and Aligarh, 1863-64.

Walī Sarhindī, *Tawārikh-i Jahāngīr Shāhī*, Bodleian, 231.

'Alā'uddīn 'Ghaibī Isfahānī Mirzā Nāthān, *Bahāristān-i Ghaibī,* tr. Borah Gauhati, 1936.

Muṭribī, *Khatirāt-i Muṭribī Samarqandī*, ed. Abdul Ghani Mirzoyaf, Karachi, 1977.

Mu'tamad Khān, *Iqbālnāma-i Jahāngīrī*, Lithographed Nawal Kishore Lucknow, 1870 and Bib. Ind. Calcutta, 1865, (for the reign of Jahangir).

Kāmī Shīrāzī, *Fatḥ Nāma-i Nurjahān Pādshāh*, (or *Waqa'i-uz-Zamān*) Bibliothique Nationale, Paris, MS 111, 1874, 506.

Kāmgār Ḥusaini, *Ma'āṣīr-i Jahāngīrī*, B.M. or 171.

Muhammad Amīn, *Anfa'ul Akhbār*, B.M. or 1761 and Asafiya Library MS. 97:43:18/9.(I have, consulted both the manuscripts).

Mu'tamid Khān, *Aḥwāl-i Shahzādgī-i Shāhjahān Pādshāh*, Bankipur, Patna.

Anonymous, *Intikhāb-i Jahangīr Shāhī*, B.M. or 1648.

'Abdu'l Ḥamīd Lāhorī, *Pādshāhnāma*, ed. Kabir Al-Din Ahmad and Abdul Ali Rahim, Bib. Ind., Calcutta, 1866-72.

Shaikh Farīd Bhakkarī, *Zakhirat-ul Khwānīn*, MS, Habib Ganj Collection Farsi 32/74, M.A. Library, A.M.U., Aligarh. Ed. Moinul Haq, 3 vols., Karachi, 19661, 1970, 1974.

Maktūbāt-i Khān-i Jahān Muẓaffar Khān wa Gowālior Nāma, B.M., Add. 859 (this collection contains a letter written by Mirza Aziz Koka to Jahāngīr).

Haider Malik, *Tārikh-i Kashmir*, India Office 1100 and the 1/510.

Anonymous, *Dabistan-i Maẓahib*, ed. Nazar Ashraf, Calcutta, 1809.

B. LATER SOURCES

Sujan Rai Bhandari, *Khulāṣatu-t Tawārīkh*, Delhi, 1918.

Bhimsen, *Nuskh-i Dilkushā*, B.M. or 23.

Muḥammad Hāshim Khāfi Khān, *Muntakhab-ul Lubāb,* ed. K.D. Ahmad, Asiatic Society of Bengal, 1869.

Ghulām Ḥusain Salīm, *Riyāz-us Salātīn*, ed. Maulavi Abdus Salam, Bib. Ind., Calcutta, 1890.

Anonymous, *Haft Risāla-i Taqwīm al-Buldān*, MS. National Library (Calcutta) Buhar Collections No.45 (it contains biographies of the nobles of Bābur and Humāyūn under the heading *Taẓkirat-ul Umarā*).

Shāhnawāz Khān, *Maāṣir-ul Umarā*, ed. Molvi Abdur Rahim, Bib. Ind., Calcutta, 1888.

Kewal Rām, *Taẓkirat-ul Umrā*, B.M. Add. 16,703.

'Alī Muḥammad Khan '*Mir'āt-i Aḥmadī*, ed. Sayyid Nawab Ali, Baroda, 1972-28.

Ghulām Murtaẓā, *Basātīn-us Salātīn*, Hyderabad Deccan.

C. EUROPEAN SOURCES

Fr. A. Monserrate, *Commentary on his Journey to the Court of Akbar*, tr. J.S. Hoyland and annotated by S.N. Banerjee, Calcutta, 1922.

Hawkins, *Purchas His Pilgrims,* ed. James Maclehose and sons, Glasgow, vol.III., 1905.

Du Jarric's account of the Jesuit mission at the court of Akbar, tr. C.H. Pyne, *Akbar and the Jesuits*, London, 1926.

Early Travels in India (1583-1619), ed. W. Foster, London, 1927.

Ferno Guerriro, *Relations.* Portions tr. C.H. Pyne, *Jahāngīr and the Jesuits*, London, 1930.

Thomas Roe, 'Journall' in Purchas IV and *The Embassy of Sir Thomas Roe 1615-19*, ed. W. Foster, London, 1926.

The English Factories in India, 1618-69, ed. W. Foster, Oxford, 1906-27.

Pietro della Valle, *The Travels of Pietro della Valle in India*, tr. Edward Gray, Hakluyt Society, London, 1982.

Francisco Pelsaerot, '*Remonstrantie*, c.1627, tr. Moreland and Geyl, *Jahangir's India*, Cambridge, 1925.

Joannes De Laet, Description of India and Fragment of Indian History, tr. J.S. Hoyland and annotated by S.N. Bannerjee: *The Empire of the Great Moghols*, Kitab Mahal, Bombay, 1928.

A Contemporary Dutch Chronicle of Moghol India, ed. and tr. Brij Narain and S.R. Sharma, Calcutta, 1957.

Peter Mundy, *Travels*, vol.II: Travels in Asia 1630-34, ed. Sir R.C. Temple, Hakluyt Society, 2nd series, XXX London, 1914.

Nicolao Manuchy, *Storia Do Mogor*, 1653-1708, tr. W. Irvin London, 1907-8.

D. RAJASTHANI SOURCES

Banki Das, *Banki Das ri Vigat*, Jodhpur, 1956.

Marwar-re Pargana-ri Vigat, ed. Fateh Singh, Jodhpur, 1968-69.

Muhta Nain-si-khyat, Hindi tr. Ram Narain Dugar, Ajmer, 1926.

E. HINDI SOURCES

Kaviraj Shyamal Das, *Vir Vinod*, 4 vols., 1868.

GAZETTEERS

Government of India, *Imperial Gazetteer*, vol.XIII.

Atkinson, *Statistical, Descriptive and Historical Account of Northern Provinces of India*, vol.III, Part II, Muzaffarnagar District, 1876.

Nevill, *District Gazetteer of United Provinces*, Muzaffarnagar District, 1903.
Nevill, *Gazetteer of Sultanpur District*, 1923.

F. URDU WORKS

Ali, Ikram, *Bengal aur Orissa men Raja Todar Mal ki Karguzari* (this work was written in Persian by Safdar Ali *Mīr Munshī* of Raja Todar Mal. Ikram Ali translated it into Urdu in 1874. I have consulted only the Urdu version).
Azad, Muhammad Husain, *Darbar-i Akbari*, Nawal Kishore, Lahore, 1910.
Josh, Sultan Haider, *Nawab Farid*, Nizami Press, Badaun.
Naqvi, Jalal Ahmad, *Tarikh-i Amroha*, Hyderabad, Deccan, 1934.
Zaidi, Safdar Husain and Shaida Husain, *Tarikh-i Sadat-i Barha*, Multan, 1990.
Saeed Ahmad, *Umra-i Hunood*, Abdus Salam Collection, Maulana Azad Library, A.M.U., Aligarh.

G. BOOKS AND ARTICLES

Abdur Rahim, *The History of Afghans in India*, 1545-1631, Karachi, 1961.
___________, *Mughal Relations with Persia and Central Asia*, Reprint from *Islamic Culture*, Vols.VIII and IX, 1934-5.
Alavi, R.A., 'Evidence on the last years of Jahangir's reign in the *Anfaul Akhbar*', *Indian History Congress*, 1975 (cyclostyled).
Asopa, Ram Karan, *Mewar Ka Mool Itihas*, (Hindi) 1939.
Athar Ali, M., *Mughal Nobility under Aurangzeb*, Bombay, 1966.
___________, *The Apparatus of Empire, Award of Ranks , offices and Titles to the Mughal Nobility* (1574-1658), OUP, Delhi, 1985.
___________, 'The Mughal Empire in History', *Indian History Congress*, 1972.
___________, 'Provincial Governors under Shah Jahan', *Medieval India — A Miscellany*, Vol.III, 1975.
Banarsi Prasad, *History of Shahjahan of Delhi*, Allahabad, 1962.
Barthold, W., *Encyclopedia of Islam*, ed. Winsinck and Co., vol.I, Lyden, 1913.
___________, *A History of the Turkoman People in Four Studies on the History of Central Asia*, vol.III, Lyden, 1962.
Beni Prasad, *History of Jahangir*, Allahabad, 1962.
Bhargava, V.S., *Marwar and the Mughals*, Delhi, 1966.

Commissariat, M.S., *A History of Gujarat*, Vol.II, Bombay, 1957.

Douglas E. Streusand, *The Formation of the Mughal Empire,* OUP, Delhi, 1989.

Findly, Ellison Banks, *Nur Jahan*, OUP, New York, 1993.

Fredrick Augustus, *The Emperor Akbar*, Patna, 1973.

Gupta, S.P., *The Agrarian System of Eastern Rajasthan* (c. 1650-c.1750), Delhi, 1986.

Habib, Irfan, *The Agrarian System of Mughal India*, Bombay, 1963.

____________ 'The Family of Nur Jahan during Jahangir's Reign — a political study', *Medieval India — A Miscellany*, vol.I, 1969.

Hasan, Ibne, *The Central Structure of the Mughal Empire* O.U.P., 1936,

Hasan, Nurul, S., 'New Light on the relation of the early Mughal rulers with their Nobility', *Indian History Congress*, 1944.

____________, 'The Theory of Nur Jahan Junta - a critical examination', *Indian History Congress*, 1958.

Hodivala, H.S., *Historical Studies in Mughal Numismatics*, Culcutta, 1923.

Husain, Afzal, 'Provincial Governors under Akbar', *Indian History Congress*, 1970.

____________, 'Marriages Among Mughal Nobles as an Index of Status and Aristocratic Integration', *Indian History Congress*, 1972.

____________, 'Growth of Irani Element in Akbar's Nobility', *Indian History Congress*, 1975.

____________, 'An Unpublished Letter of Mirza Aziz Koka to Akbar', *Indian History Congress*, 1978.

____________, 'Element of Continuity and Stability in Mughal Nobility under Akbar and Jahangir', *Studies in History*, Vol.II, No.2, 1980.

____________, 'The Position of Racial Groups in the Mughal Nobility', *U.P. Historical Review* Vol.II, 1983.

____________, 'Mirza Aziz Koka ki Jahangir key Nam Ek Aprakashit Arzdasht', (Hindi) *Madhy Kaleen Bharat*, Macmillan, 1983.

Khan, Ahsan Raza, *Chieftain in the Mughal Empire during the Reign of Akbar*, Simla, 1977.

____________, 'Babur's settlement of his conquest in Hindustan' *Indian History Congress*, 1967.

____________, 'Gradations of Nobility under Babur', *Islamic Culture*, Vol.XI, No.1, January, 1986.

Khan, Iqtidar Alam, *Mirza Kamran — A Biographical Study*, Bombay, 1964.

___________, *The Political Biography of a Mughal Noble, Munim Khan Khan-i Khanan* (1497-1575), Aligarh, 1973.

___________, 'The Mughal Court Politics during Bairam Khan's Regency', *Medieval India — A Miscellany*, Vol.I, Bombay, 1969.

___________, 'The Turko-Mongol Theory of Kingship', *Medieval India — A Miscellany*, Vol.II, 1972.

___________, '*Wizarat* under Humayun', *Medieval India Quaterly*, Vol.V, No.I, 1950.

___________, 'The Nobility of Akbar and Development of his Religious Policy 1560-80', *Journal of Royal Asiatic Society*, 1968.

Khan, Rifaqat Ali, *Kachhwahas under Akbar and Jahangir*, New Delhi, 1976.

Khosla, R.R., *The Mughal Kingship and Nobility*, Allahabad, 1934.

Lambton, A.K.S. *Landlord and Peasant in Persia*, London, 1953.

Moosvi, Shireen, *The Economy of the Mughal Empire c.1595*, OUP, Delhi, 1987.

Namier, Sir Lewis, *The Structure of Politics at the accession of George III,* London, 1963.

Nigam, S.B.P., *Nobility under the Sultans of Delhi A.D. 1206-1398*, Delhi, 1968.

Pant, Chandra, *Nur Jahan and her family*, Allahabad, 1978.

Prasad, Ishwari, *Life and Times of Humayun*, Orient Longman, Bombay, 1956.

Prasad, Rajiv Narain *Raja Man Singh of Amber*, Calcutta, 1960.

Qaisar, A.J., 'Shahbaz Khan Kamboh' *Medieval India — A Miscellany*, vol.I, Bombay, 1969.

Qazi, Mukhtar Ahmad, 'Was Bairam Khan a Rebel?' *Islamic Culture*, 1947.

Qureshi, I.H., *Akbar, The architect of the Mughal Empire*, Delhi, 1978.

Radhay Shyam, *Babur*, Patna, 1978.

___________, *Life and Times of Malik Ambar*, Delhi, 1968.

___________, *Kingdom of Ahmadnagar*, Delhi, 1966.

___________, *The Kingdom of Khandesh*, Delhi, 1981.

Ray, Sukumar, *Humayun in Persia*, Calcutta, 1948.

Rizvi, Athar Abbas, *Muslim Revivalist Movement in Northern India in the 16th and 17th centuries*, Agra, 1965.

___________, *Religious and Intellectual History of Muslims in Akbar's Reign*, Delhi, 1975.

Satish Chandra, *Parties and Politics at the Mughal Court, 1707-40*, Aligarh, 1959.

__________, *Mughal Religious Policies, the Rajput and the Deccan*, Delhi, 1993.

Sharma, G.N., *Mewar and the Mughals*, Shiv Lal Aarwal & Co. 1962.

Siddiqui, I. H., *Mughal Relations with Indian Ruling Elite*, New Delhi, 1983.

__________, *Some Aspects of Afghan Despotism*, Aligarh, 1969.

__________, 'Political role of the refugees from Delhi in Gujarat under Sultan Bahadur Shah', *Indian History Congress*, 1972.

__________, 'Diplomatic Relations between the Rulers of Delhi and Gujarat During the 16th Century' *Medieval India — A Miscellany*, Vol.III, 1975.

__________, 'The composition of the Nobility under the Lodi Sultans', *Medieval India — A Miscellany*, Vol.IV, 1977.

Smith, V.A., *Akbar the Great Mughal*, S. Chand & Co. 1962.

Srivastava, A.L., *Akbar the Great* (3 vol.) Agra, 1962-67.

Tod, James, *Annals and Antiquities of Rajasthan*, London, 1914.

Tripathi, R.P., *Some Aspects of Muslim Administration*, Allahabad, 1956.

__________, *Rise and Fall of Mughal Empire*, Allahabad, 1963.

__________, 'Administration of India During the minority of Akbar', *Journal of Indian History*, Vol.I, Part II, 1922.

__________, 'Akbar and Maham Anga', *Journal of Indian History*, Vol.II, 1932.

Trivedi K.K., 'Rajput class in the Mughal Nobility —The Bundela case', *Indian History Congress*, 1977. (Cyclostyled)

William, Rushbrook, *An Empire Builder of the Sixteenth century,* S. Chand & Co., Delhi.

Zaidi, Inayat Ali, 'Political Role of Kachhwaha Nobles during Jahangir's reign', *Indian History Congress*, 1975.

Index